THE LAUGHING GORILLA

Robert Graysmith's Published True Crime Books:

ZODIAC

THE SLEEPING LADY

AUTOFOCUS (THE MURDER OF BOB CRANE)

UNABOMBER: A DESIRE TO KILL

THE BELL-TOWER

ZODIAC UNMASKED

AMERITHRAX

Zodiac, Zodiac Unmasked, and *AutoFocus* have been made into major motion pictures by Warner Brothers, Paramount, Phoenix Pictures, and Sony Pictures.

THE
LAUGHING
GORILLA

A TRUE STORY OF POLICE CORRUPTION AND MURDER

ROBERT GRAYSMITH

BERKLEY BOOKS, NEW YORK

THE BERKLEY PUBLISHING GROUP
Published by the Penguin Group
Penguin Group (USA) Inc.
375 Hudson Street, New York, New York 10014, USA
Penguin Group (Canada), 90 Englinton Avenue East, Suite 700, Toronto, Ontario M4P 2Y3 Canada
(a division of Pearson Penguin Canada Inc.)
Penguin Books Ltd., 80 Strand, London WC2R 0RL, England
Penguin Group Ireland, 25 St. Stephen's Green, Dublin 2, Ireland
(a division of Penguin Books Ltd.)
Penguin Group (Australia), 250 Camberwell Road, Camberwell, Victoria 3124, Australia
(a division of Pearson Australia Group Pty. Ltd.)
Penguin Books India Pvt. Ltd., 11 Community Centre, Panchsheel Park, New Delhi—110 017, India
Penguin Group (NZ), 67 Apollo Drive, Rosedale North Shore 0632, New Zealand
(a division of Pearson New Zealand Ltd.)
Penguin Books (South Africa) (Pty.) Ltd., 24 Sturdee Avenue, Rosebank, Johannesburg 2196,
South Africa

Penguin Books Ltd., Registered Offices: 80 Strand, London, WC2R 0RL, England

This book is an original publication of The Berkley Publishing Group.

The publisher does not have any control over and does not assume any responsibility for author or third-party websites or their content.

Copyright © 2009 Robert Graysmith.
Book design by Kristin del Rosario.

First edition: October 2009

Library of Congress Cataloging-in-Publication Data

Graysmith, Robert.
    The laughing gorilla : a true story of police corruption and murder / Robert Graysmith.
        p.   cm.
    Includes bibliographical references and index.
    ISBN 978-0-425-23014-5
    1. Nelson, Earle Leonard.   2. Gordon, Harry.   3. Murderers—United States—Biography.
    4. Murder—United States.   5. Dullea, Charles W., 1889–1966.   6. Police chiefs—California—
San Francisco   I. Title
    HV6245.G685 2009
    364.152'30979461—dc22

PRINTED IN THE UNITED STATES OF AMERICA

10 9 8 7 6 5 4 3 2 1

The Laughing Gorilla haunted the last honest cop in San Francisco. Captain of Police Inspectors Charles Dullea felt there was nothing worse than a cop killer. Nothing worse, he thought, unless it was a dirty cop or a killer cop. In the early 1930s he encountered all three—and soon after something worse lumbered out of his darkest nightmare—laughing.

The Setting—1930s San Francisco. The city's Ferry Building, Moorish Clock Tower, and docks are a fog-shrouded region of bloody labor riots. Depression times, bad times—poverty, soup lines, and the most corrupt police department in America. The city hall, the DA, and the cops run the town as though they own it, and they do.

The Quarry—A long-armed Gorilla Man who strangles with his huge hands and dissects his victims in autopsies with a straight razor. He is the nation's first traveling serial killer.

The Protagonist—Captain Dullea, an ex-Marine, encounters a new kind of man and new kind of crime—motiveless sequential murder, "the greatest reign of terror ever inflicted on the nation's women." *Why* is the mystery he cannot solve. *Who* is the answer he never suspected.

The Antagonist—Police Chief William J. Quinn, brutal, anti-labor chief who shotguns and gases striking longshoremen as the docks go up in flames. His cops have individual bank accounts of up to $830,000. Quinn cannot be shaken from his office. Dullea intends to make certain he is.

The Prime Suspect—Slipton Fell, movie-star handsome and instantly attractive to women, especially older ones. The "Laughing Killer of Woodside Glens" lives within a half block of the Bay Hotel where "The Murders in the Rue Morgue" come to life and is identified by the staff as the killer. But is he the one Dullea's seeking? In Cleveland, Eliot Ness pursues another Gorilla Man who might also be Dullea's man.

To Brad Fischer and James Vanderbilt

ONE

As the sailor looked in, the gigantic animal had seized Madame L'Espanaye by the hair and was flourishing the razor about her face, in imitation of the motions of a barber.

—E. A. POE, "THE MURDERS IN THE RUE MORGUE"

"**ARE** you Mrs. Clara Newman?" the whispered voice asked through a slit that served as a mouth. "Are you the lady who advertised a third-floor room for rent?" The stranger's watery blue eyes fastened on Clara Newman's face, then on the expensive pearls around her neck, and finally on her frail throat. The Gorilla Man laughed, a mirthless laugh at the bottom of a dusky staircase.

The olive-complected stranger seemed nice enough, except for his vaguely simian features—broad nose, a wet mouth too long for his face, and small low-set ears. Beneath his short, straw-colored hair Clara saw a Y-shaped wound, wet as his lips, which was not quite healed. For a short man, five feet, seven or eight, he had a powerful build—as muscular as the gorillas he resembled—wide shoulders, broad chest, long arms, and short legs.

His huge hands were corded with muscle. Even in the dim light Clara could see they were covered with light-colored tufts of hair. The joints of his fingers were swollen, the balls of his thumbs extraordinarily broad and square, and the joints in the long flexors of his thumbs much longer than average. The snapping and catching of his thumb, a "gamekeeper's thumb," were due to a thickening of the sheath and tendon at the metacarpal head. The repeated action of twisting the heads off small animals forces the thumb dial deviation at the joint. His nails, a half inch long or more, curved rply inward. Even as a child his hands had been large and continuously n motion, except when clasped rigidly in prayer. As an adult he sometimes walked on them—easing forward onto his knuckles, straightening his legs and ambling forward with uncanny ease. He suffered from violent migraines that troubled him all his life. At times, the pain was so overwhelming he could not walk except on his hands.

The sanctimonious young man in the vestibule of Clara Newman's rooming house hoisted the heavy Bible under his arm as if it weighed nothing. By God, he loved that Bible! The worn, well-thumbed volume with rich leather covers and embossed gold inscriptions had been handed down from his widowed grandmother to his aunt Lillian, a rabid Pentecostal Bible-thumper. From Lillian's saintly, hated hands it had come down to him. But the Gorilla Man's own restless hands had worn away the gold leaf, scuffed the gold-sided pages, blackened the bound-in cord marker, and smeared the octavo pages where he'd double-lined, even triple-lined in ink his most cherished verses. "My aunt told me I would be a minister some day," he told Clara Newman.

While it touched her heart to hear that he loved God, she thought it would be exceedingly odd to see that long, simian mouth recite Scripture.

The Gorilla Man wore a shabby, dark gray suit; a white shirt; a wide, yellow tie with a hand-painted palm tree; and a tan Stetson too large for him. He routinely returned home in someone else's clothes. He had just been shaved and barbered, though his overhanging brows remained un-trimmed. Because he needed only a thick ridge of bone above his eyes to make him perfectly apelike, those heavy brows fulfilled that function. Beneath their canopy his deep-set eyes shimmered like well water. They darkened to indigo as Clara studied them, failing to notice their animal cunning. Turning, she led him to the second floor. On the third-floor landing the Gorilla Man's long fingers spread wide. He flexed them—*snap-snap*-catch-*snap*—and laughed.

CAPTAIN of Police Inspectors Charles W. Dullea awoke with a start, drenched with sweat and shaking. Greenish yellow light was streaming through his bedroom curtains. After a rainy night and overcast dawn, high-stepped banks of clouds to the east had parted to permit an unearthly illumination to drench San Francisco. Dullea wiped his brow as he sat up. He had been dreaming of the Gorilla Man again.

His hands were trembling as he shaved, drawing the blade of the old straight razor from his marine days across the line of his jaw. He shook the lather into the sink and applied astringent alum to a shaving cut. Dullea had been the responding officer in the Gorilla Man investigation, an unparalleled case with an unparalleled creature and a death toll akin to a war or natural disaster. A detective lieutenant then, he never forgot standing on the second-floor landing of Clara Newman's boardinghouse unable to lift a foot farther into the refurbished attic where the killer had left her nude, violated body. Dullea had actually experienced horripilation—gooseflesh that made his hair rise .

At first the local papers called Clara's killer "the Dark Strangler," but his great strength and husky apelike build soon earned him another sobriquet, "the Gorilla Murderer," then, because it looked better on the banner, "the Gorilla Man." The press bestowed no nicknames on Captain Charles Dullea. They knew him simply as "Charlie" as did a thousand in the SFPD and many more thousands of citizens throughout the Bay Area. He had an affable face, a face you'd welcome at a tavern. His bushy black hair was cut short, and though he'd make attempts at parting it, the wind always defeated his efforts. His lips were thin as razor blades, his eyes cool and lazy as the Bay and as unreadable. Like the Bay, he was filled with deep and unexpected currents. Well proportioned, a solid 205 pounds spread evenly over a trim six-foot, one-inch frame, the dignified detective was seemingly as wide shouldered as the city's Ferry Building and as tall as its Moorish Clock Tower. His movements were economical, measured, and self-confident, those of a first-rate athlete and ex-soldier. But once roused to action, Dullea was quick thinking and quick acting, filled with more passion than anyone would ever expect. Unfortunately, he was an honest cop on the most corrupt police force in the nation. He just didn't know it was dirty yet.

Dullea dressed in a freshly ironed shirt, dark vest, and six-button double-breasted suit. His throat was tight. Methodically, he knotted his red-striped tie and tucked the twin peaks of a folded white handkerchief into his breast pocket. A touch of the farm boy clung to him. His suits never really seemed to fit, and his trousers were always a bit too short. His pointed black shoes, laced to the ankle, looked uncomfortable and were.

Over a late breakfast with his wife, Winifred, and baby, John (Charlie Jr., the eldest, and Eddie, the middle child, were already at school[1]), he opened his morning *Chronicle* and read the date—April 29, 1930. Yes, it had been four years since the Gorilla Man spoke those hushed words—"Are you Mrs. Clara Newman?" Ultimately, the long-armed strangler had wriggled out of Dullea's West Coast dragnet and escaped across the country as the first traveling serial killer in the nation's history. Dullea still castigated himself for not being able to save Clara Newman and over two dozen others, including a six-month-old infant, from strangling and *then* rape. Dullea kissed Winifred good-bye, centered his high-crowned hat, and left the house. Outside he saw the sky had turned green. Not knowing what to make of this odd occurrence, he climbed behind the wheel and drove to the Hall of Justice. He watched the morning sky until no green remained, only a growing darkness.

AT 9:52 A.M. a bullet hole surrounded by streamers of light appeared in the skies above San Francisco. Pilot Bill Fletcher, at the controls of a powerful Stearman biplane, circled Mount Tamalpais to the north. Then he headed southwest and nosed straight up into the great rift. Fifteen thousand feet above the Pacific, the lens on his fixed wing camera froze over. His gloved hands became frigid. Above Fletcher, "Baily's beads" surged clockwise around a moving black hole. He switched on his oxygen, kept climbing, and ascended into a darkening fissure many thousands of miles long. As the enormous rupture crawled northeast it cast a half-mile-wide shadow over San Francisco and plunged the temperature below by nearly twenty degrees. Ground level, at the wheel of his cab, Captain Driver Harry Gibson felt his fingers grow as numb as Fletcher's. He flexed them, craned his head out the

---

[1] Charles Jr. would later become president of the University of San Francisco; John, a professor of theology at Santa Clara University; and Ed, the partner of famed attorney Jake Ehrlich who called Captain Dullea "one of the city's toughest, straightest and best cops."

cab window, and studied the blackening heavens with widening eyes. He put his cab in gear and crept to the intersection of California and Montgomery streets, all the while peering upward.

At 9:58 A.M. two well-dressed gents—paymaster Morris B. Murphy, thin, bespectacled, and nearly hairless, and office manager Max Kahn, pallid and double-chinned—exited a branch of the Bank of Italy. Under his arm, Murphy clutched a black leather grip stuffed with $4,000 in small bills. Nervously, both men scanned the green sky, flagged down Harry's cab, and scrambled into the rear seat. As the cab edged along the shadow path, the squeal of street cars and growl of motors gradually faded away. The shuffle of ten thousand feet ceased. People stopped to watch the skies. As if holding its breath, the bustling metropolis grew deathly silent. Its heartbeat ceased.

By 10:14 A.M. a third of the sun had been eaten away. Lights sprang on in diners, dingy hotels, and the half-filled office buildings of failed businesses. Hundreds atop the lofty Pacific Telephone and Telegraph Building held up pieces of smoked glass and squinted at the moon inching its way across the sun. One man lighting matches to make smoked glass set fire to City Hall. At San Quentin State Prison, "Killer" Kid McCoy and LA's crooked DA Asa Keyes (ostracized by other prisoners) caught the sun's reflection in a water bucket and watched the rare spectacle that way. The last total eclipse had occurred five years earlier over New York. There wouldn't be another for two years, and that over Maine and New Hampshire, not San Francisco.

By the time Harry angled his cab up on the bulkhead between Piers 26 and 28, the eclipse had blanketed a half-mile width. He rolled to a stop at the entrance to the Stevedoring and Ballast Company as a waiting man stepped from the shadows. "He wore a good Herringbone suit that had seen better days," Harry recalled. "The only thing new about him was his big shiny revolver."

By 10:36 A.M. half the sun was gone.

By 10:57 A.M. the last bright sliver was blotted out as the eclipse reached totality. Its shadow swept across the earth at terrific velocity—half a mile a second. By 10:59 A.M. the moving bullet hole, outlined by flickering flame, split the sky above Napa County. By 11:00 A.M. it darkened Woodland in

Yolo County. Its advance over the hills was marked by a halo fifty miles in diameter. By 11:02 A.M., amid the high altitude, tall trees, and bright flowers of Bishop Ranch in Yuba County, Dr. Robert Altken waited at Comptonville along the path of totality. He tinkered with two delicate spectrographs, adjusted angstrom units to violet blue and orange red wavelengths and captured the flickering corona as it swept over him a minute later. His bones went chill. Soaring from a lake, two amphibian planes with red stripes took up the chase until they were outdistanced. For a little over an hour dusk shrouded the San Francisco morning. Within that daytime darkness all manner of things were done by all manner of men, but in the same old familiar ways since Cain killed Abel.

BY 1:37 P.M., the time Captain Dullea arrived, the pond-size stain next to Pier 26 was barely tacky on the well-trodden concrete. As he parked his car, he surveyed the waterfront. Eleven miles of jutting piers aligned along the arched northern and southeastern sections give the Embarcadero the appearance of a gap-toothed smile that commences with the sooty factories and freight yards of the S.P. Depot at Third and Townsend. From there it curves north for several blocks before beginning its abrupt arc to the northwest to terminate at Fisherman's Wharf. Dullea could see the Ferry Building a few blocks away, midpoint in an area called the City Front. Defined on the south by even-numbered private piers and warehouses, the Ferry Building is bounded on the northeast by odd-numbered, state-owned pier sheds and industrial plants. East Street, which fronts the Embarcadero, dipped briefly into a tunnel at Market Street and reemerged near Washington Street at a huge Camel cigarettes billboard near the Bay Hotel.

Powerful locomotives were pushing and pulling Southern Pacific, Western Pacific, and Santa Fe boxcars to waterfront railroad yards to be joined to other freights. Boxcars on spurs of the Belt Railroad, a state-owned and operated railway, led out onto every pier so cargo could be loaded directly from the ships into boxcars. A Belt Line locomotive passed Dullea, wheezing mightily and trundling like a huge black beetle. Slowly, it nudged two refrigerator cars toward the Matson Line docks at Pier 30.

Dullea heard the cry of gulls and water lapping against timbers. All about him flashed the wide, unbroken expanse of the Bay—no Golden Gate or Bay Bridges. The iciness in the air had evaporated as suddenly as it had come. It was hot now. He knelt and dragged the point of a yellow pencil through an immense stain. The seepage had congealed enough to leave a definite trail. Once dry he would be hard pressed to judge its age. Already dry to his touch at the edges, it could have been paint, rust, or oil, but it wasn't. The dried blood had begun to clot three to five minutes after being shed.

The blotch darkened under the blazing sun, each moment making it more difficult to differentiate it from older stains like grease and tar. Freshly spilled blood shines a glossy reddish brown, but its ultimate hue is always black. In the open air, the slight luster on its surface faded as Dullea watched. Automatically, he calculated by the change in color how long the blood had been there. "Three hours old," he determined, though he already knew exactly when it had been shed—10:37 A.M. He was looking at drainage. A human life reduced to drainage! And that, he concluded sadly, was the origin of the lake of blood. In a few years, the Bay Bridge would pass like an awning over the loathsome stain and shroud it as effectively as this morning's total eclipse.

Dullea averted his eyes. Normally, he didn't know the victim. This time he did. So did the tough new police chief, William J. Quinn. So did hundreds of longshoremen along the crookedly smiling waterfront. The blood belonged to the most beloved patrolman on the Embarcadero, Officer John Wesley Malcolm, a thirty-two-year veteran. Big-eared and turkey-necked, this last of the old Barbary Coast beat cops had been "a friend to the downtrodden and an unrelenting enemy to the vicious and corrupt." Dullea could still see his face, lined as a street map, creased by a broad smile, a snowdrift of white hair spilling from his cap.

At the northern edge of the lake of blood, where the concrete had been beaten down by the steel rims of carts and wheels of heavy trucks, a hobnailed boot had tracked blood. Dullea followed its trail to a crowd of sullen men. All were potential witnesses—burly merchant sailors, stevedores, and longshoremen dressed in flat caps, denim shirts, and heavy black canvas pants. Every pair of Frisco pants had been patched, repatched, and restitched where they were ragged at the cuffs. Every shoe was worn, cracked,

caulked, and resoled. From every back pocket hung a cargo hook for snag-
ging rolls of hemp, grappling burlap bags, and settling disputes. Labor un-
rest festered in this foggy region of grimy waterfront hotels and warehouses.
Soon blood would run on these piers. The hooves of the National Guardsmen's horses would grind it into the pavement to blacken under the sun
until it was indistinguishable from Malcolm's blood.

Anger was in every eye, and something else—fear. Dullea understood.
It was in his eyes, too. People were losing their homes and jobs. This morning, in sympathy with new Wall Street lows of copper, steel, and rail issues,
local exchanges had dipped another 19 points (though in the final hours of
trading a small rally was being staged). Ever since the nation's employment
rate had stalled at 9 percent, desperate men had mobbed the waterfront's
eighty-two docks and 118 steamship lines seeking work. City-operated
soup kitchens were serving oatmeal, a wedge of dry bread, and watery coffee to long lines of unemployed. Once they had eaten, the men joined a
longer line for supper: a cup of thin beef stew and a chunk of sourdough.
At the foot of Telegraph Hill, Lois Jordan's White Angel Jungle was serving
casseroles. At Rich and Clara streets the Salvation Army was handing out
room chits in exchange for sawing wood. A few of those who couldn't find
work turned to illegal means like the man who murdered Malcolm.

Dullea observed a battered black taxi, spare and simple as a poker,
angled on the bulkhead, a bold white *512* on its open door. The slender
cabbie was conspicuous in the milling crowd. Harry Gibson, a resident of
725 Cayuga Street, was red haired and red complected with a long, lean
face and sorrowful brows. Harry's thin black tie was cockeyed, and he had
pushed his cap with its oversize gold medallion as far back on his head as
he could. Sweating and nervous, he squinted into the post-noon sun. Harry
wiped his face with his sleeve and shifted his weight from foot to foot. "We
pulled up to the pier," he told Dullea. "At that moment a guy stepped forward and told me not to make any noise. When I seen it was a raise, I
studied his car so I could remember it. It was a Dodge and a very beautiful
girl was in the back seat."

"A girl on a heist?" said Dullea.

Harry's fares, Murphy and Kahn, huddled in the Stevedoring Company
entrance by a white picket fence, might know more. "Just after we drove up

in the taxi," said Murphy, "I slid out carrying a black leather grip stuffed with $4000 in small bills, a typical single day's payroll. I saw a stranger standing in the shadows by the cab as soon as it rolled to a stop. I'll never forget that man's face as long as I live. It's planted indelibly in my memory. If I meet him fifty years from now I'll still recognize him. He had a narrow face, pasty complexion, a sharp nose and glassy brown eyes. He wore a soft tan hat, a garish hand-painted tie and was well dressed in a dark herring-bone suit. About thirty, five-foot-six, lean, between 130 and 140 pounds—and, oh, yes, he whispered."

AS soon as the cab stopped, the Whispering Gunman slipped alongside Murphy, speaking so faintly that Kahn next to him had not heard a word. Neither had Oscar K. Brehmer of Corta Madera working on Pier 28 as a freight clerk, nor Harry Hade of Pleasant Valley, nor Chris Claussen, erst-while port captain of the Stevedoring Company not a dozen yards off. All were within earshot. Dock men, passersby, draymen, rail workers, black lines of round-nosed Fords filled with potential witnesses cruising on Har-rison Street failed to notice the bold robbery in the bizarre midmorning darkness.

"Gimme that bag, if you know what's good for you and your friend," the Whispering Gunman said, grinding a cheap revolver into Murphy's ribs. Not until he pried the satchel from his fingers did Murphy understand his breezy confidence. Some feet away a confederate was leaning against a light blue Dodge, "a small coach model with wire wheels," and calmly smoking a cigar. Murphy memorized the sedan's license—"No. 8-D-598." Captain Louis Ellsinger, of the coastwise passenger steamer the *Harvard,* noticed the Dodge, too.

"THE second man was younger than the first," Murphy continued, "twenty-five to twenty-nine years old, dark hair, and sallow-complected—slightly taller than the first by several inches—about five-foot, ten-or-eleven . . . weight about 175 pounds. He wore a shabby blue suit and a cap pulled down over his face. He looked Italian. After only a moment I realized there was a third person in the rear of the Dodge—an attractive woman—slender, large blue eyes, brunette hair slightly waved and pulled back of her ears. I couldn't figure out what such a nice, refined young lady was doing there and with such rough men."

Neither could Dullea.

"GIVE the gunsel the bag," Kahn had advised Murphy who had done so. At 10:37 A.M. the Whispering Gunman passed the bag off to his Italian confederate—just as Officer Malcolm came whistling round the corner.

The polished brass buttons studding his dark blue serge barely shone in the odd morning dusk. The old workhorse wasn't supposed to be here. Normally he had today off but had switched shifts with another officer. Born in Santa Cruz County May 28, 1870, he had been a San Francisco blacksmith before joining the SFPD at age twenty-eight. More important, he was a close friend of Captain Dullea and Chief Bill Quinn. If the robbery had not been so quiet, Malcolm probably wouldn't have stumbled onto it. If the white noise of passing vehicles hadn't drowned out the soft-spoken robber's words; if it had not been so dark and the robber had not panicked at the sight of a uniformed cop—if—Malcolm would've gone on his way to a well-deserved day off and, when he turned sixty in a month, entered a well-deserved retirement with his wife, Emilie, in their Ellis Street home. But Malcolm walked right into the gunman.

The Whispering Gunman shoved his long-barreled .38 against Malcolm's chest (he could feel the brittle ribs) and whispered, "Up and gimme your gun." Malcolm said a few words no one heard, never took another step, never got to his own gun. But the Whispering Gunman had heard his partner snap, "Here's a cop! Give it to him," and instinctively reacted. His revolver, pressed hard against Malcolm, kicked in his hand. Two muzzle flashes lit up the dusk as two slugs hammered into Malcolm's heart, spun him around, and dropped him like cargo from a burst net. Instantly, he began forming his lake of blood. "Emilie," he whispered, "Emilie . . ."

Malcolm's blood was steaming as it ran down the incline, so much blood that no postmortem lividity took place. His radial artery still pulsed—a steady, plainly visible throbbing. The Whispering Gunman caught up with the moving Dodge and pivoted inside. The car roared northwest, weaving in and out of traffic before swinging southwest on Harrison Street. An ambulance was dispatched from the Harbor Emergency Hospital behind the nearby Bay Hotel.

"I think I know one of the bandits," Mickey Rowan, an Embarcadero habitué ventured to Dullea. "He's a mug known as a dice player along the waterfront. I think I can take you to where they're hiding."

The wide brim of Dullea's hat cast the upper half of his face into shadow, making it difficult for Rowan to read his expression. Dullea shook his head, then signaled an officer to escort Rowan to the Hall of Justice. He never put much stock in eyewitness testimony: "It's the last to look at and the first to suspect. Human memory remains the most unreliable of all proofs." No, Dullea was counting on his famous "I squad" to come up with real evidence.

Overcome by emotion, he walked pier-side to watch the *President Hoover* sail in an hour late from the Orient. The *President Hayes,* due at dawn, had been delayed by rain at San Pedro, but the Australia-bound *Maunganul* was on time. He watched her backing slowly out into the stream trailed by what he knew was a line of ring-billed gulls. Short-billed gulls, fatter and lazier, never leave the ferry slips. Inspector William McMahon scattered a cloud of feathers as he fought to Dullea's side. Handsome and square-faced, he was dressed in a gray suit that set off his arched brows, dark hair, and white sideburns. His gray, wide-set eyes were glistening. Malcolm had been his mentor since his rookie days. He and Dullea stood watching the ship traffic. McMahon spoke first.

"Malcolm, the finest old chap I have ever known, was an officer whose sage advice and help lifted me over many a stumbling block when I was a green policeman," he said. "After viewing the life blood of my dear friend, I want a special assignment to be left on this case until John's murderers are brought in to answer for their crime."

Dullea agreed. As captain of the Robbery Detail, McMahon's investigation dovetailed with that of his Homicide Bureau. McMahon knew Dullea would not leave the slightest suspicion uninvestigated. "I ran the plates,"

Dullea said, "and it came back that the licensee is Mr. M. J. Skidmore of 543A Natoma Street. The plates had been filched from his car two days ago. He filed a report at the time."

"What do you think of Skidmore?"

"Skidmore's okay," Dullea replied, studying the drifting liners and trailing gulls headed toward the Gate. He had already set the wheels of the pursuit in motion.

Inspector George O'Leary of the SFPD Auto Detail and M. O. "Jimmy" Britt of the National Auto Theft Bureau, had already ferreted out who owned the Dodge. Roland Sheehy, of the Budd Wheel Company at 1581 Bush Street, had reported it stolen last Friday. "It's going to be cast off at the earliest possible opportunity," Dullea advised Britt, who sent out an all-points bulletin over the ticker—"All cars be on the lookout for any light blue Dodges parked at curbs, especially in the Embarcadero district." Captain Thomas Hoertkorn and Lieutenant John J. Casey alerted the city's thirteen police precincts by Teletype and briefed the Berkeley, Oakland, and Alameda police departments by phone. Waterfront police scrutinized ferryboats traversing the Bay and sheriff's deputies staked out the air fields.

Chief Quinn knew all the old-timers, but Malcolm had been the best. "They won't get away," the tough Irishman said evenly as he ordered foot patrols, riflemen, and shotgun squads onto the Embarcadero. "Shoot to kill if they resist. This killing was the cold-blooded work of the worst type of gangster-gunman." His voice grew cold. "There will be no letup until we bring the murderers in dead or alive. Get the man who killed Malcolm! Get 'em and swing 'em for this trick!"

TWO

The words heard by the party upon the staircase were the Frenchmen's exclamations of horror and affright, commingled with the fiendish jabberings of the brute.

—E. A. POE, "THE MURDERS IN THE RUE MORGUE"

THE last such citywide manhunt had been four years earlier—February 20, 1926—a chill Saturday morning when the Gorilla Man rang the bell to Clara Newman's Victorian in response to a white placard in her window. "Yes, I have three rooms vacant," said the attractive sixty-year-old woman. A wealthy spinster, Clara kept her several substantial boardinghouses filled exclusively with male lodgers, whose masculine presence she enjoyed as long as they weren't drinkers or sailors.

"Could you let me see the third floor room?" He cast his eyes upward as if praying. His voice was very soft. She noted his gorilla-like appearance.

"Of course you can see the room," she said, fingering her strand of pearls.

The Gorilla Man's watery blue eyes were piercing, unblinking. Clara had seen a travelog about gorillas at the new Embassy Theatre at Market and Seventh. What did she recall? They seldom stared directly unless they were going to attack, then they beat their broad chests with cupped hands and aggressively charged on all fours. Apes use their knuckles and the flat soles of their feet in a gait known as knuckle-walking. The stranger's teeth, neat and even, were as strong as an ape's. During manic periods, the Gorilla Man lifted heavy chairs with them to demonstrate his strength.

As he identified himself as "Roger Wilson," a suspicion briefly crossed Clara's mind. In the vicinity of Sacramento and Pierce streets near her boardinghouse, women had been terrorized for months by a "Mad Dancer." He appeared completely nude in the windows of vacant houses and danced wildly before vanishing. While the young man matched the description, Clara considered him too devout to be that perverted creature. As they ascended, the Gorilla Man paused on the second-floor landing, grasped the double rails of the bannister, swayed a little, and began rubbing his right temple. "Oh, it's only my head," he apologized. "It's paining me." When he removed a JB Stetson hat with a wide brim, Clara saw the interior band bore the initials G. W. R. and a Masonic emblem. The hat was so large on him she knew it had to belong to someone else. Though his sandy hair was long and wavy on top, it was cut short on the sides where a clear liquid was running from a deep, thumb-size wound.

"Roger Wilson," born in San Francisco on May 12, 1897, suffered his first blow at ten months old when syphilis killed his mother, Frances. Within seven months his father, James Ferral, died of the same disease. The orphaned boy went to live with his maternal grandparents, Jennie and Lars. When Jennie died in 1908, the boy, taught to be so submissive he couldn't defend himself, was sent to live with his aunt Lillian Fabian. "At age ten he was riding his uncle William's bike," Aunt Lillian recalled, "when he skidded in front of a passing trolley and was struck." His head became wedged beneath the streetcar fender and was battered against the cobblestones at every revolution of the wheels along a fifty-foot path. At the hospital, doctors assured Aunt Lillian the boy would not recover. The wound, literally a hole in his skull, had left him comatose. Lillian stood vigil anyway, and when he awoke on the sixth day, she was at his bedside with the Bible. "I can see he's completely mended," she divulged. "I can now psychically peer into his mind and the accident hasn't changed him one little bit."

But it had. Now he was prone to lapses of memory; long, sullen silences; and staring fixedly at his aunt's visitors until they grew uncomfortable and fled. He flew into violent rages, refused to bathe, and swore like a sailor. When he heard voices speaking to him of religion, he clutched the family Bible to his chest and feverishly recited biblical passages. At dinner he buried his face in his plate and ate like an animal. Aunt Lillian pointed out that his antisocial behavior was countered by his devout character. "He is just like a child," she said, "and we consider him like a child, but of course we never go too far with him because there is always fear of him."

Even as a youngster, his hands were oversize and strong. He began physically tormenting his cousin Rachel. Several times Lillian surprised the "quiet, morbid" child peeking through a keyhole at Rachel as she undressed. Each time, the smirking boy dropped to his knees, clasped his huge hands and promised through moist, quivering lips never to peep again. Hadn't Grandmother told him that sex was dirty? At fifteen, he exhibited a ferocious sexual appetite. Arrested for robbery in Plumas County at age eighteen, on July 25, 1915, he was sentenced to San Quentin State Prison for two years. Paroled on September 6, 1916, authorities arrested him again in Stockton on March 9, 1917, under the name "Clark" for petty larceny and sentenced him to six months in jail. On March 23, 1918, he was again arrested in LA on burglary charges under the name "Farrell." He escaped the LA County Jail within five months.

As "Evan Louis Fuller," he got a job at St. Mary's Hospital in San Francisco. After he fell from a ladder at work and suffered a second serious head injury, the voices howling inside his head grew louder. On August 12, 1919, under the name Evan Fuller, he married a shy fifty-eight-year-old Catholic schoolteacher, Mary Theresa Martin. Their marriage was stormy. Nights he would "go out and look for work" and return days later in someone else's clothes. His jealous indignation, constant haranguing from the Bible, and threats to kill her drove Mary to an emotional collapse in 1920. As she convalesced at St. Mary's, he threw himself on her, raving that her doctor had been sleeping with her. Ripping away the sheets, he molested her before orderlies could wrest him off and ran away.

On May 19, 1921, he gained entry to Charles Summers's home at 1519 Pacific Avenue by pretending to be a plumber. In the basement he found Summers's twelve-year-old daughter, May, playing with dolls; he knocked her down with a clenched fist, and choked her. Her screams brought her elder brother, who grappled with him before he escaped. It took two cops to subdue the powerful young man. Charged with a sexual assault on a child and confined at Detention Hospital, he was diagnosed as "erratic, violent and dangerous." On June 13, psychiatric doctors committed him to

Napa Hospital for the Insane in "a constitutional psychopathic state." He escaped within a week. Police apprehended him in the bushes outside his aunt's house peeping at his cousin as she undressed. Six months later, he made another break, was recaptured, and escaped again on November 2, 1923. He showed up wild-eyed at his aunt's house wearing a crazy hat. The hospital finally discharged him on paper, "in absentia," on June 15, 1925. His family last saw him in October of the same year.

From San Francisco, he traveled to Philadelphia where he strangled Mrs. Olla McCoy on October 18,1925; May Murray, on November 6; and Lillian Weiner, on November 9. All three had "Room for Rent" signs in their windows and were bound with strips of cloth tied with a "complicated sailor's knot." He sold items of their clothing at a north-side pawnshop, where the pawnbroker got a good look at him.

The next glimpse of him came when Clara Newman admitted him to her San Francisco boardinghouse. Clara's nephew Merton Newman, a slight, dark-haired young man in glasses, passed them on the second-floor landing. He had heard the Gorilla Man's odd, knowing laugh echoing up the staircase, so he noted the mild-spoken stranger's huge hands with special attention. "The balls of his thumbs," Merton recalled, "were very broad and square, with swollen joints and nails at least a half-inch long." His eyes were cunning, hypnotic, difficult to draw away from. Grumbling about the malfunctioning furnace, Merton nodded to Clara and the man and continued on to the basement. Behind he could hear the snap and cracking of the man's knuckles.

Walking flat-footed on the soles of his feet, toes extended, Aunt Clara's prospective lodger trailed her to the top third-floor room. "It's a reconditioned attic," she apologized. As she walked, he watched her hips.

Clara's age didn't matter to the Gorilla Man. Any woman of any age he found alone would suit his purposes: she need only be a landlady with a room to let. His strict aunt, who had raised him in an atmosphere of worshipful zealotry, had been a landlady, and he hated her. As Merton worked over the basement furnace, he was vaguely disquieted. He swept out the clinkers and, above his hammering and stoking, heard footsteps padding down the stairs. "I'll be back with the rent," said a voice. That soft, mocking laugh echoed again. He heard the front door shut with a bang. After he finished, Merton wiped his hands and left without going upstairs.

On Wednesday, February 24, he called on his aunt to see if the furnace had given her further trouble. No one had seen Clara for days. His search ended at the third-floor lavatory, where he found the naked corpse of his aunt. Merton flew downstairs to call the police. When Detective Lieutenant Charles Dullea and Inspector Francis (Frank) LaTulipe climbed the stairs, they had to stop at the door to steady themselves.

"Once Clara Newman entered the room," LaTulipe conjectured when he had recovered, "the killer yanked her to him. With one hand he took some sort of cord and twisted it around her neck, leaving behind this ligature imprint." He pointed out the livid red line on her throat, almost hidden by the black marks of gigantic hands and deep fingernail indentations. "Then he choked her with his hands as she struggled."

Dullea imagined Clara fighting, her body automatically convulsing, her legs drawing up in spasms, then dropping and going limp before he stripped her. Could her missing necklace have been the ligature? Autopsy surgeon Shelby Strange would know.

His postmortem revealed an engorgement of her lungs and the right side of her heart, an unusually long retention of body heat, and an exceptional fluidity of her blood. The trachea was injected and red and the tympanum (the cavity of the middle ear) had been ruptured. When the strangler gripped her throat, the hyoid bone fractured where his broad thumbs met, though just one of his huge hands could have covered her mouth and nose to cause suffocation. Strange was pretty sure Clara's struggles had contributed to her death. The swift accumulation of fluids, saliva, and mucus in the bronchial tree had choked her as completely as the crushing hands. Through tests, Strange established that she had been raped.

"Not like any rapist I've come across before, there's a sadistic element to his crime," he told Dullea. "You won't believe this, Charlie. She was violently beaten and repeatedly assaulted *after* being strangled." The Gorilla Man was a necrophiliac, a perverse creature of abnormal sensuality compelled to copulate with a dead body.

When Merton viewed the body, he saw the deep fingernail marks on her neck. "They are at least an inch and a half deep," Dr. T. B. W. Leland, the coroner, told him. Merton then made the connection to the hulking man who had passed him on the stairs and given that long, strange laugh. "I particularly recall those long nails," he said. "He has to be the man who killed her. Look, I want to accompany her body to Detroit."

"I believe you should remain here and I'll tell you why. As you are the only man who can identify any suspects arrested as the stranger you saw. It might delay the solution of this murder were you to leave." Reluctantly, Merton agreed.

"We have narrowed the search," Dullea told his men at the HOJ, "to the mysterious stranger described by Merton Newman as having confronted him in the house sometime before he discovered his aunt's body."

But the Gorilla Man had only begun his reign of terror against women. On March 2, 1926, Mrs. Laura Beale was found by her husband; she had been strangled with a silk belt and then violated under circumstances similar to Clara's. The description of Laura's killer matched that of the Bible-carrying young man known as Roger Wilson. Alarm spread throughout the Bay Area as Dullea intensified his manhunt and staked out pawnshops in case Clara's necklace should turn up. On June 10, as armed posses combed San Francisco, the Gorilla Man appeared at a rooming house on Dolores Street run by Lillian St. Mary. She joined the others, smothered, her naked body stuffed beneath her house bed. Six days later, a self-righteous young man with a Bible visited a rooming house at 1372 Clay Street. "The man was stocky and well-built, with shifty eyes, strange blue eyes, and the hands of a giant," said the landlady, Mrs. P. A. Ford, who lived on the fifth floor. "When he asked to see a room on the third floor, I called my husband, and the stranger immediately left, saying he wasn't interested in an apartment."

He didn't go far, only downstairs to the fourth floor where he knocked on Mrs. Stidger's door. "I'm here to fix your phone," he told her.

When Mrs. Stidger expressed suspicion, the man fled next door to Mrs. Gladys Dunne, manager of an apartment house. A smile played about his lips all the while Gladys was showing him a room. Those huge hands were flexing and cracking, when a janitor appeared and he ran away again.

The next day, three East Bay women reported a man with a Bible had tried to rent apartments from them. On June 17, in Albany, California, Mrs.

Flint Huffart went to bed. Her head was filled with nightmares of the "Go-rilla fiend" who had been in all the papers. During the night, she dreamed the strangler had climbed through her window and was choking her. When he seemed about to win, she reached under her pillow and pulled out the revolver she kept there for protection. Firing full into his face, Mrs. Huffart awakened to find she had shot her own hand.

A number of strangers, trading on the Gorilla Man's reputation, carried out depredations of their own against terrified landladies and laid the blame at his door to confuse the police. The Santa Cruz police arrested a stockily built foreigner after the brutal rape of Allie Doyle, a young widow, and as-saults on two other women. A mob would have lynched him as the Gorilla Man, if Dullea had not driven Merton Newman at high speed to Santa Cruz. "That's not the Gorilla Man," Merton said. In Santa Barbara on June 24, the real Gorilla Man strangled landlady Ollie Russell with a curtain cord so tightly that blood gushed from her neck. An LA police bulletin de-scribed "the Strangle Murderer" as "probably Greek, rather high cheek bones, dark skin and a thin face."

By August 16, he was in Oakland in the East Bay at landlady Mrs. Mary Nesbit's door. He discarded her in a pool of blood in the bathroom of the apartment she had planned to rent. When several months had passed with-out another attack, Dullea prayed that the killer had burned himself out. Although Jack the Ripper, a similar random killer, had apparently stopped by his own volition, the Gorilla Man could not. He appeared to be a mania-cal sex pervert with a taste for murder driven by religious mania and a compulsive, relentless sexual appetite. "All crimes must have a motive," said Dullea. LaTulipe was not so sure. The Gorilla Man was a new type of man.

In Portland, Oregon, on October 19, he reappeared just long enough to throttle and violate three landladies in six days. He crammed Mrs. Beata Withers into an attic trunk filled with love letters from her failed romance. He twisted a scarf around Mrs. Mabel Fluke's neck and hid her in the attic of her five-room bungalow. He jammed Mrs. Virginia Grant behind her basement furnace and then hitched back to San Francisco on November 10, where he choked Mrs. Anna Edmunds to death. Following his usual pattern he stuffed her brutally violated nude body under a bed in her boarding-house. Five days later, he was in Seattle, where he squeezed the life out of

Mrs. Florence Monks and three days later Mrs. Blanche Meyers in Portland. With so many of Dullea's men hot on his heels, the random killer fled the West Coast for the Plains States, where it was cooler. Dullea was frustrated that he had come so close to catching the killer.

"I will tell you this," said LaTulipe. "Sadistic torture and murder will always follow a prescribed pattern. Not a blunt instrument one time and a knife the next, but always his hands or the cord. His set pattern will never vary: Shortly after getting a shave and a haircut he will call at any house with a 'Room to Let' sign in the window. Any landlady he finds alone he will strangle, then rape and leave nude in the offered room, usually under the bed. He will steal clothes from his victim to sell. He is a necrophiliac and a sadist. Going by his religiosity, I think the huge Bible he carries suggests a possible motive."

Dullea recognized some portion of the type—a lust killer. Was the Gorilla Man's unbridled sadism in itself an object of sexual gratification and their elusive motive? The only thing he was certain of was that the Gorilla Man's name was *not* Roger Wilson.

THREE

A gorilla . . . can make only about 20 sounds—roars, whimpers, screams,
soft grumbles. . . . Laughter is not one of them.

—*GORILLA*, IAN REDMOND

BY 3:30 P.M., April 29, 1930, the day of Officer Malcolm's murder, Chief
Quinn's patrols were still combing the city for the Whispering Gunman and
his swarthy accomplice. "I want every piece of motor apparatus in the department out," he said. "Scour the highways and alleys for the bandit car. I
want a finger on every trigger."

Quinn named his Flying Squad after the winged-wheel insignia on the
shoulder patches of its fifty-two young members (four from each of the
city's districts). He inaugurated the thirteen Harley-Davidson sidecar motorcycle units shortly after being sworn in as chief on November 20, 1929
(the same day Dullea became captain of inspectors). These "motorized bath-
tubs" were a mobile reserve capable of reaching any corner of the city
within ten minutes. Quinn's Flying Squad pulled on specially designed uniforms, high polished boots, and goggles. Each driver nudged out the kick
starter, rose into the air, and came down hard. The cycles accelerated from
the dark mouth of the underground garage, every sidecar equipped with
automatic rifles, service pistols, cases of tear gas, light machine guns, and
sawed-off shotguns.

Although the Flying Squad had been specially trained by Quinn's right-
hand man, Detective Sergeant Tom McInerney, it had been under Dullea's

command from its first day. Fifteen years earlier Dullea had been a founding member of the Shotgun Squad. When four masked gunmen knocked over the Claremont Roadhouse, Dullea, then a very young motorcycle cop out of Richmond Station, had joined in the chase down Fulton Street. He fired on the getaway to puncture its tires but, being a famously bad shot, missed completely. Two of the four robbers hunched down in the tonneau of their car and returned fire, narrowly missing Dullea. At Sixth Avenue they veered north, raced past Richmond Station to Lake Street and crashed into a low wall on the Presidio grounds. In the ensuing gun battle, Corporal Fred Cook was killed and three of the robbers escaped. To capture them, the SFPD organized the first proactive motorized anticrime patrols—squads of armed detectives who kept in contact with headquarters by street phone, the only way they could communicate. The search for Malcolm's killers would be conducted the same way.

At 4:00 P.M., Corporal Harold Leavy, behind the wheel of his "prowler," located a light blue Dodge parked at 55 Second Street in the wholesale district a half mile from Pier 26. Leavy felt the engine—still warm—then peered into the backseat. Scattered on the floor were adding-machine tapes, a packet of blank white envelopes, two dimes, and a nickel. Murphy's empty black leather satchel lay open on the seat. A half hour later, Inspector La-Tulipe, the eccentric and wizard criminologist in charge of the SFPD's I squad, reached the getaway car. He was a striking man—long, thin face; silver hair combed in a high pompadour; and a nose as sharp as a ship's prow—the better to ferret out clues.

LaTulipe popped open his battered case of photographic apparatus and fingerprint gear and unpacked sensitive plates, flashguns, bulbs, a heavy Graflex, and a scale ruler. "I began going over the sedan for prints," he said, "our first step I hoped in identifying the murderous bandit pair and their pretty little companion."

LaTulipe swirled a soft camel's-hair brush in the direction of an emerging fingerprint. His touch was so light he sometimes used a feather to develop latent minutiae. With long, even strokes he gently brushed finely ground carbon dust along the ridge flow and coaxed a perfect print on the steering wheel into visibility. He blew away the excess, then shifted photographic plates to capture two other prints from the front passenger side and rear window. Excited, he returned to his threadbare lab. In 1930, there was no national repository of fingerprints—the federal ID bureau wouldn't be up and running for two years. Until then, LaTulipe would have to resort to cruder methods. Beginning with the delta of a print, he counted the friction ridges separating it from the specific core of the pattern and visually tried to match it to prints in his meager files.

Three days later, Captain Dullea, Chief Quinn, Inspector McMahon and his partner, Martin Porter, and ninety-eight uniformed patrolmen solemnly motored to Officer Malcolm's funeral. The long line of prowl cars, lights flashing, stole silently to Cypress Lawn Cemetery. They left with sirens screaming. Dullea watched the manicured lawns and marble headstones flash by. "At least," he told Quinn, "the old workhorse died in harness."

"Those bastards," said Quinn. His huge fists closed. "I want them bad." Quinn smiled a wolfish smile. His lower teeth were small, sharp, and inclined outward. His ears were square, and his thick hair a rusty brown. He was baby faced, but with his ever-present cigar looked more like a ward heeler than a policeman.

"Since the gunman was dressed in good, but shabby clothes," McMahon suggested, "I think he's going to rag himself out as soon as he can. We'll make the rounds of local tailors."

But first he and Porter rode directly to the I Bureau to hear what La-Tulipe had to say. As they entered, he doffed his Moore-Stetson (today was San Francisco Straw Hat Day) and fanned two pasteboards out onto his scarred desk. "Boys, I got a file on two of the prints," he said. "All you have to do now is find these bums."

Mug shots are notoriously poor likenesses, but these were unusually sharp. The first card, #12014 (from the Seattle PD), was of George Berta. The second, #4718 (from the Tacoma PD), showed a man with distended brown eyes and slicked-back hair—Peter M. Farrington Jr., alias Joe Gorman, alias the Whispering Gunman.

"Berta and Farrington belonged to the gang who robbed the Nanaimo Canadian Bank in '22," LaTulipe said. "They served an eight-year stretch for that caper and only got out last year. Their partners, Tony Moresco and Lou Costello, broke jail. We're still looking for them. A fifth member, Big Johnson the Scandinavian, is still in jail at Seattle awaiting trial. Nobody ever forgets Big Johnson. That's why the big oaf keeps getting caught. As for the woman, I've got no record."

"Have Harry the Cabbie work up a composite sketch of her with one of the newspaper artists," said McMahon. With Harry's completed portrait in hand, they traced the crooked waterfront. At last they reached Tony's Place on the ground floor of a bookie joint and saw their pet stoolie behind the bar polishing glasses with his apron. "Who you want for the shooting all right are Berta and Farrington," Tony Sudoni replied. "They come in once in a while, but ain't been here for a week."

"What about her?" McMahon slid the sketch across the polished bar.

"Nah, I . . . I don't know her at all." Tony was obviously lying. Mc-Mahon leveled a murderous gaze at him. "Please, please why should I lie?" said Tony, wiping his hands on his apron. Two gold teeth gleamed. Clearly, he would squeal on the two men, but not the woman.

Disgusted, McMahon walked to a corner phone booth, called a patrolman to stake out Tony's, and returned to the HOJ. "The story's probably this," Dullea told him. "Tony knows the woman was somehow coerced into helping the two robbers. For that reason no one in the community is going to help you locate her. San Francisco's Italian community, some 58,000, is remarkably close-knit and loyal, especially toward women and particularly one of such stunning beauty."

"Charlie, I've got a theory. Canadian police are preparing to try Big Johnson for a fresh bank holdup. I think Berta and Farrington committed the Pier 26 robbery to raise money for his defense. If so, they might reach out to their pal in jail."

McMahon got to Seattle on June 7 and, from the jail, tailed two of Big Johnson's visitors. He got within a block of the Whispering Gunman before he was spotted. Farrington fled to British Columbia. A sergeant nabbed the gunman, who was in a barbershop with a hot towel over his face, a loaded .38-caliber revolver on his hip, and a crate of ammo in his hotel room upstairs. Captain Claussen journeyed to Tacoma to eyeball Farrington. "That's the bastard! The son of a bitch," he shouted. "I'll testify he's the guy who pulled the trigger on Malcolm." Extradited, Farrington whimpered to Mc-Mahon all the way back to San Francisco about his bad breaks and heart condition (which had spared him from the whip in Canadian prison). "I only read about the copper killing the next morning," he rasped, "and I was in Los Angeles when I done that."

FRANK J. Egan was a boyish, pleasant-looking man of slender build with short black hair, bushy brows, and the tightlipped smile of a schoolmaster. But his profile was a jigsaw piece—rounded forehead curving down into a long, sloped nose, an upper lip angling back to a pursed mouth, and a chin thrusting forward like a fist. His eyes, glassy as black marbles, shone with a strange light. As San Francisco's first and only public defender, it fell to him to represent Farrington. "Egan was my bitter political enemy," admitted Dullea. "A state of official enmity existed between his office and the police department, since they were on opposite sides of almost every case. I knew that Egan flattered even himself that the police were afraid of him and would like to get rid of him. He was an exceedingly clever lawyer so we prepared our case against Farrington carefully."

On September 4, Egan, in sartorial splendor, sauntered into court. Beneath a new camel's-hair coat, the public defender wore a well-cut gray flannel suit. He removed the coat and jacket and hung them on the back of a chair. Tucking his thumbs under colorful suspenders, he squared his narrow shoulders, and in shirtsleeves began pleading Farrington's case before Judge J. J. Trabucco's court. On the first day of trial, the widow Malcolm locked her eyes, filled with hope, on prosecution witness Oscar Brehmer, especially during his last half hour on the stand. But when Assistant DA Harmon Skillin questioned Harry Gibson, the cabbie could be certain only about the gunman's cap, suit, and weapon, and the widow began to sob.

In his lab, LaTulipe was wrestling with Malcolm's uniform. Its dark fabric made it difficult to define the density of powder residues blown into the bullet penetration area. How could he document this "tattooing" for a jury and demonstrate that the slugs had been fired at extreme close range? "There is one way," he thought—a test sensitive to black and smokeless powder residue and insensitive to all other chemicals except nitrates. He desensitized a piece of photographic paper in a hypo bath, washed and dried it, then immersed it for ten minutes in a warm 5 percent solution of Kodak's dye and C acid. After the treated paper dried, he placed it face-up under the uniform, made sandwiches of dry toweling moistened with 20 percent acetic acid, and ironed the packet. Clusters of dark red spots appeared that corresponded to the burned powder grains around the bullet holes. LaTulipe had his visual evidence.

Elsewhere, McMahon was grappling with other clothes: Farrington's. Labels steered him to a Stockton haberdasher who had consigned the shirts, underwear, and ties to a store at the Hotel Wolf in San Francisco. Hotel records placed Farrington at the Wolf (registered as Edward Murray of Tracy) on the same day Malcolm was gunned down.

A week later, an all-male jury began deliberating Farrington's fate. For five hours, their shouting resounded down the marble corridors of City Hall. At 10:13 P.M., as they were about to be locked up for the night, they reached a verdict of first degree murder. Because the jury offered no recommendation, it was a mandatory death sentence. Peter M. Farrington Sr., father of the killer, was in the court when C. A. Browning, court clerk, read the sentence of death. So was Mrs. William Farrington, the defendant's sister-in-law, who shrieked and hurled curses at the jury as three bailiffs carried her bodily out of court. Farrington never flinched, only listened calmly and thanked his counsel. Then, half-turning toward the jury, he whispered so softly Dullea could hardly hear, "You have made a terrible mistake."

He showed some character in the end by refusing to disclose the name of the comely young woman in the backseat of the Dodge. "Publicity would destroy her character," the Whispering Gunman told McMahon, who drove immediately to Tony's, hopeful that the barman might speak now. "She's from a fine family," he said. "Those rats, they got her drunk and that's why everybody's glad you got them," Tony spat between his gold teeth. "For myself I know nothing. And nothing's all I'll ever know."

Exactly thirteen months after he murdered Officer Malcolm, the Whispering Gunman would climb thirteen steps to a San Quentin gallows and complain no more.[2]

During the first days of Farrington's trial a gray-haired and lantern-

---

[2] In 1932, cops nailed Farrington's partner, George Berta, in Seattle after a fierce gun battle.

jawed woman had sat front row. As Egan's longtime benefactor, Mrs. Jessie Scott Johnson Hughes, "Josie," had come to cheer him on before he handed the case off to co-counsel Nate Coghlan and Ed Lomasney. At times, the fifty-seven-year-old woman's eyes brimmed over, filled with admiration for her youthful protégé. The well-to-do widow lived alone in one of the city's posh new residential districts west of Twin Peaks, an area of "respectability."

Josie called Frank Egan "Son" and "Nephew" and he called her "Mother" and "Aunty." During the 1906 quake and fire, Egan, then a lowly expressman, encountered Josie fleeing the flames. When he salvaged her luggage, they became inseparable friends. Under her motherly guidance, Egan studied law and set up a private law practice in 1914. Four years later, when the state legislature formally established the office, he was appointed San Francisco's public defender. In 1921, he was elected to the post in his own right and four successive times after that. Finally, Egan became Josie's financial adviser, and this is where all the trouble began.

First, Egan cozied away her house on Moultrie Street, then had attorney Vincent W. Hallinan (who was also Dullea's lawyer) draw up Josie's will naming himself executor. Josie already had a $5,000 insurance policy, with Egan as her beneficiary. But on February 9, 1932, he had convinced Josie she needed another $10,000 of coverage. Her insurance company had disagreed. "Ten thousand dollars is too much for you to carry," they told her, "but we will issue you a $5,000 policy."

Egan presented an $8,500 promissory note, purportedly bearing Josie's signature, and offered to pay her premiums if the company would grant a $10,000 policy to protect the note. The company issued the second $5,000 policy, designating Egan as sole beneficiary and assigning him double-indemnity clauses. Should Josie die accidentally, he would receive $20,000, and he desperately needed that money.

Though Egan earned $8,000 a year as the San Francisco public defender, three years before he had put up his residence at 225 Urbano Drive as security for a loan. Now the bank was initiating foreclosure proceedings against him to collect the overdue $9,000 note. He owed nearly that much to the estate of August and Katie Weber, an aged couple who had advanced him $5,000 in return for a promissory note. While Egan was Katie's attorney, he siphoned $3,120 owed her from the city employees pension fund into his own account. He accomplished this by banking the money to her credit, then withdrawing it with a blank check (one of many Katie had signed so Egan could pay her expenses) and redepositing the money in a dummy bank account under the fictitious name of "Minnie Peyser." "You have nothing to fear," Egan told his tool, Janet Kent. "No one will ever connect you with Minnie Peyser."

Next, he led Mrs. Weber to believe he had repaid the $5,000 loan by producing a forged bank passbook showing a deposit entry for $5,000. On November 16, 1930, Katie died under suspicious circumstances, and her husband, a retired street sweeper, began demanding an autopsy and threatening a lawsuit to regain any remaining funds.

Other shady dealings came to light. Eight years earlier, when Egan and his wife, Lorraine Kipp, were married, she had come into a sizable inheritance from the estate of Margaritha Busch, heiress to the brewery fortune. Lorraine had been her companion and nurse. Within two days of Busch's death, Egan filed a deed of gift with the county recorder, transferring a $200,000 row of apartment houses on O'Farrell Street to his wife. When Busch's Chicago relatives sued, Lorraine settled out of court for a third of the amount. When another of Egan's clients, Mrs. Catherine Craven, died from alcohol, her nieces examined her $25,000 estate and found only an empty safe deposit box and a few real estate mortgages. When they asked Egan what had happened, he threw them out of his office. Florence Cook, another of his wealthy clients, was also proving to be a problem.

Devastating losses through depreciations of securities Egan held had him reeling. The large emergency sums of money he had stowed in a safe deposit box had dwindled away. Even Josie Hughes's two modest insurance premiums totaling a mere $113.20 a month had become a drain on his limited income. The pressure was relentless. Egan, a chronic sufferer of sinus, gallbladder, and kidney afflictions, the last requiring an operation, was headed for a nervous breakdown. Harassed by creditors Egan thought of the rewards—riches, that bottomless will, the double-indemnity insurance policies. He thought of the alternatives, too—eviction, financial ruin, illness, public scandal, the loss of his powerful political position, and jail. It was enough to drive a man to murder.

FOUR

The term *Gorilla:* Since 1930: A person with gorilla-like strength; a person known for his strength and lack of intellect; a hoodlum or thug; strong-arm men, gorillas and tough guys. Specif., one hired to kill or do violence.

—*DICTIONARY OF AMERICAN SLANG*

OVER a period of seventeen months, during which Dullea had the misfortune to catch the Gorilla Man case as the first officer on the scene, the Gorilla Man strangled, then raped landladies from San Francisco to Council Bluffs and across to New York State. He traveled from Philadelphia to Buffalo, from Detroit to Chicago, and finally with the United States up in arms fled across the border into Canada. Dullea studied the U.S. death toll. Three Philadelphia landladies—Olla McCoy, May Murray, and Lillian Weiner. After eleven San Francisco, San Jose, Santa Barbara, Oakland, and Portland strangulation murders, the Gorilla Man fled to Council Bluffs, Iowa, where he choked Mrs. John Berard on December 23, 1926. Four days later in Kansas City, Missouri, the Gorilla Man garroted Mrs. Bonnie Pace. The next day, Mrs. Germania Harpin and her eight-month-old daughter were *both* strangled and violated—the infant throttled with a rag. Dullea steadied himself and continued reading—April 27, 1927, Mary McConnell in Philadelphia; May 30, Jennie Randolph in Buffalo; June 1, two Detroit sisters, Mrs. Minnie May and Mrs. Maureen Atorthy. June 3, in Chicago, he strangled Mary Sietsema with an electric appliance cord and left her disheveled on the floor for her husband to find.

One afternoon, LaTulipe walked in on Dullea and saw the big, tough

Marine slumped with his head in his hands. The case had really gotten to him. Finally, in the summer of 1927 Dullea caught a break. When the Portland newspapers printed drawings of the expensive jewelry the Gorilla Man had pinched from wealthy widow Florence Monks, three landladies recognized it and notified the police. "We rented a room to a polite, pleasant, young man who had stayed with us a few days," they said, "and we bought some of that jewelry from him." Portland police at last learned the Gorilla Man's real name just as he fled from Minnesota into Canada.

G. CHANDLER picked up the Gorilla Man along the highway a mile north of Luna, Michigan, and drove him to Noyes, Minnesota. Mr. and Mrs. Hanna gave him a lift a mile south of the international border at Emerson, Manitoba. They drove him the rest of the way into Winnipeg and let him off at Corydon and Emerson streets. Around 5:00 P.M. on June 8, the Gorilla Man entered Jacob Garbor's secondhand store on Main and traded in his blue suit for a herringbone coat, black boots, a gray felt hat, and a dollar in cash. He secured a job as a construction laborer, and that same day, as "Mr. Woodcots," rented a second-floor bedroom on Smith Street from landlady Mrs. Katherine Hill. She found him quiet, likable, and pious: "He was a very devout gentleman who always carried a huge Bible under his arm."

He gave her a dollar, all he had, with the promise of eleven more for the rest of the month's rent. Only his greatest willpower kept him from killing her on the spot.

FIVE

The city's most attractive neighborhoods were built west of Twin Peaks and south of Mount Davidson, according to a San Francisco City Guide of the period.

ON Friday, February 20, 1931, five months after the verdict in the Whispering Gunman's trial, Captain Dullea was still sleepless and dissatisfied. He drove to the HOJ to lose himself in new investigations and forget the disagreeable public defender, Frank Egan. It was bad enough that today was the fifth anniversary of the day the Gorilla Man strangled Clara Newman, but Egan's name crossed his desk immediately. Florence Cook, Egan's prosperous client, had been found dead an hour earlier. Only $3 remained in her accounts. After Florence acquired a house on Post Street, she had become friends with Mrs. Flo Knight and through her met Egan, an occasional visitor to her ground-floor dancing school. "Before that time," Florence's ex-husband, Edward J. Cook, said bitterly, "my wife had been a shrewd business woman, dependable, not addicted to drink of any kind. From then on, she began drinking heavily and lost all sense of business and reliability."

When Cook gave his wife $1,500 for her needs and another $3,500 to deposit, she turned both sums over to Egan "for safekeeping." When she served her husband with divorce papers, she confided to him, "I don't want a divorce, Ed, honey, but Frank Egan insists on it."

Before Florence died "from the effects of alcohol," she had deeded her property over to Egan, though witnesses to the signing believed they were witnessing her death certificate. Building residents warned Egan and her attending physician, Nathan S. Housman, that if they didn't take Florence to a hospital instantly they would summon an ambulance themselves. Dullea knew Dr. Housman—prim, horse-faced, toothbrush mustache, tiny round glasses. He was not only Egan's personal physician but a gangland doctor.

When one of Housman's patients, gangster Earl Leter, was shot in a blind pig[3] over at 110 Eddy Street, he died from a gunshot wound without telling who shot him. Dullea was confident that Leter had talked under anesthetic and named the shooter. "What I hope is that the doc will speak that name aloud at some point," he told Ignatious McCarty, a surveillance expert, "and if we install a powerful microphone we can pick it up."

The night of July 1, McCarty packed his needle-nose pliers, two coils of telephone wire, a drill, and a knife and broke into Housman's office on an upper story of the Flood Building, where he concealed a small Dictaphone in a seldom-used corner.

So far, the wire tap had been disappointing. Either Housman didn't have the information or he wasn't discussing it. Inspectors Percy Keneally and George "Paddy" Wafer continued to monitor the line, while Dullea attempted to solve the strangling death of Rosetta Baker by a huge-handed killer in her California Street apartment. The wealthy widow had a fondness for younger men.

July plodded by as the detectives hunkered down in their Monadnock Building hideaway at 385 Market Street, read the racing form, chewed the fat, and waited. Paddy studied the peeling paint and cigarette-littered floor with disgust. What a step down! Five years earlier, he and his partner, Detective Sergeant Louis De Mattei, had ended the murderous spree of the Terror Bandits, California's first drive-by killers. And wasn't he the one who had brought in a wounded Larry Weeks as bait and stationed then-Lieutenant Dullea by his hospital bed to capture the killers when they came to rescue their partner? In the sweltering room, Paddy scratched his stubble and

---

[3] A prohibition bar that worked under the knowledge of the police by payoff.

adjusted his headset. From his earphones fine copper wires swooped up Market Street to Housman's office.

By July 30, the two sweating, smoking harness bulls were sick of the doctor, sick of his cronies, sick of their endless babble crackling over the insubstantial lines. There was no doubt Housman's office was a hangout for the underworld. Abruptly they heard hollow laughter. "More lowlifes," thought Wafer, but reached for his pad and adjusted his earpiece, as did Keneally.

"Sure, Auntie could be killed easily," said a laughing voice. "You know, she thinks so highly of me she calls me Nephew and Son." Another laugh—snide, sarcastic, yet familiar—not the doctor's high-pitched laugh because after all these months the two bulls heard that in their sleep. "If only I had that insurance of Josie Hughes," the laughing voice continued.

Wafer and Keneally looked at each other and pressed their earphones more tightly against their ears. They'd heard this voice before directed in derision at them as they testified on the witness stand. Yes! It was Frank Egan, who had represented the late, unlamented Pete Farrington at trial.

"How much is involved?" asked Housman.

"Nearly $20,000, a tidy sum," continued Egan. "It would settle all my debts and leave me a little spare cash."

"Oh, well. She'll probably die someday."

"Not soon enough. Hell, she's only fifty-seven. Wouldn't it be funny if she got run over? But she never will. She's too cautious. I guess I'll have to kill her myself!"

"And you'd be the first man suspected. The police would find out she has got $20,000 of double indemnity insurance in your favor and they'd clap their hand right on your shoulder. For God's sake, who else would want to kill her except you?"

"Do you think I'm a dumbbell? I wouldn't do it myself and I wouldn't let it look like murder."

"Then what would you make it look like?"

"A hit-and-run accident."

Wafer and Keneally drove to the HOJ to repeat what they had overheard. "Oh, come on, boys," Dullea said with a wide grin. He leaned back in his swivel chair and put his hands behind his head. "Egan had to be joking. Imagine a man in his position planning such a thing. Whether you like him or not, he's one of the city's biggest political figures. Heck, he might even be mayor one of these days."

"He said it in all seriousness, Captain!" said Wafer. "Come listen for yourself." As Dullea monitored the open line, Egan explained how he'd establish an alibi the night of Josie's "accident." "I would go to the Friday night fights," he said. "I would have a ringside seat, and make myself very conspicuous. The whole hit-and-run thing could happen while I was there." Housman asked who would do the job for him. "Oh, there are several guys that I got out of the pen I could call on. If they didn't do what I told them I could send them back."

Dullea put down the earphone feeling morally obligated to warn the intended victim. "I sat back," said Dullea, "and pondered on what could be done to prevent Egan from carrying out his murderous plan. I could not arrest him. He had committed no crime. And we had no legal proof that it was his voice we had heard over the wires. Besides, the whole plot was so incredible for a man in his position, that even if we could prove that it was he who had done the talking, he would have no difficulty in making it appear that he had been merely joking."

Dullea spun out Josie's number on the rotary dial. He had decided that to tell her who he was would do no good and might do some harm. As Egan's benefactor, she might take it for granted that Dullea, Egan's political enemy, was trying to do him a personal injury. If she were to tell Egan, he, as an exceedingly clever lawyer, would seize the situation and turn it to his own advantage. "Egan would compel me," decided Dullea, "through a slander suit, to reveal the source of my information—and thus deprive me of my secret means of learning anything further about his plans or Earl Leter's murder."

"This is a friend," Dullea told Josie. "I want to warn you against Frank Egan. He's after your money. He wants your insurance. You are in grave danger if you have anything further to do with him."

"Warn me against Frank Egan?" Josie burst into laughter. "Why he's the best friend I have." She slammed down the phone.

Because Josie hadn't taken his warning seriously, Dullea wrote her an anonymous letter detailing Egan's plot to carry out her hit-and-run murder. This had one effect. The following day Josie complained to Alexander Keenan, her physician, "Nephew has all my money and I do not even have the scratch of a pen to show for it. Instead of me, you should present your next medical bill to Frank Egan."

When Dr. Keenan did, Egan told him Josie's funds had been exhausted. This shocked Josie who began calling Egan's office every hour or going there and pestering his steno, Marion Lambert.

Over the Dictaphone Dullea heard Egan say, "Aunty's driving me crazy to return her money. Now she's threatening to take me before the Bar Association. I can't stand it any longer. It's her life or mine." Dullea doubled the guard around her and penned another warning note, which had no effect. Finally, he dismissed the men stationed outside 41 Lakewood Drive, Josie's home, and began standing guard himself. He hadn't been able to save Clara Newman and all the other landladies from the Gorilla Man, but forewarned he could save Josie Hughes.

The next Friday night, Dullea drove to Josie's home in Ingleside Terraces. He passed Cerritos Avenue and Moncado Way, the site of the old Ingleside Steeplechase Race Track. It was gone now. Nearly twenty years earlier, developers had purchased the land for $2,500 per acre and constructed housing tracts around the site, following its straightaways and turns. Urbano Drive, built over the track, duplicated its lozenge shape, running east to west. Dullea turned onto the road and soon reached Egan's "charming many-gabled three-story" on the straightaway. He saw Egan in the window. Dullea drove on to the clubhouse turn. Nestled in the vee of Entrada Court was the biggest sundial in the world, where local ladies conducted needlework parties. Five curving roads intersected the track, and just on the other side of Ocean Avenue, they became Fairfield, Lakewood, Manor, and Pinehurst drives. Dullea crossed Ocean to Lakewood, where Josie lived.

Josie's two-story stucco stood at the end of a line of similar whitewashed Spanish Colonials crawling up and over a steep hill. Most Ingleside Terraces homes had been designed in the Arts and Crafts or Mediterranean style. The developer, Joseph Leonard, had made "crowded conditions impossible" by offering oversize lots, ranging from fifty to eighty feet in width and from one to two hundred feet in depth from four different plans. Josie's small two-bedroom had cost her $6,000.

Dullea secreted himself uphill where he could see Josie's front door and peer down on her mission-tiled roof. Her dark-trimmed bay windows overlooked the street. A small garage, virtually soundproof, lay below the master bedroom where a basement ordinarily would be. The garage was locked and empty. Josie did not drive and never allowed anyone the use of her garage.

Around 8:00 P.M. a tall, lean figure came puffing uphill from the direction of Urbano Drive and mounted the ten brick steps to Josie's door. A quick sharp buzz. When Josie opened the door, Dullea saw Frank Egan framed in the light. As the door closed, Dullea rushed down the drop of the hill but checked himself in mid-street. "Egan wouldn't act without an iron-clad alibi," he thought. "Mrs. Hughes could not be safer than when Egan is in the house with her." An hour later Egan came down the steps and Dullea phoned Josie. When she answered, he hung up. Afterward, Josie's neighbors complained her phone rang far into the late hours.

Over the next week Dullea monitored the Dictograph. "From time to time," he said, "we heard Egan refer again to the project of murdering Mrs. Hughes, and almost as frequently I phoned and attempted to convince her that she should have nothing more to do with him."

Dullea overheard Egan planning to become "the Czar of San Francisco" by murdering any political foes in his path to the mayor's seat. He even targeted his ineffectual assistant, Gerald Kenny, a man who could absorb a martini at fifty paces. But there was no more talk of killing Josie. Dullea concluded he was aware his plan was blown. As Egan's ranting grew more incoherent, Dullea decided he was either drunk or using dope or his mind was failing. If he was not in his right mind, there was no reason to take his threats more seriously than those of any hophead.

More months passed. Dullea disconnected the bug, but consulted with his lawyer, Vince Hallinan, who assured him there was no longer any danger. On March 7, the bank, as forecast, filed a foreclosure suit on Egan's house. Whatever the desperate public defender was going to do he was going to do it soon.

Anguished by indecision, Dullea decided to see Chief Quinn. Two years before, Quinn, a favorite of the mayor and police commissioners, had rocketed from sergeant to chief of police. His first official act as chief had been to lock Mrs. Frances Orlando in the Bush Street Jail for the crime of dressing in men's clothes. Quinn's promise of a clean department had been welcome words to Dullea. During the Rum Bribery Investigations in April 1922, police officers, deputy sheriffs, and their higher-ups had been arrested in every district. Police Commissioner Theodore Roche had begun cleaning house with the arrest of knife-wielding ex-cop Tom Joyce, the proprietor of a blind pig at 47 Sixth Street. "Cops accepting bribes from saloon keepers in return for immunity from arrest," Roche said, "will be prosecuted on charges of conspiracy to violate the Volstead Act [which outlawed alcohol]. Policemen accepting money from bootleggers will be weeded out. I have no use for a crook inside or outside the department."

Had corruption returned to levels equaling those wild and wooly days when every cop was on the take? Dullea's flaw was that, like most honest men, it was difficult for him to perceive dishonesty in others. But with the example of Egan, his faith was shaken. He had learned how far a respected man of the public trust could fall. Unable to endure another sleepless night, he walked down the marble corridor to the chief's office at the northwest corner of the HOJ.

The Old Girl (as they called the fortresslike HOJ) was a boxy, serviceable stone edifice with semicircular bays and tall fan windows with radiating sash bars, each like half a lemon slice. The elaborate fretwork, stone mullions, grillwork, parapets, and a long rooftop battlement failed to add a grain of cheer to the oppressive tomb. Chief Quinn's office was something else entirely.

The big front room was opulent—fine rugs, parqueted hardwood floors, and long polished tables. A photo of the chief hung alongside Mayor "Sunny Jim" Rolph Jr. next to pictures of two early civilian-appointees, DA White of the Mooney bomb plot days and affable Dan O'Brien who tried to be "a good fellow" by day and an officer-administrator by night and failed miserably at both. Quinn's latest photo showed him in action on the running board of his new armored police vehicle and Captain Mike Riordan aiming a machine gun through a gun port. In Dullea's own office was exhibited only a single photo and that of his wife and three sons.

Against one wall the chief proudly displayed shining rows of police trophy cups. In his office, Dullea had a single battered trophy he hadn't won for anything. Someone once brought him flowers in it, and he'd kept the empty cup. Next to an early lowboy radio, the chief prominently displayed the ensign of the International Association of Chiefs of Police, which he hoped to someday head. Across the room the stolid Irishman, a study in military severity, sat rigidly behind a huge mahogany desk. He was well-buffed, well-starched perfection, his superbly cut dark blue serge studded with golden epaulettes and full gold braid. A gold star, two gold stripes, and three gold buttons gleamed on each sleeve. Quinn's gilded elegance contrasted against a triangle of colorful flags unfurled on both sides of him. "Assured, resplendent in blue and gold, almost Napoleonic in his posture," Kevin Starr wrote of Quinn's appearance at a Civic Center rally, "the Chief embodied the power of established authority as it struggled to contain the increasing restiveness of the populace." That day, Quinn stood not against a background of flags but against a white sea of union placards. He was not only antiunion but antireform, especially with his own department. He routinely stifled any opposition or attempts for reform by discrediting or transferring any critic into the hinterlands.

On the same day the Whispering Gunman was convicted, Quinn had transferred, unannounced, five high-ranking officers and six policemen looking into graft within the SFPD. "The less talk about the transfers the better for all concerned," Quinn threatened as he packed off the most aggressive to work at the city jail or Potrero Station. "When you're at Potrero Station you can't go any further down," said one cop, "so if you ever get transferred from Potrero Station you must be on your way up." In a department predominantly Irish—40 percent native-born Irish and 40 percent Irish American, such a demotion was called an "Irish promotion."

Dullea carefully studied the ceiling line of the elegant office, looking for the twin wires it was alleged Chief Quinn used to bug his deputy chief's office next door. Quinn, a San Francisco native, was born April 23, 1883. He attended Lincoln Grammar School; graduated from Sacred Heart College; and studied law at Saint Ignatius College, graduating in 1925. He had been walking a beat since 1906. With a sweep of his cigar—long, thin, expensive—Quinn directed Dullea to a seat. He held his cigar between his first two fingers, thumb tucked under, and pointed down. When he had a point to make he held it like a gun. When he was of equal temperament, he held it perfectly horizontal. But when it pointed up . . . "Get to the point, Charlie. I'm busy on these robberies."

In May, a big redheaded man had pushed into the Lowe-Davis Loan Company asking for a $100 loan. "Sorry, we don't lend that much," said the manager. "Just for that, I'm going to take the whole works." Drawing an automatic, Red escaped with the money on the No. 9 Market Street car.

In July, he robbed the American Trust Company and escaped in a Yellow Cab. He and a partner then knocked over the Bank of America on Seventeenth. In this wild era of Tommy guns, sawed-off shotguns, and bank heists, there were six times more crooks in the nation than grocers. One year, six hundred banks were robbed for a loss of $3.5 million to the nation. Quinn's solution was to replace ringing alarms at the banks with silent alarms and invite the employees to the HOJ firing range to learn to shoot. He suspected experienced bank robber George "Red" Kerr. In the end, the robber turned out to be Tommy Coleman, a San Quentin escapee who was a dead ringer for Kerr, who was innocent. Quinn signed his report with a Wahl-Eversharp Gold Seal fountain pen, which had a 14K-gold point and embellishments. He turned it in the light. It was a treasured gift from Commissioner Roche.

Dullea didn't know how to suggest that a trusted, popular public official was plotting murder. Finally he just came out with it. There was a moment of silence as the chief absorbed his words. Then his jowls quivered, his watery eyes blinked, and his cigar jutted to forty-five degrees. "Which side are you on?" he snapped. His fist came down hard. "I want you to back off Egan! Get it, Charlie?"

Quinn stood and walked to the recessed window. His posture was perfect, alert, filled with fierce energy and strength. He was a big man, two hundred pounds and taller than Dullea. In spite of the spare tire around his waist, the overall impression was of power.

Clasping both hands behind his back, the big Irishman rocked back and forth, his eyes sweeping the blossoming trees of Portsmouth Square across the street. The room was pin-drop quiet. Dullea could hear a clerk down the hall pecking out a report. "Because men are human," Quinn explained in a calm voice, fighting to control his irritation, "there will be occasional scandals and some, as a matter of course, will involve public officials, but much of this is imagined in the fevered minds of do-gooders." He turned, small teeth tight against his lower lip. "I want you to back off of any sort of investigation. I will handle matters such as that. Do you understand, Charlie? For Christ's sake, Egan's a former city police officer and a fireman." The cigar dropped to half-mast. Dullea's moment had passed.

He returned to his small ground floor office with the green tacked carpet, more distraught than before. Quinn's comments had seemed overly defensive to him—as if he knew of a deeper internal corruption than Frank Egan, which in itself was horrendous. Yes, thought Dullea, curious remarks. But his problem had still not been solved. Still ringing in his ears were the last words he had heard Egan speak over the planted bug—"By Friday night all my troubles will be over." But which Friday night? And by *troubles* did he mean Josie Hughes? Or someone else? Each Friday night after that Dullea ordered a secret two-man watch be kept on Josie. There might be nothing to the threat, but he could not take the chance. He did not intend to fail another woman as he had all those San Francisco landladies in 1926.

SIX

The ancient Greeks got their 5th century B.C. word *Gorillai* from the native name of a hairy tribe in Africa and used it to mean savage.

IAN REDMOND, *GORILLA*

"AMERICA had never seen anything like Earle Leonard Nelson before or since," wrote Jay Robert Nash of the Gorilla Man's true identity. "There have been killers who were just as methodical and who carried out their brutal murders with just as much religious fervor—but none had the transcontinental intensity. . . . He was a killer apart, a killer's killer, a mass murderer who worked coast to coast with a Bible in his hand."

The era of the sex crime that followed World War I may have begun with the Gorilla Man, who terrorized the North American continent for years.

IN Winnipeg on June 9, 1927, Earle Nelson encountered fourteen-year-old Lola Gowan on the front steps of 133 Smith Street selling artificial flowers her crippled sister made to support her family, who lived on University Street across from the Vaughn Street jail. He wanted to buy some, but she would have to come to his room so he could get his money. Once inside, he wrapped a cloth around her neck, strangled her, and repeatedly violated her. Stuffing her corpse under his bed, he went to sleep.

In the morning he packed Lola's belongings and headed down Portage

Avenue to find new lodgings. On Riverton Avenue he spotted a "Room for Rent" sign in a window. He told landlady Emily Patterson he didn't have any money but would do repair work in exchange. He was seen fixing the Pattersons' screen door. That evening Emily's husband, William, returned home. "Where is your mother, children?" he asked. "Oh, Daddy, she's been gone all day," the two boys cried.

Emily hadn't been seen since that morning. After a search of the neighborhood, William reported her missing, then put the kids to bed. As it approached midnight, he grew more worried. He trudged to their bedroom and, sobbing, dropped to his knees at the foot of their bed. For almost an hour he prayed for Emily's safe return. "Please direct me to where she is," he begged. When he opened his eyes he saw little pink fingertips peeking out from under the bed. Reaching beneath, he felt an ice-cold hand. While he had been praying for Emily's return, she had been only inches away—naked, throat crushed, and raped after death. Her wedding ring was missing. The strangler had taken it along with the family Bible, $70, and William's brown whipcord suit. As was Earle Nelson's custom he left behind his own clothes.

His discards provided enough clues to send the police on a canvas of local boardinghouses that ended at Katherine and August Hill's. "I haven't taken in any suspicious lodgers lately," said Mrs. Hill. "In fact we've had no new lodgers since Mr. Woodcots last Wednesday. He's rather on the short side, dark, with blue eyes and a simian mouth and jaw."

The detectives raced upstairs to his room. As soon as they entered they smelled a sickening smell. As a detective bent to retrieve an artificial flower, he saw the body of the missing flower girl, mutilated beyond recognition. "Good God, man!" he shouted.

"To think that that fiend lay sleeping in that room all night with that poor dead girl under his bed!" August said as he shielded his sobbing wife. So horribly treated was Lola's body that Chief of Detectives George Smith permanently sealed the record.

Nelson used $10 of the stolen money to buy a fountain pen, corduroy trousers, and a plaid shirt at Sam Waldman's secondhand shop on Main Street. He left behind Patterson's clothes, then got a massage, shave, and haircut at the Central Barber Shop next door. Nick Taylor grew suspicious as he cut Nelson's hair. It was encrusted with blood from deep nail scratches on his scalp where Emily had fought back. Nelson caught a ride with Hugh Elder into Regina, Saskatchewan, two hundred miles west. He engaged a room from landlady Mary Rowe on June 12 under the name Harry Harcout. The next morning, he saw an accurate description of himself in the paper and bought new clothes from the Royal Second Hand Store. He changed into blue overalls, a khaki shirt, and cap, then caught a lift from Isadore Silverman, a scrap metal dealer, whose route took them around police patrols via back roads to Boissevain, Manitoba.

"If he's heading for the border," said Smith, "he'll have to cross prairie country where there are few towns for him to lose himself. A lone hitchhiker should be easy to spot."

Canadian constables and U.S. policemen closed in on him from both sides. When he bought some cheese and a drink at the Wakopa General Store the proprietor, Les Morgan, recognized him and notified Constable Wilton A. Gray, the only officer on duty at the Killarney, Manitoba, department.

Constable Gray was patrolling twelve miles north of the international border just outside the small farming community of flat land and tree-lined rivers and hills when he saw a man nonchalantly walking down the road and asked his name. With a shy smile, he said it was Wilson and that he was a stock hand who worked on a nearby farm. Gray was suspicious. No Canadian would call a spread this far west a farm. "We're looking for a man who is responsible for the deaths of twenty six women," Gray said, and watched for a giveaway sign.

"A mass murderer? I only do my lady-killing on Saturday nights."

"You'd better ride back to Killarney with me, so we can check your story."

"Fair enough. You fellows have to play it safe when there's a killer on the loose."

"It can't be him," Gray thought. "He's too cool."

At the ancient and tiny Killarney jail, Gray took away his shoes, socks, and belt as a precautionary measure, then double-locked him inside a cell and handcuffed him to the bars. He then walked fifteen feet away into the next room to ring Inspector Smith in Winnipeg.

"I think we've got the wrong man," Gray told him. "He says that his name is Wilson."

"That must be the strangler!" Smith said. The Gorilla Man had used the name Wilson here in Winnipeg and in San Francisco. "Don't be taken in by his innocent demeanor. Twenty-six women are dead because they made the same mistake. For the love of God! You didn't leave him alone, did you?"

Gray ran into the next room. The Gorilla Man was gone. He had picked his cuffs with a nail file he found under his bunk, opened the cell doors with a wire, and escaped without his shoes. As a posse was assembled, Smith sent four detectives to the isolated village by plane. He and another fifty followed by train. Meanwhile, Nelson, who had stolen new clothes, was fast asleep in William Allen's barn, one block from the jail. The next day, he showed up at the station to wait for a southbound train and hid in some bushes by a grain elevator.

Constable William Renton spotted Nelson, jumped the fence, and intercepted him. He studied the stranger's disheveled clothes—a moth-eaten sweater and a pair of hockey skates with the blades removed serving as shoes. "You look like you slept in the open last night, sir."

"Where do you farm?" Nelson pointed to a building by the tracks. "That's a slaughterhouse," said Renton.

Nelson began running down the railway tracks as the morning express rolled into view and rushed right into Smith's arms as he stepped from the train. Captain Matheson of the SFPD flew from San Francisco to Winnipeg to confirm Nelson's identity. He studied the strange, blank-faced man who wore a tweed suit and cap. His wide shoulders and huge manacled hands still gave the impression of power. During his trial, Nelson showed no emotion as forty American witnesses identified him. "That's the man," said Matheson.

When Nelson's aunt Lillian and estranged wife, Mary, attended, he ignored them. On November 14, 1927, the jury deliberated just forty-eight minutes before convicting him of Emily Patterson's murder. Despite his pleas of insanity and innocence ("Murder just isn't possible for a man of my high Christian ideals"), he was sentenced to hang on Friday, January the thirteenth as the thirteenth man ever hung at the Vaughn Street Jail, which was across the street from the Patterson family home. "I am innocent,"

Nelson said. "I stand innocent before God and man. I forgive those who have wronged me and ask forgiveness of those I have injured. God have mercy!" Earle Nelson's insatiable habit of strangling landladies was finally broken.

"THAT'S odd," Dullea had said as he perused the San Francisco papers. No mention anywhere of the Gorilla Man's execution in Canada. He could not be sure he was even dead. In Chicago, where there was a corrupt police force, criminals bought their way off death row or faked their executions. Perversely, Dullea hoped the Gorilla Man was still alive to return so he could have a second chance to catch the murderer.

Elsewhere the Gorilla Man stirred. His huge hands opened and closed. He was coming back to life. His eyes turned west.

SEVEN

"Gorilla" actually meant a hairy, tough man before it meant the ape; the ape gets its name from the man and not the other way around as one might think.

—IAN REDMOND, *GORILLA*

THE second anniversary of Officer John Malcolm's murder, Friday, April 29, 1932, was exceptionally cold. Inspectors Jim Malloy and Bart Lally were bundled up and parked on Fairfield Way where it curved over to intersect Lakewood Avenue and continued north to dead-end at Kenwood Way. Lally, cigar clenched between his teeth, scanned the road for the hundredth time. Malloy had been combing his wavy, silver hair straight back. Each time the thick shock had sprung back as curvy as Fairfield Way. There was scarcely a straight line in the Ingleside Terraces or in nearby St. Francis Woods' shaded, winding ways. It was as if their architect had only a French curve with which to draw his plans.

Because all the streets were curved and steep, it made a stakeout difficult and concealed any potential attack on Josie around the corner. The roads were built wide to accommodate big automobiles like the 1926 sable black Phaeton Lincoln custom touring car in front of Josie's house. Its engine was running smoothly. In those days you could get eight good years out of such a model with a radio and a speaker set into bird's-eye maple.

Mrs. Walter Bowers, a neighbor, saw the touring car at 4:30 P.M. "A man drove up in the car—owl lights, a low tonneau and extra-thick trunk," she said, "and appeared to conceal his face with a hand and his cap pulled down over his eyes." She also sensed there might be a second man sitting in the rear seat. Fourteen doors down Mrs. G. E. Little of 55 Lakewood also scrutinized the unique sedan and its driver. "A horse-faced young man, about twenty-three, with a close-cropped mustache was sitting in it," she said. "He tried to shield his face, but I got a real good look at him. I would recognize him if I saw him again. He was Verne Doran, you know, Mr. Frank Egan's chauffeur."

At 4:35 P.M., Josie rang her friend Mrs. Joseph Dennis. "It's gotten so I'm afraid to leave the house at night," she lamented. As they chatted Mrs. Dennis heard Josie's doorbell sound. "It might be someone trying to get me," said Josie, and hung up.

An hour later Mrs. Albert E. Jacks, sixteen doors up, saw Frank Egan walking within a block of Josie's home. That was not unusual because he lived so nearby. Shortly after, the Lincoln started up and came cruising north along Fairfield at twenty-five miles per hour. As it turned into Kenwood Way, Malloy adjusted his little spectacles and noted the uncommon Phaeton trunk and unique spotlight that hung from the median of its radiator, which was very unlike a Packard's jutting radiator (gangsters commonly took their victims for a last ride in a Packard sedan). Within two years, except for Fords and Chevys, the square radiator would be replaced by the streamlined radiators of the Chrysler airflow and the Pierce-Arrow's gracefully tapered front. The back and side curtains were tightly drawn, and Malloy could not see inside. The car pushed on east, swung south on Keystone Way, then rolled back around on Ocean Avenue, the local main drag, to Lakewood. The sedan crept past the lookouts for a second time. As if testing the waters, it came around a third time. When the sedan passed a fourth time traveling at sixty miles per hour, its lights were out and it quickly passed out of sight.

When the dark sedan did not return, Malloy and Lally felt secure in relinquishing their surveillance because they knew Josie never went out at night; at 8:35 P.M., they returned to the HOJ. An hour later Mrs. Jacks observed a large touring car with its lights out back away from Josie's unused garage. A second man slipped from the bushes at the end of the driveway, closed the garage door, and slid into the auto like a cat. At 9:45 P.M., the speeding Lincoln passed Rena and Warren Louw walking east from Timothy

Pflueger's new white-towered movie palace, the El Rey Theater on Ocean. They had just seen *The Champ,* a tear-jerker starring Wallace Beery and Jackie Cooper.

When the cruising auto returned, this time going west, and slowly passed the Louws, it made them nervous enough to step back into a doorway. The Louws waited until the car had rounded the curve of Kenwood and swooped northeast before they continued up the severe incline for another two hundred feet to 150 Kenwood. They reached the O'Neil home—white picket fence, weedy overgrown yard, street pole, and a dark shape lying in the road flush to the curbstone. "You don't think much finding a woman's body like that," recalled Mr. Louw. "You just feel." He ran the twenty doors down to his house and rang the police from there. "Then I went back to see if she was really dead. She was."

When Inspectors Herman Wobke, Ray O'Brien, and LaTulipe reached the scene, they saw no evidence around the body of any accident. "No skid marks or broken glass," LaTulipe remarked. "It's chilly and she's not wearing a coat or hat. She has no purse and there are no house keys on her. The car was going downhill, yet her head is pointing uphill and her ankles are crossed."

Anyone hit by a speeding car is usually thrown headfirst in the direction the car is going. No blood about the face (only the bruise marks of what looked like a fist) and no marks of having been hit before being run over. Her sole identification was a gold ring inscribed "Joe to Jessie." When this fifth unidentified female body of the year was conveyed to the morgue by Deputy Coroner Mike Brown, the best known and most respected coroner in the state, Lieutenant Pete Danahy and reporter Charlie Huse were waiting. Danahy saw no cuts or bruises on the hands, arms, elbows, feet, knees, or legs, places where they should be. "That don't look so hot to me as a hit-and-run case," said Danahy, dragging out his pad and pen, "but it sure has possibilities as an old-fashioned murder mystery."

Early Saturday morning, Egan raced down the marble steps to the coroner's clammy basement office to identify Jane Doe number five. "Mrs. Jessie Scott Hughes is an old and very dear friend," he told Mrs. Jane Walsh, the coroner's chief deputy. "It's her. I've handled her business affairs for years as an advisor, ever since I was in private practice."

"Has she any relatives?" asked Mrs. Walsh as she bent to retrieve a blank form.

"Yes," Egan said, "but she is not on friendly terms with any of the family. As Mrs. Hughes would have wished, I shall take charge of the funeral arrangements." Mrs. Walsh nodded her head sympathetically, asked if Josie had left a will and who the beneficiary was.

"I am," said Egan. "She left an estate of $25,000 and named me the executor."

"Did she have any insurance?"

"Only a $2,000 policy," Egan said as he signed the delivery receipt to turn Josie's body over to a private undertaker. "Relation to deceased: Executor," he printed.

Reporter Henry "Hank" Peters, at a cashier's window, overheard Egan and went directly upstairs to Dullea's office. "I didn't intend to get a 'raise' out of the captain," Peters said later. "All I did was casually mention the hit-and-run body from last night had just been identified by Frank Egan. But when I spoke the name of Mrs. Hughes, he almost hit the ceiling. He said the case might develop into something tremendous, and then he closed up and wouldn't say any more and told me to get out."

Alone in his office Dullea felt as if the shadow of the Gorilla Man had fallen over him again. Once more, he'd been unable to save a woman's life. He wondered whether it really was a hit-and-run accident or if Egan actually carried out his plot in front of his detectives. Without warning, Egan strutted into Dullea's office, took a chair, and tossed his expensive tan fedora onto the blotter. "I've just come from the morgue, Charlie," he said. "This Josie Hughes, who was run over last night, was an old friend of mine. This is a terrible thing. She was like a mother to me."

"Where do you suppose she was going at that hour on a chilly night without a coat?" Dullea fought to contain his fury. Under the desk his hands were clenched.

"Josie frequently went for long walks without her hat and coat."

"That's not what the neighbors say. They said she prided herself on her appearance and never even went out to hang clothes on the line without wearing a hat. She was afraid to go out alone at night, especially so far above her home on the sharp incline where her body was found."

"Oh, no, you're wrong there, Charlie. I had often warned her against walking about the neighborhood in the evening. Mrs. Hughes frequently took walks in the hills about her home attired only in house clothing and sweater—no coat, no hat. I cautioned her not to go out without her glasses—about a year ago she was almost hit by an auto—just as she was last night. Her son, James, fourteen, was killed in an auto accident fifteen years ago."

Dullea contemplated Egan's facial expressions. Was he a cold-blooded murderer or not? His placid, self-assured demeanor provided no clue. But Egan was a skilled jury lawyer and consequently a fine actor.

"By the way, Charlie, I was coming in to see you this morning anyway. Something ought to be done about the parking arrangements in front of the Dreamland Pavilion on fight nights. They're terrible."

Dullea's heart gave a leap, though his face remained impassive. There it was—the alibi he had expected. "Dreamland Pavilion? Is that where you were last night?"

"Yep. I came early and remained ringside the entire evening. On the whole, it was a pretty good card, but the parking was terrible."

"Well, you should speak to [Captain Charles] Goff at the Traffic Bureau, not me."

"An amusing thing happened, by the way. Some drunk sat behind Dr. Housman and I and spent the whole evening throwing Eskimo pies at a friend who was with me."

"It's lucky he didn't throw them at you. He'd have made a fine mess of that." Dullea indicated Egan's spotless fedora. Now he was morally certain that last night's tragedy had been the work of the man before him, but it would take more than a moral certainty to convince a jury. "San Francisco's public defender had murdered Mrs. Hughes," he thought, "yet I can not arrest him."

"Well, I have to hurry to wind up Josie's affairs," Egan said, rising. "Busy, busy, busy." On his way out he brushed past Lally, who had Louw's statement in hand. "So Louw got a good description of the car did he?" Dullea asked Lally. "Louw knows cars," Lally said. "He's a garage mechanic and saw the cruising Lincoln well under a street light."

"Fine. Now make a list of all of Frank Egan's friends and former clients, especially ex-cons and see which one owns a car like that." Then he sent for Homicide Inspector Allan McGinn, head of the Death Squad.

McGinn was a burly man, his tiny eyes and mouth lost in a broad, square face. His features were made even smaller by his prodigious nose and huge ears. He had carelessly shaved that morning, his shirt needed pressing, and in almost every respect he was drab. Only the shining gold of his shield accented his cheap suit and vest. McGinn placed his battered gray fedora where Egan had laid his splendid hat.

McGinn was in bad with Chief Quinn that morning and was consequently depressed. The day before, Louis Zanardi had been beaten to death by three unidentified men after a baseball game at Rolph Playground, and McGinn was getting nowhere finding them. "Get out to Josie Hughes's house," Dullea told him. "Find out what really happened there last night."

McGinn, LaTulipe, and Inspector George Engler coursed up busy Market Street in its generally westward path toward the Pacific and rolled up and over Twin Peaks. Some twelve thousand feet below ran the longest transit tunnel in the world (an extension of the No. 12 streetcar downtown line). The two-and-a-quarter-mile-long bore took five minutes. From 4th and Market over 20th Avenue and Ellis Street, it took McGinn forty-two minutes to reach Ingleside Terraces and call Dullea.

"Every window is locked," McGinn said, "and every door is double-bolted and locked from the inside."

"Then how did Josie get out?" Dullea asked. "She didn't have a key on her. Get inside no matter how." McGinn was smashing a window with his gun butt when Anthony J. Bell, a special police officer employed as a watchman, pulled up. Bell had patrolled the vicinity of Josie's home for several years and knew Josie and her habits. "What's going on here?" Bell shouted. "Frank Egan called me last night and told me to pay particular attention to the Hughes home and see that nobody breaks in."

McGinn flashed his badge, then climbed through into the vestibule, entered the front living room and down a hallway to the dining room. Inside, fifty canaries in fifty little cages began to sing all at once. Covering his ears, McGinn turned left into the kitchen and a small breakfast nook. Josie's frugal dinner was still laid out to be cooked. Her keys were still on the dining room sideboard. Upstairs, her hat and coat lay on the bed. He tested the locked windows, then walked out onto the little porch above the garage. He went downstairs where he and LaTulipe observed that the garage double doors had a self-engaging spring lock. "So they took her out by way of the garage," surmised McGinn. "That's the only way." He knelt and smelled a puddle on the floor—water, soap, and cleanser. But whoever had scrubbed the concrete had missed four black impressions.

"Tire marks!" said LaTulipe. "But Josie didn't own a car." Positioning his tripod directly above the treads to prevent foreshortening, he directed a light across the surface for maximum contrast and snapped a shot with his mounted four-by-five speed Graphic. Then, starting at one edge, he pressed a strip of fingerprint tape onto the print, overlapped it with a second strip by a quarter inch, and lifted the entire impression. On the concrete he found several long gray hairs, which he put into a glassine envelope.

AT the morgue Dr. A. M. Moody, the pathologist, briefed Dullea. "Josie Hughes died of a crushed liver. Her chest was caved in by the wheel of a car and the left side of her face and shoulder were covered with friction burns. She was flat on her back at the time."

"Could she have lived long enough to turn herself over?"

"No, death was instantaneous."

"Then since she was found lying facedown someone must have placed or thrown her that way after she was dead."

At the sloped table Dullea methodically went over Josie's white waist with a magnifier. Near the left shoulder the garment was badly soiled with grease, but the brown silk sweater over it had no holes, tears, or dirt marks. It was also buttoned wrong. "Her sweater was put on after she was killed," said Dullea. "Someone else dressed her and that means she was killed at home.

"Egan's accomplices, and it must have been a two-man job, borrowed a heavy car, drove it into Josie's garage, chloroformed her unconscious and threw her under the wheels of the car. They ran back and forth over her prone body *inside her own house*. They dropped her dead body into the road several blocks away to simulate a hit-run accident."

No matter where he touched in this murder wheel, its spokes all ran to Egan. LaTulipe compared the garage floor tire tracks to those pressed into Josie's skirt. "They are identical," he said.

"Frank, take some men and go out to Egan's house," said Dullea. "Compare this tire pattern with those of his Lincoln sedan. But I don't expect a match. Egan's blue Lincoln is of a much lighter shade."

At Egan's, LaTulipe jacked up the rear of the Lincoln, rolled the tire treads with ink, lowered the wheels onto a long strip of paper, and pushed the car forward one complete revolution to make an impression. While he was doing this Egan fled. "I was terribly angry at all this suspicion," he explained later. "I walked out of the house. I guess my mind snapped. I cannot remember anything else."

"This appears to be a most serious case," Assistant DA Isador Golden told the press, "with some unhappy phases." Golden ran one hand through his silvering hair. "To disclose certain facts at this time would be to defeat the ends of the police and destroy their efforts to prove the truth in this case."

Golden, McGinn, and Dullea located the death car at a garage at Turk Street and Masonic Avenue. In the low tonneau Dullea found seven long gray hairs clinging to the passenger footrest. "This is probably where Josie was dropped from the car," he said.

At the lab, LaTulipe washed the seven hairs in ether alcohol to remove all greasy matter, gave a glass slide a coat of nail polish, and imbedded the hairs there. After the lacquer dried, he removed the hairs leaving behind an impression like tire treads and compared them to a similar slide containing impressions of Josie's hairs found in her garage. They were alike.

"McGinn," Dullea said, "drive out to the 26th Avenue firehouse and see fire lieutenant Oscar Postel, the registered owner of car. He's a friend of Egan's."

An anonymous caller was telling Postel, "Get that car out of the garage," when McGinn arrived.

"The cops have already got it," Postel said.

McGinn grabbed the phone as the line went dead. He got the story out of Postel: "Egan's chauffeur, Verne L. Doran, borrowed my Lincoln at noon on Friday to take him for a ride."

"Oscar didn't see that car again until 10:45 that night," fireman Charles Lynch added, "and when he did the radiator was still warm."

On Monday, May 2, at 5:30 P.M., Lorraine Egan's phone rang. "I'm going to the Native Sons' banquet for Coroner Leland," Egan said, "and won't be home to dress as it's an informal affair."

She got another call at 9:00 P.M. "We've just taken Frank Egan for a ride," a man told her and hung up.

Shocked, Mrs. Egan called her brother, Harold Kip. "I am terribly worried, Harold," she said. "I can't understand why, if Frank were all right, he would not have left some word or called home. He is a home-loving man and never drank and has no enemies that I know of."

She was unaware that her husband, in his desperate attempts to head off financial disaster, had initiated business dealings with C. Vincent Riccardi, ex-con, disbarred attorney, and former jury fixer. For the last week, Egan had been carrying a loaded revolver in a breast holster and a reserve clip of cartridges in his pocket.

Dullea was in his office drawing up an arrest warrant for Egan when the SFPD switchboard at Sutter 1-2020 put a call through to him. Dullea grasped the waist of the candlestick phone and pressed the bell-shaped receiver to his ear.

"Captain, this is Frank Egan. Two men have got me."

"Who has got you?" asked Dullea. "Some of my men?"

"No. These men, they've got me. In a telephone booth . . . wait until I get my bearings . . . at the north end of the Ferry Building. . . . They're outside. They think I'm telephoning my wife. Help me! Charlie, you know I had nothing to do with the Hughes case. I was at the fights that night—"

"Give me more definite information. I'll shoot right down . . ." The phone clicked in Dullea's ear. He dropped the receiver onto its hook and ordered officers to the Egan home as he dashed out. At high speed, Dullea drove the half mile to the concourse at the foot of Market Street. The wide street was silent except for the distant whine of police sirens and a cab rounding the corner. Its motor faded away, the sirens waned and the thoroughfare was quiet again.

Dullea, eyes glittering with excitement, crossed to the Ferry Building. The majestic sweep of its front arcade was broken only by a protruding central entrance pavilion and four longitudinal bays arched like an ancient Roman aqueduct. Dullea eyed its multiple doors and the six pairs of Corinthian columns running its entire 660-foot length. Each opening offered a place for a man to hide. Dullea quickened his step.

Dispassionately, the great yellow eyes of the Clock Tower peered down on him, a mere speck 240 feet below. His steps echoed in the cavernous building as he jogged toward the Washington Street side, where there was a bank of pay phones. No sign of Frank Egan or two suspicious men or anyone who might have seen them. Outside, brakes squealed. His men had arrived. After a search, they came up empty. Dullea ordered all twenty detectives under him on duty to work the Hughes and Egan investigations as one case. But where was Egan?

An hour before he called Dullea, Egan was observed parking in his regular slot at the St. George Garage on Bush Street. He and another man walked to 333 Kearney Street, where they took the elevator to Egan's office. At 9:20 P.M., when the elevator operator saw the frosted glass go dark, he locked the building for the night. Fifteen minutes later, a patrolman glimpsed Egan and Dr. Housman crossing Powell Street and Geary Avenue. On Kearney Street, the pair bumped into William Otts, a private eye. "Somebody has been tapping my office phone wires in connection with Mrs. Hughes' death," Egan complained, "and I want you to investigate this."

At 10:00 P.M., hotel clerk, R. J. Fraser sighted Egan and Housman strolling along Geary near Jones Street.

This puzzled Chief Quinn. "Egan said he was in the Ferry Building," he noted, "yet we can place him either in his office or on the street at that time."

The chief arranged with NBC radio affiliate KGO for some radio time on Thursday. He reached the complex at 9:00 P.M., passed a glass-enclosed Spanish patio, which permitted a small audience to watch programs live, and strode to the microphone. Quinn loved radio and loved a big audience (three out of five families owned a radio at that time) and was at his best as he broadcast a personal entreaty to Egan at 9:15 P.M.

"As Chief of Police," he began, "I am appealing to you as a public official to appear and make explanation of your telephone conversation with Captain Dullea in which you indicated you were held against your will. It's your duty to reveal the names of the men you said have you in custody. If we do not hear from you within a reasonable time, we shall have to take other measures."

Three days later, there was the first public indication that Josie's death was more than a hit and run, but one of murder. After a conference with DA Matt Brady, Dullea ordered the entire department to search for Egan in connection with Josie's death. McGinn opted out. He was investigating another murder. O'Bryan Bemis, who had won big at the track, had just been found dead at Fort Funston at the California Rod and Gun Club range. Thus it was Lieutenant George Richards, head of the Robbery Detail, who spent the next day scrutinizing city hospital records.

In the late afternoon, he reached an old family residence at 601 Steiner Street, a weathered Victorian known as the Park West Sanitarium, and knocked on a thick oak-paneled door. He was admitted into rooms of high ceilings and richly carved walls. At the admitting desk, he located Egan's name in the register—signed in by Vince Hallinan yesterday at 2:00 A.M. "I told him to notify the police," said Mrs. L. C. Broniscoe, owner. "Mr. Egan was in a terrible condition, unshaven, clothing rumpled. He appeared to be suffering from malnutrition and said he had not eaten since Sunday only wandered the streets in a daze."

As they waited for Dullea, Mrs. Broniscoe showed Richards the basement steam chambers for alcoholics, electrical apparatus for delirium tremens sufferers, and patients strapped in canvas sheet and immersed in cold baths. "It's an odd place," she said. "The longer you are here, the less you know. A few years ago a woman hanged herself. My nurse opened a closet door on the second floor and found her body suspended from a clothes hook."

When Dullea arrived, Dr. V. Mitchell and Dr. Milton Lennon, Egan's physicians, barred him from seeing Egan for twenty-four to thirty-six hours. "He's in a highly hysterical condition with the symptoms of a man who has had no rest and is greatly worried," Mitchell said.

"Look, in a homicide matter we have the right to question anyone if there is any reason to suppose he may help us solve it," said Dullea. "When he gets well enough I want to ask him the circumstances of a homicide case in which the victim was known to him and see if he can shed any light on the investigation."

"Between you and me, I do not think he wandered in the open. He appears to have been indoors since his escape."

"It's nobody's business where he's been!" said Hallinan, who had just rushed in. "I am Egan's attorney and have instructed him not to say anything. He will not talk to the police. He does not feel obliged to explain the telephone call to you. Further, he is not going to be badgered about this thing. The whole thing is ridiculous. No order for Egan's arrest has been issued."

For the next twenty-four hours a detail of inspectors surveilled Egan for "his protection." The only inspector allowed to see Egan was McGinn. "He had his eyes closed and looks wan," he reported.

Twenty-four hours later, Dullea told Egan, "You are not under arrest, but inasmuch as you called on me last Monday night, indicating you required protection, I am now furnishing you that protection—inside a cell."

Now Dullea began searching for Woodland boy Verne La Page Doran, Egan's chauffeur. "Doran is hiding out in a mine run by a crazy old man in a rugged canyon several miles from Carmel," a snitch told him. "Be careful. He is heavily armed and guarded by his friends."

Inspectors Jim Malloy and George Page charged the mine, but Doran had already slipped in from Salinas to surrender at a San Francisco car barn.

At noon on Saturday, May 14, Assistant DA Golden summoned to his Mills Tower office Quinn, Dullea, and Doran's lawyer, Walter McGovern. Dullea shook hands with Doran (a cold, firm handshake) and told the twenty-three-year-old, "I will do everything in my power to recommend leniency, but only if you talk. Do you know anything at all about the charge that Mrs. Hughes was murdered? Did you ever talk to Mr. Egan or with any other person about taking the life of Mrs. Hughes at any time?"

"No, sir, I never knew anything about her death until I read it in the papers."

"Have you any knowledge with reference to her death?" McGovern, a pudgy man with a small, prim mouth, asked. He adjusted his wire-rim glasses. "Were you ever in her home?"

"No, no. Never," Doran answered. "I only knew where she had lived because I read it in the newspapers after she died."

"Did you ever talk to Mr. Egan or with any other person about taking the life of Mrs. Hughes at any time?" Doran said no. "You have learned that if you make a statement involving other persons, that you will be granted your liberty?"

"Captain Dullea will do everything in his power to recommend leniency."

"But of course the fact that you are innocent does not mean you will not be framed."

Before Egan provided him with an alibi, Doran had been serving a year for burglary in San Quentin. Now he not only faced fifteen years on parole violations but burglary and holdup charges in Judge Lile T. Jack's court. That afternoon, Dullea broke Doran who gave up his accomplice—Albert Tinnin (alias Robert Knight), Egan's process server. Tinnin once made a spectacular escape from the Tehama County Jail at Red Bluff. Before Egan provided him with an alibi the previous February, he had been serving ten years to life at San Quentin for the 1924 attempted murder of a Corning woman he had chloroformed and left to die. Josie had also been chloroformed. But Mrs. Marjorie Cockroff was saved when the wind blew her door open. Had she perished, her sister, Helen Kincaid, Tinnin's San Francisco live-in girlfriend, would have received the entire $100,000 shared inheritance their mother had left them. The attorney handling Miss Kincaid's share of the estate? Frank Egan.

A month before Josie's murder Tinnin left his sister's house to register at the Blackstone Hotel on O'Farrell Street. As leader of the Folsom Prison band, he bragged he was going to organize a city orchestra. A week before the murder, Egan introduced Tinnin to Doran. Four days before the murder, Egan bought Tinnin a saxophone, a $300 clarinet, and a Luger pistol. The night before the murder, Egan visited Tinnin for the seventh time at the Blackstone. The day of the murder, Doran and Tinnin rang Josie's bell on a ruse to enable them to recognize her later. Afterward, they met in Egan's office, as he called Josie and told her, "I'm bringing two friends for dinner." When Josie saw the sedan in the driveway she opened the garage door and Doran drove in. "Where's Frank Egan?" she asked and refused to get her hat and coat and join them.

"Tinnin struck her several times," said Doran, "and knocked her unconscious. He placed her in front of the right front wheel and had me drive over her then back over her. Then we put her in the car and drove to Kenwood and threw her out." After the killing, they informed Egan they had accomplished their assignment, then played Ping-Pong until 11:30 P.M. The Monday night Egan disappeared, Tinnin fled the Blackstone Hotel, carrying only his clarinet case.

"That's it," said Dullea. He slapped his thigh. "Doran's story is enough. He and Tinnin murdered Josie at Egan's directive. We have a strong case and I can't find a flaw in it. The physical facts check in every detail and corroborative witnesses have been found. Whether Tinnin now talks makes no difference. If he wants to plead guilty and take his chance with the court, that is his own business. But he will get no recommendation of clemency from me."

Golden's phone rang. He listened, then hung up. His face was ashen. "Frank Egan had escaped from jail," he said.

"It has to be an inside job," Dullea said. "Someone in the SFPD facilitated Egan's escape."

How deep the bought illegalities and official venality ran he could only guess.

EIGHT

The investigator at the scene must protect the deceased person's property, attempt to uncover any facts that tend to throw light on the cause of death, and protect the evidence at the scene.

—CRIME MANUAL OF THE PERIOD

ALL over San Francisco newsboys trumpeted: "Police deny hint escape was 'staged,'" and "Who left the loopholes through which Egan fled last Saturday?" Many citizens believed Chief Quinn had allowed Egan to escape because he knew too much about graft conditions in the city and had to stay at large. To counter rumors of police complicity in the flight, the chief went on the radio again. "We'll be glad to listen to any information Egan has of misdeeds by any member of the police department involving criminal activities," he said, then challenged him to a personal showdown to discuss the allegations.

If Egan was not speedily found Mayor Angelo Rossi said he was giving "very serious consideration to the desirability of a shakeup and an investigation into the Police Commission and police department."

"We put guards on Egan several times," Golden said, "but always had to take them off when Hallinan complained we were violating his civil rights. But if the police and district attorney were fearful of Egan's disclosures they would have passed it off as a hit-and-run accident and nothing further would have come of it. We will welcome Egan's surrender and are confident that he will turn up, dead or alive."

"By all means let him come in and tell us everything he knows," added

Dullea, "no matter whom it hits. We would like to hear anything he might care to tell us about the murder of Mrs. Hughes. Second, we'll be glad to listen to any information he has of misdeeds by any member of the police department involving criminal activities. We did not arrest Egan earlier because the DA advised against it on the grounds that it would be exceedingly bad strategy to move before we had a case on which he could be held in prison once we put him there."

Although he couldn't find Egan, Dullea knew where Dr. Housman was and arrested him. "I am innocent of any charges that might be made against me," the doc said from his cell, "tending to implicate me with the alleged murder of Mrs. Jessie Scott Hughes."

As police searched for Egan in the hills surrounding Emerald Lake, the fugitive was partying inside Hallinan's cabin with dark-haired, lovely Vivian Moore. When he heard Doran's confession over the radio, he drove Hallinan's car back to San Francisco to surrender. At the HOJ, Chief Quinn, in civvies, hat tilted over his right eye and a cigar in his mouth, questioned Egan publicly. A small tape recorder in a glass case on the desk was running as reporters and cops crowded around. Egan was dressed immaculately, plaid handkerchief peeking from his breast pocket. His mouth was drawn tight.

"Have you anything to disclose to me at this time that might show any crooked alliances between the chief of police," Quinn asked, "or all or any members of the police department and any criminals, either organized or unorganized?"

"No, of course not," Egan said flatly. "I have no disclosures to make about the corruption in the department."

"Do you feel on account of me being chief of police that you might not be at liberty to disclose any information you may have, to me, on account of my position, or on account of the fact that I may be allied with the certain criminals referred to?"

"Absolutely no. I know you to be honest and conscientious in your duties."

"Would you prefer to talk to someone higher in authority than me, the Board of Police Commissioners or President of the Board, Theodore J. Roche?"

"No. I have nothing to disclose to anybody."

Although the escape and Egan's demeanor had convinced Dullea there *was* something to disclose, he mollified himself that Egan was as bad as it would get. In the meantime he and McGinn investigated two unsolved murders. On May 15, a cousin of a municipal court judge, Will McCann, had been dumped at Marin and Kansas streets. Three days later bootlegger Luigi Malvese was gunned down in front of the Del Monte Barbershop. McGinn knew Genaro Campanello was the killer, but before he could locate him, the chief sacked him.

Quinn assigned Captain Arthur Layne, commander of the Central District Station, to replace him. Layne was a widower with five sons, $1,800 in the bank, a mortgaged home, and a reputation as the scourge of Barbary Coast gambling interests. In other words, he was an honest cop. At Central Station, Quinn replaced Layne with Captain Fred Lemon, a bull-necked thug. After Layne effectively swept the Tenderloin, arresting grifters, gambling syndicate thugs, and prohibition gangs, the chief sent him on a long vacation. Layne never returned to Central Station where he was so desperately needed, but ended his days running the Police Academy, making sure officers could type. Such was the reward of an honest cop in San Francisco.

On June 4, McGinn captured Tinnin and held him incommunicado at the Whitcome Hotel under security so tight Tinnin's own mother sought legal action to learn where he was sequestered. Tinnin claimed that the day of Josie's murder between 7:30 P.M. and 11:00 P.M., he was in Mrs. Burton Darren's hotel apartment trying to interest her in an invention. The "inventor," Frank Yelavich (with whom Tinnin had been tried for robbery in 1916), didn't keep his appointment. Mrs. Darren wasn't any more reliable. A year earlier, she had been arrested on two charges of violation of the Corporate Securities Act and one charge of Grand Theft. Egan had represented her in court. Nine days later, McGinn drove to the Salinas Hotel and brought back the register Tinnin had signed to forge "the final link in the story." Now that Dullea had all the conspirators in hand, he could pit them against each other.

Those in law-and-order circles, sick of the devious tricks Egan had been using to get guilty criminals off, had been floating a ballot proposition to abolish the public defender's office. His continued association with his ex-con clients long after their cases had been disposed of made abolition of the office a real possibility for the first time. "Naturally it cannot be suggested lightly that the office be abolished since it was created by the people," said State Senator Roy Fellom, author of the act creating the office in 1921. "It was never the intention that it was to be used for the defense of seasoned criminals, but to provide counsel for defendants too poor to hire lawyers."

It was functioning well in other California cities, but not in San Francisco, where Egan's staff seemed "unnaturally large."

The Hughes murder trial began on August 8 before Judge Frank Dunne, who had adjudicated the historic police graft cases in the 1920s. As Egan was led into court in handcuffs, a man detached himself from the crowd and lunged at him. "My wife was one of your victims," Ed Cook screamed. "You and Dr. Housman took her away in an ambulance and kept her a virtual prisoner. You placed powders in her drinks and after she signed over her property you bastards let her die."

Jailers held Cook back—"Pull yourself together, mister."

As murder charges against the conspirators were read, Doran locked his eyes on the floor, Tinnin looked straight ahead, and both moved perceptibly away from Egan. By the time the clerk finished, a wide gap separated all three. Tinnin was represented by Nate Coghlan and Egan by Vince Hallinan and William McGovern.

When the defense put former San Quentin convict Charles Colonna on the stand, he suggested Doran had killed Josie himself during a botched burglary. "I met Doran on Mission Street a week before the murder," Colonna said, "and he tried to interest me in burglarizing a woman's house by Balboa Park."

Next, Doran's county jail cellmate testified Doran said he was going to give up Egan and Tinnin "to save his own skin."

"It seems that [Egan] is to be made the victim of a police persecution," Hallinan said, "similar to another internationally known scandal that has disgraced the police annals of San Francisco."

The 1922 conviction of radical labor activist Tom Mooney had resulted from a frame-up engineered by the DA with the complicity of the SFPD. Hallinan called Egan to the stand as his final witness. By restricting his direct questioning to the murder day and preceding day he got Egan's denial on record while denying the prosecution the chance to cross-examine him about earlier events. "Josie recently had begun to let friends use her garage for parking," Egan testified, claiming she had told him by phone that she had just scrubbed the garage floor.

On September 2 at 4:00 P.M., prosecutor Golden was engaged in the last minutes of his closing argument when Vince Hallinan made "unduly loud, boisterous, harsh, offensive and contemptuous" interruptions and was hauled to the county jail for twenty-four hours. In his absence Golden continued: "You have heard what Doran said about borrowing Postel's car to take Egan riding, of later paying Postel $1.50 from Egan for oil and gasoline."

As the jury was closeted the next day to begin deliberations, Dullea said ominously, "I fear we have only scratched the surface yet."

On Tuesday, September 6, the jury was ready to return its verdict. Hallinan was not permitted to return and Acting Public Defender Gerald Kenny took his place. Though the "friendliest relation" between Kenny and Egan was apparent, he was unaware of his place on Egan's death list. In only ten minutes, the jury returned verdicts of first-degree murder against Egan and Tinnin, who were each sentenced to a quarter century in prison. Years later, when Egan's attorney, Vince Hallinan, was asked about Egan's claim of innocence he only smiled and rolled his eyes. Doran went to Folsom on a manslaughter conviction and under protection from any inmates who might injure him for having turned state's evidence. He was assigned to Dormitory No. 2, the "old man's dormitory" separated from the yard by a locked iron gate.

On September 9, the press revealed that Dullea had foreknowledge of the plot. "From what Egan had said over the Dictograph," said Dullea, "I knew in a general way where to look for his men—among the former convicts for whom he had obtained parole and given jobs."

Alameda County DA Earl Warren, when asked what he would have done about the wiretap if he were Dullea, replied, "I would have destroyed the transcripts and killed everyone who knew about them."

Nate Coghlan said he liked Dullea personally but thought he should find another line of work. "I don't see much of a future for the captain," he said.

These were tough times for Dullea, who continued to be tortured by the thought he could have saved Josie Hughes. If only he had been more forceful, if only he hadn't hesitated, if only. . . . At times a cold shadow fell over Dullea. Then he heard that mirthless chortle on a shadowed staircase. The Gorilla Man had laughed and hefted his huge Bible, and the city had been afraid, and then the nation. Three thousand miles away, for the first time in over four years, the shadow of the Gorilla Man stretched over a blood-stained carpet. A razor was clutched in his huge hand.

NINE

In New York, mobster "Monk" Eastman, barrel-chested, with long arms and a bulldog jaw, killed twenty men with his bare hands and could crack a beer keg with his enormous knuckles.

SATURDAY, October 21 was a typical New York day. Senator Wagner, the labor senator, was leading a protest against the Nazi treatment of Jews and calling for a boycott of German goods. On that day the Erie Railroad had just advertised a New York to Chicago World's Fair round trip with two nights in a hotel plus fair admission for $24.75. It was also a day of turmoil and excitement and especially of unexpected and unexplained deaths.

On that day, the best-known cabby in the Village, Edward Tyrrell, for thirty years the Hotel Brevoort's driver, died while driving his horse and open barouche to the stable. The horse knew the route and finished the trip with a dead man at the reins. On that day, on the island park in Allen Street between Delancey and Rivington streets, two gray-haired women sat pleasantly talking and eating grapes. One was poor. The other had $6,305 in the bank. Two hours passed before both women pitched onto the concrete walk—suicides by poisoned grapes. On that day, the evicted family of Joe Romola, a bookkeeper, stood freezing around a pile of their household goods. Their landlord had stacked them in front of their former home at 851 West 177th Street. He did not want to accept Romola's home relief rent vouchers because the city was slow to pay. The eldest child grew deathly ill and would not last the night. And on that day over on 70th Street in

Brooklyn, lawyer A. B. Epstein, depressed over his meager earnings, blew himself up in his basement with a stick of dynamite.

But the worst death of the day had been the last. Wilhelm Johnston; his wife, Florence W. (aka Margaret Johnston); and their two kids, William and Margaret, lived in a Washington Heights apartment. Around four o'clock they'd shopped at the A&P around the corner. They bought a pound of porterhouse for 35¢ and a half pound of chuck for 9¢. They seemed happy enough, but later that night neighbors heard piercing laughter issuing from their third-floor rooms. A voice, louder than the other, seemed to be speaking in a foreign language, possibly Swedish. At 11:00 P.M. a heartrending shriek echoed from their apartment, then a second. Finally silence. Neighbors called the police.

Two New York cops pushed past a dozen tenants and at the middle turn, where the stairs changed direction, found a large blood stain. Forcing the Johnston's door, they entered with drawn guns to find the lights blazing and the apartment in wild disorder—furniture thrown in all directions and a shattered pot on the floor. They hurried from the living room to the bathroom to the kitchen, really only a closet arrangement of a disappearing sink and stove called a kitchenette. The back of a mechanical refrigerator separated the kitchenette from the rest of the apartment—a small bedroom and the master bedroom. Florence was dead on her bloodstained bed, strangled, stripped, and horribly autopsied with a razor. But four people lived here. Where were the other three? A large stain of blood on the landing, as large as the one Officer Malcolm had left, suggested a body or bodies had been dragged down the stairs. At 11:45 P.M. police located the Johnstons' children at a neighbor's down the block. They could tell the police no more than they already knew, which was nothing, and authorities began dragging the river for Wilhelm. The Johnstons were just the beginning of a long chain of motiveless crimes that would involve a San Francisco Gorilla Man and Captain Dullea.

TEN

Safe mobs may consist of up to a half-dozen men. Their backgrounds may be varied, but the leader of the mob is usually a professional and most always an ex-convict. The leader compiles his information and lays his plans.

—CRIME MANUAL OF THE PERIOD

IT took a second betrayal to really open Dullea's eyes. This time it was one of his own men.

Just after midnight on January 27, 1933, dispatcher Paul Frasher eyed his shotgun standing in the corner and shivered. It was a frigid night at Land's End. The wind was rising, shaking the painted frame barn, and whistling over the peaked roof. Frasher heard it humming through the crisscrossing of electric wires above. He wished he were home in his cozy Irving Street apartment by the Bone Yard, a square block of abandoned streetcars. He heard sand biting the windows and the medallion reading "Market St. Railway Co." swinging violently in the gale. Other signs were for passersby farther west: "To Lincoln Park" and "California Palace of the Legion of Honor." Beyond Twentieth Avenue, sand dunes stretched to Sunset Boulevard, though in four years the dunes up to Thirty-ninth and Taraval would be gone. The Sutro car barns at Thirty-second Avenue and Clement Street (one of the main car barns of the Market Street Railroad) lay just south of a succession of precipitous cliffs overlooking Salada and China Beaches. Three sets of streetcar tracks led into a huge barn packed with white-fronted cars returned after their day's run. Frasher listened to the hiss of his tiny stove, the faint *tick-tick-tick* of cooling machinery and—

something else—tiny pebbles cracking against the front window. Frasher peered out.

While his attention was diverted, a tall, elegant intruder in a white domino mask slipped in through the rear door. The Phantom jammed Frasher's shotgun into his chest and sent him sprawling. "I'll blow out your brains," he said with fury.

Two confederates in white handkerchief masks burst through the door, the smaller hiding behind his larger comrade. They bound and gagged Frasher, tossed him facedown in an outer office, and dropped an overcoat over his head.

The Phantom was remarkably well informed. Somehow, he knew the first safe in Frasher's office was empty and the second stuffed with $2,219 in coins—the receipts of three Sutter car lines. Rapidly, the thieves chiseled off the knob and smashed the combination so silently five other workers in distant parts of the barns never heard. "We're not going to have enough time to finish it. We'll just take the safe away with us."

Somehow the Phantom knew Special Officer Frank Sheehan was due on his rounds. In spite of the enormous weight of the coins, the gang shoved the safe into a burlap sack and dragged it across the sidewalk. Outside they hefted it up into a small sedan and drove to their hideout, a little beach cottage. Frasher wriggled across the floor toward the phone, but before he reached it Officer Sheehan, a bit late, reached the barns and freed him. A tall policeman had stopped him on the street and delayed him.

The next day, Rockaway Beach Deputy Ed Winters found the blown safe discarded on a beach road near the links of Sharp's Park Golf Course. LaTulipe rushed fifteen miles from San Francisco to capture any errant fingerprints. Apparently, the gang hadn't been in such a big rush after all. They'd taken time to leisurely rub their prints from the safe.

On March 5, the nation's banks went "on holiday" for four days. Not so the White Mask Gang who kept themselves gamely employed blasting open safes all over the Embarcadero. On March 14, Dullea met with Inspector Richard Tatham, the head of the Robbery Detail, to discuss this highly successful gang of cracksmen. It was hot in Dullea's office. Tatham took off his hat and wiped his brow with a checkered kerchief. His remarkably square head, sturdy as a cast-iron kettle, was a disorderly bird's nest on top and shaved at the sides in the crop-eared style. His broad, trusting features were doughy and unfinished, as if created by the pressure of a knuckle here and the scratch of a nail there.

A terrible suspicion lurked in the back of Tatham's mind, one he was afraid to voice but one common sense told him had to be true. "My theory is"—Tatham closed the office door—"that these 'petermen' are being tipped off by someone on the inside." Somehow the Phantom had timed the movements of both special and public police patrols to the second and was granted access to every door. No matter what trap they laid, the lanky ghost would be forewarned. As Frank Egan had once been, the Phantom had to be a policeman.

"I sincerely hope not," said Dullea. His shoulders slumped as he recalled Egan had known of some great corruption within the SFPD. Was this it?

In April, the phone rang at a palm-shrouded, redbrick one-story, rebuilt in the Romanesque revival style. The Richmond Police Station on Sixth Avenue between Anza and Geary avenues was Dullea's home in his rookie days when he covered his Richmond District beat (bounded by Fourteenth and Forty-eighth avenues, Lake and Fulton streets) by motorcycle. Even when patrol cars were introduced into this northwestern corner of the city, it was still so sparsely settled that Richmond Station never assigned more than one patrolman per car to the region.

Back then, Dullea wore a round-topped billycock hat and a knee-length uniform coat with tails long enough to stow handcuffs and a serviceable blackjack, which he relied on because he was such a poor shot. Though his Marine Corps discharge papers, which he still kept in his desk drawer, had rated his character as "excellent," they listed no firearms qualifications, even as a marksman. Dullea still carried the service pistol he had emptied at a fleeing gang of robbers in the Richmond. When he ran out of bullets the robbers turned, drew their guns, and began chasing *him*.

Dullea had proudly trained at the knee of "The Dutchman of Richmond Station," Sergeant Oliver L. Hassing. Hassing, a devoted husband, a father of three, and a well-respected model officer, was dark haired, craggy-faced, and amiable. Over his twenty-three years of spotless service, the Dutchman had been attached to the Traffic Bureau, a separate entity reporting directly to the Police Commission, then as a corporal at the Mission Station before being transferred to the Richmond Station. At the police desk, the Dutch-man snatched up the receiver. "My name is Joseph Boberg," the caller said. "I'm superintendent of the Fourth Church of Christ Scientist over at 300 Funston Ave." Boberg reported he had seen a prowler around the church. "We have $500 in the safe at all times."

"Yes, sir," said the Dutchman. His expression had not brightened. His workload was considerable because he was working day and night. "I'll make a report on it, and we'll have the beat officer keep an eye on the place for you," he said. "Now tell me everything."

Boberg was comforted for at least two weeks. That was when the Phantom's White Mask Gang cracked Boberg's church safe like an egg and stole every cent of its Easter collections.

ELEVEN

Gorilla: a hoodlum. A thug, or knuckle-dragger with lots of brawn, not much brain. A criminal with a fondness for strong-arm tactics. Long-armed Abe Lincoln was called the Illinois gorilla, Al Capone's men were known as gorillas.

—DICTIONARY OF AMERICAN SLANG

ON February 17, 1934, fog bells were ringing low across the water as the first bracing portal of the new Golden Gate Bridge reached 480 feet above mean high water. This week alone the Marin-side bridge tower had consumed 570 tons of steel. Off Fort Point, the last of three eight-hour shifts were quitting work on the south pier excavation. The cabin liner *Santa Cecilia* out of New York a day late was just sailing past the Headlands to discharge forty disgruntled passengers onto the docks.

From those docks, the White Mask Gang scurried like rats into an office at 188 Embarcadero Street, hammered the dial off a safe with a center punch and heavy hammer, and drove the spindle free of the tumblers and snatched $1,000. Two nights later, within the shadow of the Ferry Building, they smashed into the Alaska Fishermen's Union at 49 Clay Street, located the safe's soft spot, and drilled the spout out. Their appropriation of $3,477 of hardworking men's cash plunged union secretary John Olson into such deep depression he killed himself.

"All through 1933 and 1934," Inspector Tatham recalled, "the burglars known as the White Mask Gang launched a breathtaking offensive, a shocking wave of crime month after month that had us at our wits' end. . . . In previous years San Francisco's police department had kept from the city all known 'petermen,' but now I was convinced we were trailing a new and clever gang who had learned their lawless trade without previous arrest or intervening prison terms. In other words, professional amateurs—an odd paradox."

On Easter Sunday morning, Dullea cursed aloud. He had provocation. Last Easter Sunday, the White Mask Gang had committed a burglary in the early morning hours. Now they'd done it again—jimmying open a side window at the Wilson Candy store on Clement Street and blowing the safe. On Saturday, May 5, the unscrupulous "yeggs"[4] propped a ladder against a building adjoining the Fleischmann Yeast Company at 245 Eleventh Street, leaped the short distance to the other roof, and scurried down a light well. They prized the door off a fireproof safe with a crowbar ("a rip job"), crammed $500 in cash into a black bag, and blended into the heavy morning fog seconds ahead of arriving workers. Inadvertently, the Phantom had swiped a fortune in registered securities. Considerately, he mailed them back. By then Tatham and Inspector Bill Mudd had already wasted a night compiling a comprehensive list of the stolen bonds. When LaTulipe dusted the envelope he found no prints, watermarks, or other identifying marks.

Midnight man John Davis was scrubbing down a delivery wagon outside the People's Baking Company at 1800 Bryant Street when he heard a hollow laugh. Sponge in hand, he peered into a deep shadow cast by an arc light. A tall man with a long white handkerchief over his face was leaning against a wagon. "Raise 'em, buddy," the Phantom said.

With his gun, he motioned Davis inside into a small office segregated from a larger office by a plate-glass window where the gang waited. They bound and gagged Davis and baker Frank O'Neill and spread burlap sacking beneath the window to muffle the sound of falling glass. The gang climbed through to the safe. They laid out their tools on a blanket—three chisels, six drills, two pliers, three punches, two drill keys, one wire pick, one copper hammer (which would make little sound if dropped), a fulminating cap, a brace and bit, and a cake of Lux soap.

---

[4] A thief, especially a safecracker, from John Yegg, the first safecracker to use nitroglycerin to break into a safe.

The Phantom consulted a small black binder—an inch of mimeographed pages held together with three screw-headed brads. He disliked torches, which tended to incinerate any money inside, and preferred the old Civil War technique of pouring gunpowder into the crevices around the door seam and sealing the fissures with soap. The modern method, the "lock shot," consisted of punching the safe by drilling holes into the lock spindle hole and stuffing them with nitroglycerin-soaked cotton. "Use the lock shot," decided the Phantom. He uncorked a small bottle of homemade "soup" brewed by slowly boiling dynamite sticks in a kettle over a fire. Nitro rises as a clear, straw-colored film that can be skimmed off—dangerous work. The nitric oxide and nitrogen dioxide created during the process can collapse your lungs. He walked as if on eggshells—that single eyedropper full was potent enough to jolt the safe's door off its hinges.

He inserted a charge of nitro-soaked cotton into a primed cartridge (a dynamite blasting cap and wire fuse) and exploded it with an electric detonator. That blast set off the larger nitro explosion. With a muffled *whump!* all four sides of the safe expanded, the tumblers released, and the heavy door—trailing smoke and sparks—launched itself through the smashed window and almost hit Davis. A second shot crumpled the steel compartment inside the safe without damaging the several strongboxes and $1,600 of currency. Leaving behind shards of glass, steel, and plaster, the gang faded away. Davis and O'Neill made themselves comfortable. They wouldn't be discovered for hours. "They were cautious, clever, and astonishingly well-informed," Davis told Tatham. "Good craftsmen. All around it was a neat job, and though I hate to, I've got to give them credit."

When the gang took the Associated Grocers on Pacific Street for $4,000 and sped off in a waiting truck, cops patrolling less than a block away failed to notice. By summer, San Francisco was strike-ridden and aflame with labor riots. For almost two years the gang had been striking with impunity, but during the bloody unrest when every cop was on overtime cracking the skulls of agitators at the waterfront, they committed no robberies. When the Globe Brewing Company at 1423 Sansome Street left its doors open offering hospitality to patrolling police, the Phantom befriended Robert Graham, the elderly watchman, and engaged him in long conversations. After the strike ended, the police left, and longshoremen got back to work. So did the White Mask Gang. Now Tatham was certain the Phantom was a cop. Graham was going to work one night when a tall, white-masked figure blocked his path. "All right, Graham," he said, "this is as far as you go."

"How do you know my name?"

In reply, the Phantom split his skull and robbed the Globe.

The Phantom's string of precisely planned capers finally began to go awry on July 29, when he busted into the Golden State Milk Company's main plant at 459 Bay Street, less than five blocks from Pier 33. The gang sealed employees Fred Frocade, Americo Frigole, and George Lombardi in the milk chilling vault. There were several dull roars, then cursing. The safe was empty. Milk worker Wayne Storey met the cracksmen going out. They pinioned his arms, debated whether to kill him, and settled for kicking him unconscious. On September 4, they smashed into the Coca-Cola plant and were almost surprised by a beat patrolman before wrangling a 1,500-pound vault containing $500 into their truck. They left it shattered on a Daly City mountain top. "I had that safe photographed and gone over inch-by-inch by LaTulipe," said Tatham, "but the only prints were those of the employees."

On October 22, the gang found the cupboard bare at the Challenge Creamery and retreated so rapidly they left their best small drills behind.

The Phantom's end came at 10:45 P.M. on November 11 (Armistice Day). Mary Mardueno, an attractive dark-bobbed woman, noticed a light across the street from her tiny flat and went to her window overlooking the Majestic Bottling Plant at 36 Beideman. Across the wide thoroughfare, shafts of light were darting about the topmost floor. When they blacked out, Mary retired. At 11:57 P.M., a heavy roar shook her from her cozy bed. As she dialed the Western Addition Police Station, the concussion was still rumbling through the neighborhood and rattling window panes. Officer John "Andy" Johnson, a blond, triangular-faced young man, who was about to go off duty, snatched up the receiver. "There's been an explosion at the Majestic Bottling Works," Mary cried. "Wait, I can see lights inside again. . . . I think they're burglars. . . . Yes! Hurry. Hurry! You can still catch them."

Sergeant Michael McCarthy, Andy, and five heavily armed uniformed officers in Sam Browne belts raced to the plant. "You are to hinder any escape by those still inside until we know what the hell's going on," McCarthy ordered.

He stationed officers McNally, Desmond, and Nilan at the front, Jim Casey at the rear, and Tom Miller and Andy in the main yard. When Andy heard faint scuffling at the far end, he scaled the fence and crawled into the open space, when a cough from behind a pyramid of packing crates alerted him. He climbed over an iron grill into an alley and shone his flashlight up a ladder tilted against the building. Two men in white masks and leather gloves were cowering at the top. One was lean, sleepy-eyed, and unshaven; the other was a neckless, crop-eared giant with a can-shaped head, and toothbrush mustache.

Though he didn't know it, Andy had half the White Mask Gang in his light. Passing his prisoners off at the front gate, he returned and heard a long, weary sigh from inside the plant. Inside, he apprehended a third man in a long black coat.

"Don't," the tall man mumbled. "Oh, for heaven's sake . . . get me out of here." The man licked his lips. "Don't take me in. For the love of God, please let me go. You know me, Johnson. I'm an officer with the police. You know what this means to me. For God's sake stand aside!"

"You . . . you stand there!" said Andy, confused at finding an officer he had known for over a year in such hot water. Suddenly, he sighted a fourth man and gave chase. "Stay there," he called back.

The tall man fled, but was halted by Casey at the rear gate. "Who are you?" Casey demanded, covering him through the steel grill. "I am a police officer. Let me out . . . the gate—Wait, I will convince you. See." He held a gold-encrusted star into the flashlight beam, but kept his thumb over the badge number and his hand up to his face as he backed away, smiling, waving, smiling and saying, "No problem . . . no problem . . ."

In the top floor office, Andy smelled the strong odor of explosives. He called Dullea, who pulled on a hound's-tooth suit, four-button vest, and gray hat and hurried to the scene, sleepy but excited. At last, some of the White Mask Gang was in custody! Leslie Orlandi, general manager of the plant, theorized the gang had entered through the basement by wriggling under a loading platform, opened a rear door facing the yard, and propped up a ladder for a quick getaway.

"Because they couldn't drill the door open," said Dullea, "they went back and got some nitro. They used too much and that's what woke Mrs. Mardueno. The strong blast only bulged out the sides of the safe, blowing open the combination, but failing to force open the inner strongbox. They must have run outside, then driven around the neighborhood to see if anyone had heard the explosion, then returned to the plant. They waited around the safe too long deciding what to do next. That's how we surprised them."

"Too bad they didn't know the safe was empty," said Orlandi grinning. "Six days ago, Election Day, it was full."

Dullea inventoried the abandoned paraphernalia—an empty burlap bag, a square copper hammer, an assortment of chisels and drills, and, most interesting of all, a small loose-leaf binder containing a mimeographed instruction book titled *The Manual of Safes*. "This tells how to open safes," he said. "It's a reference work for locksmiths or, in this case, safecrackers."

The author's name had been razored off. Under "Dials," the 120-page typewritten handbook listed "Alpine, Champion, Hall, Liberty, McNeil & Urban, Phoenix, Reliable and Victor." It contained information about drilling positions, explosives, and diagrams of dials, handles, corners, and acorns. It even advertised a tool to determine the combination of all wafer safes.

Forty minutes later Andy drove to Tatham's house for advice. "There's been a big safe job at the Majestic bottling plant," he said, "and we got two suspects in cuffs—Richard Frank [aka "Richard Frombee" and "Albert Wiener"] of 1595 Golden Gate Avenue and Kenneth "Tiny" Meyers [aka "Edward Martin" and "Clarence Wilson"] of 3578 California Street. When I went into the building I found this Station Officer. I told him to stand there. I chased a fourth man who had gone out the window, but he got away. When I returned the other man was gone."

Tatham realized he had momentarily detained the Phantom himself. "Johnson recognized the man," he said, "but what could I do? The man in question was an officer and hadn't been caught doing anything. The next day at dawn, trying to get more information, Inspector O'Neill and I drove to the City Prison to question Meyers and Frank in their cells. Meyers, though often arrested for robbery and burglary, invariably 'beat the rap,' at least on every San Francisco case.[5] I asked Meyers if there were more than three men in the gang and Tiny named Frank Fitzpatrick as one."

Tatham knew Fitzpatrick, a former bootlegger, as one of a gang of burglars once protected by Frank Egan. But nothing in his background would enable him to be a master safecracker. "We drove to Fitzpatrick's fifth floor Broderick Street apartment, but the room was ransacked. He had flown the coop. We went next to Richard Frank's cell."

"Meyers confessed there were four in the gang," Tatham told him.

"Meyers has said a lot of things he shouldn't have," said Frank.

"Well, what were you doing in the Majestic Bottling Plant at night? You are a two-time loser, aren't you?"

Frank then admitted Tiny had spoken the truth but demanded a deal before he named the fourth man. Instead, Tatham returned him to the holding tank at the end of a row of steel cages and asked Meyers, "Wasn't a policeman in on it?"

"Yes. He planned most of the jobs, sized up the safes to be blown and participated in the dynamiting operations. When he cased the Majestic Bottling Plant, he rented a flat on the O'Farrell Street side of the building and studied the comings and goings of the workers with binoculars for over a week."

The Phantom held a post at a district police station. Tiny preferred to write the name rather than speak it. "As I read the name it was still a stunning revelation," said Tatham. "It was monstrous, this charge from Meyers—it left me ragged and numb, this ghastly thing. A policeman, a man sworn to enforce the law—consorting with cracksmen and thieves. . . . It was beyond conception! I mulled it over until my head ached."

At the District Station the night of the Majestic robbery the Jekyll and Hyde cop had returned unexpectedly from a ten-day sick leave. This

---

[5] Arrested on March 4, 1918, while driving a stolen car—case dismissed; 1928, charged with attempted burglary at 1938 Post Street—case dismissed; 1930, charged for concealed weapons—case dismissed; 1932, robbery charge—case dismissed. Frank, first arrested in San Francisco on December 31, 1914, for robbery, served a year in the county jail. Sentenced from one to fifteen years in the Washington State Penitentiary for robbery, he got paroled in October 1919 and in January was sentenced to 180 days in jail at Portland for burglary. Beginning in 1920, in charges ranging from narcotics to assault to murder and battery, every San Francisco case against Frank was dismissed.

upstanding policeman, assigned to the waterfront during the strike, had been a secret partner in a garage at 351 Valencia Street with Paul Schainman, a narcotics dealer, counterfeiter, and killer who was serving time in the Nevada State Prison. Dullea, sickened by this disgraceful breach of faith, labored all Friday night, November 16, building a case. He could not in his heart differentiate between this betrayal and that of Frank Egan. The Phantom had been a trusted friend, mentor, and fellow officer. It broke his heart.

Saturday morning, gaiety reigned on the docks where the White Mask Gang had ruled so cruelly. A robust legion of confetti throwers were jubilant as the *President Cleveland*, under Captain Bob Carey, sailed away to the Islands and the Orient. As festive vacationers departed, Captain Bernard McDonald of Richmond Station solemnly drove to the Sunset District. He passed the gang's hideout at 727 Forty-third Avenue and parked down the street at 811 Forty-third. He trudged grimly up the walk to a comfortable but not extravagant home and rang the bell. A haggard man in civilian clothes answered. "You're wanted at the Hall right away," McDonald said sternly.

He drove the man, now attired in police uniform, up Kearney Street to Portsmouth Square and lower Chinatown to the HOJ. Dullea, Quinn, and Commissioner Roche were waiting inside the chief's office.

"I have nothing to say except that I am not guilty," the man told them.

"Make a report of your activities for the twenty four hours on the day of the Majestic burglary," said Quinn.

"I spent the day at home," he said, "but during the afternoon I took a walk and got a shave. I am not guilty—I did not do the things they charge me with. Are you going to take the word of a patrolman who doesn't like me against my word? I can assure you, I can prove my innocence. This is a frame-up."

When Tiny Meyers was brought face to face with him, he said instantly, "That's the man!"

Quinn suspended the officer, and Roche stripped him of his star, police revolver, and handcuffs. Captain McDonald and Inspectors William Gilmore and Ray O'Brien escorted the prisoner upstairs to the City Prison, where he printed his name in the big book on the booking sergeant's desk. They locked him in a felony cell, but kept Frank and Meyers confined in separate tanks. "It was with great reluctance," said Roche on the steps outside, "that we took the action we did. We certainly did not proceed on the unsupported word of Meyers. We made an exhaustive investigation. We are satisfied that the evidence against the prisoner is strong enough to warrant that action. He will be tried in court as would any citizen. We're on our way to his home to tell his wife. I would much rather tell her that her husband was dead."

Quinn only extolled the officer's impeccably long service. "His record had been without a blemish and outstanding," he said.

The defendant's lawyer, John J. Taaffe, alleged a frame-up in language so blue he almost came to blows with Tatham. Tatham ended the matter by stalking away. On November 20, the grand jury, after a five-hour session, indicted the officer for burglary with explosives. Through his official position, he had been able to check the activities of beat and special officers.

On January 23, 1935, as extraordinarily high seas capsized three boats off Bay Point, the convicted officer was brought in shackles into superior court. Against the turbulent background, Judge I. L. Harris's face was stormlike. "You have the mark of Cain on you," he said. "You have violated the trust of the people of San Francisco. . . . You are a man who has humiliated himself and brought dishonor and disgrace to the service."

He sentenced the turncoat cop to fifteen years. A witness further implicated the turncoat in a Los Angeles robbery, which got him another fifteen years. "I told you at the time I would see you again," Mrs. Ella King said. "I remember your face very well."

DA Brady contacted the State Board of Prison Terms and Paroles and urged the limit. "He is a peculiarly antisocial person," he wrote. "He saw fit to aid in the perpetration of the very crime he was supposed to prevent, and my experience with such persons is that they rarely change."

At the prisoner's request Dullea was to visit the Phantom at Folsom Prison on Saturday, February 23. He showered, donned a freshly pressed suit, and made the lonely drive over pitted roads to the prison. In January, on an exceptionally cold day, Deputy Sheriff Al Parker and three of the traitor's fellow cops had driven the prisoner along the same route and watched the iron gates slam behind him. Inside, he had been assigned a number, sprayed with DDT powder, and confined in a cell—seven feet by nine feet by eight feet furnished with a dirty sink, a lidless toilet bowl, and four metal shelves on L-braces, which supported two upper and two lower bunks for three other men.

Dullea checked his gun, entered a small gray room, and studied the concrete gun towers and marching convicts in formation outside the barred window. Guards ushered in a stolid, hatchet-faced man who slumped onto a wooden bench. Dullea cast his eyes on "a pathetic creature," a doting husband, father, and respected officer with years of immaculate service. Now he was a broken man, head lowered, face pale, and hair gone completely gray. His hands were calloused from hard labor at the rock quarry. His chest was racked with sobs. Dullea shook his head. By God, he would never have suspected *him* of being the Phantom. The prisoner composed himself and looked up at Dullea.

"Gambling led me to crime and gambling took every dollar I made. I just want to say I am sorry, Charlie," Sergeant Oliver L. Hassing sobbed.

Dullea turned his back on the Dutchman, the role model of his youth. "Frankly I don't care," he said, and left.

TWELVE

In four short stories written between 1841 and 1844, E. A. Poe laid down the four tenets of the modern crime story—solving a real life case, the use of psychological deduction and double bluff and the person least likely device.

—JOHN WALSH, *POE THE DETECTIVE*

THE night was clear and crisp, yet the odd apelike figure remained unresolved and broken, reforming as it lumbered from one shadow to another. It moved in a peculiar flat-footed shamble. A streetlight cast its shadow raggedly against a brick wall—that of a heavyset figure with short legs, sloping shoulders, and arms striking in their length—unnaturally long, like those of a gorilla. The light of an approaching auto made his eyes momentarily gray, then blue-brown and yellow where the beams flared. Where his coat collar was turned up a neat triangle of bronze showed in the vee. With his broad shoulders stooped, head down, and arms hanging at his side, with all extraneous detail removed, the silhouette could have been that of an ape.

His father had been an undertaker, conducting business out of their basement in Jersey, and he had been one too, or at least a morgue attendant. He recalled the fascination of rows of pale bodies lined up in the basement of Mt. Sinai Hospital. His duties had included dissecting corpses for autopsies and sewing them up. It got so he thought of autopsies all the time, and it made it hard to sleep. Vividly, he remembered the powerful chemical smell enhanced by the small space heater. He recalled the slanting floor and its central drain, the large deep sinks, and the metal table—that above all.

But he was also an adventurer and sailor plying the Great Lakes and would be one again. To the bone, he was a traveling man. A year earlier he had married a woman in Baltimore, a good, moral person who wasn't good and moral enough to stop him from heading out again on her dollar and taking more lives. The name he was using was not his own, only one of a vast catalog of identities, costumes, occupations, and different personalities he kept filed away in his head. He could be anyone at any time. The most of his true self he gave the world was the fleeting glimpse of his huge shadow and an odd, haunting laugh he couldn't control.

When the Gorilla Man was drunk, he floated in a kind of moral weightlessness. Then his will was negated and a colored curtain dropped over his eyes. Sometimes it was a red haze as transparent as silk. Other times it was a blue ocean tide that rolled over him. Europeans had been acquainted with such creatures as the Gorilla Man long before Americans. The French and Tyrolean rippers, Vacher and Xaver, had spoken of uncontrollable impulses preceded by colored hazes that compelled them to do unspeakable things. Xaver, a slightly eccentric boy of good name, felt one day an "irresistible red tide" sweep over him. Vacher also reported an "imperious and irresistible passion came on like a terrible red tide inspired by the Devil."

The Gorilla Man fought hard to control himself. Under the compulsion of those red and blue curtains of light he could not control himself. And he had been having those dreams again. When he heard of murders he asked himself, "Could it be me?" unable to admit he had committed acts of violence. "I lay down and tried to think about things I know," he confided. "I try to piece it all together. I try to reason it out. I try to think how I got this blood on my hands. I think I saw a razor. I don't know. I actually don't know."

He cast his eyes on San Francisco Bay and the nearby Ferry Building. Glad to be off the Great Lakes where he had been a sailor and back in a bustling city filled with women, he went into the nearest waterfront bar. As he listened to the chimes of the Moorish Clock Tower, he began to drink as fog rushed by the door like an express.

*   *   *

BY April 1935, Verne Doran was out on parole. Herbert Emerson Wilson, a convicted murderer in charge of Dorm No. 2 at Folsom Prison, claimed Doran had admitted he had conspired with prosecutors to falsely implicate Egan. Dullea knew that Wilson was a crony of Egan's.

On April 5, workmen completed the portion of the Bay Bridge running from the east portal of the Yerba Buena Island Tunnel to Pier E-2, a slip at the westerly end of a fourteen-hundred-foot long cantilever. On its high side, the bridge already dwarfed the Palace Hotel. Dullea gave a low whistle at the astonishing progress as he walked to his car by the Ferry Building. The big billboard atop the Bay Hotel proclaimed, "4 Proback Jr. blades for ten cents. *You* take a chance when you buy the Unknown." Next to the word *unknown* was displayed a huge gleaming razor.

Dullea got behind the wheel, humming. These days, he was a more re-laxed man. He had put his three most heartbreaking cases behind him—that of a cop killer, an ex-cop who was a killer, and a dirty cop. Dullea counted as the foremost tragedies of life the loss of a friend, the inability to save a friend, and the betrayal of a friend. He had endured all three in five years but it had made him realize what had to be done. It was odd, Dullea thought as he spun onto Market, Officer Malcolm had been murdered on April 29. Josie Hughes had been murdered on April 29. The Phantom had struck on an April 29. Now April had rolled around once more. What trag-edy would this cruelest of months bring this time? The first sign of trouble in a clear sky is a cloud no bigger than a man's hand appearing on the ho-rizon, then darkening until the entire sky is filled with fury.

That night Dullea slept well, a by-product of the sea air, the dazzling light, and the rapid construction of the two astonishing bridges that would change San Francisco forever. He would need his strength. In a matter of hours, he would be present at the birth of a new breed of man. The series of seemingly unsolvable crimes would make him wonder if the person who committed them was not human, but some animalistic creature. In fact, early descriptions would compare the suspect to a gorilla with a razor who laughed as he escaped.

As with the shooting of Officer Malcolm, Dullea's biggest case would be linked to the Embarcadero, that fogbound region of brutality, that busy crossroads of all manner of men and some who might not be men at all. The police of Whitechapel, London, would not have been surprised. Dullea learned about this creature the next day as rain beat against his office window.

THIRTEEN

Gnashing its teeth, and flashing fire from its eyes, it flew upon the body of the girl, and imbedded its fearful talons in her throat, retaining its grasp until she expired.

—E. A. POE, "THE MURDERS IN THE RUE MORGUE"

ON Saturday, April 6, 1935, Anna Lemon quit the auto ferry as soon as the hydraulic apron lowered into place with a thud. Heavy rain was pounding the raw-and-ready Embarcadero as other ferries, blasting their whistles, eased into the seven remaining slips. Commuters, in time to the beat of paddles, lifting and lowering in the waves, tramped soldierlike up one of four projecting Y-shaped gangways. On a busy day, the fleet transported nearly sixty thousand people between the East Bay and San Francisco's Ferry Building, making the Ferry Building second in foot traffic only to London's Charing Cross Station. Anna made a zigzag dash into a tarpaper-covered corridor abutting the rear of the terminal and trudged up the gusty walkway. She emerged into the Grand Nave at the second-floor level where symmetrically placed skylights let in some illumination. But in such blustery weather, the shafts of leaden light only underscored the gloom.

At 8:00 A.M., the siren sounded (it would sound again at noon and at 4:30 P.M.). To the north and south of the Ferry Building square steel doors rolled up. The stomp of heavy boots announced an army of longshoremen marching inside to unload cargo. Donkey engines near the roundhouse began hauling up stacks of lumber in clouds of steam. Among storage sheds and grimy warehouses, men began stacking, steam fitting, and repaying.

Anna and her fellow commuters, shielding themselves from the downpour, exited from the second floor and swarmed onto an arched, cast-iron footbridge. The wide span, soaring from the long, continuous double front arcade of the Ferry Building, shuddered beneath their weight and sank a little.

The driving rain had halted today's anticipated opening of the Pacific Coast League. Lefty O'Doul, an ex-pitcher/outfielder from Butchertown[6] and winner of National League titles with the Phillies and Dodgers, would have to wait another day to debut as the Seals' manager; Dullea, a rabid hardball fan, would have to wait to watch O'Doul.

Below the footbridge, alive with its tide of black umbrellas, the Ferry Building shed rain like a duck. Each of its fifty repetitive arches disgorged mouthfuls of passengers. In front twisted the Great Ferry Loop, its graceful curves accommodating ten streetcars at a time. The elegant streetcar turnaround, one of the first things built after the Great '06 Quake and upgraded thirteen years later, was widely applauded as a fine idea. It speeded loading and unloading of the streetcars, though commuters scurrying off the ferries in peak hours were often cut off by passing Belt Line locomotives. At rush hour, the freights effectively prevented commuters from boarding cars or getting to taxies on the south side. For that reason the city had constructed the wide footbridge above the Loop in 1918.

From Anna's vantage point the three sets of intertwining tracks below described the shape of a light bulb—rounded end facing the Ferry Building; base stretching up mile-long Market. In the downpour, streetcars with steamed windows lined up. Muni cars kept to the outside curve, but sometimes strayed onto the middle loop next to the Geary line. On the outer loop, a C car was starting up. Behind it a green and white Market Street Railway No. 5 car and a gray 21 Hayes Street car waited their turns.

The revolving streetcars, like lovers in the rain, waltzed around a rundown plaza. A plot of rust-stained greenery struggled to breathe next to a grill that vented toxic fumes from a short tunnel running under the Loop. Each day, eleven thousand motorists entered the 950-foot-long auto sub-

---

[6] Now Bayview.

way at Mission Street, dipped briefly under the Loop. and reemerged into daylight at Washington Street, blinking like moles. When their eyes adjusted, the first thing they saw was a gigantic Camel cigarette billboard.

On the north side of the bridge, the four-wheel dinkey to the Presidio was just leaving. Through the A-struts Anna saw the Sacramento-Clay cable car pass beneath and swing wide onto rain slick Sacramento, a major east–west downtown street. Between Sacramento and Clay, flourished a region of longshoremen's quick-lunch counters, beer parlors, secondhand clothing stores, and the Harbor Emergency Hospital. At East Street across 120-foot-wide Market Street stood the Ensign Cafe and Saloon where a call of "Captain!" at any time of day brought every man to his feet.

Anna reached the other side of the incline. There the span was welded to a wedge-shaped, three-story building with a rounded portico and a Moorish trim of iron grillwork. Its roof bristled with billboards and poles flying advertising banners. In the pelting rain, Anna gingerly made her way down two broad flights to Brundage's. The drugstore took up the slightly rounded cusp of the bridge-anchoring building. Its doors intersected the apex from Sacramento Street to Commercial Street. Advertisements reading "Bear Photo Developing" and "Ex-Lax, the Chocolated Laxative" covered the second-floor windows.

Anna turned right onto the north side of Sacramento and passed The Loop, a tavern offering Valley Brew. It had replaced a take-home family bakery that had occupied the site for years. The Loop's neon sign was clever. From the vantage point of early morning commuters one side read: "The Loop First Chance." Workers trudging home along Market Street saw: "The Loop Last Chance." Next, Bernstein's Fish Grotto's awnings advertised "Crabs, Cod and Clams In Season" and "Chowder For A Dime." Above, Harris Clothiers, signs hawked "Yachting costumes."

Anna reached her destination—24 Sacramento Street, a four-story hotel where she worked as a maid. A vertical, two-and-a-half-story neon sign spelled out, one letter atop another, three words: *Bay Hotel ROOMS*. At the bottom the word *BATH* filled a circle, as if the period of an exclamation point. Like any exclamation point, it expressed contempt, anger, enthusiasm, pain, and sorrow, the most common emotions felt at the Bay Hotel. After today, its most common emotion would be fear.

The Bay Hotel lay in the shadow of the Clock Tower. In early 1850, it had been one of three floating brigs in the Cove drawn up on the mud under a high bank. The city fathers had transformed it into a hotel at the southeast corner of Battery and Green streets, a hostelry favored by seafaring men, stevedores, Alaskan fishermen, and ladies who catered to "this salty type of clientele." There, the city honored its first elected sheriff, the greatest Texas Ranger of all. Twelve years earlier the Bay Hotel's rooftop billboard declared "ROOMS 50 Cents and Upward. Strictly Modern Improvements." Now a nifty backward sign had been painted across the entire two-hundred-foot side of the Bay Hotel, catching the eye of every arriving commuter. In mirror-image the lettering said *OWL Cigars 5 cents.*"

After the new six-story Hotel Terminal (the "Waldorf Astoria of water-front dumps") opened on the north side of Market Street, the Bay Hotel's fortunes began to decline. The Terminal had a kitchen, and its lighted sign made it the first hotel transcontinental railroad passengers saw as they emerged from the Ferry Building. In larger letters than the Bay Hotel's, their sign advertised: "European Plan Rooms, $1.00, with bath $1.50 up." That rainy day, the Hotel Terminal's colossal sign proclaimed: "Commercial & Tourist, 300 rooms 150 Baths."

Anna passed beneath a peaked roof like that of a little Swiss chalet, the canopied entrance of the Bay Hotel. Shaking rain off, she entered the lobby of the most ignoble type of hotel with the most transitory type of clientele. The Bay Hotel was cheap, shabby, and scattered with potted ferns, tattered chairs, functional couches, and sand-filled urns. The ceiling was peeling, and the elevator was barely serviceable. Signs at the reception desk advised "Please Keep Your Door Locked" and "The Key Must Be Turned in the Lock." Good advice at the Bay Hotel.

The desk was uninhabited, though the hotel register lay open. Where was the manager, Mr. T. L. Selchaw? Otto von Feldman, the night porter, had already gone. The former German army officer, reserved and polished, would not be back. By now he was halfway to San Diego. John Smeins, the night clerk, had gone home at 7:00 A.M. Anna was irritated. "It's dangerous to leave the lobby unattended," she thought as she hung up her coat and tied on her apron. "Anyone could have come and gone without being seen." She called out. There was no answer except for her echo.

Anna swept the threadbare carpet, then began cleaning the vacated rooms on the second floor and checking whether any of the hotel's property was missing. Selchaw considered that her most important duty. Around 10:00 A.M., Selchaw returned from some mysterious errand and closeted himself in his office. Before Anna knew it, the morning had passed. Like most of the working poor in San Francisco, she put in a twelve-hour day for less than a dollar. Selchaw checked in a few walk-ins and returned to his office. "Hotels are home to lonely people," he thought.

It was now 2:00 P.M., but so dim and gray out that electric lights were still burning in the lobby. Along Sacramento Street, streetlights flickered, reflected on the wet streets. The Bay Hotel's exclamation point sign shone down onto an unbroken line of black autos. Anna heard the hiss of water from tires and the complaint of metal as cable cars made the sharp turn onto Sacramento. In his office, some forgotten item was nagging at Selchaw. He walked to the desk, consulted the open register, and discovered John Smeins's note. Now he remembered. When Smeins left at the end of his graveyard shift, he had remarked, "The bloke in #309 said to give them a wake-up knock about 10:00 A.M." Selchaw called out—"Anna? Anna, go up to #309 and see if you can rouse them. If they don't mention it don't say anything about being late. And clean #315 and #317. They're vacant now."

Dutifully, Anna pushed a linen cart bristling with brooms, dustpans, and bottles to an accordion gate and worked it. The elevator, rattling and clicking twice at each floor, rose slowly. She exited into a narrow corridor. Lights were on in room 309. They had to be blazing because the crack beneath the door cut a brilliant slash onto the worn carpet. She knocked and, receiving no response, continued along the hall.

At room 315, Anna scooped up a tray, picked a wadded napkin from a cup, changed the linen, and dumped the ash trays. In her apron pocket she carried a spray bottle of carbon tet (with a little ice it got out gum) and a carton of cornstarch (with a little cold water it got out blood). She cleaned 317 to the haunting chime of the Ferry Clock Tower, so close it was as if it were in the room with her. Just past 3:00 P.M., she returned along the dusky passage. Another tentative rap on door 309. No response. A lumbering shadow or a trick of the eye, stirred by the elevator door. "Mr. Selchaw?"

No answer. She sniffed—the faint smell of musk? The dampness of rain? Another knock. No answer.

Anna fiddled with her key ring, found the passkey, gave the knob a turn, and released the catch. Inside the odor was stronger, mixed with whisky, the lingering smell of beer, cigarettes, cigars, and—a sweet smell—jasmine—gardenia—roses. Someone had crushed a rose corsage underfoot. She stepped over the broken petals. Two naked bulbs illuminated the small room in stark relief. The searing vibration revealed every detail. The bed was neatly made. But it was not what Anna smelled or saw that etched the scene into her memory. It was what she heard—her heart beating, the ticking of a watch pinned to her apron, the faint squeak of her cart, and her feet breaking the brittle nap of the carpet. Where the carpet was thin her step was soundless. Across the room, Anna heard a torrent rushing through a drainpipe welded to the building and the relentless *whoosh* and splash of passing cars below.

Someone had drawn the curtains by pulling two vertical cords passing around pulleys but left the window open. Rain was pummeling the sash, the upper pane, and a broad fire escape a few windows down. As she worked the balancing weights, her hip bumped the back of a chair where hung a woman's cheap brown print dress, a tattered black cloth coat, and a folded dark sweater. On the seat lay a red purse and small green felt hat with a bright feather. Under the chair were black pumps with three-inch heels.

Over her shoulder Anna observed an old-fashioned wooden bureau with several knobs missing. The tilted plate mirror reflected a bra, panties, and jewelry strewn on the dresser top. She turned toward the made bed. The blanket was drawn up to the metal headboard, but a few strands of long red hair showed. The woman on her back was still as a marble statue, both arms stiffly outstretched. It was odd for a guest to still be in bed this late even at the Bay Hotel. Anna approached calling out, "Ma'am? Ma'am?"

Anna tugged the upper bed covers down. Beneath was a terry cloth towel wrapped around the woman's face. The corners of the towel had been tucked under a pillow to hold it in place. Anna unwound the towel. Underneath was a lived-in face with deep scratches (such as animal claws might make) crisscrossing both cheeks. Dark bruises surrounded her eyes where fists had blackened them. Long nails had dug three deep scratches into her dimpled chin. Anna couldn't see the woman's mouth. It was taped shut with three strips of adhesive. On her extraordinarily white throat the swollen contours of a huge pair of hands were outlined in black.

The cover fell to the nude woman's chest, which was hacked. Her abdomen was discolored and bruised, and her stomach sliced to the pubic arch. But where was the blood? There should have been more. An autopsy had been conducted on the body. As a cable car rumbled by, Anna saw a breast on the night stand quivering from the vibrations. The maid's education was not vast. She knew that the nation was in the grip of a terrible economic depression and just shaking itself loose and that the police were on the take, but she knew virtually nothing of criminal history. She was familiar, though, with the Bible-spouting lodger who had a "down on whores" and walked foggy streets like San Francisco's decades ago in London's Whitechapel, an East End district like the Embarcadero. The Ripper had sought out women on the lowest rung of society (like the poor creature before Anna Lemon), nonpersons whose identities he further erased. Anna had no more knowledge of the Ripper than that. If she had, she would have recognized his last and most horrendous murder had been re-created in this cheerless room.

The room had not been disarrayed at all. If anything it was too orderly. If the strangler had taken the time to cover the redhead completely, fold her clothes, and tidy the room then he might still be . . . her eyes darted toward the bathroom door, which was slightly ajar. Through the crack she saw a naked overhead light and a washbasin with open plumbing. She heard the slow trickle of water—rain or a gurgling in the trap of the basin. It might be someone washing his hands of blood. Anna backed up, stumbling over her cart and without waiting for the elevator flew down three flights of stairs and into the arms of T. L. Selchaw, who, stretching and yawning, was coming out of his office.

"Mr. Selchaw. Mr. Selchaw!" she screamed. "A woman's been murdered!"

Selchaw thought she was joking. "Oh, is that so, is it, Mrs. Lemon?" He grabbed her by both shoulders and gave her a little shake. "Calm yourself. . . . Murdered? Where? Calm down. . . . Tell me where."

"The third floor, sir." She blurted, then fainted. Selchaw made her comfortable on the couch and took the elevator to the third floor. He saw the door standing open, the carpet bathed in light. One glance confirmed Anna's story. Selchaw retreated to his office. Anna was sitting up by now. "You were right, Mrs. Lemon," he said. "This is bad, all right, real bad, but just keep quiet. We don't want to alarm any more guests than we have to. Hush now, Anna, while I phone the police." Selchaw's hands were still quivering when he went outside to wait under the neon sign shaped like an exclamation point.

FOURTEEN

Those who kill a single person usually have a personal relationship with the victim, if only a perception that they have specific attributes which torment them.

—PSYCHOLOGY TEXT OF THE PERIOD

INSPECTOR McGinn activated his cruiser's siren by pulling a wire. It always took time to take hold and growled until it did. That's why they called cop cars "growlers." The wire broke, as it often did, and the car kept growling until McGinn, fumbling, could reattach the wire. By then he and his men had made the half mile trip from the HOJ at Clay and Washington streets to the Bay Hotel in record time. The cruiser threw up a wall of water as it hauled up in front. Its throaty growl died away to a snarl. Selchaw quickly stepped back. McGinn piled out onto the walk followed by Inspectors Michael Desmond and Bart Kelleher. The car doors banged behind. McGinn, the only inspector not wearing a trench coat, turned up his collar and growled. He hated the wet. He hated the darkness and cold. He especially hated this rundown hotel where he had been a hundred times before on vice raids. The Bay Hotel had the reputation of being a "riding academy," a place hookers took their Johns. McGinn tugged his handkerchief from the inside band of his hat, blew his reddened nose, and tucked it back.

McGinn was in a foul mood. He still hadn't gotten over being bounced as head of the Death Squad. He dropped back beneath the canvas awning, lifted the wide brim of his hat, and studied the back of the enormous billboard next door which stood as a black, coffin-shaped rectangle in the dimness. He stepped into the rain to observe the Bay Hotel window by window. Slowly his eyes rose to an open third-floor window where lights were blazing adjacent to the first red neon letter *O* in the word *ROOMS*. He thought he saw someone pull back the water-soaked drapes. Just then Inspector Harry Husted and Sergeant C. J. Birdsall roared up in an unmarked, plainclothes "eleven car" and distracted McGinn. Husted climbed out, then Birdsall, a patrol sergeant a full head taller than McGinn, planted his size thirteens on the pavement. When McGinn looked up again, the window was empty. He blinked his eyes. Possibly the wind had stirred the drapes or they had doubled back on themselves from the weight of water.

All five detectives, led by Selchaw who was trembling, took to the stairs, peering nervously into every shadowed corner and listening intently. They heard only silence, as if only the dead occupied the Bay Hotel. When they reached the third floor, Selchaw was afraid to remain and went back down by elevator. McGinn stationed Birdsall at the open door of number 309. Before they entered the room, they extinguished their cigarettes, then, all but McGinn, who was wearing gloves, buried their hands in their pockets to avoid leaving prints.

McGinn was a homicide veteran with over two hundred murders under his belt, most of them in this region of fog and long shadows, of seedy hotels, seedier sailors, and loose women. But what met his eyes in that shabby room with its flocked wallpaper and tint of rain was far beyond his ken. McGinn habitually pushed his oversize hat back on his forehead when he was puzzled. He did that now as he walked to the dresser side of the bed, leaned forward and gently drew back the section of blanket still covering the woman's legs. McGinn dropped the coverlet as if it were hot. "I have never seen such wanton and sadistic fury vented on a victim," McGinn said later. "In addition a crude autopsy has been attempted on the corpse."

One leg was crumpled beneath her, and except for a pair of torn black silk stockings, she was nude. Her lower legs shone as a mass of black and blue bruises, all inflicted by what must have been gigantic hands, certainly larger than he had ever seen.

Desmond, Husted, and Kelleher edged around to get a better look, then thought better of it. Husted was going to be sick. Kelleher murmured to himself and stepped into the hall. Desmond took off his steel-frame glasses and polished them briskly with his handkerchief, then went to the window, pulled back the blue curtains and stared absently into the rain outside and began to polish his glasses again. The downpour became a roar in his ears.

McGinn steeled himself to keep a detached viewpoint. "Seek the evidence; find the offender," he repeated.

He would call on the limited resources of his time, that of the rough science of the 1930s, and its basic psychology, which was still in its infancy. He would call on his men, whom he understood even as he did not understand what had motivated the savagery of the assailant. For the sake of his detectives, and even the big sergeant outside, McGinn outwardly remained coldly factual. Inside, he was seething and pumped with adrenaline. "There are just two answers to such a thing as this," he told his men evenly. "This is either a revenge murder or the work of a sadistic fiend such as I have never seen before. In either case this is going to be a plenty tough nut to crack."

He extracted a small notebook with a spiral binding from his jacket pocket, wet the tip of a pencil, and began printing. His hand was unsteady, but he plugged on. McGinn was never afraid of writing too much because his whole case might stand or fall on what he jotted down now. He noted the time he had arrived at the Bay Hotel, the date, and described the weather conditions—"bleak and rainy." He detailed a description of the dead body: "hair color dark red, short pageboy haircut, dark lipstick"; age: "early thirties"; build: "stocky"; clothes: "cheap print dress, cloth coat, small hat, underwear, pumps." Had the killer, in straightening and folding the clothes left behind traces of himself? He didn't see any. Were there prints on the three pieces of adhesive tape over her mouth? There almost had to be. Perhaps LaTulipe's tests for stains, tears, prints, and identifying marks would provide the answer. McGinn suspected the killer had concealed the body in a cocoon of coverlets as if ashamed of what he had done. Did this mean he knew her?

Nothing could be moved until the forensic photographer took his pictures and in all the excitement he had yet to be summoned. Slapping his notebook shut, McGinn shouted to the sergeant in the hallway, "Birdsall, call the HOJ and get the photographer."

Without touching the clawed and cut body, McGinn made mental notes on what he could see of the awful injuries themselves. First he studied the marks around her throat. In exerting manual pressure, the killer had left perfect impressions of his hands—strong, gripping fingers with unusually square thumbs and long nails that had bitten deeply into the flesh on both sides. He studied the victim's nails. Had she managed to scratch or even bite her assailant? LaTulipe would find out when he got there. There had been another case like this, but McGinn was loath to call it to mind. He reopened his notebook and entered his findings.

Husted and Desmond fanned out to search the hotel, and McGinn retrieved the steel tape kept in the growler. He took the room's exact dimensions, like a tailor preparing to make a suit. He drew a sketch of the corpse in situ on the bed, noting the relationship of the chair to the bed and chest, the location of the window to the chair, and so on.

McGinn held up her dress by two corners, then turned her purse out. Several tawdry keepsakes fell onto the wooden dresser top—a pair of tarnished earrings, a gold-plated clasp pin, a string of cheap pearls, a cheap compact, two or three loose cigarettes, a lipstick, 27¢, a mirror, and a skeleton key to some as-yet unknown house—the remnants of a sad, pathetic life. She carried no identification, but that was not unusual for the Bay Hotel and its clientele. McGinn studied the white-gold ruby ring on her left index finger.

It looked valuable, yet the killer had left it behind. Robbery was not the motive nor was this a sex crime, at least as understood by the psychology of the time. Nor, as McGinn suspected, were any of the other traditional propelling motives: greed, revenge, jealousy. If there was a motive it was one McGinn had not encountered before. "Then what the hell was his intent?" McGinn asked himself. The hat went back farther on his head. He scratched his bald scalp. He was at a loss to explain such brutality.

The victim on the bed was no beauty, yet some killer had sought her out and in his fury gone beyond the borders of civilization. The crime had to be premeditated. The killer had brought along tape to bind her and a sharp cutting implement to dissect her. Obviously, he preyed on the lower strata of life, those he had believed would never be missed. But the killer had miscalculated. His crime had been too blatant, too horrifying. It had to have been to shake such a veteran as McGinn. The press would call it "a sadistic orgy of violence in which a woman was horribly slashed and mutilated in the most ghastly manner." Regardless of the victim's station in life, she was a human being and as such was valuable. In the end, the thrust of McGinn's grim work was to prove each life important, even sacred. And like every victim, the woman on the bed deserved justice. No matter how long it took he was determined she was going to get it.

"Should we fingerprint her?" asked Desmond, who had returned.

"There will be plenty of time for that later," snapped McGinn. "She's not going anywhere."

He checked his watch. Everyone was waiting on the photographer, the coroner's deputy, Tony Trabucco, and Frank LaTulipe. McGinn couldn't even roll the body until they arrived. The weapon might be beneath it. Having done all he could, McGinn went to the open window. He watched the downpour striking the fire escape three windows away. Had the killer escaped the locked room that way and climbed up to the roof with its giant billboard? No, it was an impossible climb, though Bernstein's roof was even with the third floor. If he could fly, the murderer might be leaning against the big billboard and waiting even as they waited.

Kelleher checked the rooms on both sides. No one had heard a disturbance during the night. Perhaps the driving rain had drowned out any sounds. And her mouth had been taped. "I've got one question," McGinn said. He walked around the room and bath. "Where is their luggage?"

He rode down to the lobby where Anna Lemon confirmed the room door had been locked. Their "cold-blooded gent" had taken the hotel key away with him. He might still have it on him; the murder weapon, too, because it was not in evidence. McGinn got Anna Eve Lemon's full name and the names and addresses of anyone else who might be a witness. First was the absent night porter, Otto von Feldman, then the night clerk, John Smeins. Selchaw had no forwarding address for von Feldman, but did for Smeins. McGinn scrawled "John Smeins" on the right-hand page of his notebook along with the address Selchaw provided. "When did they check in?" he asked.

"Let's see," said Selchaw, pulling the register to himself, and ran his finger down a line of signatures. "Here it is. Smeins registered the woman and her husband registered just after 3:00 A.M."

McGinn turned the book. Two inked lines as jagged as barbed wire read: "Mr & Mrs. Meyers." The mysterious Mr. Meyers had put a period after *Mrs.*, but not after *Mr.* On the left-hand page of McGinn's notebook was a space for suspects. He wrote "Mr Meyers." "I'm curious," he asked. "How did Mr. and Mrs. Meyers explain their lack of luggage? I couldn't find any suitcases in their room."

"Luggage? I don't know. You'll have to ask Smeins. But I do know the man left a wake-up call." He pointed out the notations "3:00 A.M." and "10:00 A.M."

"I will ask Smeins," said McGinn.

Because the night clerk lived only blocks away, he ordered Desmond and Kelleher there. "Hurry," McGinn said. Exiting the Bay Hotel, the two waterfront cops passed LaTulipe coming in the front door. Only half a block away all four clock faces of the Ferry Tower were illuminated, glowing softly down on the dismal hotel. Close on LaTulipe's heels trotted the police photographer carrying the huge cameras of the time. Investigator Ray Boreas was just crossing the street. Now the detectives could truly begin finding the answer to the puzzle of the murder on the third floor of the Bay Hotel, the most horrible any of them had ever seen. Because Smeins had seen the face of the murderer and could identify him, he was crucial to their case. He might even be in danger himself. Desmond and Kelleher quickened their pace.

FIFTEEN

Do not touch, alter, or move anything until it has been measured, photographed, and examined by the persons responsible for the evidence.

—THE GOLDEN RULE OF INVESTIGATIONS

AT 4:35 on the rainy Saturday afternoon of April 6, Francis X. LaTulipe
reached the small drab room in the Bay Hotel. The falling rain outside had
tinted its walls a tea-stained blue the texture of smoke. Ever after, the expert
criminologist called number 309 "the blue room." He dragged his forensic
equipment—micrometers, microscopes, and bulky instruments used to
make meticulous measurements—from the elevator. He was a brave man to
do battle armed with only these tools. LaTulipe dropped his apparatus outside the door. Inside was a rapid succession of *pops*, the photographer
"shooting a flashlight." A final searing *crackle* resounded as he hurled one
last bulb to the carpet, having photographed the victim from every conceiv-
able angle—close-ups of the head, full face, and profile—all crucial to learning her real name. The photographer packed up, and as he left gave a
thumbs-up to LaTulipe.

When someone garroted wealthy patroness Mrs. Rosetta Baker with a
sheet in her hotel apartment at 814 California Street, LaTulipe had gone
over the death chamber inch by inch with a powerful glass. He located a
dime-size irregular patch of skin torn from a finger during the struggle, a
white button ripped from a man's shirt, the worn lift of a man's shoe
heel, and the thin wooden peg used to hold it in place. "It was a perfect

case," LaTulipe recalled. "Plenty of evidence at hand, but we couldn't get a conviction."

"Seek the evidence . . ." he thought, the mantra of Dullea's men, as he studied every inch of the nude body. "Frenzy," he said, "whoever it was was carried away with frenzy."

Yet that same frenzied someone had tidied the room, made the bed with her in it, left very little blood, and been cool enough to bring along a roll of tape. "Mutilated and gagged with adhesive tape," he wrote. "Why gag someone who was already dead? Had she been alive during the mutilation?" He hoped not. Using tweezers, LaTulipe carefully peeled away the three strips of tape crisscrossing her mouth. Beneath were three elevated, white tattoos, permanent compression marks. They were white because after death blood can no longer reach the capillaries.

He studied her bruised throat where large, powerful hands were outlined in black. Nine years earlier, the Gorilla Man's strong gripping fingers had left the same bruises. His hands, too, had been huge, with long flat nails. Gorillas have long flexible thumbs capable of stretching to grasp large branches, but almost every muscle, bone, internal organ, and blood vessel of the gorilla is repeated in man. Even their hands are relatively short and wide—like human hands.

LaTulipe examined the cuts. Were they lacerations or incisions? Lacerated wounds have ragged, contused edges split away at bony prominences with strands of connecting tissue bridging the gaps. He saw none of these characteristics. All her wounds were incised, the least common wound, and implied a very sharp razor or knife. Knives were not ordinarily carried, except by seamen.

He studied a shallow pool of blood surrounding the breast on the night table. A slicing tool suggested that the killer was undersexed. In his sadistic delirium, he had employed a cutting tool as a symbolic mimicry of sex. The pointless mutilations told LaTulipe this might be a lust murder. The lust murderer bites, dissects—slashing the abdomen, exposing abdominal viscera, and eviscerating the torso. He amputates the genitals.

LaTulipe looked for "scarf-skin"—abrasions confined to the cuticle—but found no blood or skin beneath her nails. Even if he found some he could do very little except determine blood type, sex, and race. A triangle of black celluloid-like material on the floor caught his eye. He bent and retrieved it. The killer's tight grip on his cutting tool had broken off a piece of the handle. Getting down on his hands and knees, LaTulipe peered under the bed. As his eyes grew accustomed to the darkness he saw the instrument of mutilation—a razor marked with a residue of flesh, cartilage, and crusted blood. LaTulipe bagged it and a tuft of coarse hair. He placed both in a clean pill box.

Deputy Coroner Mike Brown drove the morgue wagon to the Bay Hotel himself. The roly-poly veteran was out of breath as he wheeled his gurney into the elevator. Heavy, thick-necked, turtlelike, he was a head shorter than McGinn. Two years earlier on another April weekend, Brown had conveyed Josie Hughes's body to the morgue. "He is an ace investigator," said McGinn of Brown, "a relentless searcher of facts, one of the kindliest and most sympathetic of all men in spite of his daily work among the tragic dead."

What was the worst he had seen? Brown thought a moment. "A construction worker's suicide with a shotgun filled with water," he decided. "When he placed the barrel in his mouth and pulled the trigger, the pressurized water acted explosively and took off the top of his head."

But Brown had never seen anything like the atrocity in room 309. He took one look at the body and began sobbing. Even the cerebral LaTulipe was touched by his compassion. Coroner Thomas B. W. Leland arrived and, after viewing the body, authorized Brown to remove it. Sergeant Birdsall gathered the clothes from the chairs, and followed the gurney down in the elevator. Brown was still crying. Birdsall put his beefy arm around his shoulders.

After Brown drove the body away, LaTulipe began rooting for latents. He studied the victim's nails and the victim herself. An attacker's fingers bearing blood can actually leave prints on skin. LaTulipe decided to try a new fingerprint trick. He placed iodine crystals in a glass tube and blew lightly through an atomizer. The heat of his breath transformed the crystals into a gas that would react actively on any greasy matter. He got close and blew back and forth over the wall. Previously invisible prints appeared. But the second he ceased blowing, the fugitive brown marks began to fade.

He took a photo, fumed some more and took another. He repeated this process until his head began to ache. The toxicity of the gas in such close proximity caused his head to swim. Men had died doing this test. Staggering to the window, he stuck his head outside and took several deep breaths. After his mind cleared, he began to dust the window frame. As the cloud of finely ground carbon settled, made sluggish by the misty rain, it adhered to one good print. LaTulipe picked it up on tape, affixed it to a card, and after taking exact measurements of the blue room, locked the door and left.

DESMOND and Kelleher, walking briskly, reached the night clerk's home a few blocks from the Bay Hotel. The two seasoned waterfront shooflies had been the perfect men to send. No one knew the Embarcadero as well; no one understood those who lived there better. Kelleher's son, Tim, within a few years, would join his father as a SFPD detective. It was still raining, but lighter now. Sailors passed arm in arm with smiling women in colorful outfits. Everyone was getting ready for Saturday night. The bars were doing a thriving business. Music and loud voices sounded. Neon lights sprang on. Just after 5:00 P.M., Desmond and Kelleher reached two rows of tawdry boardinghouses with stone lions out front. They climbed the steps. It took Desmond a moment to read the mailboxes and locate the right room. He rang the bell. Neither man expected the living skeleton who answered the door.

A bald head with pinkish, hooded eyes shone luminously in the darkness. The long, grim face, beaklike nose, veined neck and prominent Adam's apple suggested a vulture. The undernourished skeleton had drawn on thin triangular eyebrows and wrapped an argyle-patterned robe around his narrow shoulders. The design added to his general angularity. His bare legs suggested to Kelleher that he was naked beneath the robe. The smell of lilac vegetal was overpowering.

"I'm Smeins," he said, then ushered them into a room overlooking the street, sat down, and daintily crossed long hairless legs. "I'd be glad to answer any questions you have," he said. He reached down and petted the calico cat curled at his feet.

"Start at the beginning, and tell us all you remember."

"The register is correct about the time—3:00 A.M.," he said in a calm, deliberate manner. He paused each time before speaking as if collecting his thoughts. "The woman and a man I supposed was her husband registered as: Mr. and Mrs. H. Meyers of Los Angeles. 'We don't have luggage,' they told me. 'We've just driven up from Southern California. We were just too tired to bring it in. Give us a quiet room. We don't want to be disturbed.'

"When the man and the woman came in, they were not walking arm-in-arm, but seemed very chummy all the same." Smeins rubbed his long, dry hands together. "She was very much at ease and not a bit shy. They were laughing and talking and addressing each other as 'dear.' He said, 'I want a room and a bath.' Then he turned to the girl and said, 'Is that all right?' She said, 'Yes, dear.' I handed her a folder listing San Francisco places of amusement, streetcars, playgrounds and all that sort of stuff. She smiled and said, 'Oh, thanks. This will help me get acquainted.' The bloke paid for the room with a $2 bill. They had no baggage with them. Then I took them up in the elevator to the third floor, to their room, #309. There were a number of vacancies but Mr. Meyers had requested that room, I was happy to oblige.

"I asked the couple, 'Is there anything else you would like?' She replied, 'No, thank you.' So I left as the man closed the door and locked it. I heard the lock click as I walked away. About 4:30 A.M., the elevator bell rang. So I went up to the third floor with the elevator, and there was the man looking cheerful. I took the bloke down to the lobby."

Desmond was flabbergasted. The monster had accomplished all that horror in less than an hour and a half.

"You know," said Smeins, "I think the same man may have stopped at the hotel last summer and maybe the summer before, but had never stayed any length of time. I think he was known around the hotel as a crewman on a coast ship by what name I don't know or even what port he was from."

"That would have been during the bloody dock strikes," said Desmond. "Perhaps he was stranded in San Francisco along with all the idled ships." The coast ships had particularly been hit hard. The crippling shipping strikes had wrecked the passenger steamer *Harvard* under command of Captain Louis Ellsinger (a witness in the Malcolm shooting) as surely as the Point Arguello rocks had sunk her sister ship, *Yale*.

"Make a check of the hotel's old register and see if you can find his name," Kelleher told Smeins, knowing that it would only be another alias as surely as "Mr. Meyers" was.

"Was there anything unusual about the man?" asked Desmond.

"What wasn't?" A huge grin crossed the skeletal face. He rocked one slippered foot.

"Now think carefully, what did he look like?"

"Von Feldman might have seen him more clearly because he went up to fix the window, but let's see." He put one hand under his sloping chin and thought. "Mr. Meyers was fairly well-dressed in a dark suit that fit snugly."

"Muscular," said Kelleher.

"Yes, I would say so."

Smeins described a burly suspect, twenty-six to thirty years old, with blue-brown eyes, a slitlike mouth, low-set ears, and vaguely simian features. "He kept his face averted. He was short and heavyset, about 5' 8" and weighed around 180–190 pounds. But he could have been taller and heavier. I got the impression he was crouching. He had a powerful build—broad chest, long arms, wide shoulder, and short legs. Huge hands and a large head. He had a strong lower jaw and enlarged canine teeth. I would say he had light to medium-brown hair and a tanned, weather-beaten complexion."

"Like that of a seafaring man," said Kelleher. "Our killer is a sailor."

"Mr. Meyers had huge hands and massive shoulders—like those of an ape."

"A gorilla man," said Desmond. A Gorilla Man! He looked to Desmond. It couldn't be happening again.

"I'd know him if I saw him again," said Smeins. "When Mr. Meyers came down into the lobby about 4:30 A.M., his coat collar was turned up around his neck and his face was partially hidden. He wore his hat pulled low. It was a porkpie, a snapbrim with a low flat crown. He was all ready to go out into the rain. He kept his hands in his pockets."

"He plunged his hands inside his pockets to hide bloodstains on them," said Kelleher glumly.

"And he pulled the hat down to hide any scratches on his face," added Desmond. "Did he say anything more?"

"Well, the bloke said to call them about 10:00 A.M. He said his wife was hungry and asked me where he could get some sandwiches. He had a soft melodious voice, I remember that much. As I recall his actual words were, 'It's hell with these women. All they want is beer and sandwiches before they'll go to sleep. That damn woman is sending me out for beer and sandwiches.' I told him where he might get some sandwiches on Market Street and he went sauntering out the door. He walked with a kind of gait, on the flat of his feet. I thought it was a bit queer at the time. He was whistling nonchalantly and gave out a kind of queer little laugh. He laughed all the way out. I thought it might be the oddest laugh I've ever heard. And when he didn't show up again and knowing what you've told me now I'm positive it was. He still hadn't come back when I went off duty at 7:00 A.M."

The cat purred contentedly at the skeleton's feet. The tiny claws flexed. The solid ticks of the clock sounded as Smeins, unblinking, stared at them in silence. The detectives left after Smeins promised to try to remember more about the sailor who had stopped at the Bay Hotel. Smeins sat down to think, then leaped up and went for the phone.

SIXTEEN

The name *gorilla* was given to the largest of the anthropoid apes by American missionary and naturalist Thomas S. Savage upon his return from Africa in 1849.

SMEINS'S very remarkable portrait of "Mr. Meyers," a unique man described by another unique man, was disseminated by the communications room at the HOJ to all Bay Area law enforcement agencies. By Teletype, phone, and radio they broadcast a description of what could only be a human gorilla who used a razor to kill. On the Embarcadero, speeding growlers were reflected in the rain-slick streets, black upon black punctuated by flashing red. Chief Quinn's Flying Squad gunned their motorcycles and roared from the HOJ like hunting animals. These ninety men and forty-five sidecar units had proven to be the SFPD's most efficient pursuit vehicles, outperforming the Buick town cars. At 6:00 P.M., Captain Dullea, because of the serious nature of the crime, assigned dozens of his detectives to fan out over the Embarcadero. "He's a husky man with big hands, broad shouldered and hunched like a gorilla," he told them. "He's very strong. Spread out and search the docks, search ships and seaman's hangouts. It's our only chance—our one lead."

Night fell, and the slanting rain ceased. In his small office, Dullea was troubled. The site of the murders—the third floor, and the method of murder—a strangling by a beastlike killer with huge hands, reminded him of the Gorilla Man. But he could not reasonably connect the two. He was dead, wasn't he? He had died in Canada, hadn't he? Yet for the second time in his career Dullea and his men were on the lookout for a Gorilla Man who strangled his female victims in rooming houses and hotels. He pushed back his chair, rose, and walked to a wall map to consider the avenues of escape from the city. There weren't many.

There was no Bay Bridge or Golden Gate Bridge yet, though both were under construction, had been for years. Yes, thought Dullea, the unfinished frameworks taking shape in the Bay would have been useless to the fugitive. The only ways to reach the city were by rail and auto up the peninsula from the south or across the Bay by boat and ferry. The region's forty-three ferryboats, each splashed a different color, provided frequent and reliable service across the Bay to and from the Alameda and Marin County shores. And though the lights on the Ferry Building footbridge were left on after midnight and the terminus lit on the upper floors, the last ferry had left at 11:35 P.M. This meant that no means of transportation across the Bay would have been available until four hours after Mr. Meyers left the Bay Hotel laughing. Perhaps someone on the Embarcadero had seen a husky man loitering at 4:30 A.M., waiting for the ferries to start running.

"You know," said LaTulipe, "I'm certain the killer's clothes might still be stained even after twelve hours. That job was bloody work. Workers don't wash often on the docks. Search the Embarcadero for someone wearing bloodstained clothes." Dullea amended his bulletin. "Be on the lookout for any suspect matching the above description who might have bloodstains on his clothing or scratches on his face or hands," he ordered.

The cops got lucky almost immediately. Down by the Ferry Building they dragged in a big fisherman who matched the description and had an enormous amount of blood on his greasy clothes. "Are you Mr. Meyers?" the cops asked wolfishly, hot on the scent and licking their chops.

Forthwith, LaTulipe began a precipitant test on the fisherman's jeans. Preparing a supersensitive solution of benzidine, he moistened the material with pyridine. He could verify that the blood was human and not animal by viewing the red corpuscles. Using a handheld lens, he watched for a clouding that never came. It wasn't human blood. "Forget it boys," he said. "It's probably only shark blood. Besides, Mr. Meyers was described as well dressed." LaTulipe was still troubled by the lack of blood in the hotel room. Where had it gone?

In his office, Dullea, working in his shirtsleeves as he customarily did, shuttled between his two small desks comparing reports. In the background an old dilapidated radio spit static as lightning crackled far out to sea. Dullea frowned. The drunken reporters on the second floor had "traded" their antique radio for his new model. Someday he intended to make a counter raid and snatch it back.

Chief Quinn had crammed all the reporters, photographers, hangers-on, bailiffs, deputies, and tipsters into two small, high-ceilinged rooms with peeling paint and floors littered with cigarette butts. The reporters played pinochle, rummy, and poker. Blue and red poker chips piled up and ashtrays spilled over. They sipped cold coffee, swam in clouds of tobacco smoke, and extinguished their butts in their cups.

Yawning, Hank Peters glanced at his cards, then through the begrimed window. Rain was falling outside again. Eddie Gillen, pecking out a report on his Remington, dropped a butt on the floor and ground it under his heel. Charlie Huse, shoes off, was trying to grab a few winks on the broken leather couch by a marble-floored bathroom that contained a single toilet for them all.

Across the hall was a courtroom. On the southern side was a rabbit warren of rooms where police questioned prostitutes. Dullea coveted this area for his captains' offices, but Chief Quinn had his own plans for this prime real estate. Because the dirty windows admitted scant light in the Press Room, the reporters kept the overhead light burning all day. By day a little light spilled from the sash windows into an open light well connecting to the grim city prison above. Swirling in the crosscurrents, the reporters' smoke was sucked up the light well. Whenever the reporters needed information from the criminal court, they simply yelled up to the duty sergeant at his desk.

In well-administrated police departments detained persons are taken to the district station, where the duty sergeant reviews the detention, asks the patrolman for the circumstances of the arrest, determines what evidence has been collected, and determines whether any further follow-up is appropriate. Then he reviews the arrest report before submitting it to the lieutenant for final approval. Not in San Francisco. There, detained prisoners go directly to the HOJ, where the station sergeant acts only as a receptionist who performs record-keeping chores and keeps an accurate accounting of property.

In the north wing of the jail, Superintendent Bernard Reilly slumped at his high wooden bench at the visitor's cage. Twenty feet away a guard paced the narrow corridor, waiting to escort another manacled prisoner along that hallway known as the "Bridge of Sighs." Next door to the HOJ, a few off-duty policemen were taking the edge off a grueling day at Cookie Picetti's Star Bar. Some were drunk. But drunk, sober, or bored—they all waited. Dullea waited, too.

Mike Brown, still shaken, delivered the body of Mrs. Meyers to the City Morgue on dingy Merchant Street. This cold, bleak place across the alley from the HOJ was marked by a blue light, just as the murder room had been. Brown waited until Dullea came down from his office and met him at the rear door. Sergeant Birdsall, who had bundled up the woman's clothing, awkwardly held the garments away from himself. Dullea took them. If all else failed, he hoped to trace the victim's identity through the small felt hat, cheap print dress, cloth coat, and tattered underwear.

"In the coroner's gloomy establishment downstairs," Dullea said later, "the inspectors and I went carefully over the clothing she had been wearing as Ray Brooker the deputy coroner prepared a written record which reflected type, size, color, store labels and laundry markings."

Dullea studied a typed carbon copy as Brooker wired an identification tag to each article. Then with a camera with a double-extension bellows, he snapped three close-up photos of the razor with the broken handle. He also fingerprinted the body—standard procedure.

"I rushed to the office of Dr. Adolphus A. Berger, the city autopsy surgeon," Dullea said, "and told him, 'Post mortem her as you never post mortemed anyone before. I need to know exactly *when* she died, *why* and by exactly *what* means she was killed, so that I can find out *who* was responsible.'"

The smell of death and disinfectant was strong in the twelve-foot-square autopsy room. Bright light gleamed off a metal gurney with the herringbone gullied pattern where Dullea had laid out Josie Hughes's clothes in 1932. He listened to the continuous sound of water trickling in a trough around the edge of the concrete floor and down a central drain. Low shelves held rows of brown bottles. Dr. Sherman Leland laid out gleaming instruments. A huge porcelain bucket was by his foot. As a steno took down dictated notes, Leland lifted the white muslin sheet and conducted a careful examination of the victim's scalp and external surface of her body. He carefully photographed the wounds in close-up alongside a six-inch celluloid scale. Next, he cleansed the wounds of blood, then rephotographed them.

With her blood type established, Leland studied her dilated pupils. The tight pressure on her neck had paralyzed the sympathetic nerves and left pinpoint hemorrhages in the whites of her eyes. "That's an infallible sign of strangulation," Leland said. Still he was not sure.

But conclusive proof of manual strangulation would come from the cracked hyoid, a thin-armed, U-shaped bone buried in the heavy muscle of the neck. This free-floating anchor for the tongue's muscles rests just where thumbs would press during strangulation. Yes, thought Leland, it is fractured on both sides. A powerful man with wide thumbs had been the strangler.

"Is there anything to indicate whether she was alive when the crushing force to her throat was applied?" asked Dullea from just outside the circle of light. His voice was tight, hoping she had been dead first, hoping she had felt no pain from the killer's "autopsy."

"She was not dead," ventured Leland. "The muscle supporting her hyoid bone had been deeply bruised. Charlie, dead bodies don't bruise."

LaTulipe would challenge that assumption. This week in London, where forensic science currently led the world under the tutelage of Sir Bernard Henry Spilsbury, Sir Robert Christison had demonstrated that a bruise from manual compression of the throat can be made up to two hours after death.

"You say she must have been lying on her back when she received the wounds," asked Dullea. "Could she have lived long enough to turn herself over."

"No. Death probably came while she was still on her back." Leland rolled the corpse to the side. "Her back is crisscrossed with lines. A nude corpse's dead weight registers the textures of any surface that exerts pressure against it. In this case—sheets."

The absence of considerable blood in the room suggested the woman had been dead before she was disassembled. "Dead bodies don't bleed."

Leland examined her throat and neck, removed her lungs and heart, and noted Tardieu spots in her heart (tiny capillary hemorrhages due to raised blood pressure). This was another sign of strangulation as the cause of death. The surgeon put down his scalpel and shook his head. It had dawned on him that this was the *second* time the victim had been autopsied that day.

As Dullea made the lonely trek back to his office, he observed the bright, cold rooms and shadowy figures at work in the morgue. There is a weird kind of fascination about morgues and autopsies, about mortality and the fragility of life. He guessed it was a job not far removed from police work. Deep in thought, he climbed the stairs. Presently Dr. Leland came into his dimly lit office with his report. "Do you think our killer might work in a morgue somewhere," asked Dullea, "and decided to try such an operation?"

"That's a possibility," replied Leland, "because that's just what Mr. Meyers has done. He's attempted an autopsy with some skill."

"Perhaps we should stake out hospital morgues in case his intense fascination might draw him there." Leland did not answer. It didn't matter, Dullea's most important questions—time and cause, had been answered by the doctor. Death had occurred around 4:00 A.M. from strangulation and hemorrhage. According to John Smeins, Mr. Meyers left thirty minutes after that.

A little after midnight (it was now Sunday, April 7), he assigned Desmond, Kelleher, and Husted to identify the murdered woman. "Get out there," he ordered. "Trace her jewelry. Wake up pawnshop dealers around the Embarcadero and find out what you can."

After they left, Dullea got an unexpected break. Routine fingerprinting by Inspector Dan O'Neill of the Bureau of Identification had paid off. Mrs. Meyers was in their arrest files as a "notorious police character" under the aliases of "Bette Davis," "Bette Coffman," "Lena Coffin," and "Bette Coffin." The police narrowed their list of the victims' names to one when a man called to report his wife, Bette Coffin, missing. He was told to come to Merchant Street. Dullea notified Desmond and Kelleher to abandon their rounds of the pawnshops and instead spend the rest of the night combing sailors' hangouts and shoreside dives tracking a Mrs. Bette Coffin's last movements.

McGinn and Husted, who were now conducting the investigation, decided instead to go to Mrs. Coffin's residence of record at 966 Broderick Street and get a list of her hangouts. It was vacant. Husted got the new address, 1207 Gough Street, from a neighbor. At the new location they learned Mrs. Coffin's husband was already at the city morgue and started there to interview him.

By 3:20 A.M. a sad, seedy little man known as Al "The Mouse" Coffin (aka Ernest Coffin and Ernest Coffman) was rapping timidly at the entrance to the morgue, which was in an alley behind he HOJ. "I've come to claim my wife's body," said The Mouse as Dullea came downstairs from his office across the alley to join him. He saw The Mouse standing quietly under the blue light with shoulders bowed, which made him even smaller than he was. They both entered. "She left the rooming house Friday night to go downtown," he told Dullea, "and that was the last I seen of her." Tears welled in his eyes. The Mouse was so threadbare, he really owned nothing of value except an absolutely airtight, ironclad alibi, which his poker buddies later verified. Besides, they were looking for an apelike man with huge hands and a deep tan—not a pale shrimp like The Mouse. Dullea believed the poor little guy was genuinely bereaved.

Mrs. Coffin's past was sad, too.

The Mouse admitted his wife had a police record as a vagrant and occasionally used dope. Dullea returned to his office to read over her file. Bette had been arrested scores of times as a streetwalker and drug addict.

"What kind of drugs did she take?" Dullea asked McGinn.

"That's it," said McGinn, who had been at a loss to establish a motive. "It's the drug connection. Mrs. Coffin is a stool pigeon for the narcotics division. She was murdered in such a horrible way as an example to others. How else could you explain such the violence of the attack. That has to be the motive. The underworld has taken its terrible vengeance."

SEVENTEEN

"If every force in the country was connected by Teletype machines in a series of strategic units; if we could spare our men from routine duties for more extended schooling. Then and only then we might make more progress against crime."

—CHIEF QUINN

ON Monday morning, April 8, over at the *San Francisco Chronicle*, Allan R. Bosworth lifted his green eyeshade. He was alone at his desk on the third floor. The great copy wheel was deserted. Thoughtfully, the editor tapped the end of his blue grease pencil and stared across the lines of vacant tank desks and rows of fat pillars. Shafts of light cut through the arched bow windows. A hint of salt air wafted through an open pivot window, carrying the clear northwest wind sweeping the Farallone Islands at fifteen miles an hour. The sea was moderate, and the barometer, at 30:14. At the Heads it was hazy with fog, but on the corner of Fifth and Mission streets, the sun was dazzling. The *Chronicle*'s clock tower was just striking 8:00 A.M. Bosworth studied the indestructible mint, with its classic Greek columns and sweep of marble steps, across the street.[7] It made *Chronicle* publisher Mike de Young proud to throw down double eagles bearing his neighbor's

---

[7] The Old Mint had been the only banking institution to survive the 1906 quake and fire, when employees, armed with only a one-inch hose saved the building and $200 million in gold bars. Ironically, with widespread poverty all around, one-third of the nation's gold reserve was stored there.

mark when he bought his Picso punches. A block away was broad Market Street and at its source workers were pouring across the curved iron bridge to begin the dreary week all over again.

Out in the Bay, the south tower of the Golden Gate Bridge had reached 540 feet (200 feet short of its final elevation) and was already 23 feet higher than the Bay Bridge's highest tower. By God, it was a race between the two bridges! thought Bosworth. Twenty-four gangs of Bay Bridge riveters, driving more than two hundred thousand rivets, had just come level with the Golden Gate's deck. For the eleventh time, the traveling derrick they used to erect the steel tower was raised into position, 480 feet above water level. It bent from the strain. No matter who won the race, it would almost certainly spell the demise of the Ferry Building as San Francisco's front door.

Early morning in the block-long city room most of the swivel-back chairs and single pedestal desks were vacant. Royal typewriters were shrouded on their stands. In the alley below, a handful of unshaven reporters were sleeping off a bad night in their cars—arms flung out windows, fingers dangling. Copy boys began going from car to car taking orders for aspirin, coffee, and bacon and egg sandwiches.

Behind Bosworth, a man in shirtsleeves sat behind a little wooden gate running his hands through his hair. "The *Chronicle* city editor," Bosworth explained, "was occupied in toning down a particularly gory bit of business for its breakfast-table audience. A girl variously described as Bette Coffin, Bette Coffman, and Lena Coffin was found dead in her bed at the Bay Hotel on April 6th, with one of her breasts sliced off. There was no special class to the story [but] it had its day on the lips of newsboys."

The *Chronicle* routinely suppressed the more gory details of murders that captured the public's imagination so they would not be too dreadful to contemplate over the breakfast table.

On Saturday, the *San Francisco News*'s scarehead had banner-lined in blue and green: "GIRL KILLED BY FIEND!; FOUND SLASHED TO DEATH IN SF HOTEL." The bank under it read, "Slayer Chokes Victim, Then Hacks Body. No Signs of Struggle." A halftone two-column cut on page one showed Smeins in his bathrobe, looking as birdlike as ever, giving his first-person account. On Sunday, the *Chronicle* ran this:

FIEND SLAYS NUDE WOMAN IN SF HOTEL. BODY HACKED AND CLAWED BY KILLER. POLICE LAUNCH SEARCH FOR MAN.

A red-haired woman known as Bette Coffin, 34, was found murdered and mutilated in a hotel room at 26 Sacramento St. yesterday afternoon. Her nude body, brutally hacked and clawed, was discovered in bed 11 hours after she had registered at the hotel with a man who gave the name of H. Meyers. . . . The woman had been strangled, her head and mouth had been bound with adhesive tape, and her right breast had been severed. . . . John F. Smeins, night clerk said he had seen the man last summer.

Lieutenant Otto Frederickson, head of the SFPD's Homicide Division, told the press she had been the victim of a sadist. "This man might perpetrate a similar crime at any point," he warned. "You haven't seen the last of him. I recall that Mrs. Ruby Allen was found murdered in a similar way under similar circumstances in a cheap Post Street hotel one rainy April."

Bosworth wondered if there was a connection between Mrs. Coffin and the slaying of Louise Jeppesen in Golden Gate Park the previous year. "What was the world coming to?" he thought. He had seen it all. After arriving in the Golden State via west Texas and the U.S. Navy, he had performed every newspaper job on the West Coast—police reporter, copy editor, picture editor, news editor, and editor of three dailies. A decade in the future he would be a columnist for the *Chronicle* and the author of three hundred magazine articles, a mystery novel, and three Western novels (*Hang and Rattle,* his most successful shoot-'em-up). Bosworth had done everything and known everyone—yet never met anyone like Slipton Fell.

But then Bosworth had never met a murderer before.

The *Chronicle* city room began filling up. A few men began monotonously pecking out stories with one finger—bell, shift, bell, shift. Copy boys assembled "books," layers of cheap newsprint that they interspersed with sheets of blue carbon paper. They emptied ashtrays and thinned rubber cement with acetone. One copy boy, a scion of a wealthy Menlo Park family, conducted his duties in white tie and tails (he had a dinner party to attend that night). He ran corrected proofs, carried retouched photos to the composing room, installed rolls of paper in the Teletypes, and kept his tux spotless.

The tempo in the City Room picked up. Rows of Teletypes began chattering. Bells jangled insistently with news from Europe. Adolph Hitler was on almost every page every day. Copy boys tore, wrapped, and bound punched tapes with rubber bands.

At 11:00 A.M. the editors arrived to hold their preliminary meeting in the conference room to decide what would go in the paper. Though newspaper circulation remained high at the *Examiner* and *Chronicle,* ad revenue was plunging. Five years earlier there had been a 15 percent loss, then a 24 percent decrease the following year, and 40 percent the next, and 45 percent after that. Six years earlier, before Cornelius Vanderbilt and Will Hearst lost a bundle and the afternoon papers merged, there had been five big dailies.

The barnlike room was filled with men and smoke, and black rotary phones on desks began ringing. So did the pay phones in a row of green booths lining the north wall. Ticker tapes spooled on the floor of the financial department. From the back, a fossilized Sunday editor sneezed violently nine times in a row, something he did every hour. Bosworth believed if he ever sneezed a *tenth* time it would kill him. He glared at the big black clock.

Still no sign of his most personable, part-time reporter.

He took a call, then fed a sheet of paper into the roller. He typed a few lines, snatched the page out, and rolled in another. He wondered why some maniac had re-created the autopsy murder of Mary Kelly, the last and most horrible of Jack's Whitechapel crimes. He scanned another headline: "Police Seek Clues in Brutal Crime," then took up the *Examiner*'s front page: "Girl Murdered and Mutilated in Hotel Here; Body Found Nude, Mouth Taped, Torso Slashed with Razor." The most famous police reporters in the city had responded to the tragedy—Fred L. Diefendorf, Hank Peters, Eddie Gillen, Rod Leidy, Jimmy Yeiser, Eddie Longan, and Charles Huse. The *Chronicle* city editor finally decided on an update, which Bosworth buried on an inside page:

POLICE HAVE NO CLUES TO SF HOTEL MURDER; COMB WATERFRONT PLACES TO SEARCH FOR SHORT SAILOR SUSPECT.

After combing waterfront hangouts and sailors' haunts all night police yesterday were still without a clue to the curiously gruesome slaying of Mrs. Bette Coffin, 34, former denizen of the city's night life. Mrs. Coffin's nude body, brutally beaten and mutilated, with one breast severed, was found Saturday afternoon in a hotel room at 28 Sacramento St. Death had been caused by strangulation and loss of blood.

Sailor Sought

Convinced that a seafaring man had killed the woman, with a possible sadistic motive or for revenge, Inspectors Michael Desmond and Bart Kelleher were searching for a sailor, short and stocky and about 26 years old. A man of this description registered at the hotel with the woman at 3 o'clock Saturday morning. He left alone an hour and a half later, saying that he was going to "get some beer and sandwiches."

Held Premeditated

That the murder was premeditated was the belief of the police, who pointed out that the man undoubtedly had in his pocket when he entered the hotel the tape with which the woman's mouth was bound, and the razor, found under the bed, with which the woman was mutilated. From Al Coffman, the woman's husband, police obtained a list of her acquaintances and planned to question them.

Around noon, the bullpen came to life, and the rhythm of work began—a machinelike repetition of cutting, rubber stamping, and time stamping. At the horseshoe-shaped copy desk, an editor corrected the Bay Hotel story, cut it to fit, capped it with three subheads, and scribbled the type size on it. He spiked the carbon and picked a battered brass cylinder out of the basket at his elbow. Rolling the typed original into it, he sealed the rubber end flap to a brass button. Glad to be rid of such an unsettling story, he fed it to a pneumatic tube in a hiss of compressed air to the Press Room out back.

The Linotype operator extracted the copy. Her fingers moved mechanically over her keyboard, converting the letters to metal type. A cauldron of lead bubbled at her elbow. There came the reassuring *click-click-click* of mats cast down the channels and across the star wheel. The instant the elevator dropped, a full line was sent to cast. Finally, she walked the full stick to the bank. The printer eyeballed it with a pica ruler, loosened the quoins, and tightened the chase. He swept the unused type into the hell box.

On roller skates, the boy in white tails delivered sausage sandwiches called hot dogs (weren't they made of dog meat?). Tad Dorgan, the *Examiner*'s cartoonist, had made "Hot dog!" an excited exclamation. For the next three hours, the reporters worked on their stories in the field, calling them back to the assistant editor or dictating to a copyboy. At 3:00 P.M. the budget meeting began as the assistant city editors brought in their lists with slug lines and stories for the next day's paper. After the managing editor decided their sequence, the photo editor offered up pictures for the stories.

At 3:30 P.M., a booming laugh emanated from the front elevators and rolled past the reception area, down the corridor and the editorial boardroom, and into the City Room. When the echoing laugh reached the barnlike room it lost its echo. The ceiling was baffled to reduce noise. Reporters frowned at such merriment interrupting their deep thoughts, especially on a hung-over Monday.

A laughing man with prepossessing features filled the doorway. He was the classic Adonis type, as good looking as a movie star, except for slightly too-thick lips. Twenty-six years old, six feet tall, and 230 pounds, he was perfectly well made, except for his long arms and huge hands. He had slate gray eyes and a smooth face full of good humor. His teeth were flashing white and his dark hair glossy and lustrous. He frequently smoothed it back using his long fingers as a comb. His ruddy, tanned complexion, deepened by weeks at sea, was rapidly assuming a healthy pink color.

He wore a rumpled, well-tailored gray suit, a light V-neck shirt with short sleeves (to show off his considerable muscles), and black moccasin-style Oxfords with no socks. He was sleek and well fed, a lusty consumer of thick steaks and whole fried chickens. He was a mystery wrapped in an enigma and instantly attractive to women, especially older ones like Bette Coffin. The laughing man lived on the same block as the Bay Hotel.

Bosworth smiled in spite of himself. With his expansive gestures and endless jokes and tales, Slipton Fell was well liked. He was a soldier of fortune—a prolific sailor and adventurer who had traveled through Alaska; wandered all over South America; and journeyed extensively in North Africa, Russia, and Asia Minor. He spoke German, Arabic, Turkish, Spanish, and Italian and had an alternate personality to go with each. "He was extremely coy about giving his real name," Bosworth recalled. "Currently he was using the name Slipton J. (for Just) Fell and I called him that."

Bosworth had assigned him to gather some colorful stories in Latin America. While there, Fell plotted a revolt (which failed) and was forced to escape on an outbound freighter. As proof, he carried a letter of introduction from a Nicaraguan consul to the bandit chief Sandino, a self-described local patriot, which he displayed at the slightest encouragement. Bosworth did doubt Fell's list of expenses in gathering the story. "He had somehow become separated from his assistants 'Upton Rose' and 'Faran Wide,'" said Bosworth, "and wanted to apprise them of his whereabouts."

If his outrageously named assistants were only other facets of Fell's personality, Bosworth didn't know so he kept all three on the payroll. Besides, he admired the young man's boldness. Bosworth waved him over.

"As I remember it," Bosworth said later, "Mr. Fell entered this pixilated place just as the Sunday editor fired another volley of sneezes—7, 8, 9 . . . and as a hundred pound 'Jap' *yawara* instructor [the subject of a *Chronicle* Sunday piece] was paving the way for some publicity by throwing a 200 pound reporter flat on his back. . . . Yet the personable young man calling himself Slipton J. Fell had no difficulty in attracting attention, despite these rival sideshows."

"Fired?" Slipton Fell asked with a crooked grin. He smoothed the wrinkles in his gray jacket.

"Fried!" said Bosworth, indicating his reporter's tipsiness. "And you seem to have cut yourself, Mr. Fell."

"I guess he just slipped n' fell," said a copyreader at the U-shaped desk.

Another booming laugh. Fell dusted the spots, smoothed back his hair and bared strong, even teeth. He had been missing since Friday, when he had been scheduled for an interview about his "Latin American vagabonding."

When Fell couldn't recall where he had been over the weekend, he replied by laughing nervously—an infectious laugh that rose above the ringing phones and cries of "Boy!"

"Where did you find him this time?" said Bosworth.

"Alkied and drying out in the drunk tank," replied a reporter who had rescued Fell from the top floor of the HOJ. He was with Ralph." When that *Chronicle* reporter was intoxicated, he hailed cabs for long pointless journeys he couldn't pay for and ended up jail.

"Just who was he today?" Bosworth asked.

"'J. Hannegan, cook,'" said the reporter. "I had to convince the sergeant he was really a *Chronicle* writer and not a cook. I sprung Fell too just for the hell of it."

"And just who was *he* today?"

While Fell was a likable fellow, his personality was a maze of different identities, "one of the singularly fey characters then peopling the city room." Wherever else he had been since Friday, Fell knew all about the murder. He never ceased begging for a picture and feature story about himself. Well, thought Bosworth, he would grant Fell his wish. The *Chronicle* would write of him: "His mouth is large and sensual when not wreathed in a fatuous grin or cleaved by his ringing guffaw."

"Run a good picture of him in his sailing costume," said Bosworth, "the one with the ascot and briar pipe." Fell had previously supplied a photo of himself at the rail of a liner sporting a mustache and dressed in a tweed cap, black vest, and expensive camel's-hair coat. His collar was upturned and shirt open in a vee as he posed. "No one knows what's in my mind, but, oh, if you only did," said Fell who left with a backward wave.

"Never mind Fell's real name," Bosworth recalled. "He got his story . . . he got his picture and went happily on his way, and when he had gone the city room seemed a quiet and sober place, and the managing editor decreed a more conservative make-up for the first edition and that damned Bay Hotel story got changed again."

At 6:00 P.M. Metro (with eight men) and International (with four men) sent out the layouts for the first edition. At 7:00 P.M. the production department returned a proof of the first edition for the outlying circulation areas. The managing editor checked the layout, quickly turned it around, and sent it back to the production department. Between 8:00 and 9:00 P.M., the reporters began heading to the bar in the alley. At 10:00 P.M., the copy editors honed their stories for the Home and Final Editions, and at midnight the Final went to print. A counting machine on the presses stopped at the circulation number. Between 1:00 and 2:00 A.M., the last papers were bailed and loaded onto circulation trucks waiting in stalls on the loading dock. Now the terrible events of the Bay Hotel could be read the next morning.

Fell was in a rush to get to his new job in Woodside Glens south of San Francisco. Though this turned out to be his last visit to the *Chronicle*, Bosworth never forgot him. A decade later he recorded his experiences with the apelike young man in a lively article titled, "The Laughing Killer of the Woodside Glens."

EIGHTEEN

An uncertainty pervaded the department as to the responsibilities of supervisory officers at all levels. There was an absence of a command structure which provides high level command decisions at night and on weekends.

—COMMISSION REPORT ON THE SFPD

THE next morning, Tuesday, April 9, the reclusive Mrs. Ada Phillys French-Mengler-Rice returned to the Woodside Glens from one of her mysterious excursions. The fifty-eight-year-old writer and former journalist lived alone atop a knoll two miles south of Woodside and four miles west of Redwood City. As the black cab glided through the foggy hills, curious neighbors parted their blinds and silently gauged its progress. With a bitter twist to their lips, they studied the rigid profile framed in the rear window. The stolid, dark-haired woman had been gone an interminable time. They knew Mrs. Rice as well to do and a world traveler, though none of them knew why she was well to do or where she traveled. She often took long journeys to other countries without notifying her husband, children, and relatives. "I've only seen her only twice in twelve years," complained Mrs. Lawrence Doherty, Ada's cousin in Oakland across the Bay.

The neighbors both hated and feared Ada Rice who, consumed with social welfare and club work, had been president of the Redwood City Women's Temperance Union. She had proven a willful, ineffectual, and spiteful leader. Her tips to the police had initiated a number of nighttime raids against her neighbors, whom she erroneously suspected of operating whisky stills in violation of the Wright Act, California's version of the Volstead Act.

Fog overflowing the brooding hills surrounding Skyline Boulevard rode the road's spine down into the rocky ravine and shrouded the cab just off the Canada Road. At the head of the long drive, Ada paid the cabbie and exited by a broken white picket fence. Her terraced summer cottage stood bleak and empty on the two and half acres her second husband, August Mengler, had bought when he still loved her. He had still loved her when he built the boxy house with his own two hands. Only one thing broke the stern, shingled squareness of the split-level vacation bungalow—a half-story penthouse with a skylight done in the Japanese style. A brick garage on the right side did project slightly onto the dismal lot. Skeletal trees stirred in the wind. Ada saw that her rock garden had been overtaken by thistles. Three steps took her to the front door. The screen door lay on its side against the house. Inside, it was silent. The winds howling down off Skyline Boulevard were screened out by the soundproofed ceiling Ada had installed. Ada's few visitors said it "looked like a museum." A crude masonry fireplace filled one corner, white concrete protruding between its flagstones. A set of andirons supported two iron pokers. Right of the fireplace was a davenport with one bad leg and a door that led to a back bedroom, where French doors admitted in gray light. On both sides, cold light filtered through double windows.

On those rare times when the fog cleared, a fenced-in redwood timber deck on the roof provided an outlook for Ada and permitted her to sunbathe there or under the skylight. While she had been gone, Mrs. Rice had stored her car on blocks in the garage. She opened the arched door and realized she would need a man to pump up the tires and remove the blocks. Ada hiked to a nearby service station, thinking over her problems as she went. First, she was thrice married. Her first husband, Fred French, a minister's son and the father of her three children, had died suddenly.

She married August H. L. Mengler, a slight, wearied sea captain and engineer, on July 8, 1930, in Martinez, California. Ada posed outdoors in a cane-back chair. In the photo of that happy day August stands stoutly behind her. Ada, in spring bonnet, white frock, and pearls, nestles a bouquet of roses in her lap, but the determined thrust of her jaw hints at trouble to come. It came on November 1, 1932, when she left the family home at Woodside Glens to travel abroad. "She's been living at an unknown address in Greece without my permission," August complained. When she extended her Grecian tour, he drove to San Francisco to see his lawyer, Joseph I. McNamara, at his office in the Kohl Building.

His signed complaint of September 23, 1933, alleged Ada had married him "more for his worldly goods, than love and affection." He cited extreme cruelty and a passion for welfare work and social reform that caused her to neglect their home. "I gave her large sums of money to make her trip," he said. "I sent more when she urgently cabled that she was stranded in Europe, but no more. I fear she will use the money for more world travel. I love her, but cannot live with her."

One thing puzzled McNamara. Not only did Ada travel under the name Ada French, but gave her forwarding address as 80 Wall Street, New York, the address of her former husband, Fred. August filed for divorce on September 21, 1933. Two days later, he was as dead as Fred French.

August collapsed in the lobby of an O'Farrell Street hotel (other reports placed his death in bed upstairs) and died as ambulance attendants transported him to Central Emergency Hospital. With August's sudden death, Ada had an incentive to return after a year away. She went to see McNamara who described her as "a woman of violent passion . . . subject to frequent outbursts of temper in my office." August's children were convinced their father's death was due to heart trouble aggravated by marital worries and fought Ada's claim as rightful heir. Ultimately, she was awarded her husband's bank account of about $2,500 and their jointly shared property, which amounted to another $10,000. They had homes at Muir Woods Park in Marin County, Berkeley Country Club Terrace at El Cerrito, Cardiff by the Sea in LA County, and the two gloomy lots in Woodside Glens, the only property August had demanded for himself in his complaint. Consequently, that was the only property Ada really desired. On that contested lonely spot of ground was the remote, square bungalow she loved so much.

Last January 29, the Reverend Jason Noble Pierce, pastor of the First Congregational Church, had married Ada to seventy-two-year-old Charles Freeman Rice, a Seattle contractor. As a member of a powerful Alaskan family, he had been the mayor of Nome in 1921 and 1922. Ada's brother, Don Carlos Brownell, was the present mayor of Seward, Alaska. Rice filed for divorce after two months for the same reasons as Mengler—Ada's pre-occupation with social reform to the exclusion of her home life. Ada's recent sojourn in Seattle had been to arrange the terms of divorce. Two days earlier, Mr. Rice requested that real estate agents John and Davenport Bromfield look to Ada for future payments on the bungalow and told her to watch for them. Putting her unhappiness on the back burner, Ada reached the service station, a single structure with glass bubble pumps and a Coke machine with glass bottles.

"Could you send a man over to my house to pump up my tires?" she asked.

"I'll do as good," said William Werder, the manager. "One of my new employees lives only a short distance from your home. I'll write down his address."

Ada went there and knocked on the door. Rubbing the sleep from his eyes (in the middle of the afternoon), a Greek god answered the door and began laughing. Almost immediately, she had liked his infectious laugh. Under a palooka shirt, worn outside his trousers and buttoned all the way to the bottom, he was barrel-chested. He had huge hands and strong white teeth. Like many other older women Ada had instantly fallen under the young man's spell, his wonderful jokes, and endless role-playing. Slipton Fell even played the mandolin.

NINETEEN

Homicide is not always murder, but murder is always homicide.

—DETECTIVE MANUAL OF THE PERIOD

BY Wednesday, April 10, 1935, five days after the Bay Hotel murder, things were not going well for the investigation. By 10:00 A.M., the SFPD Narcotics Division had already called Dullea back and gotten his day off to a rotten start. "Bette Coffin has never under any circumstances been a squeal of ours," they reported.

An hour later, Dullea's phone rang again. This time it was the FBI. "Your victim was never a drug informant of ours," the local special agent informed him. Another lead was dashed.

Dullea, working in his shirtsleeves and wearing the tie his wife had bought him, swiveled around to glare at the wall of his tiny office. A dozen three-by-five cards were tacked there. He was rearranging them as Detective Sergeant McInerney entered with reports under his arm and coffee from the Chinese establishment next door. Dullea took the coffee, then spread the reports out. The first was an unsolved San Diego case. On February 20, 1931, someone had hauled the mutilated nude body of eleven-year-old Virginia Brooks down a hill, hung it from a tree, and bound it with a sixty-foot long rope. The loops at both ends had been tied with intricate knots of the type used by seafaring men. "Since those gentlemen are notorious travelers," thought Dullea, "the killer had probably sailed for other ports immediately afterward."

Dullea was about to save the bulletin (such a madman might be back someday) when he found a second report cross-indexed with the first. Chief Quinn had made a notation in pencil on the back of a brown envelope sealed by a string that wound around a button. He unwound the string counterclockwise and dumped out a second file.

Two months after the Brooks murder, a powerful man had dragged the disfigured nude body of seventeen-year-old artist's model Louise Teuber down a slope and suspended it from a tree by a sixty-foot long double-looped line. The sailor's knots, identical to those in the Brooks murder, convinced Dullea those threads were part of the same bloody tapestry. The elusive sailor had returned to port. The brutality of the assaults recalled to Dullea the savagery of the Bay Hotel murder, so he filed both reports in his cabinet. They also called to mind the murders by Earle Nelson, who had used strips of cloth with a "complicated sailor's knot" to bind his victims' wrists.

In the late afternoon he ordered Inspector McGinn to the East Bay to interview Bette Coffin's mother. McGinn consulted his watch. While unhappy about crossing the Bay during rush hour, McGinn knew he had at his disposal a web of efficient ferryboat lines that spun out across the Bay to Contra Costa, Alameda, Solano, and Marin Counties.

Commuters either converged at the Hyde Street Pier west of Fisherman's Wharf or at the Ferry Building, the terminus for four steam railroads and five interurban systems with twenty-nine cable car and streetcar lines. At 5:05 P.M. McGinn joined the evening rush as workers spilled out of their offices onto Montgomery and Market streets. Streetcars began to pile up. Within minutes, the broad thoroughfare was packed with people pushing for the 5:15 P.M. boat. They made a dragging trudge past the Bay Hotel and Last Chance Cafe. Their heads were lowered guiltily because they had jobs and so many did not. They crossed the iron bridge spanning the Loop or dodged the Belt Line cars at the downstairs entrance to the Ferry Building.

McGinn scanned the dying tree in the plaza where dark-haired Harmonica Nell had sold papers for years. Her reedy mouth organ blues had risen above the hawking of other newsies. Her soulful eyes had wrung pennies from every commuter. Nell played best when the fog crept in and sang her finest when icy winds whistled around the Moorish Clock Tower. She vanished one day to reemerge as Mae Stockdale, widow and moll to killer Jim O'Neil. In May, police captured her in Stockton in a shootout. She was sentenced to Tehachapi Women's Prison, from which she made three escapes (Nell became known as the female Houdini). In early April 1935, poor Nell was committed to the Ukiah State Hospital for the Insane. So many roads to take, thought McGinn, but only one final destination.

A number of slips at the Ferry Building were kept by different companies. The SP exclusively used Slips 9 and 10 for its screw-driven, steel-hulled twin ferries, the *New Orleans* and the *El Paso*. Constructed in Bethlehem's Potrero yard for $1 million each, they made eight round-trip crossings a day to the East Bay. The Western Pacific's *Feather River* and the SP's *Encinal* were both heading across for Oakland via the "Creek Route." Most ferries were linked with railways. The screw steamer *Berkeley* was the fastest, but the small *Edward T. Jeffery,* which held fewer passengers and cars, got to Oakland in eighteen minutes. McGinn plunked down 35¢ for a round trip; if you brought your car onboard you paid $1.20.

The downstairs waiting room filled rapidly. On the second floor, tired workers occupying wooden benches staggered to their feet as the brass-rod fence slid away. McGinn slipped into a corridor leading to the berthed ferries, and saw the *Jeffery* getting up steam. A nervous sailor, he watched anxiously as the hydraulic gangplank lowered. A few Bay ferryboats had capsized when the water ballast at one end was too heavy and the passengers had congregated at that end. He followed a slight incline onto the main deck and then inside.

The leisurely crossings were pleasant breaks in the commuters' daily drudgery, but onboard this trip was a disagreeable ferry traveler known as "Mrs. Blight." She fought with every conductor and gate man, argued with the newsies, browbeat the waiters, and made terrible scenes with the passengers. Everyone feared Mrs. Blight who routinely filled the spaces on both sides of her seat with bundles while people all around her stood; she even put up her feet to steal more room. No one, not even McGinn, dared challenge this formidable creature—and he was armed.

He debarked at the Oakland Mole (which contained the slip for SP auto ferries) at the foot of Seventh Street and took an Espee steam train along a long reedy pier. Alameda Mole passengers rode the electric Red Train. Shortly, McGinn reached 1697 Twelfth Street in the downtown and knocked on the door of a clapboard house with yellow trim and lavender flowers. Mary Luz, Bette Coffin's mother, answered. Wiping his feet on the mat, McGinn entered and sat down on the davenport. Like Al, The Mouse, Mary had long ago accepted her daughter's self-destructive lifestyle. She suggested McGinn speak with Bette's fifteen-year-old son, Otis Leonard Coffin, who lived in Richmond with his grandparents, Mr. and Mrs. Wellington Coffin. "Will might provide more information," she said.

By hire cab, McGinn reached 1808 Eureka Street in the neighboring city. "No," said Mr. Will Coffin, "I don't remember Bette ever mentioning anyone she was afraid of, certainly not a laughing sailor with big hands and long arms."

But then Otis interrupted. His mother had a burly friend somewhat like that. "Where was he from?" McGinn asked.

This might be important, so he took out his notebook. The boy thought. "San Diego or maybe San Pedro," he said. "I think maybe he was a sailor. I saw him only once, last summer outside a tavern South of Market."

McGinn was familiar with that section of cheap saloons ("Free Lunch Today") and rooming houses ("20 cents a Room") not far from the Bay Hotel. "Go on," said McGinn, his pencil poised. "What else do you remember?"

"He had a short name with an 'H' in it, like Hank or Henry or Harry," Otis said. "But that's all I can recall of the name, only that it was short, only that I saw him that once."

"San Diego or San Pedro, Hank, Henry, or Harry," wrote McGinn. Maybe the name was important, vague but important. He closed his notebook.

"Poor Bette," said Will Coffin. "Nothing ever seemed to work out for her. If you ask me, it's that husband of hers you should take a closer look at."

The photo on the mantle showed a bright young woman in the days before she became an addict. "No one should have endured what she had," thought McGinn. Coffin brought coffee to fortify him for his cold voyage back.

Onboard the ferry, McGinn got a little sick. The sea began to kick up. A patchy fog was floating just above the surface. Powerful waves were buffeting the hull. Spray pelted the windows in the forward saloon deck where McGinn sat. He knew exactly when they passed Alcatraz, with its pelicans and black-crowned night herons. The Klaxon at the north end bleated twice and the one to the south once—a kind of moan—*Ohhhhhh, Gawwd!* He heard the draft in the smokestack, the slap of the paddlewheel, and the measured, rhythmic thrash of strokes in the huge cylinders.

The choppy crossing took forty-one minutes, a minute above the average. Too seasick to file a report, McGinn wobbled home on unsteady legs. He knew he wouldn't sleep. He was curious about this Hank, Henry, or Harry Somebody. What motive could there possibly have been for such savagery? The next day, McGinn promised himself, he would check to be sure their quarry hadn't been arrested for another crime, but wasn't hopeful. He was convinced the Gorilla Man had sailed out on a freighter immediately after he left the hotel, probably one bursting with wild animals like Frank Buck collected and where a Gorilla Man would feel perfectly at home among his own kind.[8]

WINIFRED and Charlie Dullea passed the evening at the gilded Orpheum at Eighth and Market. It wasn't "bank nite" or "tin can night" (when each movie-goer brought a tin can of food for the needy) so they paid 80¢ apiece, the evening rate for the double bill. The second film was *Mister Dynamite*, set in San Francisco by Dashiell Hammett, a former Pinkerton man, who once wrote copy for Samuel's Jewelers on Market. He once skipped out of the Hotel Pierre wearing all the clothes he owned in layers. Edmund Lowe in the title role played "a man of many schemes, most of them shady." Dul-

---

[8] Frank Buck was an American collector of, and authority on, wild animals. He had collected more than twenty-five thousand specimens of wild animals, including gorillas; in 1931 he wrote the bestseller *Bring 'Em Back Alive.*

lea shifted in his seat after the first two murders and a suicide. He could think only of McGinn out in the fog trying to piece together Mrs. Coffin's last hours. Where had she been before she entered that room colored blue by the rain? What stranger had she met that last night? And where? Winifred could tell her husband was troubled by some secret he knew or suspected.

TWENTY

Gorillas are intelligent. They use simple tools, such as a branch, to ascertain the depth of a swampy pool.

—2003 SCIENTIFIC REPORT

"I was a dog robber in the marines," Captain Dullea told McGinn the next morning. He laughed and explained, "A dog robber is an orderly for a commanding officer." Dullea had attended Franklin Grammar School and graduated Lowell High, clerked a while and when still a very young man joined the Marines in 1908. "Yes, we marines saw the world all right—at least the Philippines and Mexico." As a corporal, Dullea had been a member of the first Madera campaign forces. Discharged in 1911, he always kept his Marine Corps discharge close at hand. Presently, the papers were in the middle right-hand drawer of his desk, along with personal letters, trinkets, photos, keepsakes, and drawings his boys had made for him.

From the time he joined the SFPD in 1914, Dullea's fellow officers had admired him for his endurance, agility, strength, and facility in self-defense and apprehension. He could bring in a man with a minimum of force and was courageous in the face of danger. He "showed street sense" in his dealings with criminals and informers and people on the border of criminal behavior. He was "alley-wise," demonstrating calmness in the face of complex situations such as family disturbances, potential suicides, robberies in progress, and accidents. Most of all, they credited him with initiative, effective judgment and imagination, and exceptional skill in questioning witnesses of crimes and suspected offenders.

They respected him for advancing through the ranks and for the military efficiency with which he ran his department. The few honest cops admired him for his high level of personal integrity and ethical conduct. Dullea never had accepted favors or a bribe. When he joined the police department in 1915, all the cops still sat at old-fashioned inkwell-imbedded schoolroom desks. He found it laughable to watch the big detectives trying to straddle the small chairs as they filled out reports.

After the long, monotonous routine patrols, broken by life-threatening situations, he followed the regular course of advancement. Dullea became a police corporal in 1921, a sergeant in 1923, and a lieutenant later that same year. He made captain in January 1929, then chief of inspectors, captain of detectives, and finally captain of inspectors on the same day Quinn was elevated from sergeant to chief: November 20, 1929. On the average, it takes a patrolman thirteen years to become a sergeant, nineteen years to become a lieutenant, and twenty-three years to become a captain.

"Dullea's biography," said the papers, "is the story of San Francisco's big cases. Remember the Jepson case? Dullea was in it. Remember the attempted diary delivery payroll robbery? Dullea was in it. Remember the capture of Stevens and Kessel? Dullea was in that. And everyone knows the still famous Egan case and that of the Whispering Gunman. He was there—in every phase of the detective work."

The hard-hitting detective chief took each job that crossed his path, did it right and never gave up. He was easygoing when things were easy and tough when tough cases cracked his way.

While Dullea was fabled for his honesty and morality, Chief Quinn was not. It bothered Dullea that when Egan escaped jail rumors that the chief had allowed it had been widely believed. Had corruption really taken hold of the department again? Whether Quinn was a party to it or blind to the facts, he did not know.

Both he and Quinn had been bred "South of the Slot," so called after the slots in the tracks that cut the town in half at Market, the widest thoroughfare in town. The two inside tracks were reserved for the Market Street Railway. The outer two were for the city's own Municipal Railroad. At rush hour the "Roar of the Four" was deafening as the cars rushed along the odd four-track system. When Dullea and Quinn were kids, they pitched pennies at the slots and "nipped the fender" by riding on the folded cowcatcher on the trailing side of the Muni cars.

By Thursday night, April 11, six days after the Bay Hotel autopsy murder, Dullea was still having difficulty getting his mind around the unfathomable Gorilla Man. He had stopped asking Who and Where? and was now, like McGinn, wondering Why? No motive seemed to apply, not robbery, passion, vengeance, or gain of any sort. "In God's name," thought Dullea, "what had the killer hoped to accomplish by such butchery? Bette Coffin was too poor to be worth robbing. She was not excessively desirable, nor a beauty or in her youth even attractive. Still, she was a simple mother who deserved life as much as the next. The killer had whistled and laughed as he lumbered away. Could such a man even be human?"

Dullea kept an anxious eye on the docks. Forty-seven years after Jack the Ripper invented motiveless, compulsive murders in London, America had her own motiveless serial killer. Someone was killing prostitutes in the rundown section of a great city apparently for the sheer pleasure of it. As reporter Fred Diefendorf later wrote, "This Bay Hotel murder was only one of several crimes in the U.S. that were to parallel in horror the series of ghastly murders committed by Jack the Ripper in England some decades ago which shocked the entire civilized world."

There was a much better analogy than the Ripper thought Dullea. He put on his coat and hat and went out. Yes, a more apt analogy, a story he remembered from his childhood by Poe, the story of an ape wielding a razor. Down by the docks salt spray peppered his face. Wind tore at his coat, and the most robust foghorn on the Bay began booming from the Ferry Building as if calling for help. *Ohh, Gawd! Ohh, Gawd!*

AFTER a meager supper, Dullea had no sooner unlocked the door to his office than he made a giant stride in his search for the Gorilla Man. After his homicide detectives had searched the Bay Area for any unsolved murders that matched theirs and found none, they had requested by mail that all West Coast detectives be on the lookout for a killer with huge hands and the loping stride of an ape who may have committed an autopsy murder in their city. Finally, Dullea attempted to establish a pattern with other unsolved girl murders in widely separated parts of the nation. As part of his plan, thousands of circulars had been distributed through every seaport in the United States asking detectives to be "particularly on the lookout for a fiendish 'Jack the Ripper' who might be a seafaring man."

Dullea looked down at his desk. The eight-by-ten manilla envelope bore a New York postmark. He slit it open and spread out several yellow pages on his blotter. He read the first paragraph and sat bolt upright. "The report inside," he said later, "was very enlightening."

If the subject matter had not been so grim, a broad grin would have crossed his face. Before his eyes lay a connection between the San Francisco murder and an unsolved New York City homicide case from almost two years earlier. At last!—a concrete link to the Bay Hotel killer and a crime exactly like it clear across the country. In answer to his bulletin the NYPD had forwarded to Dullea all they knew of the tragedy of Wilhelm Johnston and his wife Florence W. Johnston in Washington Heights. He laid the first page down, flattened it, and began to read silently. About 11:00 P.M. on Saturday, October 21, 1933, Mrs. Flo Johnston was found strangled, stripped, and horribly autopsied with a razor. A huge stain on the second-floor landing and bloody streaks on the stairs suggested a second body, that of her husband, had been dragged down the stairs.

Dullea had little more information at this point, except for the last paragraph. The NYPD had searched abandoned buildings in the area and probed the river for Wilhelm Johnston without success. This was interesting, Dullea thought. If this was their man from the Bay Hotel, the Gorilla Man was not only a cross-country murderer of women, but of males, too. Such wandering journeymen were almost impossible to catch. It meant that there could be other murders as ghastly as Mrs. Coffin's they might never know about. Just because the Bay Hotel creature was elsewhere didn't mean he had stopped being who he was and doing what he did for whatever reason he had. Dullea had to start at the beginning again and look for what he had missed. The answer was right in front of him.

TWENTY-ONE

Investigation is the process of uncovering the unknown details of an incident by systematic search and patient inquiry—the truth of the matter.

—CRIME MANUAL OF THE PERIOD

BECAUSE night clerk John Smeins's description of the deeply tanned Mr. Meyers indicated the murderer might be a sailor, the SFPD search had centered on the Embarcadero. The dockworkers were a rough lot of multilingual, mostly single and lusty men who kept 135 brothels running all night and 150 gambling dens and three hundred bookie joints running all day. "You could play roulette in the Marina," columnist Herb Caen wrote, "shoot craps on O'Farrell, play poker on Mason, and get rolled at 4 A.M. in a bar on Eddy."

The waterfront's population changed constantly as sailors shipped in and out, returned from long voyages, and embarked on longer ones perhaps never to return. Every year, seven thousand ships and forty million commuters and travelers arrive and depart this second busiest crossroads in the world. The detectives spread out over the waterfront, an astonishing setting for the saga of the Gorilla Man.

Inspectors Desmond and Kelleher treaded amid creaking winches and sheds marked "Pago Pago" and drank their way through barrel houses and the lowest dives. They always ended up back at the city's most celebrated landmark, the 240-foot-tall Clock Tower as much an icon to San Francisco as the Eiffel Tower is to Paris. On bright days they watched the campanile's shadow, as if a sundial, extend across the Great Loop and, with its inexorable scythelike sweep, touch the Bay Hotel. Page Brown, who died young, had modeled the Neoclassical clock tower after the Giralda, the Moorish tower of the Cathedral of Seville and adopted portions of Venice's Piazza San Marco. After the 1906 quake jolted loose the Colusa sandstone that sheathed the tower, they restored it with reinforced concrete.

The Clock Tower marks the midpoint of the Embarcadero, which would grow to over twelve miles long, with eighteen miles of ship berthing space along forty-two piers. There were also two deep water channels—Islais Creek and China Basin. Other Bay ports were expanding, too. Dock workers were already unloading bulk oil, ores, and sugar at Pinole Point, Ozol, Port Chicago, Oleum, Selby, Crockett, Martinez, Avon, Benicia, Hercules, Port Costa, Valona, and Antioch. Within two years, Redwood City would open as a deep-water anchorage to join the well-established dry cargo harbors of Oakland, Alameda, and Richmond.

Normally combing the docks for a Gorilla Man would have been effortless. Certainly, a man of such a striking appearance, of such strength and unholy habits, with such huge hands and vaguely apelike features and eerie laugh should be easy to locate. Surely, his monstrous appearance would betray him. And yet he might not be as fierce as thought. They had only Smeins's word to go on. He might have been tall and walking hunched as he fled the Bay Hotel. Perhaps he was only a very powerful weightlifter and not repellant, even attractive enough to entice a woman to follow him. Police had yet to learn that evil sometimes came in ordinary, even attractive packaging and that not every homicide had a motive.

Five years before everyone on the waterfront had gone the extra mile to find beloved Officer Malcolm's killer. Captain Chris Claussen had traveled all the way to Tacoma to finger the Whispering Gunman—"That's the bastard!" Those days were gone. Since July it had been impossible for cops to work along the waterfront. "Unbelievable," said Dullea. "They are no help at all. . . . People assail the police department but do not take into account their own lack of civic consciousness in failing to testify or to help us. In serious cases I have consistently met with refusals by citizens to appear as witnesses against defendants."

None of the waterfront regulars was talking. The sole exceptions were the city's grimy waterfront hotels and boardinghouses who depended on police protection for survival and city permits to keep operating. So they were cooperative—a little. But they were the only ones. Longshoremen hated the police with a cold fury because of "Bloody Thursday." The previous summer, the Embarcadero had been a tinderbox awaiting the first spark. Chief Quinn had furnished that spark.

During California's worst strike, dockworkers picketing for better working conditions through the International Longshoremen's Association (ILA) had been bloodied, even murdered by the SFPD. The chief's special antistrike force had so alienated the city's most exploited group, that it would be years before Dullea and his men could regain their formerly cordial relationship with the longshoremen. In 1933, the peak year of Communist-led agricultural strikes, Quinn had answered Alameda County DA Warren's call for "a coordinated statewide assault on Communist provocateurs by the lawmen and prosecutors of California." The previous August, Quinn, Mayor Rossi, and other anti-Communist officials, contriving a Red scare, attended an Oakland meeting of the California Peace Officer's Association.

The previous April, the longshoremen had been organizing for a strike when Ignatious H. McCarty, a crackajack salesman with the Lake Erie Chemical Company, rang up Chief Quinn. His fervor for the mechanics of police crowd control verged on the pathological. He was forever searching for more effective riot control tools.

"Tell me, Chief Quinn," he gushed, "just what do you need?"

"For one thing the clubs are too light," complained Quinn. The Alameda sheriff had advocated the use of railroad brake sticks (four-foot-long wooden poles rounded like baseball bats that conductors used to manage mail sacks onto trains).

"Too light? Let me see what I can do with that," said McCarty. He wrote his superior: "These cops here, when they hit a man over the head, are not satisfied unless he goes down and a good split occurs. Our clubs are too light for this purpose. Could you contemplate making them heavier? Advise."

The new extra-long, extra-heavy riot clubs, nightsticks with a lead core, were forthwith shipped to San Francisco to the delight of Chief Quinn, who addressed his next concern. He was a little leery of the effectiveness of the tear gas being offered him. For the last decade, the SFPD had kept tear gas and mustard gas bombs in its arsenal for routing barricaded criminals and dispersing strikers, and he found it too mild.

"Oh, the new stuff is not the usual tearing kind," explained McCarty. "These are canisters of a powerful vomiting and nausea gas. The longshoremen won't know what hit them."

"Really!" Quinn's sales resistance shattered quicker than a cracked skull. "I'll need several crates of the sickening gas before Easter."

"Chief Quinn was determined to be nobody's Sentimental Alice," wrote historian Kevin Starr. When the longshoremen struck the previous May, Quinn ordered his antistrike squad (182 patrolmen, 17 mounted policemen, and 5 prowl cars) to Pier 35 where the Industrial Association—the powerful San Francisco business interests intent on breaking the unions—were moving cargo by truck convoy. They were also conveying two hundred scab workers (some dressed as policemen) to unload the *Diana Dollar.* "Bear down hard on any threats of disorder," he ordered as longshoremen blocked the convoy.

Along the Mission-style facades of the Matson Navigation Company piers, sixty cargo ships specializing in the Hawaiian trade were idled. Three American-Hawaiian freighters had anchored in the stream to save wharfage duties. Another two were abandoned in their berths. On May 28, 1934, Mayor Rossi ordered Quinn to "put every man in the department on the Embarcadero if necessary to preserve peace and order."

The chief's detachment of five hundred mounted and foot patrols armed with sawed-off shotguns and tear-gas bombs rushed strikers at Pier 20. "Some of you boys with shotguns fire into the crowd," Lieutenant Joe Mignola ordered. "If bricks start floating at us again, somebody will wind up in the morgue and I don't think it will be any of us."

Patrolman Emmet Honore shot a striker in the back, a police car knocked two girls to the pavement, and a mounted policeman rode over a twelve-year-old girl. Women leading a parade were clubbed, officers aiming "for the soft parts of their anatomies." Three days later, Mignola's officers ran amuck again near Steuart Street, attacking activists with blackjacks and clubs. In response the ILA struck all West Coast ports, effectively shutting down two thousand miles of intercoastal trade.

The steamer *City of Los Angeles*, the Grace Line steamer *Santa Rosa*, and the coastwise six-hundred-passenger transport *H.F. Alexander* (which routinely sailed between Seattle, San Francisco, and Los Angeles) were idled. Travelers and crewmen alike were stranded, including a burly figure whose shadow fell on the doors of the Bay Hotel.

His long arms were as muscular as a weightlifter's and he moved with an eccentric, flat-footed shamble. The figure upturned his nostrils as if sniffing the wind and, overcome with an overwhelming desire for sleep, entered the lobby. Behind the desk, John Smeins noticed the guest's expensive well-tailored gray suit, but not his face. Quite soon, his attention was diverted to the roving mobs outside. The Gorilla Man intended to stay a few nights, until the ships were moving again and the police had retreated from the docks.

In his room, he studied his large hands. On the dorsum, the skin was not soft and yielding as is usual, but tough and thick to stand wear and covered with a fibrous septa. He washed his hands in cold water, shook them for several minutes to stop them from tingling. His thumbs made a snapping, cracking sound as he flexed them and then went to bed. The next two nights, the hotel staff heard him alternately laughing and sobbing. Once he screamed aloud.

ON July 3, seven hundred policemen in gas masks rolled a line of boxcars into place to seal off the south side. At noon, five trucks chaperoned by eight police patrol cars edged south toward the warehouse at 128 King Street, an area Quinn had so far kept free of strikers. Suddenly, pickets broke their lines near the S.P. Depot, surged around a pile of bricks, and began hurling them. Inspector Desmond was hit under his eye, Inspector Cornelius in the head, and Officer John LaDue in the leg. A rock crashed through the cruiser window and grazed Sergeant McInerney as he was tossing gas bombs. A brick narrowly missed Quinn, who was crouching in the backseat and showered him with glass. Gas oozing from overturned cars threatened to ignite, and he barely escaped. He was certain now that Communists had been drawn to the city to turn the strike into an actual revolution against national law and order. "I am carrying on the important work of suppressing the radicals who seek to destroy our government," he said. "This is not merely a bitter strike, but a well planned revolution."

An hour and a half later, strikers blockaded the Belt Line at Second and Townsend streets to prevent police from using the tracks. "Let 'em have it, boys!" Police Captain Thomas Hoertkorn shouted as his men fired shotguns into the crowd. In revenge, longshoremen "patrolled like vultures" for scabs, and when they found one, they kicked out his teeth or laid his leg across a curb and snapped it like a twig.

On July 5, Bloody Thursday, thousands of city workers cheered a union parade of about 150,000 members. Quinn armed eight hundred cops with the new heavy riot sticks and canisters of vomiting gas. At 8:00 A.M. a state Belt Line locomotive dragging clouds of black smoke and carrying dozens of cops prodded two refrigerator cars toward the Matson Line docks. Near the roundhouse near Pier 30, marksmen hugged the slanted stairs of the coal car. Fire trucks played high pressure hoses on thirty thousand strikers and their sympathizers. The employers' group, the powerful Industrial Association, had agents riding with the police. Sirens screaming, Quinn's shock troops, in a sweeping front south of Market Street and east of Second Street, marched over strikers who withered beneath gas and shotgun and machine gun fire.

At 9:30 A.M., at Piers 38 and 40, picketers held their ground as mounted police, protected by a broadside of rifle and pistol fire, swept up Rincon. At 1:00 P.M., a pincher movement by two phalanxes of cops south and north closed upon the ILA headquarters at 113 Steuart Street. Police split heads with nightsticks, and mounted patrols ran over those who fell. Cornered, the strikers made a wild surge on a police car and rocked it until two police inspectors leaped out. "If any of you sons of bitches want to start something, come on!" one cop taunted and spun around, shotgun locked into his cheek. He kept his forehand elbow down under the fore end and the grip hand's elbow out to his side. His weight was slightly forward as he fired. He dropped the shotgun to waist level and took a second shot from a low assault position. Discarding the shotgun, he fired slugs from his revolver until it was empty.

Howard Sperry, a sailor, and Nick Counderakis, an unemployed cook, had just completed their shifts in the longshoremen's relief kitchen when they were mortally wounded, Sperry at Steuart and Market streets and Counderakis near the corner of the Audiffred Building on Mission Street. Charles Olsen was hit in the arm, face, chest, and leg and lay near death. Thirty-two strikers were shot and over three score gassed or badly injured. "Still the strikers surged up and down the sunlit streets among thousands of foolhardy spectators," the *Chronicle*'s Royce Brier wrote. "Panic gripped the east end of Market St. Soldiers in San Francisco. War in San Francisco." By midnight tanks were rolling along the Embarcadero.

On July 9, thousands marched somberly from the Ferry Building down Market Street to Valencia Street for Sperry and Counderakis's funerals. Theaters, restaurants, and shops hung signs in sympathy: "Closed Till the Boys Win." No streetcars, buses, or taxis were running. The only transportation were railroad-owned ferryboats, because they carried the U.S. mail from the southeast end of the Ferry Building. Federal law forbade their crews from striking.

On July 17, two regiments from the 40th Infantry Division of the National Guard occupied the Embarcadero from Fisherman's Wharf to China Basin. "If it is a question of you or the rioters, get them first," Lieutenant Colonel David Hardy ordered his 159th Infantry and the 125th Coast Artillery troops. "If you are attacked clip them, then bayonet them, then use bullets."

They blocked both ends of Jackson Street from Drumm to Front with machine gun–mounted trucks and raided the ILA soup kitchen at 84 Embarcadero.

Widespread violence ended two days later, and the strike two days after that. Ship owners agreed to settle by arbitration and Australian immigrant Harry Bridges, head of the ILA, sent his men back to work. The ILA gained control over the waterfront hiring halls, the key issue of the walkout. "San Francisco has stamped out without compromise an attempt to import into its life the very real danger of revolt," said Mayor Rossi on national radio.

On April 12, 1935, the city's establishment praised Chief Quinn "for the strong stand he had taken against Communists during the summertime maritime strike."

His round, baby face beamed with pride. An hour later, Dullea got a call from Desmond and Kelleher. While combing shore-side dives and flea-bag hotels they had found three witnesses who had seen Bette Coffin with the Gorilla Man. They were to be in Dullea's office first thing in the morning.

TWENTY-TWO

Putrefaction causes color changes and bloating. Often the features thicken until they are unrecognizable.

—FORENSIC TEXT OF THE PERIOD

ON April 13, eight days after the Bay Hotel murder, Dullea's intense manhunt on the waterfront yielded the first sighting of Bette Coffin in those missing hours before she checked into the Bay Hotel. The three dock workers took chairs in Dullea's office. Their hatred of the chief had been overridden by a sense of moral outrage that a woman they knew had been butchered. Besides, they liked Dullea.

They had seen Bette about 11:00 P.M. the night of her murder at Fifth and Market streets, ten blocks from the Ferry Building. An hour later they spotted her again a block away at the Old Mint.[9] The *Chronicle* clock tower cast light directly onto the steps under the portico where she sat with a stocky young man. His drunken laughter was so distinctive that the trio heard it long after the fog and rain had swallowed the couple up. The man's face had been shadowed, so the crucial hours between 1:00 A.M. and 3:00 A.M., when Bette and her "husband" registered at the Bay Hotel, remained a mystery, but it did get Dullea to thinking.

---

[9] Plans were already under way to close the Mint and move operations to a new mint. During World War II, Dullea and a skeleton crew of officers would protect the Old Mint and even camouflage it in black paint to conceal it during any air raids.

Had they been so drunk that they were turned away at various hotels until they were accepted at the Bay Hotel? LaTulipe compared the foggy east side of London's Whitechapel and prostitutes and the foggy east side of San Francisco's Embarcadero and prostitutes. More than fifty years earlier at 1:00 A.M. an inebriated Catherine Eddowes had been liberated from Bishopsgate Police Station. Turned away from her lodgings, she was drunkenly wandering Mitre Square when she met the Ripper.

As for Slipton Fell, the laughing reporter, Dullea had no way of knowing that he often took long, unexplained voyages to Latin America, San Diego, and New York under the guise of gathering news. Right now he was cruising just outside San Francisco. In the months after hurriedly deserting his apartment several doors down from the Bay Hotel, Fell had felt out of sorts. His multiple identities kept bumping into each other, keeping him preoccupied and sleepless. Who was he today? His identity was defined by the roles he chose to enact and the masks he wore. The powerful young man was what Ezra Pound termed "a broken bundle of mirrors . . . a streaming sequence of selves." So many personalities, all warring with each other inside his handsome head, had to hold an equal number of jobs and thus Fell found himself very busy indeed. He needed all those aliases.

The previous October, Fell had been working at the Pacific Gas and Electric Company in Oakland, when he reported his paycheck stolen. A replacement was issued, but when he cashed both drafts, the pilfered check was traced to him, and he was fired. Then he got a job at a Richmond gasoline service station, forged another check, and was sacked again. In the following November, Fell obtained a job at an auto assembly plant, where he met Joseph Anthony, a thirty-two-year-old oil service attendant at the Cutting Boulevard station. Anthony, who had come to California from Marshfield, Oregon, four years earlier, spent his free time inside his second-story apartment behind the filling station. He had no friends and no known enemies, except for Fell. Somewhere in the mix was a woman—there was always a woman—and the two men had fought over her. When Fell left the plant at the end of December, that should have been the end of the feud, but apparently wasn't.

On January 7, 1935, someone climbed the stairs to Anthony's apartment and slugged Anthony as soon as he opened up the door. After a furious battle, the visitor knocked Anthony out, carried him to his bed, and trussed him hand and foot with wire he had brought along. Then he propped Anthony up with a pillow, stuck a burnt cigarette in his mouth, and buried a carpenter's ax in his skull with tremendous force.

Mr. and Mrs. Gerald Shaw's grocery shop took up the ground floor of Anthony's building. When Mrs. Shaw had not seen Anthony for some time, she went upstairs, discovered his body, and called police. Richmond detectives initially suspected a woman of the killing because of the long fingernail scratches on his cheek, neck, and ears. But a strong man had to have carried Anthony to the bed and buried the ax so deep. He had left two fingerprints in blood on the haft of the ax. The only item stolen was Anthony's gold watch. As for Slipton Fell, he possessed four watches of which he was immensely proud. All of them were gold.

One of the jobs Fell did in the guise of yet another of his personalities was at the Woodside garage near lonely Ada Rice's house. Under the name of Jerome Selz (Jerry to his friends), he pumped gas, wiped windshields, and repaired the occasional engine. He was the All-American boy in this role. Though Will Werder, the station manager, had recommended Fell to Ada, he personally didn't like him. "Jerry was not popular with men," Werder said, though this was not the truth. "Of course, he didn't seem vicious or dangerous. In fact the reaction of most of us was that he was a conceited bore. No matter what subject we brought up, Jerry always knew all about it. He was the expert. He had done it better than anyone else and done it first. His favorite trick was to bet the firemen at Woodside that he could lift them from the ground by their belts using just his teeth. Jerry always won that bet."

Obviously, Fell had the public trust because the neighborhood let him act as a night watchman for the community. He was a very likable man, especially to older women. To promote himself at the Woodside garage, Fell had his other personalities—Ralph Jerome Selz, Ralph Sells, Charles Oliver, Slipton J. Fell, Upton Rose, Faran Wide, and more—write letters to the personnel department and home office of the big petroleum company that owned the Woodside station. The stream of letters lauded his charm, courtesy, matchless efficiency, zeal, and the blue-ribbon work he did. The same company had already discharged him once, but from their Oakland branch and under another name. When they rehired him as Jerry Selz, nobody was the wiser. The letters, all in the same handwriting, were so effective that, under his new name, Fell got a raise from the same company that had fired him.

TWENTY-THREE

Homicide is the killing of one human being by another. Compared to other major crimes, the statistics on homicide are low. Fortunately, homicides are few and far between in the overall crime picture.

—CRIME TEXTBOOK OF THE PERIOD

IT was now Tuesday, April 16, eleven days after Bette Coffin's murder. The waterfront was cheerful, filled with bright sunlight. There was a slight breeze out of the west. The docks trembled with activity. For the moment, everything seemed right to Dullea. Gazing at the hoards of travelers, he observed, "All roads lead to the Ferry Building."

So did his greatest cases—the shooting of Officer Malcolm, the "kidnapping" of Frank Egan, and the Bay Hotel murder across the street, a tragedy forever linked to the Ferry Building and its daggerlike Clock Tower. The sweeping panorama of blue mountains, sky, and water lifted Dullea and McGinn's spirits. As they ate crab, Captain Coombs's *Lochgoil* glided in like a feather from Rotterdam and berthed alongside Pier 33. Dullea asked McGinn if, with the jailing of the Phantom, they had seen the last of large-scale corruption within the department. McGinn shook his head. "Maybe, Charlie" he said, "but I doubt it." He said no more. Sometimes it was wiser not to know too much.

The motor ship *Ele* under Captain Selbje of the north German *Lloyd* (with Princess von Preussen aboard) tied up alongside. The *Lloyd* got under way immediately and headed toward Oakland as Captain Blanquie's French Line motor ship *Washington* sailed for France and Antwerp. As vessels came and went, an elderly man at the end of Pier 45 fell into the water. Captain Eddie McCarthy of the lookout service and his pal Al Bartlett dove in and saved him.

The south tower of the Golden Gate Bridge had risen another 20 feet from its concrete base, striving to match the tower on the Marin shore at a full 745 feet. The welders and riveters were making better progress than Dullea's men, though his homicide squad had an astounding clearance rate of 80 percent. (Today, 20 percent is considered phenomenal.) But in the lovely light, the terrible murder at the Bay Hotel was fading in everyone's memory. Only its exceptional horror and Dullea's persistence kept it alive. Dullea returned home, tortured that he'd overlooked some essential clue. "But I can't quite put my finger on it," he told Winifred over dinner.

It was elusive, tantalizing. A vague, yet important bit of evidence lay undiscovered—plainly visible, yet somehow invisible. He couldn't escape the fact that he already knew the answer. He knew the secret of the Laughing Gorilla, and he knew his name.

Before dawn on Sunday, April 21, Dullea and his family joined forty thousand San Franciscans trudging up Mount Davidson (Blue Mountain) south of Twin Peaks and west of Glen Park. As the city's highest natural point, one of its three tallest peaks, it is visible fifty miles at sea. Through a cold, wet fog, the worshipers followed the narrow path the WPA had just improved. Now women could wear high heels during the Easter pilgrimage.

At the 925-foot summit a bitter wind chilled the celebrants. It was a typical San Francisco day—dismal to sunny to foggy to windy, so they had dressed for both warm and cold. Dullea's double-breasted, worsted kept him snug, but he feared for the women in their spring dresses. They gathered in front of a new 103-foot-tall east-facing cross. Plans had called for a 100-foot cross, but because they'd had concrete and steel left for three extra feet—why not? The March before, President Franklin D. Roosevelt had illuminated the cross via telegraph from the White House. The cross, 10 square feet at the base and 16 feet into solid rock, tapered to 9 feet at the top. Dullea saw twenty-five bullet holes fired by cops during a drunken orgy pockmarking the cross.

The sun broke through to reveal an array of colorful Easter hats swaying like golden yarrow on the hillside. Faces uplifted as they sang "The Old

Rugged Cross." As Dullea bowed his head, he remembered the last time he had prayed for guidance—the day Josie Hughes had lost her life through his failure to act in time.

OVER at the *Chronicle* Allan Bosworth was working a Sunday shift. The socialite copy boy was dressed more traditionally today, but still skating figure-eights around the rows of pillars. The Sunday editor was still sneezing nine times in a row, and Bosworth was still secretly praying for a fatal tenth sneeze. A skeleton crew at the horseshoe copy desk was sipping coffee, cigarettes smoldering in ashtrays. Reporters were playing cards and working off hangovers. The police speaker was squawking. Business as usual, except for Bosworth, who was troubled. Slipton J. Fell had known too much about the Bay Hotel mutilation murder. "Ha ha!" he had laughed callously. "The killer had put her breast on the bedside table and taken away her nose."

"At the *Chronicle* we were ignorant of a few facts," Bosworth wrote later. "We did not know that when Slipton J. Fell visited us, any Latin American adventuring was in his past, and that his last sea voyage was only from Alcatraz to the Army pier. He had been in the disciplinary barracks of more than one post and come to Alcatraz Island as an Army deserter."

In 1925, Fell, under an alias, enlisted at Vancouver, Washington, barracks, then "bought" his way out. Four years later, he rejoined the infantry in San Francisco and again paid his way to freedom. In fall 1930, he attended Oregon State College at Monmouth, from which he was expelled for poor grades and inciting a riot as an outgrowth of "communistic tendencies." He traveled to Los Angeles; lived in San Diego for a while; and journeyed to Mexico, Nicaragua, and all the other glorious places he spun tales about. In April 1931, he enlisted in the Army Air Corps and was transferred to March Field, Riverside, and then Randolph Field (Texas), from which he deserted in September. Two months later, he was arrested in San Francisco and sentenced to one year at hard labor at Fort Winfield Scott. So Fell was not only a liar (though many of his adventures would prove to be true), thought Bosworth, he was a deserter.

Bosworth would later discover Slipton Fell was also a murderer.

The editor settled back in his swivel chair and lit a cigarette. The paper had gone to press—forms locked up, photos etched in copper-backed zinc, cardboard mats made, hot metal poured, and curved plates strapped to huge presses. The loud warning bell rang loudly for the Monday edition. Presses began rolling in the basement, a distant throb like a pulse. On the loading dock, printed papers were bailed in wire and driven away by trucks.

"As for Fell's real name . . ." Bosworth said. "Never mind that. Who has the time?" He hit the space bar on his typewriter, rolled a page into place, and began to type. Except for his hunt and peck, it was silent in the long brightly lit room. Bosworth considered Fell one of the most unusual individuals he had ever met. "I became involved," he typed, "in the remote fashion of a news editor in assembling and presenting the story of his crime, and his dubious and equally mirthful confessions. It was an incredible story."

THE first time Mrs. Ada Rice met Fell she appreciated his tumultuous roar, the same booming gaffaw that so unnerved and annoyed editor Bosworth. She found it charming, even infectious. Most of all, Ada saw him as a rambunctious boy full of adventure yet possessed of a sensitive soul. Such individuals as Fell rarely display bizarre psychotic symptoms but give serious attention to appearing normal and covering their tracks. Fell, fascinated with the workings of his own mind, had recently taken a personality test in a magazine to try to understand himself.

He answered the questions methodically. "The questions asked what I liked and disliked in life and what I hoped to do about it," Fell said. After twenty minutes he turned to the back page to consult a key that told what sort of character he had as determined by his answers. "Well, I didn't get a very good rating. The answers I gave, according to the magazine, indicated I am inclined to be sulky. It also said I am the type that whines and complains when things go against me. I ask you, am I whining and complaining now? Don't I seem to be in a jolly mood? Am I not a good Joe—the salt of the earth? Also the character analysis said I am subject to outbreaks of brutality and that I have abnormal ideas as to rightness and I don't mean righteousness because by no stretch of the imagination can I be termed a righteous man."

To almost everyone but Bosworth (who had suspicions) and Werder (who was jealous), the very likable Mr. Fell appeared sane and sober, though egocentric. "I am absorbed in what I am doing," Fell explained, "and the quiz said that I look on things from my own tangent, that I am unreasonable and have no respect for individualism and want things done my own way. I am inquisitive. Well, I ask you, is that me? Well? It said I am inclined to flare up and lack accomplishment."

Mrs. Rice didn't agree. The first day she met Fell she judged him a man of great accomplishment. As a world traveler (like herself) he spoke English, French, and German (like herself). As they returned to her house along a wooded path, he told her about his rip-roaring adventures in revolution-torn Latin America. As proof, he stopped under an oak and showed her a consul's letter of introduction to the South American "patriot" Sandino whose insurgent forces Fell had tried to join. This fascinated the romantic Mrs. Rice. It went to the core of her social consciousness. They had so many things in common.

At the house he reinflated her car's tires and removed the blocks; when Ada asked him inside for a drink, he agreed. The sun was just going down, and the chill fog was tumbling into the ravine by its sheer weight. Fell energetically stoked the logs in the hearth until sparks fanned out. When the fire was crackling he grinned broadly, leaned back on the divan, and sipped his drink. Ada sat at his feet as he told her about the *Chronicle* feature story on himself ("Yes, I will get you a clipping") and how he had attended the Olympic Games in Holland in 1928.

"I was doing freelance work for the magazines," Fell recalled. "I had no passport and they kicked me out. So I went to Belgium, and from there I was kicked out to Germany. I was kicked out of most of Europe. Hell, what's the use of a passport anyway? I traveled all over South America without one. One way of seeing the world is to just let yourself get kicked around." He paused, recalling some unpleasant experience and covered his real feelings with a robust laugh. His perfect teeth flashed in the dimness. "I traveled through Western Canada, just working my way around, and practically covered all of the U.S. wandering."

To Ada, the bungalow seemed bright and cheery for the first time since her husband left. Loving his laugh as she did, she suggested that Fell move in, and he did on the first of June, though his version of the story differed from Ada's in one respect, the most important one. "I first met her when she drove into the service station where I worked," he said. "One day she came into the place. Her car was acting up a bit, and I began to tinker with it—I'm pretty good with machinery—and fixed it. She offered me a tip which I refused. Company regulations, you know! But I guess that gave her a friendly feeling for me, because pretty soon she asked me out to her house. We found we had a lot in common. We'd both traveled a lot—the same places in some cases—and we both liked to talk about our travels. We talked a lot about books, too, and really had fine times together. Finally she told me she'd just talked herself into taking a trip, and she asked me if I'd like to rent her house while she was away. It is a swell little house and of course I jumped at the chance. Wouldn't anybody?"

Just as Frank Egan had called Josie Hughes his "Auntie" and Josie in return had called him "Nephew," Fell called Ada his "Woodside Mother" and she called him her "Woodside Son." She already had a son, but Fell appealed to her motherly instincts, as Egan had appealed to Josie's. "He has never really had a mother to guide him," Ada thought, "why couldn't I be his?"

But Fell had a real mother who had given birth to him in San Francisco in 1908. Until recently, she had lived in Berkeley where she taught school under the name Anna J. Selz. She returned to Oxnard, her birthplace, to work as a high school principal. As far as Fell was concerned, he didn't have a father. He hadn't seen him since he was five and had been totally self-supporting from age twelve.

"Do you have any siblings?" Ada asked. Fell smiled mysteriously and said that he had a thirty-one-year-old brother somewhere in the Bay Area. Residents of the Woodside neighborhood later recalled Fell introducing a man as his brother at the local tavern. It puzzled them that the brother bore no resemblance to Fell and spoke with a vaguely foreign accent. Apparently the "Woodside Brother" remained in the vicinity for only a short time, certainly no longer than a December evening, when he told them he was "going up to see 'Jerry' at the bungalow" and vanished.

Fell also introduced an aged woman to the tavern crowd as "my little mother." "She's taking care of me and cooking at the house," he said. That "mother" disappeared abruptly. Fell, who had been speaking constantly of her for months, never mentioned her again. Afterward, he was seen digging at night in the rocky yard encircling Ada's bungalow.

For a while Fell's wisecracking, multiple personalities, and stories kept Ada entertained, his incandescent smile and that wonderful dark hair, those broad shoulders and muscular arms made her life worth living again. For the first time in years she felt fulfilled enough to forget her multiple husbands and quarrelsome neighbors. He diminished her wanderlust, though it could never be completely extinguished. At night the rocky glen was lit up and filled with music.

ADA was a solitary woman, and when she mysteriously vanished one night, few neighbors took particular notice (they hadn't seen that much of her before). Those who did thought she was traveling abroad. Fell did nothing to dispel that notion and gave them the impression that she was traveling in Greece or the Balkans "or somewhere over there."

"And how do you know she's in the Balkans?" police later asked a neighbor.

"Why, that nice young man who lives in her house told me," she said. "That's how I know Ada was traveling abroad. She went away to the Balkans as a foreign correspondent." Given a moment, the neighbor would even be able to name Ada's young traveling companion. "He told me that she'd gone away with a Bulgarian cavalry officer named 'something—itch.' Oh, yes, I remember—'Michael Baronovich.'"

The existence of this dark, distinguished Bulgarian officer on leave was confirmed by two more sources. Bill collector Lawrence Maloney had visited Mrs. Rice's Woodside Glens home. "At the door," he recalled, "I was introduced to a man of distinguished appearance . . . a tall dark man with a black wavy brush of hair."

When Maloney returned again, both Mrs. Rice and the Bulgarian were gone. Instead he was greeted by Slipton Fell, who cheerfully paid the delinquent bill for her and told him he was the new owner. "I bought the cottage for $1700," Fell said, cinching his robe. According to Fell, Ada asked him to come up at night and leave some things because she was leaving the next day. "When I drove up in front of the cottage it was pitch black. There wasn't a light about the place. That struck me as funny."

The second source was Mr. and Mrs. Albert Johnson, proprietors of the Woodbank Auto Camp on Cooley Avenue in East Palo Alto. Several times last year, Mrs. Rice had told them of a "beautiful boy with black wavy hair" who was traveling in Turkey and coming from Bulgaria to visit her. As proof, Mrs. Rice gave the Johnsons, who collected stamps, envelopes from Athens and Turkey. The envelope from Turkey, postmarked June 28, 1934, had a notation on the back: "From I. Reikdjan, 11-13 Topham, Kele Cadds, Istanbul." I. Reikdjan, Mrs. Johnson conjectured, might be the real name of the "beautiful boy from Bulgaria."

Those closest to Mrs. Rice, her estranged husband in Seattle and her bankers, weren't too concerned about her absence. She typically left the country to live at unknown addresses overseas. Wasn't that why August Mengler had divorced her? Wherever Ada was they knew she was alive hot on a story or writing a book or being a self-righteous pest. Besides, the tracks of her industry were factually documented on the backs of checks. The banks saw drafts bearing Mrs. Rice's very recognizable signature pass through their hands. All had been written after she had gone away.

A letter with a return address of Coxsackie, New York, requested that her bank transfer $135 from her savings account to her checking account. No one noticed that the envelope was postmarked Redwood City, a town only four miles from Woodside Glens. Hugh and Phyllis, Ada's children in New York, still received reassuring typewritten letters from her with a syntax and style of writing consistent with their mother's and bearing authentic-looking signatures.

County authorities could also point to a signed paper naming Slipton J. Fell the new proprietor of Ada's Woodside Glens bungalow along with some $5,000 worth of property. Ten days after Fell moved in, Mrs. Rice had deeded him her home, some Skyline Boulevard property, and an El Cerrito parcel of land in reciprocation for some Sierra County mining claims on which he had filed. The Downieville mining site was worthless, and Fell owned only a fraction of it and that under an alias.

Considerable time would pass before even one person genuinely missed Mrs. Ada French Mengler Rice. Charles Rice did, only because he had court papers that needed her signature. "I made several unsuccessful attempts to find her during the divorce proceedings," Rice said. "And there were no answers to the divorce action notices which my attorneys ran in California papers."

If need be, he would go to the higher courts to get her signature. He would not let up until he found her.

Much later everyone, Mr. Rice included, conceded that Ada Rice had gone up in smoke. And along with her, Michael Baronovich, her handsome young friend, had evaporated. The timing was intriguing. The pair had "gone traveling" just two months after the Gorilla Man killed Bette Coffin a half block from Slipton Fell's San Francisco hotel room. Ada had vanished less than two weeks after Fell moved into her home.

IMMEDIATELY after the autopsy murder the Bay Hotel's night porter, Otto von Feldman, the ex–German military officer, had moved to San Diego. He would recognize Fell from a photograph in the *Chronicle* feature story that Fell had cajoled Bosworth into running. It would be widely reprinted when Fell was arrested for two murders and suspicion of four or five more. But von Feldman would not make that association with the Bay Hotel and Fell until March of 1936. At virtually the same time, John Smeins, the Bay Hotel night clerk, would reach the same conclusion.

"My God," von Feldman would say, gripping the paper and locking his eyes on the portrait of Slipton Fell, a mosaic of tiny dots. Otto's breath would catch in his throat. "My God," he would whisper, "that's 'Mr. Meyers.'"

TWENTY-FOUR

Knock, knock.
Who's there?
Gorilla.
Gorilla who?
Gorilla my dreams.

—JUVENILIA 1930s

ON May 27, Captain Dullea, Police Commissioner Theodore Roche, and Chief Quinn went to lunch at the St. Francis Hotel. Roche wanted to discuss the Hassing scandal; Quinn wanted to bury it. Lunch promised to be interesting. Overall the chief was cheerful. *True Detective Magazine* had just named him "a far-reaching officer whose handling of his department has made it one of the most effective crime-combative and crime-preventive agencies in the country."

From their cab Dullea heard the reassuring *click-clack* of birdcage traffic signals and the pleasant rumble of a Powell Street cable car. Across from Union Square he saw the majestic St. Francis Hotel. Unlike most other hotels in town, it wasn't a copy of another great edifice. The Fairmont Hotel on Nob Hill, a replication of Madrid's Royal Palace, had gone bankrupt. But the St. Francis survived because it was architecturally unique, had no mortgage, and was privately owned. Its owner, Templeton Crocker, riding out the tough times on his yacht, the *Zaca*, seldom meddled in its daily operation. The addition of a fourth wing in 1913 made it the largest hotel on the Pacific Coast. Silent film star Roscoe "Fatty" Arbuckle made it the most notorious.

On Labor Day weekend 1921 baby-faced Fatty and his loyal pal, deadpan comic Buster Keaton, motored up from Hollywood in Arbuckle's $25,000 Pierce-Arrow. The 266-pound comedian, known for his Mephistophelian marksmanship with pies, had begun his career in San Francisco. He ended it there. Homicide Chief Louis de Mattei led Arbuckle, a raincoat over his pajamas, into the HOJ and booked him for the "rape-murder" of starlet Virginia Rappe during a wild party in room 1221 of the St. Francis. Though innocent, Hearst's *Examiner* gleefully tried Fatty through three trials. He was acquitted in all, but was a broken man.

Ahead, Dullea saw taxis and limos arriving and departing in clouds of exhaust. A few idled in front of the hotel's sedate gray-and-white canopy on Powell Street. A doorman in mid-street blew his whistle and raised a flutter of pigeons as they climbed out. The lobby had an ornate carved ceiling, dark marble pillars, sofas, chairs, writing desks, fireplace, and a Viennese Magneta clock, which controlled every clock in the hotel. They paused at the bar for a drink in the comfortable, oak-paneled Club Room. When it was remodeled with chrome, Lucite, and black patent-leather walls, the name changed to the Coffin Room. The dining room had been called the Rose Room, the Garden Room, the Fable Room, the Embassy Room, and the Empire Room, but its new pastel paintings of a sleek blond goddess were so praiseworthy it was renamed the Mural Room.

Swiss headwaiter Ernest Gloor, a moon-faced man in tiny silver spectacles, escorted the three men to a well-situated table. Where he seated you in the Mural Room demonstrated your degree of importance. Paradise was the first five tables, everything else—Siberia. Gloor was rarely intentionally rude, but when he was, it was well deserved and executed with exquisite, icy politeness. Gloor's sole occupation was to remind high society how important they were and how unimportant everyone else was. Upon the death of Mrs. Eleanor Martin, the queen of San Francisco Society, Gloor had assumed her place and single-handedly transformed Monday lunch at the St. Francis into an awesome ritual. Everyone who was worthwhile attended.

Dullea listened to a string quartet, the hum of talk, the tinkling of glasses, and the giggling from under the tables—children playing at the feet of society mothers dressed in silver furs and I. Magnin's latest. Below, in the hotel's steamy laundries, kitchens, and boiler rooms, workers were slaving for $20 for a six-day week. The previous year they struck for better wages and were preparing to do it again.

Dullea brought up the successful fight police officers had waged against a Senate bill during the last legislative session. "The bill," he said, "would have made inadmissible as evidence a confession or statement by a defendant which was not given before a magistrate and recorded verbatim by a court reporter. If such a law were in force our hands would have been completely tied. We not only have to prove that a man is guilty beyond a reasonable doubt, but we have to sell our stories to twelve jurors. If one disagrees with us there is a mistrial. Still the sob sisters on the *Chronicle* are worried that someone's wrist shall be slapped every time we take in a criminal."

The chief grunted his assent. He loathed any kind of press, any kind of dissent.

"Honeycombed with graft and inefficiency!" Quinn said, his face reddening. "How many times have you heard that phrase?" The big hands clinched. "Why should such ugly charges as 'graft' and 'inefficiency' be so often linked with the police in the average citizen's mind?" He thought the answer obvious: "Undeserved and untruthful publicity, reams of it! In the mouths of pseudo-experts, alarmists, and malcontents, these two words have carried in the public press from one coast of America to the other. Up, down, and across the country they have ricocheted until they have become not merely words, but by-words." Quinn railed against these "verbal battering rams" used so often that their mere mention "conjured up the mental image of a crooked policeman."

He paused and picked up the tall menu. He had worked up an appetite.

After the waiter took their orders, Roche mentioned the Hassing scandal of December. "All the unpleasantness of the last few years on the waterfront has been ended," Quinn assured him. "The White Mask Gang is no more. It's over." He challenged him to find any instances of actual police corruption. "Egan and Hassing were *former* San Francisco policemen." There had been crooked DAs, too. Asa Keyes, the Los Angeles DA, had sold his position in the $50 million Julian Petroleum scandal. They had placed him in the Old Man's Ward at San Quentin under the charge of the head trusty, Herb Wilson, whom he had sent up.

The chief blew out a column of smoke from his cigar, poured coffee from a silver pot, and took a sip. "Take the SFPD which I believe to be absolutely representative of a typical American police department," he said. "Look at the facts, and endeavor to find out just how much corruption, graft and inefficiency our department really contains. You hear criticism. Two to one, it's in connection with the alleged shortcomings of some other police department. By repetition these false charges have done their insidious work. The policeman, like the doctor or the lawyer, is a public servant, the one whom you can turn to in an hour of need. Just as there are occasional dishonest policeman like Oliver Hassing, so too there are occasional dishonest doctors like Dr. Housman and crooked lawyers like Frank Egan. But you can't look with scorn upon a whole profession because of these few dishonest practitioners. Why, then, brand the police departments of America with the stigma of crookedness because a few policemen do go wrong? Remember that each police department is a separately governed unit. The scandal in one, or the broadcast inefficiency of another, cannot destroy the hundreds of smooth working departments and the thousands of honest policemen."

Dullea shifted uncomfortably. Egan's escape from the HOJ had never been explained. Someone higher up had allowed it. And someone higher up had provided Sergeant Hassing (way out at Richmond Station) with the confidential schedules of both waterfront and special patrols. Was Quinn that higher up? At best, Dullea thought, he was ignorant of the far-reaching decay. At worst, he blindly countenanced the corruption within. But Quinn, with the unanimous backing of the mayor and Police Commission, was invincible. He had the power to fill key positions and was in charge of the Inspectors Bureau—Auto, Burglary, Fraud, Homicide, Missing Persons, Traffic, and Patrol Divisions—and headed up Administration and Personnel.

Above the chief was the Police Commission. Quinn was answerable to its three civilian members who are appointed by the mayor and who serve at his pleasure. The degree of a commission's independence varies with the mayor and the extent to which he tries to influence management of the police department. If the commissioners come into irreconcilable conflict with him, they are obliged to tender their resignation. A primary reason for placing civilians, not policemen, on the commission for four-year terms is that a civilian commission is better able to maintain the delicate balance between liberty and restrictiveness required to preserve both freedom and order. They all had full-time jobs and in being detached from the SFPD's daily operations had more perspective than would sworn personnel. Blatantly, Quinn extolled the virtues of the commission past and present. According to him, no such animal as a crooked cop could survive under the watch of such an "alert" police watchdog.

"Over the last 20 years," the chief said, "Mayor Rolph had achieved honesty and efficiency through a 'hands off' policy and the appointment of sterling Police Commissions. The current Commission's president, Theodore J. Roche"—Quinn smiled wolfishly at Roche—"is a brilliant lawyer, a law partner of U.S. Senator Hiram W. Johnson and of the Hon. Matt Sullivan, former Chief Justice of the California Supreme Court. His $100-a-month goes to charity. He's a man money can't buy.

"Commissioner Jesse B. Cook is an experienced, successful former chief. Commissioner Thomas E. Shumate—progressive, able, a leading physician is proprietor of a chain of drug stores and a breeder of blooded horses. Commissioner Frank J. Foran—vice-president of the King Coal Company, Olympic Club secretary, a golfer and prominent all-around sportsman. Can you conceive of such a mayor and Police Commission countenancing graft or inefficiency and corruption? They haven't. They don't. They *will* not!"

Their lunches arrived on covered silver platters. The china was of the hotel's own design. Roche grew thoughtful as he ate, partially convinced that the SFPD was nurturing vipers at its breast. Because men were human, Quinn often said, there would be occasional graft scandals and bad apples and some would involve cops. Roche studied Dullea. Sometimes one good apple survives in a barrel of bad apples. But one honest cop could do only so much. "The Hall of Justice was dirty and reeked of evil," columnist Herb Caen observed when all the facts were in. "The City Hall, the DA and the cops ran the town as though they owned it, and they did." The SFPD was the "toughest gang in town."

If Dullea wanted the SFPD swept clean, he would have to dislodge the mayor, the chief, and the police commissioners—his bosses—and do it himself. To speak out without proof and without powerful political friends in his corner was to be immediately exiled from the department. At the end of lunch, Quinn paid, then looked down at the change in his palm. It had been polished in a silver burnishing machine and rinsed and dried under hot lights until mint clean and germ free. For the last three years, only the St. Francis washed its coins. The chief went away jingling the gleaming silver, feeling a little better. Dullea hoped there weren't thirty of them.

AS they left the St. Francis, another luncheon was ending in San Rafael to the north where John V. Lewis, collector of Internal Revenue, was delivering an anticipated club address. His final words brought gasps from the audience. "And so we have discovered one retired SFPD officer," he said, "whom we have asked to pay his long delayed federal tax on a personal fortune of $110,000!"

Lewis's revelation of such wealth in such economically troubled times precipitated a stunning series of developments. Chief Quinn didn't really enter the picture until the owner of Club Kamokila got angry.

The comely Mrs. Alice Campbell was Hawaiian royalty. Her mother was Princess Kuaihelana of Hawaii's royal ruling house, and her father, Jim Campbell, was the multimillionaire Pineapple King and Sugar Czar. Alice, a guileless woman known as "Princess," had opened a nightclub in a former Methodist church on downtown Bush Street as a venue for her vocal aspirations. When Central Station officers began shaking her down, it irritated her that they never harassed the hookers working out of lavish upstairs rooms along nearby Lysol Alley. Not that Princess didn't employ equally friendly women in grass skirts from the Powell Street sidewalks, she just didn't like to be unfairly singled out.

In short order, special-duty officers arrested her bartender and manager, convinced neighbors to file noise complaints, challenged her dance hall license, and stationed a permanent detail of six uniformed officers in her doorway to discourage customers. In each of the city's fourteen districts, two to four special-duty men, a vice contact group (disrespectfully referred to as "bucket men" or "collectors" behind their backs), operated as aides de corps to the district captains. The captains were not only unsupervised but answerable to no one (not even the Bureau of Communications) as to their whereabouts at any hour of the day, even in emergencies, and exercised considerable authority subject only to minimal review by their superiors. Being virtually accountable to only their unaccountable captains, the bucket men were ripe for graft.

"The Kamokila Club is a dive, one of the worst in town," said Captain Fred Lemon, the bull-necked commander of Central Station. "This woman is not fooling anyone with this society bull and I'm going to close the place every night."

Princess's lawyer, Jake Ehrlich, the legal representative for the police department, didn't question that graft on a large and grand, well-organized scale existed, flourished, and excluded all competition but advised her against paying off. Next he filed a $20,000 slander suit against Lemon based on Lemon's known salary, which represented only a tiny fraction of his true income.

When Princess could hold out against Lemon's Central Station extortionists no longer, she paid them, then dialed the SFPD and asked for Chief Quinn personally. "I want to check on the bribe I just paid to your men," she said. "I want to be certain I haven't been overcharged." Princess was a careful woman.

"Overcharged?" asked Quinn.

"Well, you tell me. Is $150 the right amount to pay six policemen for protection? Should I have demanded a receipt?"

Quinn dropped the receiver back on its hook, legally obligated to call Mayor Rossi and DA Brady. Instead, he called Captain Lemon, who was "a very great and good friend" of Tom and Pete McDonough. The two brothers (and their nephew, Harry Rice) ran the underworld's post office where they extorted, refused, threatened, and obliterated anyone who impeded their brutal management of the city's gambling, dope, graft, and organized vice rings. They protected pimps, bankrolled madams, and kept an eye on the nightly take of every hustling girl on Eddy Street. "They knew to the dollar how much gambler Bones Remmer or Eddie Shahati took in a night play," said Ehrlich, "and had the drawings on any burglary, con-game or safe blowing that happened *before* it happened—or it *didn't* happen. Tammany never ran New York City as completely as the McDonoughs ran the right to break the law in San Francisco."

Having learned their trade during the corrupt Abe Ruef administration, they suborned witnesses, tampered with judges, paid off police, and bribed officials to pass or amend city ordinances beneficial to their enterprise. As the not-so-secret overlords of the underworld ("the Fountain Head of Corruption" according to the *Examiner*), they commanded an army of crooked cops, daylight stickup artists, pickpockets, fast-money specialists, burlesque queens, grifters, lamsters, and shoulder strikers.

That Captain Lemon was a good friend to the McDonoughs was not remarkable. Numerous police officials, judges, and even the DA were their friends, too, and beholding politically. Big-bellied, cigar-smoking Tom McDonough even possessed a $2,500 IOU bearing DA Brady's name. The two Irish-Catholic brothers had founded the nation's first modern bail bonds business. The cops, underpaid at $200 per month, commonly got kickbacks for recommending arrestees use the McDonoughs for bail. They provided it from their one-story bail bond brokerage at Clay and Kearney streets—so near the HOJ that Chief Quinn winced every time Pete raised his voice in anger.

Princess's next call was to Ehrlich to make doubly sure she hadn't been overcharged. He was furious that she had paid. "And you could have demanded a money back guarantee too," he said. "Where did you get the idea?"

"Well, Jake, there was this used car salesman who knew someone in the mayor's office who said it was better if I paid."

"When you start playing ball with the right people, Princess, you can turn in your grass skirt and head for the showers as far as I'm concerned." He believed that the reasons grafters flourished so long and so openly were peculiarly San Franciscan. "Always a robust-minded town, San Francisco had convinced itself that vice was a necessary evil." The cops had convinced themselves that they were expected to pick up extra dough by the most expedient means possible and above all please their captain.

That evening Ehrlich drove to the HOJ to speak on Princess's behalf. "All other San Francisco nightclubs have dancing and we are going to have dancing too . . . beginning tonight. The police have made a circus of Princess Kamokila's attempt to start an honest business in San Francisco and it's going to have to stop. This is to advise you that the police are going to have to break down the doors of the club if they want to get in from now on."

Both Central Station and the HOJ began to pressure Princess to stop her calls to the press. She was subpoenaed to appear before the grand jury the same day action was tabled on her club's dance permit and a telephoned threat was made against the life of her little daughter, Pineapples McFarlane. Princess locked her inside her Fairmont Hotel penthouse, hired a bodyguard, and got a gun permit. Somehow the cops got to her anyway. By the time she testified she no longer recalled what the shakedown officers had looked like.

But Chief Quinn knew the Central Station bucket men who most logically would have accepted the payoff. When they refused to testify under oath, he fired them. An investigation was promised, but Princess had a better idea. "San Francisco is on trial," she told reporters as she left the grand jury chambers, "and reeks of bought illegalities, official venality and under-the-table deals. . . . When the community is not courageous it must expose vice and crime. The city should hire an investigator and pay him $100,000 to clean up this Sodom and Gomorrah."

It is surprising that the economically strapped city did just that.

DA Brady, without notifying Quinn or the Police Commission, enlisted a commercial policeman to conduct a secret graft inquiry of the SFPD. His special investigator, Edwin Newton Atherton, was a handsome former G-man with the "open smile of a casket salesman." He was also a man in need of dollars. Before Rossi and Brady knew it, Atherton would have $100,000 of theirs. In rapid succession, Atherton set up a posh headquarters in the Keystone Apartments on Nob Hill's west side, organized three boxes of files in two cabinets, and began spending the city's money as fast as he could. He even bugged Ehrlich's office. Atherton's style was to get as close to his quarry as he could, "wheedling, flattering, threatening and promising," and then snap the trap. Stealthily, Atherton set to work like a mouse gnawing a live electrical cord.

TWENTY-FIVE

The E. Howard Clock Co. of Boston had designed the four clock faces (each looking to one of the compass points) of the Ferry Clock Tower as the world's biggest—11-foot-long minute hands, 7-foot-long hour hands on an outer dial 22-feet in diameter with 3-foot-high numerals.

—INFORMATION GUIDES FOR SAN FRANCISCO'S FERRY BUILDING

DULLEA had been at the Ferry Building since early morning working the multiple murders of sailors. It was evening now, and a tired army of blue-collar workers was trudging homeward across the wide cast-iron bridge. He watched them rising up and over the inclined span as they passed the Bay Hotel. This crime had touched Dullea and his men, even reduced the seasoned deputy coroner, Mike Brown, to tears. In his fury, the Gorilla Man had made a tactical error. The frenzy of his autopsy, one of the most horrific crime scenes the SFPD had ever encountered, had filled the detectives with a sense of vengeance.

Dullea had a solitary dinner, then finished briefing his men. Before he knew it, it was 11:00 P.M. Sore from his workout that morning as a member of the South End Rowing Club, Dullea paused midpoint on the bridge and scanned the Loop below. He was expecting an informant who claimed to know who had murdered the sailors. The eerie light of the immense bridge construction in the Bay cast a glow over the docks. The terminal's electrical system (which powered all the waterfront's foghorns, chimes, and whistles) kept the pier lights on all night long, because stevedores loaded ships all night. The footbridge lights would be extinguished in an hour. The ground floor of the Ferry Building was already dark (though the second floor was still ablaze). Like pretty much every great building in San Francisco, it was a copy of some great building somewhere else, in this case Charles Atwood's railroad station at the Chicago World's Fair.

While the power to operate the Embarcadero's lights surges from the Ferry Building, the force powering its Big Clock comes from a suspended nine-hundred-pound weight. Its intricate springs, valves, and wheels are wound weekly by a crank fitted to an axle. Dullea glanced at his watch. As usual, the Big Clock was running two minutes fast, had been since 1906. That made little difference since most watches were set by it. Unlike the Big Clock, Dullea couldn't gain a minute, and he was counting on every one.

If the night clerk Smeins could be believed, their quarry did resemble a gorilla. Crouching, a gorilla is tall as a man though he weighs three times as much, almost all muscle, and has bones correspondingly thick to support his upper body's tremendous weight. Dullea theorized his quarry was not civilized and really might be a Gorilla Man, at least on a psychological level. Something compelled him to act as he did, some broken mainspring, like the clock's, which made him run fast. Dullea believed that Gorilla Men (as their name implied) were some sort of throwbacks. In the years after World War I, these creatures had been thankfully rare, but in the last decade, the nation had been infested with them. The Gorilla Man, a victim of an irresistible impulse to perform his irrational acts, had no choice. He *had* to commit another autopsy murder. Dullea was driven too. Though he would never stop protecting defenseless women like Bette Coffin, Jessie Hughes, and Mrs. Johnston, he sometimes felt as powerless as they. Was he incapable of ever providing such women justice?

Wind cut spray into Dullea's face. He buttoned down his double-breasted suit and cinched his raincoat. The wind could never dislodge his new hat with its latex sweatband that adjusted itself to all the irregularities of the human head. Below, the massive black trains of the Belt Line made their last cargo runs. The fire marshal drove by, lights flashing, checking for hazardous cargo, then U-turned toward his office on China Alley at the south end annex. Most of the piers were shuttered now, their massive facades closed until morning, when the Anna Lemons of the world put in another exhausting twelve-hour shift. The final Belt Train chugged past, pushing a line of SP boxcars. Dullea waited.

Freighters and rusty tramps rose and fell all about him. When the moon reaches its highest point above the Bay, the stream runs high, courses over the slick rocks of the strait, and lifts vessels along the waterfront about nine inches. Six hours later, when the moon dips behind the Farallone Islands, the ships sink lower. Actually, the entire region from Montgomery Street northeast to the Bay was floating on water, shifting sand, jettisoned cargo, and abandoned Gold Rush vessels. But no building on the waterfront is as sturdy as the Ferry Building, which sits on a foundation of thousands of creosoted Oregon pines sunk eighty feet into bedrock. In 1850, during the Gold Rush, South Seas ships had brought the ships' worms whose descendants were still nibbling on those pilings.

Dullea heard the whine of winches, and from a dense shelf of fog discordant jangling bells, bleats, and whistles. The Ferry Building's deep foghorn out-shouted them all. Out to sea, a deep, drawn-out bass sound repeated. He heard waves faintly slapping the hull of one of the 170 ferries bound daily for San Francisco from Marin and Oakland. Somewhere in the tulle mist a lost ferry was looking for San Francisco, which in itself is only a point of fog.

When the final streetcar departed, swinging around the Loop on the spur track, so did Dullea. He descended the slick steps to the foot of Sacramento Street. Several doors down, the Bay Hotel sign shimmered. The lights of the Harbor Emergency Hospital behind the Bay Hotel illuminated sailors out drinking and young women plying their trade. Farther down, the street was hushed. At the alley formed by two multistoried buildings, did something exit a window, hold briefly with one hand from the fire escape, and drop silently to the road? Was that a silhouette with long arms against the brick wall where the alley made a sharp turn? Was that a vague figure melting away? Dullea walked to his car. That the SFPD would lock horns with the Laughing Gorilla again was the only thing he could count on in the treacherous mist, on the shifting ground in that point of fog.

ON a quiet street, the Gorilla Man laughed to himself—as if he could ever stop laughing. Traveling here and there, back and forth, he sailed and drank, and lost himself in blue-tinted rages and tried to forget. There was a rhythm and a flow to his outbursts, a compulsive timetable that he least of all understood, but reminded him most of the tides he sailed. Whenever he had been drinking, a curtain of blue lowered and made him do things. Sometimes the curtain was red, but whatever color it always took away his reason. When that curtain parted, he was able to blot out most of what he had done, but not completely. Faint memories remained, like footprints on the shore. Sometimes it all seemed like a dream. He shuddered. They couldn't hang a man for a dream, could they? That the local press had forgotten him didn't mean the Gorilla Man didn't exist. He still moved in his odd, flat-footed shamble, hands buried to hide their size.

He had been among Dullea and his men before, close but unseen except as a fleeting shadow. He intended stalking the Embarcadero tonight, trolling for unsuspecting women at seedy waterfront hotels. He felt off-kilter. The Ferry Building is not square with Market Street but at a slight angle aligned with the arcade anchored to the seawall. It lies directly on the axis with Market and Commercial streets, but parallel with the Embarcadero. He paused at a tavern door south of Market. Drinking scared him because it was then he lost control—as if he could ever give up drinking! He went into the tavern. Tony Sudari was behind the bar cleaning a glass with his apron.

ON Monday, August 12, 1935, the two dozen men assigned to hunt the Gorilla Man were detailed to other cases. Yet the hairs on the back of Dullea's neck still tingled when he passed the Bay Hotel. Though a dozen other serious cases needed his attention—George Gordon, slain in a Utah Street factory, and Paul Hanson, killed at Lake Merced when he defended his date from a gang rape—he still studied every open doorway and followed long-armed strangers along the piers. Somewhere a laughing gorilla would continue his murderous ways in whatever port he landed. All sea routes eventually led back to the Embarcadero and all roads led to the Ferry Building, the second busiest terminus in the world. He would be back.

Inspectors LaTulipe and McMahon were camped in Dullea's office. The rush of passing traffic came in through the open window as fog tumbled past in the typically frigid summer air. The Bay is an estuary filled with tidal marshes where fresh and salt waters combine. Moisture and prevailing northwesterly winds at least had the square in bloom. Dullea pawed through some circulars, then sat back wearily. McMahon wasn't tired. After all, he was still looking for the beautiful unknown woman who'd accompanied the Whispering Gunman five years ago. "You're smitten with her," Dullea kidded him, pointing out that he kept her sketch, yellowed now, thumb-tacked over his desk.

The sun was just going down. Everyone in Dullea's office was drinking, mostly Scotch. LaTulipe opened a binder and laid out photos of Mrs. Johnston, Mrs. Coffin, and a woman strangled in Golden Gate Park. "No, no, put them away," snapped Dullea. "I don't have the stomach for them."

The criminologist put them away and took out a card marked "Bay Hotel." Two types of hairs—coarse guard hairs and soft, thin down hairs were taped to the card. "The coarse hairs are animal," he thought. "Or they might be from a chair since animal hairs are used as fibers to manufacture upholstery. If 'Mr. Meyers' is really a sailor perhaps he picked them up on a freighter transporting wild animals. What if they were an ape's? Wouldn't that be something?"

They left the HOJ to grab a bite at Il Trovatore Cafe. Busboys Vic Gotti and his brother Roland enthusiastically greeted them and brought menus. Dullea opened the tall menu. On weekdays, a complete dinner (hors d'oeuvres, soup, salad, spaghetti or ravioli, choice of entrees from the menu including filet mignon, vegetables, potatoes, dessert, coffee, and a small bottle of red house wine) cost 50¢. Because it was a Saturday, each would have to cough up an extra ten pennies.

Over ravioli, LaTulipe ventured that the Gorilla Man was mentally subnormal and morally depraved. "His subnormality removes the inhibitions that hold his sex urge in check," he said. "He may not be more lustful than the average man, but an example of what happens when a man with a powerful libido feels he has nothing to lose. Remember Earle Nelson, the first Gorilla Man?" Dullea turned away as he felt the past drop over him like a shadow. He could still hear the killer's laugh on the shadowed landing. "He was a strangler too with huge hands," said Dullea.

"He's not our 'Mr. Meyers,' if that's what you're thinking," said LaTulipe. "The original Gorilla Man was a sex killer and religious fanatic. *He* had a motive. Besides, he's dead, executed in Canada. I checked."

But the Gorilla Man was alive, if only in Dullea's tortured dreams. "The greatest reign of terror ever inflicted on the nation's women began in San Francisco," said Dullea. Those had been bleak and terrible times—his first big case and his worst—until now.

TWENTY-SIX

Conscious of having deserved punishment, it seemed desirous of concealing its bloody deeds, and skipped about the chamber in an agony of nervous agitation, throwing down and breaking the furniture as it moved, and
dragging the bed from the bedstead.

—E. A. POE, "THE MURDERS IN THE RUE MORGUE"

ON the outskirts of San Francisco, a healthy grassland was flourishing. In
Woodside Glens, the neighbors had observed an unusual thing about Slipton Fell. After he moved into Ada Rice's bungalow, he would sit shirtless
on the grass playing soulful tunes on his mandolin but seemed afraid to
enter the house. As evening fell, he would cast long, fearful looks at it, then
around five o'clock, as the bungalow cast its shadow over him, he would
start as if he had sighted a moving figure in the skylight. As the sun sank
that optical effect was heightened. Then Fell's eyes would widen, his face
maple, and a light sheen overlay his brow. As fog overflowed Skyline Boulevard and rode down into the basin on the wind's back, he would rouse
himself with effort and, shivering, trudge inside.

He kindled the flagstone fireplace, stoking the logs with a poker. But as
the fire cast flickering shadows along the wall, they too suggested a figure.
Returning to the fire, he stabbed with the poker until sparks rose and the
flare washed away the shadow. All night those passing on the road above
heard his laugh.

Daily, Fell grew more nervous. He hated the square bungalow by day
and feared it by night. He loathed its emptiness and the hollowness it im-

parted to his voice. When he did sleep, his nightmares frightened him, but not nearly so much as the terror that he might talk in his sleep. Finally, he stopped sleeping in the house altogether. "Where does he sleep?" wondered the neighbors. They studied the dark windows and speculated. "If not inside the bungalow, then where?"

Fell had concealed Mrs. Rice's car (with different plates) and a second auto in a private garage in nearby Burlingame. When the sun went down, he left the fearful knoll with relief, unlocked the garage, and crawled into the backseat of Ada's car. It was barely capacious enough to contain his 230 pounds and six-foot length, but it soothed him because the seats had the familiar smell of old lace. It made him realize that he had genuinely liked the older woman. But even in the familiar surroundings of Ada's car he slept only a few hours. When he was composed enough to drift off, he would cry out and suddenly awake. What had he said? Shaken he looked around the little garage. Seeing he was alone, he pulled his rumpled suit over himself and dozed off again.

In the morning light he saw Ada had left a few personal items in the car—her passport and some insurance papers. A finance company still held title to the car. He realized if he reported it stolen he might get a few extra bucks to tide him over.

After filing a claim and collecting from the insurance company, Fell began taking long midnight drives along the coast highway. At each hairpin turn, his lights stabbed into deep canyons. He studied them as if they held the solution to his problem of the haunted bungalow. For whatever he expected to find on his lonely nocturnal drives he was well prepared. He had packed the trunk with a rolled blanket, adhesive tape, cotton cloth, a bottle of ammonia, a container of chloroform, and a sixty-foot length of rope with loops at both ends tied with a sailor's knot. And as he sped, feeling the cool air against his face, Fell laughed as loud as he could but found no release. He couldn't endure many more sleepless nights in the cramped garage. His mouth and throat were dry and his head throbbed. What could he do?

BY September 13, 1935, only one person still missed Mrs. Ada French Mengler Rice. That was Mr. Rice. He desperately needed Ada's signature, and she was nowhere to be found and hadn't been since mid-June. At first, the San Mateo County Sheriff's office seemed interested in locating her and though inclined to serve the divorce papers they weren't exactly putting their backs to the wheel. Understandably, it was hard to keep their attention. Things rarely happened in their placid county and never in Woodside Glens. Only a case as big as murder could shatter their torpor. By February 1, the deputies would stop asking questions altogether, because on that day Mr. Rice would finally be granted his divorce in absentia and thus no longer be interested in the fate of Ada Rice. But for now, they continued their less-than-dogged hunt for the journalist.

So far not a shadow of suspicion had fallen on Slipton Fell. All the neighbors knew was that the house on the knoll sat vacant and presumably uncomfortable enough to compel him to sleep elsewhere. To the inquisitive neighbors he had explained away Ada's absence with good news. Ada and a handsome young cavalry officer had taken a sudden trip to Bulgaria, perhaps, he winked, to elope. Ada had found happiness at last. And with that Fell, flexing his long arms, had returned to the house.

The next day, John and Davenport Bromfield, Realtors (told by an irate Mr. Rice to now look to Ada for mortgage payments), materialized at the Woodside Glens bungalow. Fell answered the door.

"Ada's in New York and I've taken over the property," he told them.

"But so far you've failed to make any payments," said the Bromfields.

"I'll get back to you," he said and closed the door. After that the Bromfields were unable to locate Fell. All the neighbors could tell them was that the young weightlifter and eccentric adventurer was off somewhere on another of his excursions, his destination as mysterious as Ada's. After three weeks, the Bromfields initiated legal action to regain possession of the lonely house on Canada Road.

In San Francisco, Dullea knew Mr. Meyers to be a seafaring man. What he didn't know was that the devious Slipton Fell was an international sailor. Unlike some of his stories of adventuring, government toppling, and bandit joining, this was true. He had gone voyaging now, leaving the lonely and presumably haunted estate in Woodside Glens empty. The strange square house would hold its secrets until his return. Now, wherever Slipton Fell was, he could sleep again at last.

*   *   *

ON September 18, in the rivers, woods, and swamps of Cleveland (at the time the sixth largest city in the country), citizens were suffering at the hands of a motiveless sequential killer, another necrosadist. The fever that had gotten into the nation's blood in San Francisco had spread to Ohio. The Gorilla Man's children were at work, and they were industrious. Like the San Francisco and New York killings, the Ohio murders were something new in the United States—motiveless, random murders.

The Cleveland detectives' only clue was that all the victims had been dismembered with a surgeon's scalpel by a laughing man with long arms. Was there a link with Dullea's sailor who laughed and killed without motive? Cleveland resident Edward Andrassy probably knew the identity of the fiendish killer, but he was too busy running for his life to do anything about it—a laughing Gorilla was out to get him.

TWENTY-SEVEN

Wild gorillas are vegetarians, feeding on buds, leaves, ripe fruit, barks and herbs. Beginning at dawn they travel all day, selecting plants growing within reach of their long arms. Only captive gorillas eat meat and the only captive gorilla in the nation in 1935 was in Cleveland.

—GORILLA, EYEWITNESS BOOKS

"IT'S not as if there hadn't been warning signs of impending trouble," said Mrs. Helen Andrassy. She had felt vague rumblings over the last year, like that of an approaching storm. The very air above Cleveland seemed charged. Last September the headless torso of a young woman, coated with a sticky, odd-smelling fluid, had washed ashore on Beulah Park Beach at the foot of East 156th Street. This "Lady of the Lake" had floated from the Kingsbury Run down the Cuyahoga River and along the lake front. Two days later and thirty miles east near North Perry, a man gathering driftwood on Euclid Beach encountered more of her bare bones—scarified by the action of sand and as white and broken as the rocks. These findings were so distressing, even Mrs. Andrassy's twenty-nine-year-old son mentioned them.

"What is the matter with you?" Mrs. Andrassy asked on Wednesday, September 18. She got no reply and went back to mopping the kitchen linoleum. "You've been acting strangely for over a week."

"He's coming." The gaunt figure shifted in his chair.

"Who's coming?" she asked.

"He's coming to kill me, Ma," he said. "I tell you I'm going to die."

Mrs. Andrassy pushed back the gingham curtains in the tiny kitchen window and peered out on the gray afternoon surrounding 1744 Fulton

Road. Northwest winds were sweeping this blue-collar section of the city, where she shared a modest home with her husband, Joe, and son, Ed. Joe would be working late at his tiny, failing factory tonight. For the last two weeks, Ed had been unaccountably fearful, his large expressive eyes fixed on the door, jug ears cocked to catch the slightest sound. He had been more secretive than ever, his unaccountable comings and goings occurring at all hours. Ed had strange friends, too, scattered all over Rowdy Row, a section bordered by East Fifty-fifth Street, the Kingsbury Run, and Prospect Avenue. He also frequented a cheap saloon on the corner of East Twentieth Street and Central Avenue.

His mom had given up wondering why Ed's marriage hadn't worked and why he couldn't hang onto a job. Since 1925, he had twice been an orderly in the psychiatric ward of the City Hospital, a door-to-door magazine salesman, a bellhop, a laborer, and eight other jobs—all lost. Ed was shiftless and that was that. His only notoriety was as a police character found intoxicated and dozing in a graveyard. Four years earlier cops had imprisoned him in the Warrensville Heights Workhouse.

"An Italian gang is after me, Ma," Ed had said to explain the ice pick he carried. Two weeks before, a stranger had hammered on their door and threatened, "Ed, I want you to leave my wife alone!" Now another fierce banging shook their door. "Don't open the door, Ma. If you love me, don't open the door!" As Ed scurried into his room, the front doorknob rattled as if by a gale. Mrs. Andrassy peered out and saw a man with stooped shoulders on the mat. The cold wind stirred his tattered coat. A few leaves drifted across the cracked walkway. "He was stocky, but not fat," she recalled, "and about five-feet, eight-inches tall." Mrs. Andrassy opened the door a crack.

"Let me see Ed," said a coarse voice.

"He isn't here," she lied. He gave a cheerless laugh in response. "There was something weird and inhuman about that laugh," Mrs. Andrassy said. "He had unusual eyes—hidden by shaggy eyebrows and buried in their sockets. His eyes were large and luminous—brilliant. He had massive shoulders and long arms. His fingers were long too, tapering and steady. His face was thin, but there was a mysterious power and strength hidden in that face. It was kind of like an ape's."

"Tell Ed he better watch out," the stranger said. "Tell him something's going to happen. And he knows just what that something is." His lips shut into a thin line and he lurched down the walk with a peculiar gait. He was lost in the lengthening shadows of late afternoon. On the wind she heard his laugh again.

Mrs. Andrassy knew Gorilla Men existed. In January, Ohio's "Human Gorilla" had proved that. The full moon shining down on the Steubenville plant of the Wheeling Steel Corporation was as bright as the open hearth furnaces spilling onto the snow-blanketed yards. Beyond stretched the Ohio River and blue West Virginia hills. As shifts were changing at 11:30 P.M., steelworker A. A. Lashley saw a Gorilla Man shoot down Fred Melscheimer, a new train service engineer. "With his head down and powerful shoulders stooped, he looked like a gorilla," said Lashley. "Honest to God. His arms were extraordinarily long, almost touching the ground. He was dressed in dark trousers, a jacket belonging to an overall suit, a soft hat [like the kind the mill police wore], a pair of mill-issue work gloves and a black cloth mask that hid his features."

He loped away in a sort of dogtrot and effortlessly vaulted the fence separating the plant from Mingo Boulevard two hundred feet away. Under a blood red moon fifty-four days later, he pumped six bullets into James Bartlett, another train service employee, before escaping behind the mill's blast furnace. In July, he gunned down two more three hundred feet from the first shooting, then, muttering incoherently, he trotted to the river and escaped in a rowboat.

On July 28, mill police, acting on a tip, were waiting and captured him. Lieutenant C. H. Bailey ripped off the black mask. The Ohio Gorilla was David D'Ascanio, forty-seven, a mill railroader and sweeper in the plant's new process department. "His lips were a long thin line in the midst of a broad square face," said Bailey. "He was short, swarthy and powerful."

A slit in his canvas overalls allowed him to access his .38 caliber Colt Police Special in a cloth holster. His cap and slicker had been stolen from a mill policeman. D'Ascanio was taken to his Lincoln Street room. He had covered the windows with double shades and plugged the keyhole. "Have you any friends?" Bailey asked.

"No," the apelike man replied. "You've got to have money to have friends. I've got no money and I've never cared much for women. I kill nobody!" But police found a black mask in a drawer and a trunk full of .38 ammo.

"So there were other Gorilla Men," thought Mrs. Andrassy, and one had just visited her son.

It was not D'Ascanio. He would be sentenced to death next month. Ed Andrassy had barricaded the door to his room by wedging a chair under the brass knob. It was a small, spare room—one chest, one bed, five nature magazines with nude pictures of men and women playing volleyball, two medical books on gynecology, and a small red address book that he kept hidden. Ed went without dinner that night and didn't eat all day Thursday, only moped in his room repeating that somebody was going to kill him. "Edward lived in constant fear of his life," his father said later. "He always told us to mind our own business when we tried to straighten him out."

As soon as it was dark Ed peeked out at an empty tree-lined street. It was poorly lit. Anyone could have been waiting there. In spite of that, at 8:00 P.M. he slipped on his blue coat and crept out without a word.

As a rule, the Andrassys made little commentary on their son's erratic comings and goings. Like his other failings, they had come to accept them. If not for the long-armed man and Ed's dire remarks about a gang, the family wouldn't have given his absence a second thought. They spent all of Friday morning without any real sense of trepidation. By noon Mrs. Andrassy had discounted the alleged threats and by evening was waiting for him to return as usual. Saturday and Sunday passed with little concern. By Monday morning the family was barely troubled. It was Ed's way, they told themselves and went about their lives as if nothing were wrong at all.

AFTER school on Monday, September 23, Jimmy Wagner and Peter Kostura went to play on one of the raw hillocks overseeing the timeless furrow of the Kingsbury Run. A run is a midland creek that sometimes rushes with powerful currents and at other times is dry. Breathless, sixteen-year-old Jimmy and twelve-year-old Peter came out on the shapeless heap of Jackass Hill on Cleveland's East Side.

On the eroding summit at the end of East Forty-ninth Street, a few houses were cloistered among a thicket of white and black willows. The fruit of the white willows had been yellowish and drooping in June. By the end of June, the black willows had gone to seed. By July, both kinds were spotted green and white, August heat made their berries swell, and by September they were drooping in dense blue clusters. The big sassafras tree retained its red, club-shaped pedicels, but its empty fruit cups were trilling in the wind.

Straggly sunflowers poked through tin cans by a rusting bedspring where the boys spent a while jumping up and down. Downy shad bushes, brown-headed wool grass, and seedy spikes of sawgrass—itchy stuff—caught at their trousers. The boys flew kites in the sweeping winds and peered down into the isolated run at a spot where the Erie Gully and wider run met. The wind was raising dust clouds along the flat-bottomed gully—the arid bed of a creek. Sections of cliff sheathed away onto vacant tin-roofed buildings, corrugated iron sheds, a refinery lime house, and the Erie Railroad shops below. Two switch engines were working the yards as strings of freight and passenger cars on sidings about the broad arroyo shook in the wind.

Two Rapid Transit System trains crossed the basin at an angle, linking the economically depressed downtown to the swank suburbs of Shaker Heights. They brought every manner of man to the gully from every manner of place for every manner of reason. Thirty pairs of sooty tracks filled the run for most of its length. Beyond Forty-ninth Street the tracks split, and the Erie line diverted into a little gully of its own as the Shaker, Rapid, and Nickel Plate Railroad lines continued. As the canyon swung southeast from the industrial area out to East Ninetieth Street, its rushing waters were diverted into subterranean sewers. At the Thirty-seventh Street Bridge these sewers emerged to create a stagnant pool that flowed into the Cuyahoga River. From the southern shore of Lake Erie, the valley formed by the excessively polluted Cuyahoga (the only U.S. river to ever catch fire) cleaves the city into an east and west side. Toward Lake Erie, the gully became a canyon lit along its bluffs at night by vats of molten slag and the sulfur-belching stacks of steel mills. It was hell.

When Jimmy and Peter's softball rolled over the steep sixty-foot slope, they started after it, pushing their way through tangled underbrush. Halfway down Jimmy broke free into an open sedge hollow and crawled down into a shallow indentation. "Peter, there's a man down there," he shouted. "And he doesn't have any clothes on!" The body, clad only in black cotton socks, lay on its side. "Or any head!"

They slid the rest of the way down and flagged a watchman who phoned the Erie Railroad police. Sergeant Arthur Marsh and Patrolman Arthur Stitt heard the story and rang the Cleveland PD. By 5:15 P.M., Lieutenant Gorman and the No. 6 Police Emergency Team were at the scene. Five minutes later, Chief of Police George J. Matowitz, a round-faced administrator in full gold braid, contacted Detectives Orley May and Emil Musil, and within twelve minutes they, too, had reached the Erie yards.

A squad car carrying Inspector Charles O. Nevel arrived at the leaden trench. His silver hair was striped with black, his thin lips were drawn tight, and his blue eyes were intent beneath wire-rimmed glasses. Nevel, May, Musil, and the two railway dicks trailed the boys up the steep grade. Nevel's keen eyes took in every twig and footprint. Except for the boys' flight path he saw no broken branches or disturbed earth. Near the body lay a white shirt, trousers, checkered cap, and blood-stiffened blue coat. They rolled the nude body, which had not only been decapitated but emasculated. "It appears the body has been here only a short time," said May.

"Forty-eight hours at the outside," said Nevel.

"This means that the missing head and uh, the rest, might be nearby."

"There's not enough blood. He was killed elsewhere and carried to the scene. There's only one reason to mutilate a body in such a way—to conceal its identity. May, Get Coroner Pearce out here." While light remained they searched for the head. Musil, about thirty feet away, gave a cry.

"Did you find the head?" said Nevel.

"No! My God! Here's another body."

The second male, nude, headless, on its stomach, had been cleanly dismembered at the shoulder by cuts around the flexure of the joints. All the skin edges, muscles, blood vessels, and cartilage had been cut squarely. The head had been severed by a long, sharp knife through the intervertebral discs, then wrenched completely out of the joint cavity by a powerful twist.

Musil flipped over the second butchered corpse—emasculated, too. Both sets of severed genitals lay together.

The first victim was young and lanky, his wrists marked by rope burns. The second fiftyish and heavyset, had unmarked wrists. The older victim's tattoos suggested he was a sailor. His torso was also painted with a pinkish, odd-smelling fluid that came off on Musil's fingers. "Some kind of lubricating oil?"

May discovered a two-gallon water bucket half-filled with the same sticky substance.[10] "I think it's meant to preserve the body," Nevel said. "If so it failed."

The gases of decomposition emitted a nauseating odor. Putrefaction had advanced from a greenish discoloration to a general darkening and bloating of the whole body. The darkened veins looked like Venetian marble. Bacteria in the intestinal tract had multiplied, breaking down tissues and was now busy reducing the corpse to its basic chemical compounds. The sun and insect life had done the rest, but not all. Someone had tried to set the body on fire.

"After luring his victim to his home with promises of money or sex or drink," theorized Nevel, "he strips his victim of clothes, immobilizes him in some way, then emasculates him with a surgeon's scalpel. He cuts his victim's neck, severs it before he can cry out, and with the next stroke and a strong right hand twist beheads his victim."

The killer had been sane enough to bring rope, a railway lantern, and a bucket of preservative. Jackass Hill was an odd choice for a dumping ground. Nevel had seen sectioned bodies disposed of at widely separated points—backyards and basements, rubbish heaps and rivers, farms and fields, even a swamp. Two months earlier, two young wards of the Carmelite Orphanage at Hammond, Indiana, were passing through the swamp where Al Capone hoodlums John Scalisi, Albert Anselmi, and Joseph Guinta had been dumped when they found a dead man in a basket. His legs had been cut off and a knotted rope drawn tightly around his neck. The victim, missing Chicago grocery clerk Ervin Lang, had been slain elsewhere. Lang's

---

[10] Car engine oil, decayed blood, and long strands of black human hair.

mother-in-law, Blanche Dunkel, had lured him to Evelyn Smith's apartment, doped him with whisky and ether, strangled him, and sawed off his legs, which she packed in a little trunk.

As the sun slipped behind the shapeless knoll, Coroner Arthur J. Pearce, mustached and jowly, reached Jackass Hill. At night, the sounds of the dreary run were amplified—the rustle of small animals and the staccato *click* of trains on distant tracks and the lonely call of their whistles. Stitt and Hill dug by flashlight and, in a shallow grave, found the young man's head. Stitt lifted it by its hair. Flashing wigwag signals and the checker-board lights of a passing Shaker Heights commuter train revealed their ghastly expressions. Caught against the swaying treetops the mouth held an ironic smile, clouded eyes looking sightlessly at their own truncated body. The older man's head was seventy feet from its body in an exagger-ated stage of decay—sagging dead skin and the right eye squeezed shut as if winking.

"And these fellas were emasculated and decapitated while they were still alive," said Nevel.

The wind rose, a whispering laugh among the willows.

DETECTIVE May was exhausted, yet oddly excited. Detectives Blackwell and Stubley had spent the late evening questioning workers in the Erie Railway shops while he went up-spill to a huge encampment where a few inelegant wooden bridges spanned the trench. The Flats District, the valley formed by the river, was home to a hard-nosed colony of casual workers, alcoholics, addicts, ex-cons, and down-and-outers. They survived off refuse dumps lining the gully. From the Erie Railroad tracks this Hooverville of lean-tos, dilapidated board shanties, oiled-paper tents, and corrugated metal houses crept up the steep slope.

At the crossroad, May smelled sewage from the gully. "Its filth blows in the winds, assails the nostrils, and offends the eyes," locals said of the Run.

From beneath the dry sand, came the sound of rushing waters. He listened to the rhythmic burbling of the underground sewers as he scanned the dark windows of packing case huts and linoleum houses. Chicken feathers eddied in little windstorms. Rats scurried beneath makeshift flooring. Dogs

Inspector Allan McGinn taking notes and Captain Charles Dullea with his hand on the headlight of the touring car used to run over Jessie Hughes.

Quinn (on the running board) and Lieutenant Tom McInery (behind the wheel) in the chief's armored police vehicle. *Courtesy Kevin J. Mullen Collection, as appeared in his book* The Toughest Gang in Town, *Noir Publications*

All photos are from the collection of Robert Graysmith, unless otherwise noted.

The Bay Hotel with the Ferry Building visible at the end of the block.
The arrow indicates the murder room.

Aerial view of the Ferry Building on San Francisco's Embarcadero and the wide iron
bridge across the Great Loop leading to the Bay Hotel.
Courtesy of The Californian Historical Society

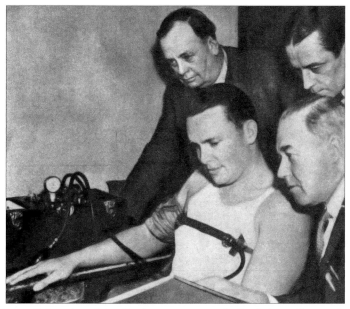

Slipton Fell undergoing a lie detector test at the Berkeley police station.
Left to right are Deputy Thomas Maloney; the suspect M. L. Britt;
and Ralph Pidgeon, the polygraph examiner.

Harry Gibson's cab on the bulkhead between Piers 26 and 28,
the site of Officer Malcolm's shooting.

Scene of the murder. Ada Rice's Woodside bungalow interior.

Ada French Rice

Ada Rice's Woodside bungalow exterior.

Ada Rice's remains, inside a wicker sarcophagus, being recovered by the coroner's men from her burning lime grave in the wilderness.

Peter Farrington,
"the Whispering Gunman."

Mrs. Jessie Scott Hughes

Inspector Allan McGinn examining the Bay Hotel murder scene.

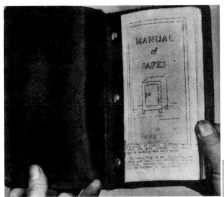

LEFT: The white-masked Phantom's safe-cracking instruction book.

BELOW: Inspector Allan McGinn and an officer examining Bette Coffin's effects at the Bay Hotel.

Jessie Scott Hughes's home and garage surrounded
by detectives and reporters. Dullea studies the murder garage.

Attorney Vincent Hallinan (left) and Chief William Quinn (right with cigar)
flank public defender Frank Egan as he is arrested for murder.
Courtesy Kevin J. Mullen Collection, as appeared in his book
The Toughest Gang in Town, *Noir Publications*

Frank Egan

Public Defender Frank Egan's home on Urbano Drive
nearby his benefactor Josie Hughes's house.

Inspector McGinn pointing out where Josie Hughes's body was found.

Officer John Johnston who caught the Phantom during a safe robbery.

Inspector William McMahon.

Inspector Richard Tatham,
the head of the Robbery Detail.

Captain of Detectives Charles Dullea.

Taxi driver, Harry Gibson.

Tiny the White Mask Gang member who turned against the Phantom.

Earle Nelson

Ramon Hughes, strangler and Gorilla Man suspect.

Officer John Malcolm

Captain Dullea after being awakened after midnight and rushing to a crime scene.

Jean Montgomery was also found murdered in her hotel room in San Francisco.

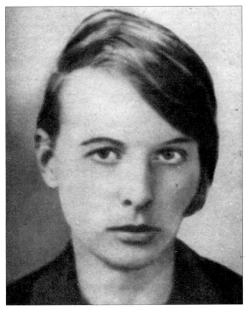

Irene McCarthy, The Laughing Gorilla's last hotel victim.

The Gorilla Man behind bars at last.

growled. Just beneath Commercial and Canal Roads vagrants had burrowed caves into the cliffside. Against May's light they pulled their tarpaper doors shut.

Nearby, Jackass Hill towered bare and forbidding, hunched like an ape. On its summit one house was lit. In the early minutes of Tuesday, September 24, May canvassed it. Out front, a housewife gazed over the bleakness of the Run. Streets in neighborhoods near the Run were rarely lit, and those that were were lit as poorly as Ed Andrassy's street.

"Have you seen anyone on the hill?" May asked.

"Sunday night," she said, "I saw two men coming up the slope. They'd just seen a man below wiping his hands on a bloody towel and wanted me to call the police, but I refused. I thought they were making the story up."

May slid to where the two boys had made their grim find. The *clang-clang-clang* from the cross-back at the grade crossing warned him before he was blinded by a blaze of light. A train flew by. For two hours he scoured the hillside, came up empty-handed and disgusted, returned to his car, and drove to the Cleveland morgue.

Coroner Pearce was completing postmortems on numbers 44996 and 44997. Both had been expertly decapitated with a swift, confident stroke by a curved scalpel between the third and fourth vertebrae. The fact that both victims had suffered an emasculation operation before death puzzled Pearce. "This element doesn't fit into the picture of a sex-crazed killer," he thought. "Then again the emasculation suggests a lust murderer—that's a motive of sorts."

As far as he could tell, the motive was not lust, revenge, or money. "These crimes are something new in the modern annals of crime in the U.S., not sex murders, but motiveless murders."

The motive was that there was no motive.

At 9:00 P.M. Chief Matowitz, Nevel, May, and Sergeant James T. Hogan studied Pearce's findings. Hogan was the toughest third-degree man on the force, but now his lean Yankee face was chalk white; his dark hair streaked with sweat. The younger victim was Ed Andrassy who, for his last meal, had eaten vegetables, the main diet of the Flats District vagrants.

"For some reason the killer didn't care if we learned who Andrassy was," Nevel said, "yet he removed every mark of identification from the older victim who must have had some connection to the murderer. Until we can find who the older victim is, we must learn everything we can about Andrassy. The severe rope burns on his wrists showed he had been tied, awake, and struggling when decapitated. He was lured to his death and struck unawares, perhaps even given a 'mickey,' chloral hydrate. Andrassy knew the killer and whatever means he employed to incapacitate his victims and would have been forewarned. That's why he had to dope Andrassy and tie his hands. Ed was a very morbid young man and might have been involved in the first murder."

The older victim had been killed three weeks before Andrassy. "Maybe *he* left a clue behind. If he knew the identity of the fiendish killer he took that secret to his grave."

Inspector Nevel drove to the Andrassy home. "Edward knew he was going to die," the mother moaned. "Four or five days ago . . . last Wednesday, a man came to the door. Edward was frightened of him . . . I didn't like his eyes." She repeated his description, that of a gorilla with heavy brows, and recalled his weird laugh.

"He must have been lying in wait and watching your house," Nevel said.

Andrassy had been killed the first night he set foot outside. Using his medical ID badge, Ed often took advantage of women in the guise of administering a physical examination. One gynecological exam of an acquaintance's wife ended in sodomy just as her husband surprised them. "Perhaps," Mrs. Andrassy said, "the man who came to our door was the outraged husband of one of those unfortunate women. We don't know any of Edward's friends. I do know he used to work in a hospital."

The killer had demonstrated surgical skill, but Ed had been a hospital orderly, not a doctor.

By dawn, Nevel had matched every name in Ed's address book with a phone number. Andrassy had a "boy friend" named "Eddie" who sold the aphrodisiac Spanish Fly. Or was "Eddie" only Ed? Mrs. Andrassy, in tears, pushed the mug books away, able to recall only her visitor's haunting laugh. A Cleveland newspaper named the killer "The Butcher," associating the animalistic qualities of the crimes with that profession.

Chief Matowitz believed both victims had been beheaded in a soundproof and private place. "Somewhere in this city," he said, "is a murder laboratory. We've got to find that hidden lab before he uses it again."

Hogan was to find the knife—a short, high, curved scimitar-shaped knife like the Persian shamshir. The majority of Cleveland's million citizens were foreign born, some eighty nationalities making steel. Large tracts of Persian, Polish, Turkish, Lithuanian, Russian, Syrian, Greek, and Bohemian immigrants sprawled near the Run.

Detectives Peter Merylo and Martin Zalewski, the latter a former beat cop in the Jackass Hill area, began the search there. Zalewski spoke seven eastern European languages; Merylo was nearly as proficient. Because the odd dust on the older victim's clothes originated around railroad tracks and flophouses, they visited every dive, slum, hobo camp, and rail yard. Chemists subjected his clothes to tests, unaware that some laundry's unique symbols can be invisible, printed in a patented ink revealed only under ultraviolet or infrared light. On November 23, when the Missing Persons Bureau failed to match him with any missing person on file in Ohio, his prints were airmailed to the newly named FBI in Washington. At roughly the same time in San Francisco, LaTulipe sent the FBI the single unidentified print he had found in room 309 of the Bay Hotel. The Federal Identification Bureau prided itself in answering all queries within thirty-six hours, except those from the Pacific Coast. "Always a bridesmaid," thought LaTulipe.

TWENTY-EIGHT

Anthropometry is the science of fingerprints. In the 1930s the theory that the shape of the third or ungual phalanx of the finger was unique to each individual was considered a surefire method of identification.

—CRIME LAB HANDBOOK OF 1937

THE tall, silver-haired criminalist, reading glasses tilted on his brow, counted the modest tools at his disposal in his SFPD lab—outdated texts and unreliable equipment, everything taped, tacked, nailed, patched, and jury-rigged or invented by himself. LaTulipe envied the new bureau with it unlimited budget.

Arguably J. Edgar Hoover became the FBI's first director because of prison official A. J. Renoe's limited budget. From November 1923 to July 1924, the Department of Justice employed as custodians of the Federal Identification Bureau housed at Leavenworth Penitentiary at Kansas the most unlikely examiners of all. The ID file was run by convicts inside the prison. Budgetary constrictions had compelled Renoe to rely on "trusties" to conduct print comparisons for authorities from coast to coast. In 1903 New York's Sing Sing Prison (then Napanoch, Clinton, and Auburn Prisons) adopted fingerprints as a means of infallible identification. A year later, St. Louis became the first major American city to convert completely to fingerprints. U.S. law enforcement had been slow to recognize the value of fingerprints as an evidentiary tool, favoring instead Alphonse Bertillon's anthropometry system, a complex series of eleven caliper measurements of bony lengths of the face and body to differentiate individuals from each other. All that had changed when an African American prisoner, Will West, arrived at Leavenworth to serve a life sentence for murder and discovered another William West already there serving a life sentence for murder. The faces and bone measurements of both were perfectly alike. Only their fingerprints were different.

In May 1923 New York City Police Commissioner Richard Enright, head of the International Police Conference (IPC), called for a meeting of the powerful International Association of Chiefs of Police (IACP) to remedy the fingerprint situation.[11] A few days later Major Richard Sylvester, superintendent of the Metropolitan Police in Washington, D.C., barged into Assistant Attorney General Rush L. Holland's office. The hawk-profiled, long-haired jurist listened as Sylvester described the scandalous work being done by Leavenworth convicts. Holland sent for his close friend Chief Hugh D. Harper of Colorado Springs, who was returning to El Paso County by way of Washington. "When a particular record vanishes from the files," Harper said as he settled his considerable weight into a chair, "I am certain convicts who are naturally not sympathetic with police activity have destroyed it."

"I've just spoken to Major Sylvester," said Holland. "He suggested Leavenworth's records be consolidated with the makeshift fingerprint bureau being maintained by the IACP in Washington. I want you to personally take over the print bureau at Leavenworth."

"No. It's in horrible shape," said Harper, aghast. "It's not a job for one man. It's a job for the government."

"Then who? What if I detail William J. Burns, head of the Bureau of Investigation, to the June meeting?"

"Mr. Burns does not stand 'ace-high' with many of the chiefs. If he went to Buffalo he would merely antagonize them. But there is an assistant to Mr. Burns named J. Edgar Hoover, a bright, efficient young fellow and very affable. The Chiefs would take more kindly to Hoover than Burns."

---

[11] Among the chiefs from forty-seven states set to attend the thirtieth annual convention at Buffalo, New York, on June 11, 1923, were Chief Harper; Joseph M. Quigley, chief of Rochester, New York, Police Department; Michael T. Long, chief of Newark, New Jersey, Police Department; John A. Curry of Niagara Falls, New York; and William P. Rutledge, superintendent of police in Detroit, Michigan.

"Now that you mention it, I do prefer his company." Holland called Hoover "Speed" because he rushed in, rattled off his words with Gatling-gun rapidity, then whisked himself out. He didn't know Hoover spoke fast to mask a crippling stutter. Sharp-featured, bulldoglike and stout with black curly hair, Hoover came down, chatted with the two men for fifteen minutes, then left like a rocket. "You know, Hugh, he always reminds me of 'Off again, on again, gone again, Finnigan.' But he's intelligent, has a splendid personality and the drive it will take to put the matter over in the proper way. Yes, Hoover is the properly qualified man to send."

In Buffalo Commissioner Enright advocated a national repository of fingerprints be housed within the Department of the Interior. The powerful IACP, which favored the DOJ, won out.

"Do we have any legal right to move the present fingerprint bureau from Leavenworth Prison to Washington?" Attorney General Harry A. Daugherty asked Holland.

"Yes, I checked with various acts of Congress and I couldn't find anything that denied the Attorney General such authority. Naturally, the appropriation for maintaining the bureau is carried in the appropriation for the Leavenworth penitentiary and that ties it pretty close to that institution."

"Well, some of our political friends out that neck of the woods will probably raise heck about it."

"Well, dammit, General," Holland said, "I'll be the goat and take all the blame."

"You will do nothing of the kind!" said Daugherty. "Take the bull by the horns and I'll stand back of you." With that he authorized Holland to ship the convict fingerprint records from Leavenworth to the Washington bureau and discard their two hundred thousand Bertillon measurements "into the limbo of forgotten things and useless antiquities."

In September, the IACP, using DOJ funds, transported their records of 150,000 fingerprints to Washington and consolidated them with the Leavenworth file of 650,000 prints. The result, "pretty much a jumble," was run by two employees who tied fingerprint cards into 50,000-card bundles and stacked them in the corner. For six months the nation was without any identification bureau at all.

When Daugherty entangled the bureau in the Teapot Dome Scandal, President Calvin Coolidge forced him to resign. "Daugherty left the government service," Holland said, "the most cruelly and brutally maligned man I have ever known in public life."

On May 10, 1924, Attorney General Harlan Fiske Stone named J. Edgar Hoover as acting director of the Bureau of Investigation. He strong-armed Congress into funding a permanent Identification Division within the Bureau, then negotiated with William A. Pinkerton and St. Louis Chief Martin O'Brien to consolidate the bureau's existing fingerprint files with the IACP records. With Congress's first subsidy of $56,000, twenty-one new employees were added to the Identification Division in the Old Railroad Building.

On November 24, 1932, the lab—with a borrowed microscope, ultraviolet light equipment, and a helixometer (to examine the inside of gun barrels) that did not work—was finally up and running. By November 1935, the lab had $100,000 of new equipment and was able to compare the Jackass Hill victim's prints with its five million fingerprint records. There was no match.[12] Next his prints went to a new Civil Identification Section (140,000 prints of government employees, military recruits, and civil defense workers and 30,000 prints of civilians who had volunteered as a precautionary measure). The Single Latent Fingerprint Section included partial fingerprints and palm prints. When John Dillinger had his fingers scarified with skin grafts and acid, his prints still showed a sufficient number of points to establish positive identification. But the Jackass Hill victim's prints were not in these files either. The tattooed sailor would never be identified.

THAT same day, LaTulipe decided to approach Chief Quinn about his poor lab equipment. He had to admit Quinn did have some far-reaching ideas. A long string of loan company and bank holdups two years earlier had given him an idea of how to combine his two great loves: police work and radio.

---

[12] By December 1935 the records would swell to 6,292,383. During the previous fiscal year, the FBI had made 304,033 successful criminal identifications from prints, a success rate Hoover gleefully estimated at 47.8 percent. Of the total prints identified 4,403 belonged to fugitives from justice.

At that time, the only way to dispatch officers already in the field was to have uniformed vehicular units call stations through pay phones and request instructions. Quinn's idea was that they use commercial radio to summon police. Regular radio programming would be interrupted, a gong sounded, and listeners would hear the chief say: "Neighbors and friends hearing this broadcast will confer a great favor on the police department by notifying all police officers of this message . . ." Within a few moments, the streets near the various police headquarters were thronged with reporting officers and volunteer citizens.

During a dry run over the KGO microphone, Quinn called patrol cars by number and told them to report to 111 Sutter Street, the NBC studio. Microphones in front of the station picked up the sound of the cars arriving and each driver reporting his arrival. Then he had a better idea. "What if we had high-powered radio-equipped autos patrolling all districts 24 hours a day and available for every police department?" he thought. "What if we had a radio channel dedicated to police communication and installed receivers in police cars? Then dispatches about crimes in progress could be flashed to officers on patrol."

Quinn put Ralph Wiley, chief of the Department of Electricity, in charge of KGPD, a shortwave radio station. Communications were forwarded from the SFPD's private, low-frequency radio transmitter in the Jefferson Square Central Fire Alarm Station to twin Eiffel Towers to Quinn's new Automotive Radio Patrol Unit—a fleet of nineteen radio cars, four solo motorcycles, and detail cars equipped with earphones. While radio car officers still could not talk to the dispatcher, the radio allowed several cars to simultaneously converge on a crime scene. In extreme emergencies KGPD could be patched into KGO on the NBC radio network to alert citizens.

Day after day, the chief put his radio patrol cars and motorcycle officers through dry runs—how to surround a bank, wait for backup, and cut off all possible escape routes. Somehow he found funds for nine police operators to answer forty incoming phone lines. "If only we had money to hire extra men, money to finance prolonged manhunts across the continents and overseas," he said. "We are striving toward it, but it is uphill work. However, year by year, we secure more alert recruits; we train them longer and more thoroughly, and we can obtain more modern equipment, employ more modern methods. Then and only then we might make more progress against crime."[13]

LaTulipe walked the marble corridor to the big corner office and knocked decisively. An hour later he thanked Chief Quinn and returned to his office heartened by his words. By July 1950, the SFPD would have spent over $100,000 to make LaTulipe's lab the best in the state—a modern ballistics-comparison microscope, bell jars, meters, spectrographs, enlargers with bellows, and other machines for magnifying and evaluating evidence and catching criminals with invisible evidence.

At the new ID Bureau, LaTulipe's unidentified print from the Bay Hotel was compared to their foreign files (the FBI exchanged prints with sixty-eight countries) and was finally identified. It belonged to the missing Otto von Feldman, the former Bay Hotel porter, the one employee LaTulipe hadn't printed. With that avenue closed, LaTulipe now began looking for strangulation/dissection murders comparable to Bette Coffin's. Perhaps the Cleveland cases could teach him something about the kind of man who committed such brutal crimes and why he did what he did.

---

[13] On May 1, 1932, LAPD Chief Roy E. Steckel got his department its first FCC license.

TWENTY-NINE

Bloating and disfiguration of the skin begins in a "floaters" fingertips within a few hours, and covers the complete hand in about twenty-four hours.

—CRIME MANUAL OF THE PERIOD

IN Cleveland, along Praha Avenue and Bragg Street at the foot of solitary, steep-sided Jackass Hill, people passed briskly if not at a trot. On Sweeney and Francis streets and across the Kingsbury Run on Kinsman Road neighbors heard laughter on Saturday night, January 25, 1936. It was a mirthless chuckle at first but took on such a heartless tone that folks cowered in their homes and children hid under their beds. Cautiously, some drew back their curtains and peeked out. A stooped figure carrying a sack was trudging along the curved rails at the turn. His tracks filled with snow behind him. The bare limbs of ice-encased trees shown like glass in the moonlight as he lumbered toward a deserted factory at 2315 East Twentieth Street. The temperature dropped further and hardly a soul was out but one.

It was freezing Sunday morning and the temperatures in Cleveland the night before had plunged to near zero. The next night would be as cold. Raw winds whispered among the abandoned freight cars. Grass alongside the rails shivered with a brittle rattle. The howling of a dog rose to meet the frigid gale. Pedestrians near Charity Hospital turned up their coat collars against the piercing wind and rushed about their business. None of them paid much attention to Nick Albondante's howling dog, Lady.

Neighbors heard Lady's howl up and down the east side of Central

Avenue in the Third Ward, "The Roaring Third," a torrid region of speak-easies and houses of prostitution that Ed Andrassy once frequented. At 11:00 A.M. a black woman entered the White Front Meat Market at 2002 Central. "There seems to be some hams setting outside near your back door in a couple of baskets," she told the butcher. "You should bring them in."

"Sure," Charles Page said, laying down his cleaver.

Lady continued baying, her breath a frosty cloud, tiny sickles dripping from her nose. Behind the brick plant, Waite's off duty cabs filled a bleak lot. Beyond, dense woods stretched to a double curve of railroad tracks and a line of corrugated metal sheds. In the distance, thirty feet in the air, an iron railway trestle spanned the tracks. Across it a train glided toward East Forty-ninth and the frozen knob of nearby Jackass Hill. A band of black children playing along the tracks heard Lady and ran up the snowy slope to see her scratching at two wicker baskets. At 11:20 A.M. Page stepped from his rear door.

A minute later Sergeant McBride got Page's call. "My God, there's another body without a head," he cried. "It's in two half-bushel baskets behind the Hart factory. And it's worse, much worse than those others."

He had instantly made the connection between the butcher murders and a body dumped near the tracks of the run. Orley May, and Lieutenant Harvey Weitzel started for the plant, but Sergeant Hogan, head of homicide since November, got there first. At 11:25 A.M., his howling siren died away in front of Crescent Manufacturing. Chief Matowitz's patrol car, and cruisers D-2 and No. 3 converged right behind.

Within the baskets were two burlap sacks containing a blackish-streaked package that accommodated a solidly frozen right arm, right hand, two thighs, and half a woman's nude lower torso imbedded with coal dust. "O.K., begin the search for the missing legs and head because all we've got now is a bloody jigsaw puzzle," Matowitz said.

"The same thin curved knife was used," said Pearce. "The head was severed between the third and forth vertebrae in the same professional manner."

But were the incisions truly professional? Even the great London forensic expert Lord Spilsbury had erred in judging a similar dismemberment. At Charing Cross Station someone had checked a round-topped, wickerwork trunk. Inside was a stout female body divided into large pieces at each shoulder and hip joint. The constable who found the body took his job seriously; he refused to allow the remains to be removed until a surgeon certified she was dead. "Clean dismemberment of parts suggests an experienced slaughter man," Spilsbury wrote but, after finding hesitation cuts, corrected his assessment. "Two tentative cuts, one opening the peritoneum and the second at the back of the right knee, should have told me the operator was unskilled."

Cuyahoga County Coroner Sam Gerber concluded their impossibly strong, right-handed killer had been in a state of fury. After breaking the skin, he wrenched her arm from its shoulder socket, roughly disarticulated her knee joints, and fractured the midportion of her lower legs.

Fingerprints on the severed right hand matched those of an Ashtabula, Ohio, native, Mrs. Florence Sawdey Polillo (aka Florence Martin, Flo Ghent, Florence Ballagher, Flo Davis, and Clara Dunn). Her file listed arrests for vagrancy, disorderly conduct, and prostitution. The stocky forty-two-year-old, who had dyed chestnut hair and brown eyes, was currently on relief and resided somewhere in the slums. Heavy snowflakes were flattening on stoops by the time Nevel and Hogan located her rooming house at 3205 Carnegie Avenue. Mrs. Ford, a red-haired and fiery tempered landlady, answered Nevel's knock.

"What do you want?" she snapped.

"Take it easy! This isn't an arrest," said Nevel. "We want some information about Sawdey Polillo. She had a room here."

"She owes me a month's rent and she run out on me a week ago. Maybe if you find her, you'll get my dollar and a half back."

"You're never going to lay eyes on that dollar and a half. Mrs. Polillo is dead. We found her torso in some old baskets this morning. Did anyone come to see her recently?"

"Well, sure, lots of men came to see her, but not during the last week. She had a few boyfriends—Martin a tall, blond truck driver with the Cleveland Transfer, a lover named Eddie and a Great Lakes sailor named Harry."

Until four weeks earlier a peddler lived with her until he threatened to "cut her all up." Mrs. Ford last saw Flo on Friday at 8:30 P.M. "Sawdey was a heavy drinker and argued a lot when she was drunk," she said. "Her only bad habit was that she would occasionally get a quart of liquor and drink it all by her lonesome in her room. When she was drinking she was pecky—quarrelsome. But Saturdays she usually stayed home and ironed."

Upstairs in a tidy furnished room Nevel and Hogan found a dozen smiling dolls arranged on the davenport, bed, and chairs. Each had her own name neatly printed on a card. Hogan fingerprinted the clock, kitchenette stove, even the grinning dolls.

On Tuesday, Flo's ex-husband, Andrew Polillo, a mail clerk, drove in from Buffalo to identify the torso. He hadn't seen her since she walked out on him six years earlier, but he knew about an old abdominal scar from the removal of a tumor "It's her," he said.

At 5:45 P.M., February 7, a Bennett Trucking Company employee passed behind a vacant house at 1419 Orange Avenue SE and stumbled over a heap in a slight depression strewn with chicken feathers, coal dust, hay, and charcoal. Beneath were Mrs. Polillo's lower legs and left arm frozen to the ground. Police never found her missing head. Chief Matowitz said, "There is nothing for us to do but wait. Some day he will make some little slip."

His worst fear was that the butcher had chosen his victims indiscriminately. But the seemingly random victims *were* linked—Matowitz just didn't know it yet.

THIRTY

In America, as in Europe, sex crime became increasingly frequent after the end of the First World War. The American police . . . found it difficult to deal with. Sex crime often appears to be motiveless.

—CRIMES AND PUNISHMENT

ONE Friday neighbors saw Fell looking refreshed and strumming his mandolin on the lawn. Wherever he had been, he had taken along his multiple personalities like well-worn luggage and probably opened each at least once. He stretched in the vaporous evening and began his exercises: a series of jumping jacks, thrusts, and deep knee bends. Yet, Fell still could not bring himself to sleep inside the house. All would be remedied if he could convince someone to move in with him. He asked his co-workers at the San Mateo gas station, but no one was interested. This stung the likable Fell because it indicated a lessening of his powers of persuasion and charm. It was for the best. He feared what he might say in his sleep that someone might overhear. It was an impossible situation—alone he couldn't sleep and with someone he dared not sleep.

Fell, under the nickname "Bromo," was now a full-time student at San Mateo Junior College. First he charmed Dean Taggert of the University of San Mateo to enroll him "in order to complete a geology course to be financed by an oil executive." The boisterous freshman was so popular, students nominated him as a candidate for class president (he would be defeated by a female student). "At one of our highjinks," said a classmate later, "everyone wanted Bromo to enter a hog-calling contest because he was so brilliant at it."

The handsome weightlifter, now twenty-seven years old, was truly not himself these days. A year ago he'd been smitten with Wilma Heaton, a pert girl at Vallecita Place in Berkeley. Wilma's mother recalled that her daughter met Fell while he was working in a Richmond auto plant. "He impressed me as quite gentlemanly," she said, "but he seemed a little too mysterious."

On Valentine's Day, Fell appeared at the Alameda County Hospital where Wilma was a waitress. "I have an appointment to meet with Ben after work," she told him, "and I can't keep our engagement this evening."

"Who's Ben?" Fell ran to his car and returned with a gun under his coat. One moment he was threatening Wilma; the next moment he was begging for forgiveness. "I wouldn't hurt you, Wilma" he cried. "I couldn't bear the opportunity of hurting anyone or anything. I'd like to hunt you with a camera, not a gun." To prove this he dashed outside again and stowed the pistol away. He returned with pictures of a yacht floating before an island. "I promise you," he said, "we'll go on a tropical cruise."

Another lie. For weeks Fell had been attempting to trade the Woodside bungalow for a powerful cabin cruiser, though he knew conflicting claims on the property made such an exchange illegal.

When Oakland fireman Benjamin Larsen arrived for his date with Wilma, Fell shouted, "I'm going to kill you."

When Larsen phoned the police, Sergeant Herman Bernstein and Patrolman Vince Spooner responded. "That man has threatened to kill Miss Heaton whom he is waiting to see and who has spurned his attention," Larsen said. He pointed out Fell lurking at the entrance.

"He said he would kill me," Wilma said, "and then kill Ben if I didn't go out with him. I don't want to prosecute. I just want him out of here."

After a brief struggle, Bernstein and Spooner wrestled him into another room. While Spooner kept him covered, Bernstein searched Fell's car.

He popped open the glove compartment and discovered a .38-caliber revolver. Fell only grinned. He produced a badge, deputy's credentials, proof he was a night watchman, and a permit to carry the gun signed by San Mateo County Sheriff James J. McGrath, the fattest sheriff in these parts.

All the cops could do was escort him to the city limits and warn him not to return to Alameda County. Fell laughed as he sped away, but his ears were burning. He was not used to being rebuffed by any woman and it made him angrier than he could remember.

On February 17, he drove to the Redwood City public library. "I'm looking for this book on poisons," he told librarian Clara P. Dills, "*A Manual of Toxicology* by Albert Harrison Brundage."

"We'll have to request that particular book from the state library in Sacramento."

"Well, hurry! I've got to have that book before March 15."

"I'll see what I can do to expedite it." Dills put a rush tag on it.

Fell had urgent use for that book, but for whom? Did he intend to poison Wilma Heaton who had spurned him? Or was it for someone he had yet to meet?

Ten days later Fell took one of his frequent nighttime rides at a point above El Camino Real near San Jose. As he turned round a wide bend his lights framed a lovely young woman down on her knees. Her travel-worn suitcase had burst and scattered her belongings. She stood as he pulled over, shielded her eyes and studied the handsome man in the headlights. He was tall and perfectly made. She was twenty-five years old (though she looked nineteen), petite (about 112 pounds), with mousy dark brown hair, high cheekbones, long eyelashes, big eyes, and a ready smile with a little too much lipstick. She wore blue denim, bell-bottom hiking pants instead of a skirt. The bicycling craze two years earlier had given California girls an excuse to wear trousers like Marlene Dietrich's. She had rolled her white cotton socks over the tops of black dancing shoes, and Fell could hear their taps click on the pavement. Across her scoop-neck sweater she had a picture of the Bambino, "the Sultan of Swat," slamming a ball out of the park. George Herman Ruth had hit 714 homers in his twenty-two professional seasons. In 1930 and 1931, when everyone else was out of work, "The Babe" was making $85,000 a season. Fell loved the Babe, even though he had been in a slow decline since 1927. "Roots still in there," Ruth once said on live radio. "He breezes the first two pitches by—both strikes. The mob's tearing down Wrigley Field. I shake my fist after that first strike. After the second I point my bat at those bellerin' bleachers—right where I aim to park the ball. I hit that fuckin' ball on the nose—right over the fuckin' fence for two fuckin' runs."

"That's odd apparel for thumbing a ride," Fell said. "More like a stage costume."

"I wear this outfit when I compete in walkathons," she said.

"I'm Jerry," he called as he flashed a fake card that said he was a deputy sheriff. That relaxed her.

"I'm Boots," she said, though she used different monikers during her wanderings: Dorothy Farnum, Dorothy Farmen, and Dorothy Wanworthy. Like Fell, her names were as interchangeable as hats. Boots's real name was Winifred Hemmer, though from age two to fourteen she had lived in a Grand Rapids, Michigan, orphanage as "Dorothy Hemmer." "I've three brothers and sisters, but I don't know where to find them," she told Fell. "I know nothing about any other members of my family, or if there are any at all."

"That's my story too. What's the rest of yours?"

For the previous two years, Boots had been hitchhiking around the country living in hobo jungles and riding the railroad brake beams from Michigan to Florida to California to Washington State and back down to California. She eked out a meager living as a walkathon champion and itinerant marathon dancer. In December, Boots had taken third prize at the North Bend, Oregon, walkathon and so had a little money. "I have to conserve it," she said, patting the cash in her breast pocket. Fell was intrigued. He had been scratching around for money like a chicken after feed and not only that she was cute. Boots, a stage performer of specialty songs and dances, was headed for San Francisco to enter a dance competition and talent show.

"Look," said Fell, "I can get you a new suitcase so you can make your trip in comfort. Hop in."

He had a nice smile so she got in. Boots was always able to find a man who could give her a room for the night or a bite to eat. "He seemed to feel sorry for me," Boots said, "and offered to give me a better suitcase for my things. I thought I was safe when he invited me there. Jerry was a bona fide cheerful friend." He cracked jokes as they drove to Woodside Glens. At the bungalow, he invited her inside to change clothes while he got down a replacement suitcase from the penthouse. Boots dragged the bag over to the hearth and in the flickering light read an engraved name: Ada French Rice. Now who was that? Jerry didn't say.

"Why don't you stay with me for awhile?" he asked. "I work nights. Why don't you get rested while I go back to work." Boots was agreeable. Fell left the Bungalow, but instead of going to work, he spent another uncomfortable night in the Burlington garage. The next morning, he returned to the bungalow. "I've got some time off," he told Boots. "Tonight I'll sleep here."

When he awoke, he asked, "Did I say anything in my sleep?"

"No, of course not. Why do you ask?"

"Oh, no reason. Are you sure you didn't hear anything?" She shook her head. "Well, that's good."

"He treated me all right," Boots said, "and was very much a gentleman. I am sure he would never have harmed me. Why, there wasn't a thing improper in our relationship. I slept on the davenport near the fireplace. I wasn't afraid of Jerry, but I was afraid of his bedroom. There was a side door and I didn't know whether I could lock it. I was just a guest."

Mrs. Rice's money finally ran out. Fell, with the added expenses of attending college, travel, paying the bungalow mortgage, keeping up two cars and now feeding a guest, would have to resort to other means. That night he discussed his finances with Boots in front of the fire. The winds on the road above were howling and they both felt cozy. "Guess I could go to Hollywood and try out for the movies."

Fell had often fantasized about turning his movie star looks to advantage on the silver screen. Boots knew all about making movies. "With his looks, gee, who wouldn't hire him," she thought. "He is so athletic and strong, I just have to encourage him." "I could see you in Gower Gulch," she said aloud.

It wasn't really a gulch. The corner of Sunset and Gower in front of the Columbia Drugstore was where all the aspiring actors hung out waiting for a call from the single booth there. A cowboy actor had once been shot down there, "dry-gulched," and that's why folks called it a gulch. "With those arms you could play a gorilla," she said. A number of actors made excellent livings portraying apes in movies.[14] Emil Van Horn, who did the "gorilla stuff" for Republic Pictures, assumed the characteristics of an ape even off camera. George Barrows and Janos Prohaska portrayed gorillas too, but Charlie Gemora, "a little Filipino guy," did the best impersonation. Ray "Crash" Corrigan was the most successful.

At six feet, eight inches, the handsome lead of Republic's serial *Undersea Kingdom,* not only had the athleticism for the role but a hand-sewn horsehair costume. His head-to-foot suit (bushy padded shoulders, coarse matted fur, and a headpiece with functioning oversize teeth) had cost him $5,000 to make. But it was so heavy that every time Corrigan took a few swipes with his paw he'd have to sit down, remove the articulated gorilla head, and catch his breath. "How much does that thing weigh?" asked Buster Crabbe.

"About a hundred pounds too much," Corrigan gasped. "I didn't ventilate it properly. It's hotter than hell in this get-up."

He kept passing out under the hot lights. Finally director Fred Stephani, incensed at the constant delays, walked over, stared down at the unconscious Corrigan and snapped, "Why the hell couldn't we have hired a real gorilla?"

When stuntman Steve Calvert drove to Corriganville Ranch he got a crash course in the psychology, mannerisms, and walk of the great ape. "Human posture ruins the animalistic effect," Corrigan told him. "To be a Gorilla Man you have to reverse your human instincts and thought patterns. You don't walk around, you lumber. You act ferocious—not because you're antagonistic, but to scare the humans away." "I actually became a gorilla," Calvert said later. "Not too many people can say that. I guess it was just in me." But Calvert could only exhibit his animal nature while wearing the headpiece. "If I tried it barefaced, I'd just freeze up."

Boots was convinced Fell would be able to submerge himself completely

---

[14] Gargantua, the Ringling Brothers star ape and the 1933 film *King Kong* had excited Hollywood about gorillas. Both Republic and Columbia Pictures started off their movie serial production schedules with jungle films featuring gorillas and starred famed wild animal trainers Clyde Beatty and Frank Buck.

in the personality of an ape. He slept well that night, dreaming of stardom and content because he had a companion at last. He didn't say a word in his sleep.

On leap year day, February 29, time and circumstances finally caught up with Slipton Fell. It was the same day visiting playwright George Bernard Shaw leaned at the rail of the British liner *Arandora Star* and made disparaging remarks about the unfinished bridges in the Bay. "Those beastly red poles with ropes strung between them," he snorted. And San Francisco? "It is frightfully one-horse, I should say, but no worse than the rest of your country."

Leap year day was the same day eighteen-year-old Teresa Hawkins ended a week-long bout of intermittent laughter. Since taking a stressful shorthand test, she had alternated between spasms of laughter and semiconsciousness. And laughter filled the air in the secluded bungalow and echoed in the redwood canyons of Woodside Glens.

Leap year day was the same day Fell phoned the San Mateo police. "I want to report that the gas service station where I work has just been held up by three men," he said. He gave them the name "Jerome Braun von Selz" (there was identification in his possession also naming him both Heinrich Fritz von Braun Selz and Ralph Jerome von Selz). The responding officers got to the Woodside gas station and dutifully wrote down everything he said.

"I was held up by three men and robbed of $12," Fell said. Such a pitiful amount of money, yet he felt compelled to see it through. That money would get him to Hollywood.

"Can you describe any of the holdup men for us, Jerry?" asked Officer Tom Burke. "Let's see," he began, visualizing the first robber. "He is deeply tanned with ruddy cheeks. He's about my age . . . dark brown hair and slate-gray eyes and has big white teeth. He is big, six-feet tall, 220–230-pounds . . ."

Burke looked quizzically at the other officer. Fell's astonishing ego had just provided a flawless description of *himself*. Burke, now convinced the robbery was a hoax, arrested Fell for filing a false report. At the San Mateo station, he immediately confessed, offering to not only replace the stolen $12 but another $16 he had previously lifted from the till. The judge sentenced him to thirty days in the Redwood City Jail. During Fell's incarceration the oil company owners were perplexed. Though their employee was in jail, they continued to receive letters lauding his stellar performance at the gas station.

AT the HOJ in San Francisco, Inspector George O'Leary of the SFPD Auto Detail caught a routine case, read the file, then sat straight up. That Mrs. Ada Rice seemed to be missing did not interest him. It seemed not to interest anyone in her neighborhood. In Seattle, Charles F. Rice wasn't interested—he had gotten his divorce on February 1. She had no other relatives that O'Leary could find, and her children were back East. What got O'Leary's heart pumping was that Ada's car had been reported stolen—ahh, that was his meat! Let's see—the money had been paid out to an individual with the dubious name of Slipton J. Fell. Slipped and Fell.

Someone with the same name had just been arrested in San Mateo for staging a hoax holdup. O'Leary walked the file over to his partner, M. L. "Jimmy" Britt, special agent for the National Auto Theft Bureau. Britt, in his polka-dot tie and three-piece gray suit, was the epitome of an insurance salesman. But the investigators were good at what they did. Six years earlier they had swiftly tracked down the owner of the light blue Dodge driven by the Whispering Gunman. They decided to forgo lunch and drive out to the Redwood City Jail, meet the young man, and dig a little deeper into this coincidence.

THIRTY-ONE

Knives are not commonly carried in this country except by seamen. The knife is at least a cleaner weapon than the poker or piece of lead piping favored by young men who set out to murder old women.

—LORD SPILSBURY, WHOSE VOLUMINOUS FILES SHOWED WHOLE YEARS WITHOUT A SINGLE MURDER BY KNIFE

DEPUTY Sheriff Thomas F. Maloney of the San Mateo Jail was fascinated by what his jailers told him. "Jerry laughs aloud in his sleep," they said, referring to Fell, whom they knew as Jerry.

"He what? You're kidding."

"Seriously. Not only that, Jerry sobs in his sleep. Sometimes he cries out."

Maloney was further intrigued when he learned that Fell had been living by himself at Mrs. Rice's house. Then where was Ada? At 12:30 P.M. O'Leary and Britt got to the jail. Maloney, still curious about the striking young man, asked to sit in on their interview. Britt said, "Sure." Big, beefy Maloney, broad shouldered and double chinned in a dark suit and argyle tie, was hard to ignore, but once he pulled his hat brim down, stuffed his hands into his pockets, and leaned into a corner everyone forgot he was there.

"Is this about the robbery?" Fell asked, looking from Britt to O'Leary in his friendly, inquiring, doglike way.

"No, Jerry, this is something else entirely," began Jimmy Britt. The slender man was about half the size of Fell. Like the deputies, Britt took to him right away. "We see here that you reported an auto stolen [in December]. A finance company held title to the car."

"That's correct, Jimmy." Fell always spoke in a positive manner followed by a big smile and a slicking back of his hair with his fingers.

"And that insurance was paid to you," said Britt.

"Yes, Jimmy. I received $18 for my equity and it sure came in handy."

Throughout the full two and a half hours of questioning, Fell cracked jokes. "He's as good as radio," admitted O'Leary. But really all they got in answer to their questions was laughter. Finally, they went outside. Britt had an idea. He would offer Fell a promise of no prosecution if he led them to the missing car. Fell thought about the offer, and late in the afternoon he led Britt, Maloney, and O'Leary to the private Burlingame garage. Inside was Mrs. Rice's missing car and a second vehicle, both affixed with stolen license plates. As Maloney stood in the dark garage, he felt a stab of fear. For the first time he was concerned for Ada's safety. He poked around in the backseat and realized that Fell had been sleeping in her auto for some time.

"Jerry, why can't you sleep at the house alone?" Maloney asked. "What's in Ada's house that frightens you so?" No answer. "Why do you cry out in your sleep in jail? Is it because there's something on your mind?"

"What? Why do you ask that?" said Fell. "Do I do that?" He looked mystified, then lowered his chin to his chest. "What did I say. Did I say anything last night?" He composed himself, and his megawatt smile clicked on again.

"And what's all this stuff, Jerry?" asked O'Leary, who had opened the trunk. Maloney and Britt went around to the rear where they saw a box hidden under a tan blanket. Inside were rolls of adhesive tape, three bottles of ammonia and chloroform, cotton, and a long rope with loops at both ends tied with sailor's knots.

"God, I forgot about that," Fell said. He fingered the rope as if it brought back memories. "Let me explain. I've been keeping those things in the car for safety. There're for a couple of fellows who have done me injury and I'm out looking for them at night. It's quite a story and will take a while to tell."

"We've got the time," said Maloney, who sat down on the running board and crossed his legs.

"Well, I've been driving around looking for a couple of fellows who had done me harm—two former prisoners, 'Boston' and 'Jiggs,' I met in 1931 at the Alcatraz Island disciplinary barracks. After they got out, they kept after me and tried to involve me in a 'hot car' racket. They persisted in trying to use my garage as a place to bring their stolen cars. I couldn't break away from them, so I planned first to knock them out with ammonia, tie them up and turn them over to police. Then I got a better idea. I thought I'd study this book on toxicology, which I asked for at the library, and find some poison which would just stun them so I could turn them over to the authorities."

Maloney got up, squeezed into the car, and rooted in the backseat. Under the seat he found Mrs. Rice's passport (she had been Mrs. Ada French when it was issued, but the picture was undoubtedly of her). If Mrs. Rice were traveling overseas what was her passport doing here? How had she left the country? "When did you last see Mrs. Rice?" asked Maloney. His eyes narrowed.

"I drove her to the San Francisco financial district with a Bulgarian army officer, Tom. I was just helping in an elopement."

They returned the prisoner to his cell. By then Fell's mood had brightened again. "So long, Tom. So long, Jimmy. So long, George," he called after them. Solemnly, they made the journey to the square house on the knoll, each man lost in his own thoughts and worrying what they would find. The sun was going down by the time they reached the Canada Road.

Inside the bungalow they rummaged through the ground floor. In a small low closet Maloney ferreted out Ada's canceled checks, thumbed them, then showed O'Leary. "Look at this," he said. "All of the checks were written and dated after Ada had 'gone traveling.'"

This was not a good sign. Neither could they unearth the mine stock Fell claimed to have given Ada in exchange for the house or the deeds to her other property at El Cerrito, Muir Woods Park in Marin County, and Cardiff by the Sea in LA County.

The next day Maloney drove to Ada's bank in Palo Alto to examine a letter supposedly written by Mrs. Rice from Coxsackie, New York, that requested $135 be transferred from her savings account to her checking account. He noticed something the bankers hadn't. The postmark showed the letter had actually been mailed from Redwood City. Next Maloney questioned Ada's neighbors to find out more about the handsome young Bulgarian cavalry officer who Fell claimed had "gone away" with her. "Oh, Mrs. Rice went away to the Balkans as a foreign correspondent," they all said.

"And how do you know all this?"

"Why, that nice young man who lives in her house told us," they said.

Next Sheriff James McGrath, an enormously fat man, visited Ada's bungalow. He surveyed the earth surrounding it. It was nearly all rock and thick clay. No bodies were buried here. If there had been, county workmen digging in the yard all this week would have discovered them. Signs of their activity were everywhere except around Ada's rock garden, which was over-grown with thistles and weeds. Undaunted, McGrath began pulling aside the rocks. He had solved a similar missing person's case back in May 1930 when Frank Roderick, a LaHonda rancher, vanished. McGrath had trapped William Woodring, the ranch handyman, and Mrs. Minnie Roderick into confessing they were lovers. They led McGrath to a deep well where they had buried Roderick's body.

When McGrath located Fell's worthless Sierra mine stock, it suggested a possible resting place for Mrs. Rice's body. What if Ada were buried in one of the Placer mine claims in the Downieville region mentioned in the stock? McGrath ordered a search of the diggings and bottomless shafts there—an impossible task. Ada might never be found. The deed to her house was also missing.

Maloney was more practical. If they were going to find Ada and her Bulgarian friend, Fell was going to have to show them the way He suspected Ada had fallen for the handsome young man. "Fell's the type that motherly old ladies wring their hands over because he never had a mother to guide him," he told Britt. "He's the kind that sob sisters insist 'couldn't possibly have done a thing like that.'"

Britt had concluded early on that threats would never work on Fell. Maloney suggested a psychological approach to break through Fell's wall of mirth. "His actions are those of an overgrown kid," he told Britt. "He appears clever, cunning and cagey, but responds to flattery with an intensity

I've never seen before. I think we'll have to play to that if we're going to get anywhere. And most of all we've got to treat him as an equal, as a friend, and get him to help us."

The young man's hale-fellow-well-met personality concealed a reservoir of loneliness. Yes, they would win him over by becoming his friends. Like his jailers, they called him Jerry without fail. That night at the jail, Fell alternately laughed and sobbed in his sleep once more. Maloney stood by his cell and listened. Fell spoke a few words, but the lawman could not decipher them.

NEXT morning, as Bay Bridge workers erected the final steel trusses between the anchorage and Pier W-1, Britt and Maloney signed Fell out of jail. He traveled with them to Ada's bungalow in good spirits, pointing out wildlife from the window and laughing. It was a hot day, and they were all glad to get out of the heat. Inside the bungalow, they stopped dead. The ceiling was crawling with a black, buzzing tide that hadn't been there 48 hours earlier. "Blow flies," said Britt. Bluebottle and greenbottle flies lay their eggs in rotting meat. As carbohydrates and proteins break down, thousands of fly-blown maggot offspring are produced in a short time. Britt, the smallest, got a ladder and climbed above the rafters. Balancing on the top step, he pulled himself up into the narrow crawl space just above where the flies buzzed. The heat was terrific and it was hard to see between timbers and the cloud of flies. There was the sweet smell of rot. Finally, Britt gave up and climbed down. "Nothing is inside there—now," he said.

In the afternoon he and Maloney drove their prisoner along lengthy Skyline Boulevard, a f͟a͟v͟o͟r͟ite spot since Prohibition days[15] for gangsters to dump their victims. Back and forth like a shuttlecock they drove, while attempting to create the impression they were just old friends out for a drive. In a way they were. The mood was light, but Maloney scrutinized their prisoner, looking for any reaction as they passed likely burial sites. Huge

---

[15] Prohibition began on January 16, 1920, with the Eighteenth Amendment and later reinforcement of the Volstead Act. It was repealed in December 1933, and the country made legally wet again.

redwood canyons rolled away by the hundreds and dropped into bottom-less canyons. Shadows grew longer. Fog rolled in from the sea and covered over Skyline Boulevard until only twenty yards of the woods were visible from the road. At one spot Maloney noticed a shallow depression—black-ened and crawling with blowflies such as they'd observed on Ada Rice's ceiling. The flies gave Maloney an idea. "This looks like a grave," he said. "Back it up a bit, Jimmy." Maloney stuck his head out the window and studied the swarming spot. "Yes, sir-re-Bob! And wouldn't that canyon over there be a fine place to throw a body—nobody would ever find it. What do you think, Jerry?"

Fell said nothing.

The next day Fell called out to Maloney from his cell, "Say, Tom, do you believe in premonitions?"

"No, Jerry, I don't. Why?"

Fell laughed. "Well, yesterday up on Skyline, you made a couple of remarks that were just too close to suit me!"

"So," thought Maloney, "Mrs. Rice is buried somewhere along Skyline Boulevard. But it's a long, long road and those ravines are deeper than hell. He's going to have to show us and he's not going to do that."

"Do you think I'm screwy, Jimmy," called Fell to Britt. "What is the consensus of opinion on that?" He bared his strong white teeth, tossed his hair back, and told a joke he'd heard on the radio. Britt laughed and went over to the cell. "Jerry, you can tell me," he said, putting his hand on his shoulder. "Why can't you sleep at the house alone?" The little investigator felt fatherly toward the tortured young man. Some time ago his pretense of friendship had blossomed into honest affection for Fell.

When he showed Britt his letter from Sandino, the investigator replied, "Why that's just wonderful, Jerry." Maloney discovered that Fell was a tremendous eater with a terrific craving for two-inch-thick steaks and whole fried chickens. As part of his plan, he had the best restaurant in town send over chicken and steak dinners for him. "Don't put cuffs on him," he told the deputies when the trays of sizzling food arrived and were laid out on the bunk. He handed the cuff key over to his men. "Let him eat with free hands. Allow the man some dignity."

"I appreciate that," said Fell genuinely and dove in.

Maloney flattered him outrageously and Britt paid attention to every word Fell had to say. Both laughed at his every quip and in the late afternoons took him for pleasant automobile rides. In the evenings, they continued to feed him steaks and chickens. "I can see he's developing a liking for me," Maloney told Sheriff McGrath. "I want to take over the questioning alone." The sheriff agreed.

As Britt and Maloney ate with Fell, they spoke conspiratorially about what might have happened to the flighty Ada Rice and wondered aloud if they could help in any way. "Do you have any ideas, Jerry?" they asked.

"Gosh, fellas, I don't know, but I'll sure enough think about it."

"I wish you would, Jerry. It would sure enough help us out of this dilemma."

Maloney perceived that Fell was very receptive to suggestion. If he planted an idea as a seed in a garden, it might grow as the fruit of Fell's own fertile mind. Yes, Britt agreed, it was possible to direct the growth of an idea through the flow of their conversation. "We might get him to lead us to the body if he thinks he has a rational explanation for the murder," Maloney told Britt out of earshot. "Let's give him an out next. Let's plant the idea of accidental death in his mind. If he fears no punishment he might tell us where Ada Rice is or at least give us his version of how it happened." Britt agreed.

"We know there's a body up there, somewhere in the wilderness, Jerry," said Britt. "If it were your sister or mother, you'd want it brought in for a decent burial, wouldn't you? Think about that. How would you feel?" Fell who had laughed throughout the meeting, stopped now and surprisingly became angry for the first time. His fury shocked Britt.

"I'll be damned if I'll confess to something I didn't do!" Fell stood, swaying, and clinched his fists, then sat back down as the passion drained from his body. "No one knows what is in my mind."

"But you cry out in your sleep because there is something on your mind," said Maloney. "You know Mrs. Rice was killed." A pause, then Britt brought up the hypothetical accident. "Look, Jerry, maybe there was a fight over the deed to the house. Maybe Mrs. Rice fell and hit her head—perhaps there was an accident. I figure it this way—she tried to burn the deed to the property [since the investigators had been unable to find that document this was a distinct possibility], and there was a struggle and she was killed in that fight." Maloney and Britt had planted their seed and now waited for it to take root. Sure enough, a version of their scenario, only slightly skewed burst from Fell's lips as soon as he forgot its genesis.

"That was a hell of a fight, all right. I'll give you that," Fell said with a smile and a wink. "You should have seen it." His smooth, pink-and-white face beamed. "But give me time to think." Another fabulous lunch was brought in. "Let me think, let me think," he muttered and reached for the ketchup. "Let me think," he said as he dug into the steak and home fries.

All eyes were on him. "He not only responds to friendship and attention," Maloney thought, "but craves the spotlight. He's a one man vaudeville act. An audience makes him feel important. As long as he is in the spotlight, he is going to drag out his time on stage. There has to be a way to accelerate the process, but how?"

From their long conversations it occurred to Maloney that they might tap Fell's honest dread of the FBI. "He has the same fears as a kid. He's fearful of authority, especially the Secret Service. Not only that, he is intensely patriotic. Defrauding the government certainly would go against his grain."

Maloney called Captain Thomas Foster of the U.S. Secret Service in San Francisco and asked him to drive out to the Redwood City Jail. As soon as Foster arrived he began enumerating to Fell the serious penalties involved for misuse of the mails and defrauding a national bank by removing funds without permission. Foster reached into his briefcase, took out Photostatted copies of Ada Rice's forged checks and waved them under the prisoner's nose. This stopped Fell's laughter for the second extended time. His terror of federal charges so shook him that he agreed to tell his story or at least *a* story over supper. His first version made no mention of a murder or a body. It was a great story, a thrilling story, and one that brought a tear to the eye.

Nobody believed a word of it.

"Would you take a lie detector test?" asked Britt finally.

Fell studied the forgery evidence on the table and the grim expression on Captain Foster's face with more than a little consternation. He thought about his options, put down his knife and fork, wiped his lips, and twisted the cap on the ketchup. He replaced the bottle on the table, and said, "Sure, why not?" He gave them a blinding smile.

Britt was so pleased he briefed Dullea on the case. The captain of inspectors was always interested in the deaths of lonely, older women who had fallen under the spell of younger men and met fatal ends. Britt had no idea why, but suspected it had to do with some great failure on his part.

THIRTY-TWO

On Carlyle: He goes about with his Diogenes dark-lantern, professing to seek a man, but inwardly resolved to find a monkey.

—ROBERT LOWELL

ON Monday, March 9, by order of Sheriff McGrath, Fell was to endure a lie detector test in Berkeley across the Bay. By morning, the Bay Area was sweltering in a heat wave. By afternoon it was even hotter, especially for Frances Hall sweating inside a cab idling outside the Folsom Prison gates. Inside, George Hall, a condemned double murderer, was unwrapping the two loaded pistols she had smuggled to him. Taking the warden's secretary as hostage, Hall cut across the prison yard and made a beeline for the outer gate where his wife was waiting. At the last minute, guards battered him into submission and arrested his wife. Now, Frances was in a cell, too, and it was still hot. By late afternoon, the day was torrid. By evening the heat was unbearable. Only a strong northeast wind kept the temperature from climbing any further.

As Maloney, Britt, and Fell reached the University of California the hot wind was so brisk that small craft warnings were posted. They parked at the Berkeley Police Station and, fighting the gale, entered and were escorted to a small room. "Well, here's the queer machine," said Fell. He felt relaxed among Maloney and Britt, his prized friends who clustered around him as if to cheer him on. "How'm I doing today?" he asked, eyeing the long tubing and dials. The "Enigma Man" stripped down to his sleeveless white undershirt and placed his right arm, elbow to wrist, flat on the table to his right. His muscles were impressive and shining with perspiration in the heat. Fell was confident in his ability to spin stories, but these police technicians had not only developed the polygraph at the Berkeley station but perfected it there.

Former Berkeley Police Department Chief August Vollmer, now a University of California professor, had made Berkeley's Scientific Police Department renown the world over through his scientific innovations. In 1923, Leonarde Keeler, a young Berkeley police recruit, devised a portable lie detector that registered stress in a person's breathing rate, pulse, and blood pressure and plotted each on a long paper trace.

Inspector Anthony Bledsoe, the examination monitor, watched as Inspector Ralph Pidgeon, the polygraph examiner, attached a pair of plates, the electrodermal response unit, to Fell's fingers and then clipped the electrodes of the galvanometer to the fingers of his left hand to measure skin resistance. Ten years earlier, Keeler added a device for registering skin resistance to electricity. Pores exude small quantities of sweat when a person lies and skin resistance drops. Pidgeon wrapped a black sphygmomanometer cuff around the prisoner's considerable right biceps to detect fluctuations in blood pressure. He inflated the blood pressure cuff with air sufficient to partially cut off circulation and make his arm numb. Next, with some difficulty, Pidgeon stretched a pneumographs strap around Fell's barrel chest to measure changes in the depth of breathing.

The room was comfortable, soundproof, and pleasantly lit. When Albert Riedel joined the Berkeley force six years earlier, he realized Keeler's machine was not foolproof. Noise, any distraction, and the environment of the test room affected the subject's reactions. Riedel limited questioning to blocks of three minutes interspersed by long breaks, then a repetition of the questions. As a subject tired, his adrenaline dropped, and he ceased reacting when being deceptive.

Pidgeon signaled he was ready to conduct the test. The chart was started. He placed a hand on Fell's shoulder as if to calm him and began by asking irrelevant questions to compare Fell's responses to later more important questions. He spoke softly. The upper lines on paper track showed Fell's breathing; the lower recorded his heart action. A needle with an ink reservoir registered Fell's heartbeats on a tape down to a fifth of second, the length of time between breaths. Another needle logged his changing blood pressure. At the beginning both horizontal lines traveled side by side uniformly in response to innocuous questions like "Do you smoke?" (question 4).

"Yes," said Fell, "roll your own and spare your roll."

A 5¢ sack of tobacco made about thirty-three cigarettes. Fell wisecracked at every turn. Pidgeon had to reign him in constantly. Bledsoe knew there were ways to outwit the machine—aspirins swallowed with Coca-Cola, iron self-control, drugs, alcohol, hunger, and pain (a tack in the shoe). One other flaw. A madman might pass the test.

Question 5: A direct question about Mrs. Rice's death—"Did you shoot her?"

The broad grin left Fell's face for the first time. "No." The machine registered a sudden surge of blood pressure, and there was a visible flinch of his muscles. Fell saw the chicken scratches become a seismographic explosion. "I'm in for it, aren't I?" he whispered to Britt. Embarrassed, Britt studied his shoes.

Question 6: "Did you kill Ada Rice? You did kill her didn't you?"

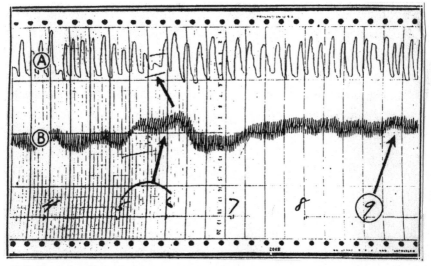

Fell's Berkeley PD lie detector results revealing his crucial deception, question no. 9.

Fell's breath line receded until it hardly registered, but his blood pressure shot up. His heart registered trip-hammer activity, the biggest spike in the test.

"Maybe she needed it!" said Fell. The needle leaped. For a moment it looked as if he would tear off the cuff, but Britt put a calming hand on his shoulder. "There, there, pal."

Question 9: "Did you destroy the body with acids or alkaloids?"

Silence. Fell's blood pressure bolted again.

Afterward they went over the test with Fell. They held the long paper track so he could see where he had failed. His face retained a trace of a smile until he saw the twin peaks of questions 5 and 6 and the huge rounded mound of question 9. Pidgeon circled the spike with his pen. "You have guilty knowledge," he said. "There's no doubt about it."

Unstrapped from the machine, Fell put on his shirt, plunged his hands into his blue zipper jacket, then said he might begin a confession. "But not now. I may talk later." Most of all it unnerved Fell that Maloney repeatedly asked about the murder of Bette Coffin and if Fell had lived near the Bay Hotel.

"Why don't you give McGrath a break?" said Britt as they got back in the car. "We know there is a body up there, somewhere." Britt was sweating and loosened his tie.

Fell thought a moment and replied, "You've been swell to me, guys, Jimmy, Tom. I'll tell it all when we get back."

Britt decided not to hurry him. "Let's go get something to eat," he suggested. "Sure, why not."

So instead of returning him to the Redwood City Jail, Britt and Maloney took Fell to the most popular restaurant in Berkeley. He smiled when they arrived, even executed a snappy tap dance for them on the gravel of the parking lot—"Me and my baby . . ." Fell's lighthearted mood vanished when he spied a hoard of East Bay reporters converging on them. Outpacing the mob, they dashed inside. When an attractive waitress came over, Fell began kidding her. She found it impossible to believe such a "personable young man" could be in police custody. She delivered their order of T-bones and fries, steaming coffee, rolls, and pie, then, seeing the reporters outside, asked Fell to autograph her starched white collar. He scrawled his initials there. "Boy—won't she get a jolt when she finds out who I really am!" Fell said.

After dinner, they drove to Ada's El Cerrito home (two carloads of reporters still behind) and made a fruitless search for her corpse in Fell's presence. Next they got to the Rice house in Woodside Glens to find the stout Sheriff McGrath and two other men outside. The rocky area around the knoll had been completely dug up. Everyone climbed the steps and went up to the door. Dorothy Farnum answered the door in her blue jeans trousers, gray sweater shirt, and brightly colored suspenders. Her tap shoes gleamed in the light from the porch.

Once inside, they allowed Fell to bathe, shave, and don fresh clothes—gray trousers with a neat crease, a light gray V-neck sweater, black Oxfords with no socks, an Ascot scarf, and a blue zipper jacket. He combed his thick dark hair back until it was smooth as a phonograph record. He was happy to be spending some time with his "friends." This respite allowed him time to consider what he was going to say. The police were thinking, too. Disturbing new information that threatened any conviction had come to light. Two of Ada's neighbors were positive they had seen her alive and well months after she vanished.

"I am positive I saw Mrs. Rice one day last August," Mrs. Ted Rawlings said. "I remember wondering why she had returned, for we hadn't seen her since June 13. It was in the daytime and she passed within a few feet of me, driving her car toward her home. I couldn't be mistaken."

Mrs. Fred Walther also told Britt she had seen Ada in a Woodside Glens election booth during the August elections. "We had talked together about the elections," Mrs. Walther said, "and as I was leaving one election booth I saw her entering the next booth and said hello to her."

It was dark out now. There was no fog and wouldn't be until the heat wave ended. Fell came out and helped the officers down into the basement where it was cooler. "Perhaps you will find something there," he said and indicated a corner of the basement where gophers had pushed up the earth. "Why don't you look there?"

Britt saw a red spot on a windowsill. "Is that blood, Jerry?" he said.

"No, it looks more like catsup to me," Fell said. They went back upstairs and DA Gilbert D. Ferrell, the stout Sheriff McGrath, court reporter William Girvin (ready to take notes in shorthand), Maloney, Britt, and Fell took their seats at the big round table. Boots brought them cold drinks and then was ordered into a back room to wait.

Fell stood by his claim that Ada Rice had gone away with an army officer to marry and was on her honeymoon this moment. At first McGrath asked his questions in a serious vein, but this elicited only silence. From then on, by prearrangement, no one spoke of a confession, only traded stories informally as if they had been buddies gathered together to play cards. Of them all Fell was having the best time.

But after a bit, the officers fell silent, tilted back their heads and stared fixedly at the chandelier around which blowflies chased each other. The only sound for minutes at a time was their droning. Odd, Britt thought, blowflies aren't usually active at night. Hypnotized, Fell watched their metallic bodies shimmer green and blue in the light. Then the five men lowered their eyes and began telling jokes and drinking again.

"How do you get the rooster to stop crowing on Sunday? Eat him on Saturday."

With knowing winks, Fell nudged the policemen as they attempted to kid him into a confession of one murder and maybe four or five others. He was a big kid trying to please. "Draw one down for Gracie Neff," toasted Fell. "She never screams; her mother's deaf." Nervous laughter. The drink washed over Fell, made him feel warm and confident he could bluff this out. "Drink one down for my old frail, she told her pa, now I'm in jail."

The detectives, who knew they sat in a house of death, became silent again. The psychological war between the detectives and their suspect continued.

"You know," said McGrath, "funny thing about those blowflies." He laced his fingers over his ample belly, lifted his chins, and peered upward. The flies continued to circle and lose themselves in the dark corners of the bungalow. "Now I wonder what they are doing. I wonder . . ." he tilted his head farther back. Everyone followed suit. More minutes of silence elapsed as everyone studied the flies. Round and round.

Now the cops began to speak again, not of a confession, but about prime bangtail. Fell was having a fine time. Because most cops on the SFPD were Irish, he told his Irish jokes. "What's an Irish beauty?" he asked and answered, "A woman with two black eyes." "What's Irish confetti?" he asked and answered, "Bricks."

Drinks went round and everyone drank until McGrath and his men put down their glasses, fell silent, and studied the circling flies again. Transfixed, Fell followed their gaze. "Now I wonder about those flies," said the sheriff. "I wonder what they're doing."

"Stop it! Stop looking at those damned flies," Fell cried. "Stop talking about them." He pointed his finger at the light, then darted it from man to man accusingly. "Stop looking at them! Stop looking at me that way . . . let me think . . . let me think." He folded his arms like a child.

After more chatter and another silent treatment, Fell put his head between his hands. The only sound was the monotonous buzzing of flies.

"Well, Jerry," said the sheriff with his biggest smile, "aren't you going to tell us what you did with the body."

"No, I'm not and you're never going to find it! You'll never find it, because I won't tell you where it is." He thought about what he had said, then laughed at himself and looked a little sheepish. His friends seemed disappointed in him.

Close to midnight, Fell stood solemnly. "All right, fellows," he said calmly as all his breath ran out, "if you want it, I'll give it to you."

Girven reopened his pad, licked the tip of his pencil, and poised to take shorthand. McGrath lit a cigarette and took a puff. Britt looked the saddest Maloney had ever seen him. "You were right," Fell said haltingly. He put both hands on the table palms down and sat down. His eyes were wet. "Yes, I killed her—but you'll never find the body. I have taken good care of that. I killed her with a poker, but her death was an accident. I returned to the darkened house on the night of last June 13—a night I will never forget. Ada had told me I could come up that night and leave some things. She was getting ready to leave almost any day. When I drove up in front of the cottage there wasn't a light about the place. That struck me as funny." He chuckled throughout at himself and at the oddness of the events that had brought him to the remote bungalow with his friends.

"As I walked into the living room I had a 'sixth sense' feeling that somebody else was in there, although I couldn't have seen my hand in front of my face. I sensed the presence of two persons in the room. I still couldn't see. Then somebody sloughed me. It felt as if somebody had crowned me with a sandbag. I was dazed, but went down fighting. I fell to the floor and I guess I must have fallen in front of the fireplace. I felt my hand close over the poker. I don't know how it got in my hand. Anyway I grabbed the poker, and came up fighting. Again I sensed—still I couldn't see—that someone was standing in front of me. I couldn't see a thing but I began swinging thinking I was hitting at a man. I lashed out with the poker and it hit something. I struck again quickly and I hit again! I heard a body thud to the floor. Then I heard someone burst through the French doors there in the back." Fell pointed toward the room where Boots was sequestered out of earshot.

"I heard him run out and away. There was enough moonlight outside for me to see. I saw a husky man as big as myself running away with a saber in his hand and slashing at the darkness behind him. I was still a little punch drunk from the blow I had received and it took me a minute or two to pull myself together. Finally I turned on the lights and saw Mrs. Rice lying on the floor, clad only in a pair of step-ins. She was almost naked. Blood was running from her nose and ears. Her head had been bashed in with a heavy fireplace poker. I had killed Mrs. Rice."

Fell explained how he wrapped the body in a quilt and sat down to think things out. "It looked bad," he told Britt and the others, "although my conscience was clear. How could I explain how I came to kill a woman in her own home? Would anybody believe the truth?" He feared the authorities would discover he'd served time in the Alcatraz disciplinary barracks in 1931 and hold that against him. "Well, I figured it all out and decided the only thing to do now was to hide that body where no one would ever find it."

He felt confident people knew Mrs. Rice had planned to take a trip and lease the cabin to him while he went to college. Later he could say he received a report that she'd died abroad and in that way explain everything.

"I carried her body out, loaded it in the back seat of my sedan and drove down the Skyline Boulevard. I knew the country pretty well and I knew a good spot to hide it." He paused and looked each of them in the eye.

"Say, if you want a sensation, fellas, try hauling a corpse around the country at night and have the owls hooting overhead. Whoo-ooo! Whoo-OO-OOO! Hooooot! I can still hear those owls laughing at me. Say, I haven't had any breakfast yet. You guys got any gum?" Britt shook his head. It was silent except for the buzzing flies until Fell continued.

"I turned off at the Saratoga Gap and onto a side road, turned four miles on the road to Big Basin. I lugged the body away from the car a piece and rolled it down the hill into a canyon, then drove back to the cottage and went to sleep." All the next day he thought about his problem and finally decided to fix the body so that nobody would ever find it. "I left her nude body under the trees for two nights. The next night I went into Palo Alto and stole two bags of lime from a warehouse and went back on a motorcycle bringing along a shovel." When he found the body just as he left it, he dug a little foxhole through the grass about three feet deep and broke the shovel handle in the process. He couldn't make the grave deep enough, so Fell buried her in jackknife fashion, with her head down and hands behind her back. "I loaded the grave with lime and put the lady in it. Then I poured the rest of the lime over her and covered that with dirt. Then I kicked the rest of the lime around so it wouldn't be noticed and left."

That seemed to be the story. The sheriff got up and went back to talk with Boots, a woman he considered a "tough proposition, one of the toughest" he'd ever stumbled across.

"It's nobody's business I lived with him," Boots told him. "It is strictly my own and nothing to be ashamed of and nothing to discuss. He treated me all right and was very much the gentleman. Why, there wasn't a thing improper in our relationship."

"Did you know he was a confessed murderer?"

Her eyes grew large; the slender girl flushed. "Goodness, no." She paused. "He isn't. Aw, you're kidding me, aren't you? T'aint so! Why, it can't be so. Why . . . why. . . I refuse to believe it. I don't believe it!" She shook her head violently. "Anyway, I don't know anything about it. I thought I was safe when Jerry invited me to stay." She ran her hand through mousy hair. "Is it so? That nice fellow?"

"It's so. He said he's going to lead us to the spot where Mrs. Rice is buried."

The petite woman's eyes grew wider. "I am sure he never would have harmed me. My suitcase fell apart," she said, "and he gave me another. The writing on it said, 'Ada French Rice.'" The attractive girl rambled on. After a minute or so she said, "I'm going to have to start keeping a diary. That's the one thing I haven't got even if I have been traveling for two years."

"Do you love him?"

"Shucks, no—I don't hardly know the fellow. I didn't even learn his real name. I just called him Jerry."

"Have you ever been in trouble before?"

"I'm not in trouble now am I?"

"Have you ever been in jail before?"

"No."

"Well you are now, as a material witness."

She shrugged. "You've got to learn to take it on the chin," she said. "I'm used to that. There are good and bad people all over the country. That I lived with Jerry is strictly my business and nothing to be ashamed of or nothing to discuss. As far as I can tell it's simply something that's causing a great deal of fuss for no apparent reason. It's just a lark. But I tell you I yearn for the road right now. I just know I'm going to miss the Dallas walk-athon."

Fell entered and smiled at Boots. "All right, Sheriff. Come ahead. I'll show you where it is." He led the way to the sheriff's auto. McGrath, Maloney, and Britt followed. "Well, Jimmy," Fell said to Britt, "Win, lose or draw, we'll still be friends. I'm going to Hollywood when I get through here." He sat next to McGrath and Britt took the wheel.

Following Fell's directions, they drove down Skyline Boulevard under a high moon. Every tree was tinged with silver. Four miles south of Saratoga Gap close to the Santa Cruz County line at the junction of Skyline Boulevard and Boulder Creek Road was a desolate area. As they drove, they could hear the rush of the nearby San Lorenzo River. Finally, about eleven miles northeast of Saratoga, Fell asked Britt to turn off the main highway onto a lonely side road. Two hundred feet along the narrow twisting path and about fifty feet from the highway, he raised his hand and signaled. "Stop here," he said. "In there."

All four stepped into a region of wild mountains and dense growth. Fell led the group a hundred yards off the road to the rim of an embankment, then halted. His bravado had faded. He would go to the edge but no farther and tottered there as if held by an invisible hand. "The body is down there," he said in a choked voice. Fell took the sheriff's flashlight and shone it below. With the light he directed Britt and Maloney as they descended the steep incline. The beam crawled over the ragged surface until it settled on the bank of a little ravine.

Fell remained above with McGrath, who was too fat to make the descent. "No, not there, Tom" Fell said, pointing with the light. "Four feet over." He was shaking now in the heat and the light darted nervously. "A little more to the right. Over there. Hold it. There!" The beam circled on a white pile of powder by a slight depression. "There she is, right there. . . . I don't want to see the body. I know everything's just as I left it because I dropped out this way about three weeks ago and found everything O.K. But when you come out to get her you'd better bring better equipment than I did." His booming laugh echoed through the canyons. "That acid has had plenty of time to work. I had to bend her like a jackknife to make her fit."

Britt confirmed that the scattered powder was caustic quicklime, the residue of two bags. "Well, he didn't fool us," called the sheriff. "If the lime is there the body must be there. It can wait. This is all we need. We'll let the coroner take care of this. Come on back." Britt and Maloney clawed their way up the steep incline to the car.

"Thanks, Jerry," said McGrath. "You told the truth." He patted his shoulder. Fell was as embarrassed as a schoolboy.

"I don't know why I couldn't leave the road and approach the grave," Fell apologized. "I guess I was afraid I'd get my best suit soiled." He began a slow soft shoe dance on the gravel—dancing on the grave of his victim. "Oh, Jerry, Jerry," said Britt. Minutes later they all started back to the county jail.

"How many bodies have they found down there?" Fell asked as they drove.

"Two," Maloney lied.

"How do they look, pretty good?" Fell turned to the sheriff. "Say Jimmy, did you ever get the wire off the other fellow?"

McGrath stiffened, but said nothing. He only smiled, a faint crescent in the moonlight.

"No, we haven't found a body tied up in wire."

"Well, I might as well tell you about this one too."

It was now 3:45 A.M., Tuesday morning.

THIRTY-THREE

The temperature of the water and the fat of the body plus gases within will cause the corpse to surface, just as gas in a balloon gives it buoyancy.

—CRIME MANUAL OF THE PERIOD

OUTSIDE Woodside Glens the prowl car slowly returned from Ada Rice's lonely moonlit grave. As they snaked north of the Saratoga Gap, the detectives and their prisoner grew reflective, their faces silver in the light. The truncks of tall trees, exposed in their headlights, slid nakedly by the cruising car. Neither Fell nor the fat sheriff had made the steep descent to the burning grave, but the smell of the lime bed clung to them as surely as it clung to Britt and Maloney's clothes.

"What's this about?"

"Oh, the man with the saber who struck me and fled—I killed him too—with a blow from a revolver," said Slipton Fell blithely.

McGrath said nothing.

"I didn't learn until later who the man with the saber was, the man who slugged me and ran away. I learned that when he came to blackmail me, to bleed me under the threat that he would expose me. We fought with guns. I clubbed him to death with his."

Fell's smooth face broke into a fatuous grin. McGrath looked glum.

"You see," Fell continued, "Mrs. Rice was going to elope with this fellow Baronovich, this Bulgarian army cavalry officer. And he was the guy who was in the house when I killed Mrs. Rice the night I came to move in my belongings. After the night of June 13, Baronovich kept calling me at the service station and hounding and blackmailing me for money as his price of silence. After several demands, he handed me Mrs. Rice's bank passbook, suggesting I draw out $135 and pay it to him to keep silent. Otherwise he would disclose my first crime. And so I was forced to forge a check in that amount. I paid him all I could and finally told him I couldn't raise anymore.

"Well, one night either late in November or early December I came home to the cottage, and found him sitting in a chair in the living room. He had a .38-caliber revolver in his lap. We talked a little. I refused to pay him more and this started a quarrel. Suddenly, he jammed the gun on me. I pushed it aside, reached for my gun, then got an arm lock on him. He was a big man so we had quite a fight.

"I overpowered him. He dropped his gun and I picked it up, just happened to get it barrel first. He made a rush at me. I clipped him a couple of times on the side of the head. I hit him some more with the butt with all my strength, cracked his skull and pretty soon he was dead. He fell like a log and I realized I had killed another person almost in the same spot in front of the fireplace where I unwittingly killed Mrs. Rice. The first had been an accident pure and simple and the second had been a case of another man's life or my own. There I was with another body to get rid of. I figured that if this sort of stuff went on I'd have to acquire a private cemetery."

"What did you do with the body," asked the sheriff. First Fell claimed he had incinerated the corpse in the oil tank of a locomotive, then provided a more plausible story. "For two days I kept it hidden behind the davenport. There was a heavy bunch of baling wire on the place, so I wrapped up what was left of Mr. Baronovich in fine style with wire from the radio antenna. Guess I must have wrapped him up and weighted him down in 80 pounds of wire by the time I finished. I wrapped him in a blanket and heaved it into the back seat of my car along with two big hunks of railroad iron, heavy railroad clamps, and a bunch of iron plates to fasten on.

"With him in the back of my car, I drove around the Bay for a while figuring a better way to dispose of it than the way I disposed of Mrs. Rice's. I happened to recall that the men who had kidnapped that fellow down in San Jose had dumped his body off the San Mateo-Hayward Bridge."

On November 13, 1933, Harold Thurmond and Jack Holmes kidnapped Brooke Hart, the twenty-two-year-old son of Alex Hart, president of the DeAnza Hotel Company and the second biggest department store in San Jose. The boy's abductors demanded $40,000 in ransom, then drove to the bridge where they knocked Hart out with a brick. They trussed him with wire, weighted him with concrete, and tossed him off the bridge alive. As he drowned, Thurmond fired several shots at the boy. Hart's wallet later washed up on the guard rail of a tanker in the Bay and two weeks later two duck hunters found his corpse in the Alameda marshes a mile south. After Holmes and Thurmond were arrested, a rioting mob smashed their way into the Santa Clara County Jail and lynched them across the street in St. James Park.

"It was about 3:00 A.M. when I reached the bridge with Baronovich wrapped in a blanket in the rear of the car," continued Fell. "I fastened the two weights to the head and feet. I tied several fishplates [the heavy iron oblongs used in railroad building to tie down rails] on the body. Then I lifted it out of the car. It was heavy with all those weights on it, but I'm strong and I didn't have any trouble handling it. But when I tried to push the body out between the rails, the space between them was too small and it wouldn't go that way. So I had to lift the body over the rail top. That was quite a job, I'm telling you. This guy weighed 200 pounds and I had almost as many pounds tied onto him. But I'm pretty husky myself and I finally had to lift it over the rail top, hoist it up and let go. I heard a big splash as he hit the water. I threw his gun in after him. Then I drove back to clean up the cottage. Now you can see why I didn't feel guilty of any crime in connection with these two killings. Why do you think I could sleep and eat so well if I did?"

Maloney took Highway 92 south of San Francisco. When they got to the deserted bridge, the sheriff got out. He had no real proof except Fell's word that Baronovich existed. The wealth of details was convincing, though. The sheriff peered over the side. The water was cold and black as ink, the current powerful. They could do nothing until daylight to find exactly where Fell had put the chained body over. "Let's go back," said the sheriff and they started for the Redwood City Jail.

Elsewhere, the bloodless body of an unidentified man laden down with chains and weights had shot to the surface. It was estimated it had been thrown over the side of the nearby San Mateo-Hayward Bridge by a very strong man. Dullea caught that case.

SOUTH of San Francisco, the Bay tides were running strong and swift. Getting the waterlogged bundle onboard the Coast Guard cutter was arduous. The sailor was bound in chains just like escape artist Harry Houdini in his recent performance at the Orpheum but had been substantially less successful in breaking loose. Link by link, the guardsmen snipped away the chains with a bolt cutter. When the mutilated corpse was released from his irons, a singular feature stood out—he had not one drop of blood in his veins.

Britt had briefed Dullea so he knew about the victim Fell weighted in chains and threw from the San Mateo-Hayward Bridge. All Dullea knew for sure was that someone was killing sailors in grisly ways. Unfortunate seamen had been found in the water, suspiciously murdered on the docks, thrown out windows, stabbed with a combination of stilettos and butcher knives, and fatally beaten. Dullea thought the crimes might be linked, but if the sailor killings were part of a sequence held together by a substantial motive, what was that motive? It was the same problem he had in the Gorilla Man case.

Dullea took a deep breath of Bay air. It cleared his head. The early morning was crystal clear. Gulls wheeled above as the police launch cut south. Barges passed by, delivering large steel beams to the Bay Bridge skeleton, and derricks were lifting them into place. In spite of eight months of setbacks (they lost the trestle twice in storms and once when a ship rammed it), the bridge was nearing completion. Architect Charles Purcell had designed it as two distinct structures, conjoined mid-Bay (exactly between two earthquake faults) at Yerba Buena Island to span the widest navigable stretch of water ever. When the two main sections were in place, the hard rock men would bore a tunnel through the island's center to connect them.

Dullea saw the Coast Guard cutter ahead. A minute later, he was aboard and minutes later followed the cutter back to the dock in the police launch, having learned the bloodless sailor wasn't Baronovich. "Including the sailor in chains we dragged up, Raoul Louis Cherborough," Dullea said, "that makes the sixth mysterious killing on San Francisco Bay in two years.[16] All the victims were seamen very active in union disputes." The fifth victim, Chief Engineer George W. Alberts of the freighter *Point Lobos* had been stabbed with two knives.[17] Dullea's informant, Matthew Guidera, told him, "A.M. Murphy of the Marine Fireman's Union, and I are roommates in the Terminal Hotel on Market Street [adjacent to the Bay Hotel], so we both could be near the ships and docks in case of a dispute involving members of our respective unions. A union leader dispatched a bunch of men to kill Alberts and the rest."

---

[16] 1. Santo Batista: fractured skull, March 1934, aboard the *S.S. Susan V. Luckenback*. 2. Vincent Torres was hurled to death from a window of the Ship Scalers' Union in September. 3. Otto Blaczensky, deck engineer aboard the freighter *Minnesotan*, was drowned in mud. 4. William V. McConologue was murdered on the steamer *Cottoneva*.
[17] The *Point Lobos* would strike a rock in heavy fog on June 22, 1939, and go to the bottom.

THIRTY-FOUR

Business has picked up 100% since the organ grinder traded in his mon-key for a gorilla.

—VINTAGE CARTOON SHOWING A GORILLA HOLDING A PASSERBY BY HIS
ANKLES AND SHAKING MONEY OUT

AS the first rays of Tuesday's daybreak streaked the sky, McGrath got a cup of coffee and signaled two trusties to load long-handled shovels into his car. As he drove to the solitary grave, several carloads of reporters and deputies kept a less than respectful distance behind. He turned onto the little-used side road and parked. So did the reporters. The trusties hauled out the shovels and made a leisurely descent of the slope, this time by ropes secured to the auto bumper. The portly sheriff saw that workmen had been excavating very close to the grave. "We probably would have discovered the corpse very soon no matter what," he said. The deputies and trusties, all in shirtsleeves, unbuttoned their vests and hefted their shovels and pickaxes. McGrath, badge pinned to his black vest, used the rope and joined them. He didn't bother to roll up his sleeves, just hefted his pick and struck a blow as flashbulbs exploded.

Blowflies were buzzing. You couldn't see them in the faint dawn light, but you could feel them. Diggers removed two feet of leaves and debris and a second layer of earth discolored by quicklime. The lime had seared the earth to a depth of another foot. Sunrise was filtering through the trees when they uncovered the decomposed body of Mrs. Rice another two feet down. A reporter became ill at the sight. "This is all we need," said McGrath.

"We'll let the coroner take care of this." The attendants lifted the body, placed it in a round-ended wicker sarcophagus with handles at both ends and made the treacherous ascent, the lead attendant walking backward and pulling as his partner pushed the casket.

McGrath returned to the jail to find the press assembled around the prisoner's cell. At first Fell had been grumpy (the jailers had awakened him early), but after breakfast and a look at the front pages, he was in an increasingly playful mood. "So you've been digging, eh?" Fell said as they entered. "Well, you boys will want a lot of pictures now, but try to make them better than the last ones. They weren't very good." He flexed his muscles under the tight black T-shirt, smoothed back his hair and chided them. "My rollicking, highly amusing little escapade hasn't been big news until now, boys. Well, it'll be on the front page now. I'm going to run Hitler right off the paper."

"Do you think you'll hang?"

"Hang? Well, I don't know. Sheriff McGrath is a grand guy and I'll vote for him the next time he runs for office if I'm in any position to vote. If the sheriff thinks I ought to hang that's his business and I don't hold it against him. I guess I've done my part to help Sheriff McGrath who's a fine stout fellow."

"How many people have you killed, Jerry?"

"I wouldn't say," he replied, smiling his brilliant smile. "Aw, hell, I wouldn't tell you that on a bet." He winked.

"Have you ever been on the stage," a reporter asked the movie-star handsome prisoner.

"Sure, once, but they kicked me off on the desert near Utah. As I recall it was a Pickwick stage."

"Murder is a joke to him," a reporter wrote. "To him murder is no crime. It's an uproarious prank with a laugh in every phrase. He is the happy killer. He carefully sets the stage for his effects—and they are always comedy effects."

"Stand behind the bars, Jerry," a cameraman requested, "and face us from that position."

"Oh, no, guys. I don't think bars would make a good frame. I like the ones taken inside the cell. Come on inside." A photographer entered with a bulky camera and dazzled Fell with several shots. Abruptly he retaliated by grabbing the camera, bracing his foot against the bars and taking the photog's picture. He stood for as many pictures as they desired. He tilted his cheek against his hand and rolled his eyes upward "in a familiar cherubic attitude." He posed lit from below with his penetrating eyes staring directly into the lenses. "Hypnotic is the only word that would do that look justice," remarked Britt. Fell performed an impromptu clog dance for the newsmen. "Two weeks ago I was going to San Mateo Junior College," he said as he spun around, both arms out, "—just working my way through school and getta load of me now. Wow."

"How long have you known Dorothy?"

"Who's that?"

"Dorothy Farnum."

"I don't know her."

"The girl at your place."

"Oh, that girl. She told me her name was 'Boots.' I don't know Dorothy well. I got in the jug right after I met her. But go easy on that stuff about my living with a hitchhiker. I've got my social prestige to think of."

While his cute little hitchhiking pal enjoyed the luxury of regular hot meals and a bath, she had the wandering bug again. McGrath decided to free her. Starry-eyed, she said, "Oh boy, Sheriff, I can be just in time for a walkathon in Dallas." Boots set off briskly with a new suitcase, not Ada's but one that McGrath bought her with his own money. She and Fell were very much alike the sheriff thought and watched Boots tap-dance out of sight.

"Once again Jerry, why did you order a book on poisons?" Maloney asked. Fell's toxicology book had arrived that morning. As far as Maloney was concerned Boots, who thought the whole thing "just so much balderdash over nothing," had narrowly escaped death.

In the afternoon Fell was returned to Mrs. Rice's grave. While the deputies dug for any other bodies, Fell posed gaily for the photographers. "It was just an accident," he told them. "Just one of those things. Anyway they wouldn't stretch me. I'm too young to be stretched. But you know, boys, hanging is a damn sight better than life imprisonment—but they won't hang me because the murder was not of my own volition."

*   *   *

BEFORE dawn on Wednesday morning, March 11, McGrath, Maloney, Britt, a *Call-Bulletin* reporter, and a photographer drove Fell to the bungalow so he could reenact both murders. Fell was dressed in a black V-neck undershirt, black gabardine pants with striped black and white suspenders, and loafers with no socks. First Maloney got down on one knee and took measurements of the living room with a tape and marked the location of the davenport, corner fireplace, andirons, and the gilded full-length mirror on a map.

"Step here," Fell stage directed the camera man, "and I'll show you just how it was done. Ha, ha!" He drafted Britt to play the role of Ada Rice. With a smile he raised the poker Maloney had entrusted him with. "I came home that night and although the lights were out, I felt the presence of someone. Then suddenly I was struck a heavy blow which knocked me into the fireplace. I seized this poker and swung it twice—this way."

Grinning broadly, Fell held the poker by the point and brought the handle end to his left shoulder, then swished it mightily right and left. "I heard someone fall, turned on the lights and found I had killed Mrs. Rice. She lay near the fireplace, clad only in scanties." All along Fell had been chuckling at his own jokes, kidding, winking, and nudging what he called "my jovial policemen," but now he steadied himself against the door. "Hold on—(a look of horror crossed his face) I've got a rotten taste in my mouth."

"Is it from memories?" Britt asked.

"No. Hell, I haven't got any conscience. But say, don't put that in the paper—(he turned toward the *Bulletin* man) that I haven't got any conscience; they'll think I'm cruel."

Now Britt stood in for Michael Baronovich.

"I met Baronovich in the murder house," said Fell. "He had taken all the money I offered him. He pulled a gun. I knocked it like this." Fell made a graceful lunge. "We had a terrific fight." "He was a big man, so we had quite a struggle. I went down like this." He went down on his left knee. "At one time, and it seemed a question of self-defense, he raised the gun like this and I grappled for it. He had great strength and it looked like I was going to lose." Fell put his left hand on Britt's right shoulder, and crossing over grasped his arm at the wrist. "I got an arm lock like this behind him, twisted his arm. He dropped the gun. I clipped him on the head. I hit him again and again." It was like watching a Hollywood film.

The detectives left the bungalow so he could show them another grave, a watery one this time. "Gee, you fellows are too fast for me," Fell said. "I've got to get some sleep. Baronovich isn't going anywhere. Let's let this go until tomorrow." He yawned.

"No, we have to do it now," said McGrath sternly. He needed to know exactly where the weighted body of Baronovich had been consigned to the depths from the San Mateo-Hayward Bridge. The party traveled in silence to the icy waters where divers were still searching. "I threw the body there on the night of December 6," he said. "I remember seeing a stalled vehicle when I drove out onto the bridge to the place I had mentally picked. I found a green truck parked there. I stopped behind the driver and asked him if he had broken down and needed any help. 'No,' he said, 'I'm just taking a nap—just sleepy,' he told me. So I got back in my car and drove further on, one mile east of the drawbridge. About 200 yards east of the curve past the toll house, I finally stopped the car and hauled out the body. I remember they were fixing the concrete here and some of the sand is still here. Also I remember the red light. See that newly patched section of the guard rail. They were just repairing it when I drove out here with his body. I tried to roll the body through the concrete rails of the bridge. You can see they're too narrow. What a job that was." McGrath bent to look. Yes, the spaces between the triple-railed span were too narrow to permit a body to slide through. Below in a rowboat Lawrence Nieri in overalls and Adolph Waldeck in a hat and three-piece suit were probing with long poles.

Jack French of the *Chronicle*, the only cameraman there, snapped Fell directing operations from the bridge, leaning over the rail and giving a thumbs-up to Nieri and Waldeck. Fell offered to demonstrate to journalist Fred Glover how he tossed Baronovich over and started to lift him over his head. Glover would have gone in the drink, if Fell hadn't been cuffed.

Only when they were on the official launch speeding south across the water did McGrath unmanacle Fell. About a mile from the drawbridge McGrath's trusties, taking advantage of low tide conditions, were sweeping the Bay floor with grappling hooks. By now the iron wire had probably rusted, and as the weights dropped away, the body would be free. "Probably the tide had swept it out to sea," thought McGrath.

The hooks sliced into the cold water until they snagged a "leg" that turned out be a log. A few bits of cloth came up along with two feet of twisted baling wire. "That looks like some of the wire I used to truss up Baronovich," said Fell. Dredging continued. Divers plunged into the black water. At end of the day their grappling hooks caught a heavy object. "No attempt will be made to raise it until low tide in the morning," said McGrath, though he was anxious to see if it was a body.

Next morning, they brought up something that might have been flesh, but that was as close as the authorities ever came to finding Baronovich.

THIRTY-FIVE

With "Floaters," persons submerged in water for a long period of time, the palmar regions will have the appearance of 'washerwoman's skin.'"

—CRIME TEXT OF THE TIME

SHERIFF McGrath returned Fell to his Redwood City cell, and within minutes the prisoner was snoring loudly. He slept straight through until morning when the jailers roused him. Fell had no sooner awakened than he called for the papers. A broad grin crossed his face as he read the bold headlines. "Say, Sheriff, this is good!" he chortled. "Take a gander at this front page. Why, I guess this makes me a mass murderer." Fell gave a boisterous laugh and slapped his leg.

When Maloney discovered a lodge uniform among Fell's belongings, he pleaded, "Please, Tom, hide that outfit from the press." But a reporter independently stumbled upon it and wrote that Fell had the costume of a gravedigger from Holy Cross Cemetery. Thus, when *Chronicle* scribe Ray Leavitt asked, "Jerry, tell us about the time you went to school in Stockton?" Fell was furious. "How did you find that out!" he snapped, then regained his composure. "How did you find that out?" he repeated mildly, as if this revelation were only one of many more still to be uncovered.

"I found a book in the Stockton schools with your real name in it," said Leavitt, who wrote, "The Adonis Killer is colder than William Edward Hickman; more nonchalant than Elton M. Stone [two of the state's handsomest and most fiendish killers]. Everything seems to be made to order to suit his fancy. It is as if he wrote his own mystery thriller, cleverly concealing the denouement so he alone could supply the key, and then reserved for himself the role of hero in his own miserably sordid play."

"This murder case against me went just boom! boom! boom! Like that," Fell said. "A chain of circumstances involved me. Anyone would have done as I did under those circumstances. Except, perhaps what I did with the bodies after making corpses of them. Now I'm sorry that I tried to cover up. I may have trouble proving self defense. But let me tell you until you got situation like this you have no idea how you will react. Now if I hadn't felt justified in these deaths I would have not pointed out Mrs. Rice's body would I? I will admit that things don't look too good, and that really is not a laughing matter. If they ask for my neck, it may be just too bad.

"No, I don't feel so good with two deaths on my hands. I am a happy-go-lucky fellow by nature. I've roamed a lot and laughed my way through life, but fellows, I am not laughing now, no matter what you may think. Right now, I'm not interested in any defense. I believe in capital punishment. As for me I'd rather be dead than imprisoned for life. I would even be willing to write my life story for $1,000."

"How many murders would you admit for that much money."

"Oh, say twice thirteen."

Sheriff McGrath questioned Fell about the unsolved shooting death last year on a San Mateo street of Kathleen Robinson. Fell studied a beach photo of her in a one-piece bathing suit—winsome, short dark hair, dazzling smile, pixielike. "I had nothing to do with that. I was not even in the locality at the time, but on one of my trips."

McGrath whisked Fell to the Redwood City Morgue—another salvo in his carefully orchestrated campaign of psychological warfare. If he confronted him with Mrs. Rice's decomposed remains, he might wring additional murder confessions from him. After viewing x-rays, Dr. James Rinehart and Dr. A. H. Head, pathologist at the Mills Memorial Hospital, had jointly determined Ada's cause of death. "Death was from a definite cerebral hemorrhage brought on by a terrific blow on top of the head and instantaneous. Tremendous depressing force indicates that more than one blow was struck."

Seeing the corpse had no effect on Fell. Instead, he was elated at the educational opportunities afforded by viewing a long-buried corpse. He studied the skull from every angle, asked about the depressed area, and engaged in a technical discussion with Coroner William Crosby about skull fractures. Crosby was stuck dumb by his series of jokes. Even the bleached skull was grinning as if at some private joke.

"Is that the body of Mrs. Rice?" asked McGrath.

"It might be her," said Fell, smiling. "You got her from the place I put her, didn't you? And she's got a crack on the side of her head, hasn't she? It isn't in very good condition, is it? Ha ha!" he roared "Hell of a looking thing, isn't it? Teeth? No—ha ha!—they don't look like her teeth to me. But, hell, it must be her. I killed her and put her in there! Now I want a big beefsteak." Just minutes after the viewing, Fell was eating a thick porterhouse steak with Britt. "Nothing like a nice, juicy one," Fell said jovially.

"Boy though, this is tough."

"Here have a piece of mine," said Fell, cutting his steak in half. "Say, Jimmy, did you ever see a corpse walking?"

Britt put down his knife, took a sip of coffee, and carefully wiped his lips. "No, Jerry, I can't say I have."

It was a rough day for those passionate of heart. When San Francisco clerk Henry Ohley shot himself in front of his girl's house on Clipper Street, the bullet penetrated his lung. As he lay near death at Mission Emergency Hospital, Ohley gasped out a story of romance blasted by the girl's father. At the San Francisco airport, officials encircled a nude long-legged blond. Miss Florence Cubitt, "the Flying Nudist," had left San Diego wearing only a beaming smile. "She'll keep her clothes on in our planes if it takes every pilot and stewardess on the line to make her do it!" said the airline officials. And in Seattle, Charles Rice finally learned what had happened to his ex-wife. "I was unaware Ada was dead—naturally I was shocked," said the elderly contractor who really had loved her.

That afternoon Inspectors George O'Leary and Ed Hansen of the SFPD police Auto Detail drove Fell downtown. He claimed that last June he dropped Mrs. Rice and the Bulgarian out "somewhere in the San Francisco theatrical district." "I think I can pick out the spot," he said. "Ah, there it is." Fell indicated a hotel at 493 Eddy Street at Hyde Street. Inside, the clerk recalled that two weeks before Fell's arrest a letter had come addressed to a Baronovich. "But we had no such guest," he said, "and so the letter was sent to the dead letter office." O'Leary and Hansen took Fell to the HOJ so he could go through their missing persons books on a chance of finding a picture of Baronovich. He could not.

A smirking photo of Fell was etched onto a copper plate and trimmed to fit with a metal table saw. It was inserted onto a page and rolled to the stereotyping machine, which automatically cut off four large blotting sheets, pasted them together, and mashed onto the page until it fit every indentation. Bent into a half circle, the dampened matrix was placed in a type-high casting box, then strapped to the high-speed press.

By evening, Fell's face was plastered across every front page with colorful names to match his personalities—"the Enigma Man," "the Laughing Killer of the Woodside Glens," "the Playboy Murderer," "the Poker Slayer," "the Laughing Murderer," and the "Burly Lothario." Fell kept himself in the news by doing anything the reporters asked, except admit to other killings. John Smeins, the Bay Hotel night clerk, studied a series of these pictures in the *Examiner*. "I know that face," he told himself. "I know he's been here before." Then it came to him.

"That's the man!" Smeins said. "That's the laughing Mr. Meyers." Smeins dialed Inspector Otto Frederickson. "I examined some pictures published in the papers and I'm absolutely convinced he's the man who registered with Mrs. Coffin and disappeared from the hotel a short time later."

"Are you certain?"

"I'll never forget those ruddy cheeks and his smile and that laugh. He told me, 'All these women are alike,' just those words exactly. 'They want beer and sandwiches before they go to sleep,' he said. I'm positive Fell accompanied Bette Coffin and registered them as 'Mr. and Mrs. H. Meyers of LA' before he took her up to a third floor room."

That night Inspector Engler interrogated Fell for three hours. At the first mention of Bette Coffin his big smile vanished. "You're on the wrong track," he snapped, angrily denying he had committed such an atrocity.

"All right," said Engler. "In that case I want you to write something for me. I want you to write 'Mr. and Mrs. H. Meyers City' on this pad." The Laughing Gorilla had indicated San Francisco as his place of residence by printing "City."

Fell wrote the words several times and with both hands. He copied the name "H Meyers" twice so they were not exact replicas. "The handwriting is very similar to that on the hotel register," Engler said. "I believe you're denying this crime because in this case you can't square it on the grounds of self defense as you are endeavoring to square the San Mateo killings."

"That hotel clerk got me wrong," said Fell. "I tell you I've never been in that hotel. I gave you my handwriting to compare with the register and didn't try to fake it. They'll find it doesn't match. You'll see. That murder was a lot more horrible than I would ever commit and I'm ready to take another lie detector test on that case any time. That little machine is the greatest thing ever invented. It certainly told my story. I know what I have done. You can give me that test or any other test."

Engler took the sample to LaTulipe. "There is some similarity between Selz's writing and that found on the hotel register," he said, "but not much." Fell had omitted the period after the initial "H" and after "Mr." and "Mrs." Other experts saw a great resemblance in the capital "H" in both exemplars, but the comparisons went no further.

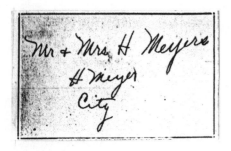

Fell's exemplar for comparison.

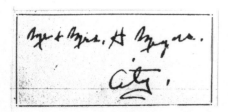

The Laughing Gorilla's handprinting.

When Smeins saw Fell in person he was more positive than ever that he was "Mr. Meyers." "Well," Frederickson asked Dullea, "is Fell the Bay Hotel Murderer or not?" "I'll settle this once and for all," said Dullea. "Bring in Otto von Feldman, the former Bay Hotel night porter, to corroborate Smeins' identification."

Frederickson located von Feldman in San Diego. He had earlier recognized Fell's photo in the paper. Frederickson brought him up and in person he found Fell's features "even more similar." "That's him," he said. "That's the man who registered with her. That's 'Mr. Meyers.' I'll never forget that beefy build and disarming smile."

Then Fell stood and von Feldman saw he was taller than "Mr. Meyers." This confused him. But the killer's odd hunched walk could be accounted for by a tall man crouching.

Out in the Bay, workers were completing half of the steel deck trusses between the anchorage and Pier W-1 on the west suspension bridge as newsies cried on the streets—"Triple Murder Suspect . . . Linked to Hotel Murder". . . "Youth Confesses Two Killings." Dullea picked up a *Chronicle* and read:

DEATH SUSPECT LINKED WITH HOTEL KILLING. IDENTIFIED BY CLERK AS THE MAN REGISTERING WITH COFFIN WOMAN.

REDWOOD CITY, MARCH 10—"That's the man!" John Smeins, night clerk at the Bay Hotel, 24 Sacramento St., San Francisco, thus today identified the confessed slayer of Mrs. Ada French Rice and of a mystery man named as Baronovich. . . . He had accompanied the ill-fated woman to a room in the hotel. Ill-fated, because the next morning she was found dead in bed. Her mouth had been taped and she had been slashed about the body with a razor. But death had been caused by strangulation, an autopsy revealed. . . . Her companion on that last night of her life was heavy set man of 27, with ruddy cheeks and a disarming smile. Smeins forgot all about him until a startled hotel employee the next day found the nude and mutilated body of the woman.

Maloney could not understand why Fell accepted liability for two other murders, but not to being "Mr. Meyers." "We know you were responsible for the murder of Bette Coffin in the Bay Hotel," he told Fell. "For God's sake, you bragged about it!"

"No, Tom. think back, I said that Baronovich killed Bette Coffin."

"And you killed *him,* didn't you."

"Tom, I'm just a poor boy working his way through college. On that night I was working in a San Francisco oil station."

The press claimed Fell had a wife who had mysteriously disappeared two years ago, but the only proof of her existence was an application form dated August 25, 1934, that mentioned her address as 1625 Fairview Street in Berkeley. McGrath obtained the actual oil company form, which contradicted the rumor. Fell's mother had lived at that address.

McGrath was worried. He could only tentatively identify the lime pit remains as those of Mrs. Rice. Without an official identification, the DA had no assurance of a conviction. Their case now hinged on two very iffy dental reconstructions being done at Palo Alto. Remarkably, Fell had provided the information that Ada had her teeth worked on shortly before their first meeting. Both dentists completed a chart of the dead woman's teeth, but their comparisons were inconclusive.

Neither could Ada's nephew, Lawrence Doherty, a Clay Street lawyer, conclusively identify her when he visited the Redwood City Morgue. Doherty contacted Hugh French, Ada's son in New York, who had written him in June that he had been "worried about her." "Your mother has been murdered," the lawyer wired. "The murderer has confessed."

Hugh and his sister, Phyllis, started West. The last hope for a firm identification lay in their hands.

Fell, always fast with a quip, grew solemn and borrowed a fountain pen from Britt. "For the first time," he scrawled, "I am beginning to realize that maybe it's not so good for me to laugh and josh about these killings. Maybe it's given folks a wrong impression about me, made them believe I am cold and heartless. San Mateo police called me the most brutal, ruthless and remorseless killer they had ever known. But the fact of the matter is that I have nothing on my conscience and I couldn't do anything else. The whole mess is just one of those unfortunate things that could happen to anybody. It just happened to me, that's all."

He didn't feel sorry because he didn't have anything to feel sorry about. One killing was an accident, pure and simple, and the other one was in self-defense. "Of course, I feel sorry for poor Mrs. Rice. She was a nice old lady and I was very fond of her. And I feel sorry that Baronovich is dead, after all, it was his life or mine and I'd rather be alive myself than be dead with Baronovich alive. Can't blame me for that. Any normal person would have done the same thing as I did." He signed his true name, Heinrich Fritz Ralphe Jerome von Braun Selz.

Psychiatrists, attempting to explain Fell's joviality, chalked it up to superegoism. "Because he believes he was justified in slaying two persons," said one expert, "the rest of the world should feel the same way, according to his philosophy. Fell is not insane, but his friends always considered him 'strange.'"

Undersheriff George Brereton of San Diego, lured by the news that Fell had lived near the two San Diego victims during April 1931 and displayed a "strange familiarity with them," rushed to San Francisco. "Did you kill Louise Teuber, a seventeen-year-old artist's model, and eleven-year-old Virginia Brooks in San Diego?" he asked Fell. Their mutilated bodies had been bound with a double-looped rope tied with a sailor's knot such as found in Fell's car. "I know all about that," Fell volunteered. "Well, maybe I did that and maybe I didn't."

Richmond Police Chief L. E. Jones's men, Inspectors George Bengley and Harry Connelly, arrived on Brereton's heels anxious to connect Fell to the January 7 ax murder of Joseph Anthony the previous year. "I left the service oil station late in '34," Fell told them, but admitted to living about a block away from Anthony. "Your fingerprints to some extent resemble the single bloody print on the haft of a carpenter's ax," said Bengley. Fell looked at the print card. "Well, I guess they look like my fingerprints all right, but I can't tell you about the murder. I know nothing about that. The fingerprints may be similar, but they're not mine. I was over in Alameda employed at a Richmond auto assembly plant about the same time. I'm guilty of this Woodside killing, but not that one. If you keep on investigating you'll get your man, but it won't be me."

"We'll settle this," said Bengley, who inked up Fell's fingers, rolled a set of prints, then hurried back to Richmond to make enlargements. They were not identical. Fell was never charged for Anthony's killing. Next the San Mateo police unsuccessfully tried to link him to the murder of an elderly merchant in Santa Ana on October 24, 1932. The next day was Friday the thirteenth, the jinx day.

THIRTY-SIX

I recorded Fell's dubious and equally mirthful confessions of having done away with a doubly dubious Bulgarian cavalry officer.

—*CHRONICLE* EDITOR ALLAN BOSWORTH

FRIDAY the thirteenth turned out to be lucky for many people. Over on Haight Street a mother saved her two small children from a gas leak just in time and got them to Park Emergency. On Jackson Street two workmen were lifting a thirty-six-hundred-pound marquee over the Woey Loy Goey Restaurant's door when it dropped on them. It is surprising that they suffered only fractured left heels. Every Friday the thirteenth the Anti-Superstition Club rented room 1313 at an exclusive hotel and drank black cat cocktails, ate coffin ice cream, broke mirrors, and walked under ladders. Nobody died. In San Mateo, a passerby saved an infant from a burning car. It would be a lucky day for the Laughing Killer, too. Fell began the morning of the thirteenth by taking two phone calls from Anna, his mother in LA. At noon he had a steak. Then, to the shock of everyone, he stopped grinning; hired John McCarthy, a San Francisco lawyer he had known for some time; and saved his own life.

"I don't want to hang," Fell told him.

"You won't."

Two hours later, McCarthy and attorney Bruce Fratis were at the Redwood City Court House conferring privately with DA Gil Ferrell and

Assistant DA Louis Dematteis. All four crossed the street to the jail where they surprised Sheriff McGrath grilling Fell about the Bay Hotel murder. Five minutes later, Fell, surrounded by officers and lawyers, walked two blocks to the store court room of Justice of the Peace Edward McAuliffe. The stout McGrath puffed to keep up. Once inside McAuliffe's tiny court, they agreed that Fell be held for superior court trial and rushed him along the street to the gray stone courthouse. Officials, assuming Fell had recanted his alibi, came on the run. At every stop, the procession of bystanders, guards, and lawyers increased as if drawn by the defendant's magnetic personality. Swiftly, Judge A. R. Cotton's courtroom was jammed beyond capacity with cops, lawyers, court reporters, and pretty secretaries who had deserted their desks to watch Fell. Everyone was there except a handful of deputy sheriffs out searching for a giant Japanese gardener, Frank Mayeda. He had hacked a woman to death with an ax, then turned on her daughters, who were recuperating at a nearby hospital. Mayeda, hands drenched in blood, staggered to the City Hall to give himself up, but the doors were locked, the phones ringing, and no one answering. Everyone was at the courthouse. "Where is everybody?" he asked, then walked to Walter Hobart's Hillsborough estate to surrender to their chauffeur. "I am sorry, very sorry for this terrible thing," he said. Officers Martin McDonnell and William Cotter locked Mayeda in the same jail cell Fell had so recently occupied, then joined everyone else at the courthouse.

At 3:55 P.M., after a brief arraignment, McCarthy waived Fell's preliminary examination. Fell's hands were clasped, his face set and flushed. He was shirtless, his blue polo sweater open at the throat showcasing his muscular chest. Dematteis had no sooner begun questioning Fell than the defendant signaled Judge Cotton, who had just fixed the degree of the crime as murder in the first degree. The interruption put him off stride.

"Do you wish to plead now?" he asked Fell directly and not his attorney.

Fell nodded.

"Wait a minute," said McCarthy.

Things were happening too fast. Cotton silenced McCarthy with a wave. "What is your pleasure?" he asked.

Stone-faced, Fell said in a frail voice: "I plead guilty."

"My God, he's copping a plea," whispered McGrath. "He's just saved himself from the gallows."

"Before sentence is pronounced," said Ferrell, who privately believed that "unofficially" Fell was responsible for the Bay Hotel, San Diego, and New York murders, "I wish to say it is recommended the supreme penalty not be imposed. By his willingness to plead guilty, he has saved the State much expense. I would like to point out that he cooperated fully with the officials. This is the sensible course to take. It saves the county time and money. Besides Fell was the only one who could have identified Ada Rice's body. Had he changed his story we might have had a situation." He turned to Fell. "You have a right to a delay of sentence from two to five days."

"No, I want to get it over with," said Fell. "I don't want to hang. They said maybe I'd get life if I pleaded guilty. I want to do that."

Still, the sentence of life imprisonment rocked Fell back on his heels. The deputies affectionately pumped Fell's hand and patted him on the back as he had achieved some great accomplishment. "What about Baronovich?" asked the press.

"There was no intentional omission," Ferrell told them, "in our failure to charge Selz with the Bulgarian murder. We had witnesses to Fell's other confession, but the Judge just didn't call for them and I thought he would bar any testimony of the second confession. Police are still dragging and if they ever find Baronovich's corpse we will charge Fell."

"Will you see your mother," a reporter asked Fell as he lit his pipe outside.

"I expect to soon."

"How do you feel about going to prison?"

"How would you?" he shouted back. "I'm not down in the dumps."

The hearing was so brief it set records. Only fifty-five minutes after he pleaded guilty, Fell was on his way to San Quentin with McGrath, Britt, and Maloney. One of the reasons Fell had confessed was to help his "pals." On board the ferry to Sausalito, passengers flocked to the dining room to peer at him. Fell, ascot around his neck, white teeth wolfish, was getting in one last attack on a juicy steak. Holding a steak knife, he poured ketchup over his steak and fries. "It's the last good dinner I'll get for a long while." He beamed. Next to him, Britt was having a steak, too.

"Who wants to buy my overcoat?" Fell quipped to the crowd.

"I wouldn't take it as a present," said a voice from the back.

"Do you feel relieved?" someone asked.

"I haven't decided yet. I feel like a dog getting out of water who hasn't shaken himself yet. Some people might be surprised by my action today, but it wasn't a sudden decision. I'd been thinking about it all the time. As I've said no one knows what is in my mind."

"Jerry, I think you're crazy," a spectator said.

"And can you prove you're not?" said Fell.

By 7:30 P.M., Fell was at the prison gates to start serving a life sentence as prisoner number 58,769. The former weightlifter towered over Warden James Holohan, whose first words to the new inmate were fierce. "Take that pipe out of your mouth!" he snapped. "You're just lucky they didn't string you up down there."

Fell stopped laughing as if he had been slapped across the face. Britt and Maloney had never spoken so harshly to him during his long interrogations. His face grew pained. Taking off his snap brim felt hat, Fell held it over his heart and addressed the newspapermen with one foot inside San Quentin and the other on free ground.

"Fellows," Fell said, "there's just one thing I'd like to say, 'I'm sorry.' I know I've caused a lot of grief especially for the relatives of the deceased. I want to thank all of you for your kindness. I'm going in now to do my damnedest to make good," he said jerking a thumb in the direction of the prison. "You can count on that." He gave a hearty wave of his hand. "So long, Boys!" he called.

He considered many of them friends, had even rehearsed his good-bye speech with Maloney, whom he considered the best of them. It was not hard for the reporters to see why Mrs. Rice had fallen for Fell. In his dark outfit, with no shirt or socks, and in yachting shoes he was a very handsome man. He had charmed the reporters, too.

"Good luck, Jerry," they cried. His huge hands closed around Maloney and Britt's hands as he bid them farewell. "Thanks, Jimmy," said Fell. "Thanks, Tom." His eyes brimmed over. As the steel gates slammed behind him, the press heard the warden say, "Put some handcuffs on him!" A minute later the big man's hearty, booming laugh was echoing down the cell block. Fell was his old jocular self (or selves) again.

"Good-bye, Jerry!" the newsmen called after him as if parting from a loved one. They still stood there as a group taking it all in as night fell.

FOR months after, the Richmond Oil Company continued to receive letters lauding the excellent work of Jerry von Selz at their Woodside station. The letters, all in different handwriting and signed by different names, bore one thing in common—the postmark of San Quentin Prison. Fell did keep his word. He made good inside as captain of the prison's tumbling team, champion weight lifter, and prison strong man. But when he took up pole vaulting, guards cast a nervous eye toward the low walls, calculated his superb physical condition, and scrapped the program. Finally, Fell, desperate to fight for his country, attempted to enlist. Army doctors rejected him as a "constitutional psychopathic inferior" but did order him to a minimum security facility at Chino. Fell obtained maps of Mexico, shipped his prized mandolin ahead, and strolled away from the honor institution. He never got to Mexico, but did reach Minnesota where he enlisted with the draft board as Corporal Ralph Jerome "Tiny" Morgan, a physical education instructor. Identified by his prints, he was extradited back to California to serve out his sentence. Fell was never discharged of the murder of Michael Baronovich. That would have been impossible. How could he have killed a man who had never lived? With the help of some makeup, Baronovich was only another of Fell's multiple identities or, at the very least, a product of his frenzied and imaginative dream mind, the only place he was real.

"WHY are you so glum, Charlie?" asked LaTulipe. "We put Bette Coffin's killer in Q yesterday." Dullea turned in his chair and stared out the grimy window. The trees were still bare. "Slipton Fell either killed for gain or by accident," he explained. "He was a greedy boy who just wanted to be liked, but hadn't the stomach for murder. Remember how his killing of Mrs. Rice so unnerved him he couldn't sleep in her house? No, Fell wasn't the Gorilla Man."

Then who had killed Mrs. Coffin and committed the brutal murders in San Diego, New York, and San Francisco? Was there a connection with the Butcher in Cleveland? The only suspect the Cleveland police ever had "that amounted to a nickel" was a Great Lakes sailor named Harry who once worked in a morgue doing autopsies. That was enough to make LaTulipe wonder all night.

THIRTY-SEVEN

An absence of a command structure on all levels made high-level command decisions at night and on weekends impossible. Under Quinn the
lines of authority throughout the department were unclear.

—REPORT ON THE SFPD

THE grand jury investigation into alleged police graft and extortion pro-
gressed in secret. Ed Atherton, the DA's $100,000 privately contracted in-
vestigator, liked it that way. Such stealth gave the former G-man, officer in
the foreign service, and private investigator the opportunity to apply a little
extortion of his own. It helped that he lacked sympathy for the little fellows,
the foot soldiers of the system. He considered them sacrificial lambs to find,
publicize, prosecute, and annihilate to give the public the impression they
made up the entire San Francisco underworld.

The forty-year-old Atherton had studied law at Georgetown University,
entered the consular service during the Great War and served in Italy,
Bulgaria, and Jerusalem before joining the DOJ in 1924. While with the
FBI, he moved to New York, Boston, Detroit, and finally Los Angles where
he helped capture a neo-revolutionary army of Mexican nationals at
the border. Over the following two years he headed the FBI office in San
Francisco. After he resigned in 1927, he started a private investigating firm
in LA with his partner, Joseph Dunn. Atherton's local snitches included
Louis Bucchiers, a bootlegger, extortionist, greengrocer, and night janitor at
the *Chronicle*. Bucchiers pointed him in the direction of a waterfront cop,

a balding, former heavyweight boxer, Lieutenant Henry "Dutch" Ludolph of the Harbor Station.

"I respect you because you have the reputation of being the straightest straight-shooter in town," Atherton told Ludolph. Atherton didn't interrogate as much as insinuate himself into the confidences of those he interviewed. He turned one cop against another by convincing him that another cop had already talked. "I have no intention of hurting you in any way or bringing about your prosecution," he said smoothly. "All I want are the higher-ups. Play ball with us." Ludolph kicked over his chair and went to see his attorney.

"He's trying to get me," Ludolph told Jake Ehrlich.

"Who?"

"That man, Atherton. I tell you, Jake, I never took a nickel of graft in my life. I'm clean as a whistle or I wouldn't come to you. He wants I should put the finger on *everyone;* on all the other guys in the business." A cop in San Francisco was never "on the force," but always "in the business."

"Atherton isn't willing to settle for a squealing Ludolph," Ehrlich thought. "He wants a broken, destroyed and thoroughly stigmatized victim." Ludolph claimed to have amassed his fortune of $50,000 (twenty-three times an average man's annual income in 1936) by picking winning horses and prizefighters. He could document every wager, but began with his bet on Battling Nelson against Joe Gans at two a half to one odds. "I took the Swede for $250 (Ludolph's present month's salary). I won. I got a stake. From then on I was just lucky, lucky but careful. I bet on the horses where I can't lose. I never blew no money on the hotsy-totsies." Recently, he had won on Hidden Sight in the eighth race at Narragansett, which paid sixteen to one. "Atherton claims I've been collecting for me, for the mayor's last campaign, for the organization; all that kind of crud."

On the west side of Nob Hill, Atherton was fine-tuning his seventy-page grand jury report, which mentioned a hundred crooked cops by name and smeared another hundred honest ones. "At gathering general information, near information, rumors, whispered asides and irresponsible scandal," said Ehrlich, "he was an ace at rounding up documented fact that could be turned into legally admissible evidence. Atherton was an ace with a broad A."

Though he calculated vice in the city grossed $1 million a year, the real figure was closer to $4 million. Gambling and prostitution alone accounted for $2.5 million. Atherton listed 135 houses of prostitution. There were actually 580, and 300 of those within arm's length of the HOJ. The Palm Hotel was "close enough for the girls to read Chief Quinn's morning mail without binoculars." Atherton quit just short of any real information but leaked enough to terrify the SFPD brass.

At the HOJ, Dullea was despondent for the honest men on the force tarred by the same brush. He was sickened by the chief's repression of any departmental dissent and apparent ignorance of widespread corruption. Much of the criminality could be laid at the chief's feet because he was responsible for the tone of the department, even if it was one of favoritism and political influence. Dullea was working in his office when Chief Quinn entered. He stood at the window, legs apart, eyes sweeping the skeletal trees of Portsmouth Square. Yellow-eyed brewer's blackbirds and starlings flitted in the lowering light. Quinn began to speak of his future. It was odd how Quinn, when he revealed his innermost thoughts and dreams, almost always turned his back on the listener.

"Charlie," he said, his face briefly lit by his Optima cigar as he drew in smoke, "if all this should go away"—he swept out a beefy arm to encompass the room—"I would like to devote myself to radio work in which, as you know, I have had considerable experience and I modestly must say great success." Fifteen years earlier commercial radio didn't exist. Now it reached into almost every home.[18] Quinn loved radio and if given a choice would rather have gone into that field than be chief. During the hunt for Frank Egan, he had issued an effective plea over the radio and enlisted the public. As a child, he'd had a crystal set—a long stained board, mounted with a wooden tuning dial and a bit of quartz crystal beneath an inverted see-through glass guard and tuned with a roving "cat's whisker." Fifteen years earlier a radio you had to assemble cost $120. Preassembled radios now cost $5. Quinn was proud of his Atwater Kent from Ernest Ingold's.

---

[18] From 1927 to 1937 was San Francisco radio's Golden Decade, when many nationwide network broadcasts originated there. Both NBC and CBS maintained production centers in the city, and a third NBC network, the Pacific Orange Network, re-created the same programs heard in the east on the Red Network.

The powerful one-dial, six-tube receiver in a two-tone brown crystalline case sat in a place of honor in his office. It had knobs for volume and tuning in stations, a lighted dial window, and a separate speaker resembling a circulating fan. Radio, which allowed eighty-five million Americans to escape the harsh realities, now seemed very inviting to the chief. It was now Tuesday, April 28. The events the next evening would be the first tentative cuts of the chisel into the big Irishman's tombstone, though it was made of very tough granite.

IN his cell on Alcatraz in the Bay, "Scarface" Al Capone, insane from syphilis, was thinking of grand juries. The quick-tempered mobster thought he had found a legal loophole that would free him. It relied on the use of "a" instead of "the" in a statute covering the manner in which grand juries may be extended. Captain Dullea was thinking of grand juries, too. On Wednesday, April 29, the anniversary of the murders of both Officer John Malcolm and Josie Hughes, Dullea took the elevator to the fifth floor of City Hall and sat down outside its largest, most ornate courtroom. At 8:00 P.M., the county grand jury convened. "The Grand Jury is inquiring into charges of corruption and rumors of graft and vice involving the SFPD," jury foreman Mott Q. Brunton announced. How deeply the chief was involved Dullea couldn't prove, but as long as Police Commissioners Theodore Roche, Thomas Shumate, and Frank Foran backed Quinn he was unassailable. The corrupt cops weren't.

First to take the stand was Captain Thomas Hoertkorn, commander of Southern Station and the man who had ordered, "Let 'em have it, boys," during the bloody strikes. "I don't know what my financial position is," Hoertkorn told DA Matt Brady, who had grown white-haired and bow-backed during the last year. "Go ahead and subpoena my wife. She knows all about the family finances and is the fiscal agent." Hoertkorn ran one hand through his brushy hair. "Can I go?" He could.

The next night, Mrs. Emma Hoertkorn failed to appear at 8:00 P.M. with her bank books and records of any family financial transactions that might impact her husband's finances. This put the DA in a dilemma. Because no charges had been brought against Captain Hoertkorn, his wife could not be forced to appear. Within the hour, Emma's physician, Dr. Emil Torre, sent the court a letter. "Mrs. Hoertkorn collapsed the minute she accepted service of the Grand Jury subpoena to appear at City Hall," he wrote. "She has had a partial breakdown and is on the verge of hysteria. She has been ill for some time [Emma had been injured in an auto accident on Geary Street the year before] and will be in no condition to testify for at least a week."

The DA didn't want to wait a week to get an explanation about the $7,000 her husband had cached in an old bait can for the last fifteen years.

On May 4, he grilled Sergeant Patrick Shannon. "Do you serve under Captain Fred Lemon?" he asked. Lemon, who had replaced honest Captain Art Layne, was the commander of Central Station. "And is it true that you are responsible only to Captain Lemon?"

Shannon refused to answer.

"As a special duty man, did you ever take a gift of money from the keeper of a house of prostitution or a gambling house, or a bootlegger, or any illegal or unlawful enterprise?" Silence for a full minute from Shannon. "Are you prepared to answer?"

"Wait a second, will you. Hold your horses. I want to protect my rights."

"Well, do you refuse to answer on constitutional grounds?"

"Yes," said Shannon, "I avail myself of my constitutional rights. My real reason is that I want to get the advice of an attorney."

The real reason was that Shannon feared *any* answer might incriminate him and lead to criminal prosecution. He was already suspended, but if the charges of gambling, making a false report, and giving false testimony were substantiated he faced summary dismissal. The DA had already connected Shannon with the operation of two bookie joints on his beat and a store that was missing jewelry after he investigated a suspicious fire there.

"Do you realize refusing to answer is an act of contempt?" said the DA.

"Yes, I understand that."

Over the next half hour Shannon refused to answer whether he would answer. And what about the $25,000 Shannon claimed he had won at Tanforan Race Track and hidden in a woodpile? According to him a mystery bangtail picker named "Monk," a Gorilla Man of another sort, ran up Shannon's $2 bet to $25,000. After Turf broker "Cabbage Head" Winchell swore he was Monk's partner, a photo of a well-dressed monkey in glasses reading a racing form appeared in the *Chronicle* with a cartoon depicting three monkeys wearing police caps captioned, "See no evil," "Hear no evil," and "ESPECIALLY speak no evil."

Patrolman Joseph Brouders, another tightlipped special-duty man under Captain Lemon, took the stand next. The tough ex–Eagles' Hall bartender had joined the department the same year as Shannon but never risen higher than beat cop. Brouders refused to answer any questions regarding his bank accounts, property holdings, or conduct as an officer. "Do you refuse to answer on a constitutional ground?"

"I refuse to answer whether I refuse to answer on that ground."

While an officer is entitled to the exercise of his constitutional rights, he is not entitled to keep his job if he refuses to cooperate. "While a man has a constitutional right not to testify against himself," Justice Holmes wrote, "he has no constitutional right to be a policeman. The refusal to relate facts concerning performance of one's duties is ground for immediate suspension or dismissal."

Whereas Shannon had been calm, Brouders was edgy. With a cry, he ran from the court with his hat over his face. Ignoring the elevator, he dashed down four flights where three friends waited outside in a running car. As the reporters caught up, Brouders wheeled and reached for his hip pocket holster. "The first bastard that takes a step toward me—!" he said furiously. He backed onto the auto's running board and was driven away.

"Ashamed of Something?" the *Chronicle* captioned pictures of Shannon and Brouders with their hats and fingers over their faces.

A few days after the grand jury investigation got under way, Officer Jim Coleman, a twenty-nine-year vet under Captain Lemon, retired suddenly and went fishing. Dullea could find no record of Coleman's retirement. He knew that an officer with such a long service usually received comment in the press or best wishes from his fellow policemen and superiors. "Mrs.

Coleman is lacking in the usual degree of knowledge that a wife would have of her husband's whereabouts," said the DA.

Dullea drove to the Coleman's home. When nobody answered, he peered in. The dog and all the furniture were still there. He went to Fulton Street to question their landlady. She had been sworn to secrecy. "Mrs. Coleman has left town too," she whispered. "I can only conclude Coleman's taken a run-out," Dullea reported to the DA. Now he had to uncover what he could about Coleman's personal fortune, which was now estimated at $90,000.

"If the police have been bribed by gamblers and prostitutes," Brunton said, "and members of the SFPD are engaged in a conspiracy to ask and obtain bribes, we want to lay blame where it belongs no matter the cost."

While the crooked cops had plenty of money, the grand jury didn't. Although the DA could legally tap his graft fund for money to prepare a grand jury transcript, only $10,000 remained, scarcely half of what was needed. Mayor Rossi would have to be convinced to provide it. There was a certain urgency about the matter. Judge Robinson had uncovered a plot to destroy the only record of grand jury testimony. Every word taken down existed in twelve longhand steno notebooks in the care of T. J. McIlveen, the official stenographer. Under guard, Robinson had the notebooks placed in envelopes, sealed with wax, and locked in two downtown bank vaults until the transcripts could be made.

Supervisor Brown found the mayor at his florist shop, which he had kept throughout his tenure, and asked him to use some of his emergency reserve fund to pay for transcripts. On May 6, the mayor expressed willingness to recommend a further appropriation. "I hardly think the $25,000 already appropriated to delve into police corruption is sufficient," he said. "Without transcripts any future prosecution of the officers would be fatally handicapped. Besides, there has already been sufficient testimony before the Grand Jury to show that there is more to find out."

A procession of defiant witnesses and recalcitrant officers marched into the Grand Jury room and marched right out again. The following night Mrs. Emma Hoertkorn, attractive, brown-haired, motherly, and nervous hobbled to the witness stand supported by her son Harold, an accountant, and her lawyer, Chauncey Tramutolo. Harold patted her back as he eased her into the chair, but she hardly needed consoling. She was tough as nails.

"I have some rights!" she snapped at the first question about her husband's vast array of bank accounts, stocks, and bonds.

"Are you aware that you are committing an act of contempt?" asked the DA.

"I guess I am."

She was dismissed and limped away. Using other testimony, the DA established Hoertkorn's fortune as $70,000 ($47,000 in three separate bank accounts and $23,000 in real estate). At 9:20 P.M. Shannon was called into the Grand Jury room where he admitted to four savings accounts: two in the Anglo Bank, one in the American Trust, and one in a Bank of America branch (each of his five children had an account at the Eighth Avenue Bank of America branch). He emerged ten minutes later with sweat on his brow. "They threw me out!" he said. "But I've talked too much already." Then he vanished into the stairwell.

"Thar's gold in them woodpiles, Pat," a reporter called after him.

Brouders staggered out next. "Somebody give me a cigarette," he said. His hands were shaking as he lit up. He sprinted down the stairs so fast he overtook Shannon.

Captain Lemon was still a no-show. The next morning the chief summoned Acting Surgeon D. M. Campbell into his office. "I want you to thoroughly examine Captain Lemon," he told him, "and see if the arthritis he complains of is really debilitating or even exists. But even if it is shown conclusively that he is physically fit to appear before the Grand Jury, I am still powerless to do anything about it. From my knowledge of the law, I would say that the Grand Jury has the power, if it sees fit, to convene in Lemon's home. But I am awaiting your report with interest, doctor."

About the same time, the DA was saying, "I want to see if Lemon is faking," and sent Dr. Louis Oviedo to examine him and get a second opinion.

Near midnight on Friday, May 1, four uniformed Taraval District officers pulled up in front of Police Commissioner Shumate's drugstore at 901 Taraval Street, one of a chain of thirty. Two of the officers smashed the glass in the front door, and Officer Sydney Hinson left prints on the glass as he picked out the shards. Three witnesses saw the cops reemerge, stack crates of liquor in their cruiser, and drive away. When assistant manager John Collins arrived at the store at 8:00 A.M., he went directly to a concealed drawer. The hidden money was missing, yet money in plain view in a stamp box by the register was untouched. "Only five people had knowledge of the hiding place," Collins told Dullea.

Outraged, Dullea personally filed burglary charges against the four patrolmen—John Farrell, radio car Officers Hinson and Thomas Miller, and station keeper John T. McKenna, the only officer not suspended. Yet Mc-Kinna had the worst record—fined for intoxication and unofficer-like conduct and twice charged with neglect of duty he once shot the door lock off the Cairo Club. In April 1930 McKinna visited his estranged wife on Leavenworth Street and, when barred from entering, climbed a drainpipe that broke and dropped him two stories into a light well. While still recuperating, he was involved in a hotel room shooting in which a woman wounded herself in the thigh. But after the four cops were formally booked, the chief released them on $250 bail each. "Why are they not in jail," curious reporters asked. "Is discrimination being shown them because they are officers? Who are the witnesses?"

"I will not identify the witnesses publicly."

"Are you afraid they will be intimidated?"

"I just want to be sure they are available to testify," said the chief.

Immediately, the reporters tried to identify the witnesses. "The area is in darkness by midnight and at that time wholly without pedestrians," they speculated. "That leaves the rows of houses on 19th Avenue with front windows providing a clear view of the drugstore entrance."

A few hours later, Quinn's close friend and secretary of the Police Commission, fifty-one-year-old Captain Charles Skelly, went to lunch in North Beach. After parking in front of La Compagna on Broadway, he went inside. One of the indicted patrolmen, John Farrell, was eating there. The lean, dark-haired young man spied Skelly. "I ought beat the hell out of you," he barked. "If I had a gun, Skelly, I'd kill you and I will kill you sooner or later."

Farrell mistakenly believed Skelly had granted "virtual immunity" to Patrolman Hinson in exchange for testifying against him. Farrell swung at

Skelly, but the former Olympic Club boxer who had once knocked out World Heavyweight Champ Jack Johnson, dodged and tagged Farrell with a powerful right. Two of Dan Barbini's waiters and noted bartender Joseph Toschi overpowered Farrell. "You're under arrest for making threats against a superior officer," Skelly said.

Toschi called for a cruiser. Just as the patrol car arrived Farrell threw another punch, and Skelly knocked him cold. After Farrell was jailed, Chief Quinn said, "We simply feel that this man is dangerous to Captain Skelly's life. I demand the highest possible bail." But next morning, Farrell was out again, on an even lower bail than his cohorts. When Dullea demanded Farrell's indictment for the attack and burglary, his fury inspired several police officers to seek out Atherton to make a deal.

Three days later, another police fortune was revealed—$35,000 in cash and stocks inside a pine box. "It's been my habit to keep large sums of money in just a little box," said Lieutenant Ed Copeland, another Central District cop under Captain Lemon. He had been a steamship company storekeeper for $100 a month, then a policeman for fourteen years, but never filed a federal income tax. The year before he had paid a state tax of $7.98.

City Treasurer Duncan Matheson, a dour Scotch Presbyterian and former captain, came up with a proposal to help Quinn. "A police chief is ham strung when he has to face political pressure in his official acts—either from a mayor or anyone else," he said. "Under the present conditions a police captain names his own special duty men and the chief has little to say about it. Under proper Charter provisions preventing Quinn's removal from politics, he would be in a position to wield full authority over his captains and other officers."

The image of an un-fireable Chief Quinn was on Dullea's mind as he stood on a sandy beach south of Fleishhacker Pool. Snowy plovers were diving as eight patrolmen and three fire searchlight truck crews ended their all-night search without result. Now only gawkers in their cars clogged the shore road above. A prayer book lay amid the purple needle grass and monkey flowers. Dullea picked it up and read the name inside: "Rev. Father Walter Semeria, S. J." The depressed logic and philosophy teacher habitually took sun baths at the beach to aid his recovery from a serious operation. Dullea found Semeria's auto with his hat and coat locked inside and concluded the worst.

Dullea, a very moral man, was more deeply disturbed by the corruption rumors than the average man. During World War II, when half the city's regular police officers were conscripted, he would order every known brothel closed to reduce the incidence of venereal disease. "We cannot substitute hygiene for morality," he said, "and any attempt to evade the moral issue, or pass over it lightly is bound to end in tragedy."

At war's end, when drunken sailors and soldiers packed Market Street and eleven died during a three-day orgy of looting and rape, Dullea would express his disgust with "the unbridled and unrestrained acts of a lot undisciplined men in uniform." He returned from the beach to City Hall to discover more special-duty men had defied the grand jury.

Even worse, Dullea knew most of them: Captain Art de Guire, commander of Harbor Station, was relieved of his badge and gun; Lieutenant Henry Ludolph was having his second brush before a Grand Jury; and Harry Gurtler, fat and many chinned, and Alec Mino (two Southern Station duty men) refused to be sworn. When Gurtler produced a doctor's note to excuse his absence, the DA threatened to call all captains and special-duty men of the other thirteen districts to testify. That day, two officers from the Ellis-Polk Station applied for sudden retirement. Now those suspended for refusing to answer questions numbered an even dozen. Captain Lemon, seeing the furor wasn't going to die down, climbed out of bed, walked into court, refused to be sworn, and became the unlucky thirteenth man.

"Honest police officers, ashamed to put on their uniforms since the graft hearings began," Commissioner Roche said, "are entitled to be exonerated as thoroughly as possible. If captains named honest men there would be no cause for complaint." But he also admitted there was a definite need for the special-duty squads. "They have work to perform that cannot be done by the man on the beat. It is not advisable to abolish a position because of the man who holds it unless you find a suitable substitute."

That afternoon a well-dressed man who claimed to be a high official of the SFPD offered Atherton a bribe.

On May 19, the Police Board dismissed Brouders from the force. When Shannon argued for a secret hearing, his lawyer Vince Hallinan, a former boxer, got in a knockdown-drag-out brawl when opposing council Paul Dana made the mistake of calling Shannon "Woodpile Pat." Hallinan began it by sucker-punching Dana at a fourth-floor water cooler. When the board unanimously fired Shannon for "over-talkativeness," he questioned their authority over him by raising the specter of Frank Egan, who was serving twenty-five years in San Quentin. Egan had challenged the mayor and supervisors' power to fire him for failing to cooperate at the coroner's inquest into Josie Hughes's death. Judge Harris settled that legal question. "When Egan took the oath of office," he said, "he pledged himself to support the constitution of the United States and that of California. When he subordinated his official duty to his personal rights he violated his official pledge and, therefore, was clearly guilty of official misconduct. . . . [T]he Supervisors had the power to dismiss him after finding him guilty of misconduct." Shannon's firing was legal.

Shannon began dickering with IRS collector John Lewis to pay federal income taxes on his $100,000 fortune. Lewis wasn't in a dickering mood. He wanted cash in full along with all penalties, special assessments, and accrued interest from unpaid taxes since 1914. The total came to $25,000—the exact amount Shannon had hidden in a woodpile.

May 21 began with a dawn fire that burned all day, eating away the oil-soaked pilings and lumber along the channel from Third Street to Seventh Street. Seven ships were cast adrift, and the Bay Bridge was damaged. Patrolman George Lillis, a Central Station bagman, was suspended for contempt. An hour later, the grand jury ordered the McDonough brothers to testify on May 27, the anniversary of the luncheon club speech that had initiated the probe.[19] Lewis had been talking about former Captain Stephen Bunner and now demanded Bunner pay his long-delayed federal tax on a

---

[19] The McDonoughs finally outsmarted themselves when they tried to pass legislation to corner the bail bond market in the state. In 1941 their tiny bail bond brokerage office at Clay and Kearney became just another dusty cigar store after Dullea and the newly-formed state insurance department made it a crime for anyone with a criminal record to run a bail bond operation.

personal fortune of $110,000. Though Bunner was onboard a steamer chugging through the Panama Canal, Lewis stripped him of a large portion of his wealth. Eventually Bunner would pay double penalties and assessments stretching over many years.

Harold Boyd, chief deputy tax collector, ordered Patrolmen Gurtler and Ed Christal, Captain de Guire, and Joe Nolan of Central District (who also was suddenly up for retirement) to appear before him about paying income tax. "I will take you to municipal court unless you settle with the city," Boyd threatened.

As word spread, twenty-three other officers made appointments with Boyd to quietly talk over their liability. Many more called on Jake Ehrlich to defend them; so many, his offices resembled the squad room at Central Station. San Francisco was such a wonderfully corrupt town that the word *hoodlum* had originated there. A local reporter, instead of referring directly to local gang boss Muldoon, spelled the mobster's name backward and changed the initial letter to arrive at *hoodlum*.

Lieutenant Mark Higgins, Western Addition, revealed $46,000 in cash and assets, Captain Will Healy told of $24,000 in cash, and Lieutenant Martin Fogarty of Harbor Station apprised the grand jury of his $44,000 fortune. "The amount of my wealth has been misquoted," said Fogarty, a good-looking man with a high pompadour and thick mustache. "For twelve years I was at the Ferry Building where I gave $1.50 daily to stranded people to get across the Bay. And there's no chance of getting any graft at the Ferry Building." He admitted $8,200 in three bank accounts of which $2,200 was his own.

After the DA did a little spade work, he invited Fogarty back. "Are you not a joint holder with your brother William in the following accounts— Just how did your mentally disturbed brother come by $16,000 in cash?"

"He was a frugal man."

Chief Quinn transferred Fogarty from Harbor Station to Potrero Station just as another of Captain Lemon's bucket men, Patrolman George Lillis, a former gripman on the old Union Street cable line, refused to take the stand. "Rule 19 of the SFPD orders officers to testify before the Grand Jury," Roche informed him.

Assistant DA Leslie Gillen, who had once covered City Hall as a *Chronicle* reporter while studying law, conducted the next questioning. The DA was exhausted. Patrolman William Quinlan of Richmond Station listed his stocks—242 shares in the Owl Drug Company at $10,000 a throw, 114 shares of AT&T, 283 shares in Transamerica, over 2,000 shares in PG&E, 40 shares of General Motors in a safe deposit box at Wells Fargo, and $92,000 in securities. Gillen, an inflexible and humorless man, showed uncharacteristic surprise.

"Where did you get the money to make such big investments?" he asked.

"Out of my savings as a patrolman."

"On a policeman's salary?" Gillen shook his head.

Quinlan had entered the department on March 29, 1905, at the age of thirty-two as a teamster earning between $35 and $80 a month and "his keep." He had $52,000 in cash stockpiled, he said, out of a policeman's salary of $200 a month over the last six years.

"I have other sources," said Quinlan, who shifted in his chair and smiled. "I never gamble, though I once won $91 on a $4 bet." He said he had inherited $3,000 from his brother, James, a veterinarian who mysteriously vanished and was declared legally dead in 1930. He also owned three vacant lots in the Bayview district and had a fifth interest in a two-story frame house on Folsom Street. He had accounts in banks all over town—Hibernia, Crocker First Federal, Bank of America—a total of $34,003. Then there was a category Quinlan called "found" money, which amounted to $100,000 in cash and stocks. He had made out an income tax report once, but forgotten to file it. Like most of the nontestifying cops, he had never paid a cent of tax.

With disgust, Gillen dismissed him. Quinn's close friend Inspector Charles Gallivan, a former $20-a-week butcher, came next. He operated out of the chief's office as one of his two private investigators, though his expertise was in bunco. He admitted $13,247.83 in cash in two bank accounts and a safe deposit box containing $43,575 in stocks—AT&T, Sears-Roebuck, Consolidated Oil, Anchorage Light and Power, and Kolster Radio. He rattled off a dozen real estate deals, concluding with the purchase of a southwest corner property on Fillmore and McAllister streets for $65,000, which sold for $80,000. "When I sold the McAllister property," he said, "I found myself in possession of about $43,000 in cash." All told he admitted to $56,822 in riches, but had paid only $30 in federal income tax and $10 in state tax. He seemed proud of that.

THIRTY-EIGHT

"The Murders in the Rue Morgue" first appeared in book form in a thin leaflet in tan-colored wrappers in 1843 for 12½ cents.

—*THE PROSE ROMANCES OF EDGAR A. POE*

IT was a crisp night. A tall, good-looking young man walked into the HOJ and admitted strangling a woman in a hotel room. "I want you to hang me," he said matter-of-factly. His voice was calm, well-modulated, and he was neatly dressed. Inspector Alvin Corrasa looked up from his desk and into his pale blue eyes. The man was not drunk. "No, I mean it," he said. "Get it over as soon as possible please. I've killed a girl in a hotel, strangled her with my bare hands, and I've come to turn myself in."

A strangling? In a hotel? Dullea would be interested, but first— "Show us where." Corrasa and his partner, William Stanton, followed the young man to 840 California Street between Powell and Stockton streets. It was not far from Nob Hill and offered a splendid view of the Bay. Inside the room, they followed a trail of clothes—a blue wool sweater, pink slip, silk underwear, and a pair of brown slacks, which led to a folding in-a-door bed. When Corrasa pulled it down, the nude body of a tall woman, bent in half, tumbled out.

Her head was drawn back tautly by a pair of brown silk stockings knotted to the brass bedposts. Dark, ugly marks had been dug into her throat, and her eyes were bulging. She had been strangled by a huge pair of hands. What struck Corrasa was that the victim's hair was the same red as Bette

Coffin's. Had they found the Gorilla Man at last? Corrasa was doubtful because of the young man's slenderness and height.

The young man sat down on the edge of the bed, placed a cigarette in an ivory holder, and began calmly smoking. "Oh, why I do these crazy things is beyond my comprehension," he said. He crossed his legs and swung one foot back and forth. "Crazy me. Only when my sanity returns do I realize the consequences of my foolhardiness. In my depression I can do nothing but run away to relieve my mind of its many, many burdens and the pressures put upon me."

He was Albert Walter Jr., the twenty-eight-year-old son of a Boston real estate broker. He had been a law clerk, butler, chef, lumber man, salesman, and soldier in the Army Medical Corps, had even served a disciplinary term on Alacatraz, where Fell had been imprisoned. Inspectors Harry Husted and George Engler and Assistant DA John McMahon joined Corrasa and Stanton. In the next hour the five men learned a few things about a new motive for murder.

"I used to live out here in 1926 and after we went east," Walter said. "I still made a trip back here about once a year. When I was last in San Francisco six months ago a wealthy importer invited me home. I knocked him unconscious and stole his gold watch." He smiled. "I guess I was not cut out to be a good guest." He looked down at the body. His face was expressionless. "I killed her because I hate all women. I hate them. I've always known that someday I would kill one of them."

"And now you have."

"Now I have."

"When did you come to San Francisco?"

"Just fourteen days ago, this trip. The girl is Blanche Cousins."

Walter, unable to endure more of his ten-month marriage and sick of managing a restaurant, caught a bus west out of New York City. Blanche Cousins boarded at Salt Lake City and she and Walter began talking. By noon of the next day at Sacramento, they were good friends. Blanche, the daughter of an Idaho Falls rancher, was on her way to attend business college. The next night in San Francisco she checked into the YWCA. "I'm counting on seeing you a lot," Walter told her. "I don't have many friends in the city," she told him. "Neither do I," he said.

"She moved from the YWCA hotel into this apartment," he continued. "That first night she cooked dinner for me here, a sort of housewarming I guess. Last night she cooked dinner for me again. I came in about 7:00 P.M., and we had a couple of cocktails before eating. Afterward we sat on the davenport talking for a while and then we did the dishes. We went back to the davenport after that and talked for a while about her work at school, what she did back in Idaho Falls, and what I intended to do about getting a job and staying out here—you know, the usual thing.

"Then I began to make love to her. I had tried to several times before but she always resisted. This time she said something about not being too hasty about things. I didn't see why she should resist me and I went blind with anger. Suddenly, I grabbed her by the throat and began to choke her. Then she didn't resist anymore. I lost my head—I guess. I don't remember all the details. I didn't know whether she was dead or not and I didn't care. I took down the folding bed and lifted her onto it. I pulled off her sweater, slacks, and slip and threw them across the room. *Then* I ravished her." There was silence in the room. Walter had stayed in the room doing unspeakable things for an hour, then tied her stockings around her neck and knotted the ends to the bedposts.

"Why?" asked Corrasa. "She was already dead."

"I suppose so. I felt for her pulse and listened for her heart. Why does anyone do any mad thing?"

Another necrosadist, to use LaTulipe's term, thought Corrasa.

"I've tried to lead a normal life," Walter said, "but this hatred and bitterness keeps cropping up in spite of me. I left my wife twice in New York because I was afraid I'd kill her. When Blanche Cousins repulsed me, it all surged up in me again. She symbolized all the things I wanted and couldn't have. That's why I choked her. I've hated women, but I couldn't stay away from them."

Walter left his room about 11:30 P.M., visited a cocktail bar or two, then bought a bottle of whiskey and registered in a hotel over on Mason Street. He drank until 5:00 A.M., then dropped off to sleep. At noon, he dressed, left the hotel, and walked along the Embarcadero and through Chinatown for hours. "I just wanted to be left alone—and to walk—I wasn't sorry then, I'm not sorry now." He had gone back to the hotel, packed his suitcase, sold all his belongings at a pawn shop—then around 8:30 P.M., walked to headquarters to turn himself in.

All night Corrasa questioned him about numerous unsolved sex crimes involving red-haired women and stranglings recently perpetrated in San Diego, on Bette Coffin and Mrs. Ruby Allen and Louise Jeppesen in Golden Gate Park. Walter shook his head.

"Nope, I don't know anything about them, especially Mrs. Coffin," he said. "You're going to have to be content with solving just this one murder. Why don't you just let me go ahead and die and get it over with? I'm sick of life."

Conscientious public defender Gerald Kenny, whom Frank Egan had targeted for assassination, was Walter's lawyer at trial. As a child Walter had suffered head injuries that might have affected him, and he had contracted VD, which had a bearing on his adult behavior. But tests showed Walter did not have a sexual disease and Dr. Marvin Hirschfield determined him to be "a psychopath with psychotic episodes." Dr. E. W. Mullins of Agnews Street Hospital for the Insane, Dr. Joseph Pohrim, and Dr. Frank Sheehy testified that Walter knew the difference between right and wrong. Albert's father, Albert Walter Sr. and his wife, Angela, made a dramatic plea for his life by telling of insanity in the family and his son's aimless wanderings and unnatural sex life. When the jury went out, father and wife, unfamiliar with courtroom procedure, left the courtroom thinking a recess had been called. Kenny told them of the death verdict outside on the sidewalk twenty-three minutes later. "Don't worry. I have no intention of committing suicide in my cell," Walter told Judge Jacks. "All I want to do now is to hang—as soon as possible. My only regret is I won't hang sooner. I just want to be hanged and forgotten." And he was. They hung the silk-stocking strangler at San Quentin a month later.

THIRTY-NINE

We called the new HOJ the Marble Orchard. I had the pleasure of working at the original HOJ. The word was that you had to have a lot of juice in those days.

—HOMICIDE INSPECTOR DAVE TOSCHI

ED Atherton, the DA's investigator, traveled south to meet with Melvin Purvis, credited with engineering the slaying of bank robber John Dillinger and Republic's first choice to play Dick Tracy in their new serial. Over the weekend, the two former G-men selected four federal agents to sniff out the big lies in the testimony. But to get to the big man behind the corruption, Atherton would have to request another two payments of $25,000 each.

LIEUTENANT Joe Mignola of Ellis-Polk Station, who had commanded his men to fire buckshot into the strikers at Pier 20, refused to be sworn. After him Lieutenant Mark Higgins of Western Addition Station admitted to $46,000 in cash, an expensive auto, and ritzy home though his yearly salary was only $3,000. He was a bit hazy as to whether he used money from his secret safety deposit box or bank accounts to purchase stock. "It's my wife's habit to just hand me money in an envelope and I usually just dropped it in the box," he said. With a disarming smile, he admitted he often got "surprise packages" of $4,000 and $12,000.

During a long grand jury session, Lemon's attorney, Edwin McKenzie, accused Roche of bias. "I am perfectly willing to step down," Roche said, "and have Mayor Rossi name a man to take my place. I have been in the department for twenty-four years and it is difficult for me even to contemplate this action because it would look like an admission of bias and a desire to avoid my duty. I don't want to resign. To do so at this time would seem like quitting under fire and shirking my duty."

On Friday night, May 30, the commission heard arguments by the attorneys for nine policemen under fire on whether Roche should be disqualified from hearing the proceedings and whether the whole commission should be disqualified. Without a beat, the mayor backed Roche. "The proceedings are entirely legal," said Roche, "and there is no chance for the disqualification of any member of the Commission."

"Then Captain Lemon pleads not guilty to all the charges against him," said McKenzie.

Patrolman E. J. Christal, nine years a special-duty officer, defied the jury, too. "You cannot force me to be a witness against myself," he said, and brought up a technical point—the charges were insufficient in that they were sworn to before Chief Quinn who was not empowered to administer oaths.

ON June 1, Richmond Station Patrolman James F. Madden, the third witness of the night, took the stand. Dullea studied the florid, baby-faced vet as he eased his bulk into the witness chair. There was a discernible creak. Had the grand jury at last uncovered a $200,000+ copper still pounding a beat? For weeks, the papers had been hinting at just such a revelation. Dullea doubted it would get that bad. Gillen reviewed the facts aloud. Madden had joined the SFPD in 1908 at a salary of $122 a month and a savings account of $2,000 saved from his $12 to $18 weekly wages as a teamster. Madden pushed back his porkpie hat and revealed thin dark hair. He clenched a cigar in his mouth, then began fishing around in his front pockets and patting on both sides of his loud tie. His hands were too small for such a big man but finally did the job. Pulling back his sleeves like a magician, he extracted ten bank books and balanced them on his chubby knees.

When an aunt died, Madden had been enriched by a bequest of $1,000. He had property on a lot at 166 Oak Street. In 1910, he invested in two flats at 1460 Waller Street and lived in one with his wife and son. From 1918 to 1921 he received $100 a month from a Haight Street garage property and "dabbled in securities," beginning with shares in the Rolph Coal Company. Three years later, he purchased 100 shares of BancItaly stock at $136 a share. "Gee," he said, "before I knew it, I had $44,000." His fat face was wreathed in a smile. He took up another book and began reeling off figures that had the jurors goggle-eyed. "I reaped a harvest of dollars from the buying and selling of horseflesh in partnership with my late brother, Dr. J. O. Quinlan.

"Then things went like wildfire," he said with a wave of stubby fingers. "I split up my stocks, divided them, the bank bought me others, they all went up, and pretty soon I owed the bank $80,000. Well, sir, I paid that off and still had a lot of money and stocks left. I paid the mortgage on my home, then, and decided to sell my stocks and concentrate on bonds. The crash came but I didn't lose anything. The bonds went up; I sold them. Then I bought stocks again, sold them, bought bonds, sold the bonds, bought stocks, until I guess I must have had an awful lot of things."

Gillen's head swam. Hard pressed to keep up with his pencil, he rapidly jotted down figures. Madden was far from finished. From his back trouser pockets he withdrew another ten books, laid them out and thumbed through them. "I got a few safe deposit boxes for my cash," he said, and read off $100,000 items without batting an eye.

"Is it true that between 1910 and 1935, these sums passed through your accounts?" said Gillen, looking down at his pad.

"Yes, I guess that's about right."

"Is it also true that in 1929 you deposited a total of $126,415.27?"

"Yes, that's also correct. Let me tell you about that. I decided to borrow some money from the banks and I got $300,000 from them."

"On what security?"

"On my stocks and bonds." He said he played the market at a loss in 1931 when he dropped $3,612.96. The following year he lost $1,414.22, and the year after that $20,775.03. In 1934 he lost $4,246.94.

"During 1934, did you deposit $143,209.34?"

"Yes," said Madden nonchalantly, "but mostly in the last quarter of the year. You see, there was a lot of reports that the State was going to the dogs, so I sold many of my bonds temporarily, sold most everything and laid low in 1934." As he testified over the two-and-a-half-hour Grand Jury session Madden was at perfect ease.

Asked if he had ever paid any income tax, Madden estimated he had paid $7,400 over a ten-year period. From his vest pocket he plucked out six more bank books and began to read nonchalantly. Gillen's pencil flew as he added. The grand total was—*$834,021.12!*

"I'm exhausted, bewildered and thoroughly flabbergasted by the amount," Gillen admitted. He ran his hands through his hair and sat down.

"I am a thrifty man," said Madden matter-of-factly.

"It would take a Philadelphia lawyer six months working day and night, to fathom your resources."

And these were 1936 dollars, as the nation was crawling out of the depths of the Depression. "We know that his fortune is large," said the DA to Dullea, "so large that I'd have to put my entire staff on it for the rest of the summer to get an accurate estimate."

How Madden had accumulated such wealth on less than $200 a month was mind-boggling.

FORTY

It was as if a compulsion had seized him and guided his hand, not so much against his will but without his knowledge. He seemed to recall only flashes of his acts, but enough to satisfy the detectives that they had the Gorilla Man in their grasp.

—*CHRONICLE* NEWS ITEM

JUST before rush hour, a nondescript man in a wide-brimmed hat staggered east along Ellis Street. He was thin, sickly, and bore a deep cut above his left eye. The backs of his hands were lacerated and bleeding, his eyes glazed and staring. Tears coursed down his stubbled cheeks. He wore an ill-fitting jacket over sailor's whites and had drawn both arms up to his chest. Crowds parted as he shuffled for three blocks—four blocks. "What's the trouble, Bud?" At the fifth block, he tottered into the bustling intersection at Stockton and Market.

Heads turned as he crossed against the Wiley signal bell that rang *ding-ding-ding* when the light changed. "This guy's just come from the mother of all drunks," the cop thought, "or been hit by a truck." The sailor held out his arms, opened his hands and offered a piece of tattered flesh to the cop. Screams erupted from those closest. One woman fainted. The crowd melted away as if fearing contamination.

"I just killed my wife," he said. His chest was heaving. "I'm the one who called the police." "Show me where," said the cop. Without hesitation he led the traffic cop back to a Tenderloin hotel at 510 Ellis Street. Inside the double hotel room on a bed was a body, nude, bloody, and unspeakably mangled. It was still warm. Her hair was titian red.

"If you don't tell me about the arrest, you sonuvabitch, I'll blast you all over town," the "Iron Duke" bellowed. The Iron Duke wasn't his real name. That was Bill Wren. He wasn't a duke, but might well have been. As the *Examiner*'s city editor, he ran San Francisco. The police commissioner, the DA, and the mayor went in person to his office at Third and Market to curry favor. He only had to say to high officials, "Bill Wren wants" and "desire became command."

The belligerent, Boston-born editor kept his power by devious means. His men worked the same way. His columnist Bob Patterson once called up Bones Remmer, the notorious gambler. "Somebody told me an embarrassing story concerning you, Bones," he said. "I'm going to have to run it in my column. I hate to embarrass you, but business is business. Of course, I might be persuaded to not run the story if you were to give me $500."

When Bones came over to Patterson's office to give him the money, the doors flew open, flash bulbs popped, and the next day's paper had a front-page picture of them exchanging money—"Bones Rimmer Tries to Bribe *Examiner* Columnist." In retaliation, Bones offered records of Patterson's long criminal history and prison time to the other papers. None would print it. They had their ethics. That was what passed as journalism in San Francisco.

It hadn't taken Wren long to find out someone was in custody for the Bay Hotel murder—after all these years. Chief Quinn had called first. "There's been another autopsy murder in a hotel," he said. "A sailor confessed that he'd just killed and mutilated a woman."

As soon as the chief hung up, a chambermaid, one of the dozens on Wren's payroll, called. Like Anna Lemon, she had unlocked a room door and discovered a partially dissected body. Then a uniformed officer rang him. "We've got the Gorilla Man," he said. "He's just confessed to another hotel murder and mutilation. I spoke to him myself. Keep it under your hat. I'll call back with more." The Iron Duke hung up, then looked to the framed motto over his head: "Tell me nothing in confidence." "Copy," he bellowed.

He needed his best reporter who was whiling away the afternoon hours at one of the newspaper watering holes. Since the repeal of prohibition in 1934, the word *saloon* was out and *tap room, juice joint, cocktail lounge,* and *tavern* were in.

The story spread in the hot afternoon. Reporters heard the news at Jerry and Johnny's and Jay Hurley's near the *Examiner*. The buzz, like a current of electricity, flowed on to the House of Shields across from the *Call* on New Montgomery. Word of the arrest passed among the tipsy scribes at Murphy's Spa at the Market–Grant intersection and at Gallagher's saloon at Mission and Fourth streets, where most of the *Bulletin* ink-stained wretches hung out. At Hanno's behind the *Chronicle,* the printers took off their square, folded-newspaper hats, threw them in the alley and began buzzing about the news.

Dullea's patrol car, siren screaming, reached the Tenderloin's epicenter, Eddy and Leavenworth streets. That tawdry region encompasses the area between Geary, Van Ness, Market, and Mason streets. Dullea and Husted entered the Ellis Street Hotel and ascended to room 516. On a chair by the door sat a traffic cop in uniform with his head buried in his hands.

The curtains were closed. The room was stifling. The man on the other side of the room was flanked by three uniformed officers. His chin was trembling. His head was lowered. Dullea saw the slashed, strangled body of a young, red-haired woman sprawled across the bed. When he remembered that Bette Coffin's hair had been the same shade of titian red, his heart began to pound.

"I'm the one who told the police," the bloodied sailor said. "I did it." He shook his handcuffs.

"Why did you do it?" asked Dullea, walking to the bed and looking down on the victim. "Make us understand. What was your motive?" He was very interested in motives these days. Dullea knelt. An expertly made hangman's noose had been tightened around her neck and some razor-sharp cutting implement had been used to cut away a portion of her torso. Not only had the sailor sectioned her body, but he had printed a message across her stomach in makeup pencil: "Honey I Love You." Dullea noticed that she had drawn her eyebrows on with the same pencil. A second note pinned to the sheet said essentially the same thing. The killer had gotten the idea from that day's *Examiner* story about film star Barbara Leonard who had been beaten in her bathroom by two men who tied her up and wrote on her back in blue makeup pencil: "LAST WARNING." They wrote it in reverse so she could read it in the mirror. Dullea agreed with Husted that the mutilations were remarkably similar to the Bay Hotel homicide. But this time the strangling and slashing hadn't been enough for the killer. He had bashed her head in with a wooden rolling pin.

When he got no answer from the killer, Dullea went to the mantle and used his handkerchief to pick up a whisky bottle. He tilted it. Only dregs remained. Maybe the bottle was the motive. He returned to the bed and studied the suspect's face. It was bleak and remorseful. Ramon Lee Hughes, a thirty-six-year-old sailor, was a good looking guy, with a full head of hair. But when remorse overtook him his face collapsed like puff pastry. Hughes rose. He could hardly stand. He tottered across the room and sat down heavily on the edge of the sofa. Blinking rapidly, he laced his fingers together like a second set of handcuffs. Heavy gold rings on each of his fingers glinted. Raising his arms, the sailor laid his cheek along his manacled hands as if making a pillow of them. He was sobering up quickly now and regretting what he had done.

"He's the most pitiful hangdog drunk I've ever seen," Dullea whispered to Husted. "In no way does he match my perception of the Bay Hotel killer."

But then neither had the handsome, likable Slipton Fell (whose face also lost its attractiveness when he broke into an insensate grin). Hughes didn't even have Fell's strength and size. Eventually, he stopped sobbing, composed himself, and told Dullea why he had done it. "Jealousy, I guess, that and drink," Hughes said, "damn drink-fired jealousy that's all. She meant everything to me."

The staff of the Ellis Hotel knew the victim as twenty-three-year-old Genevieve "Jean" Montgomery (her birth name was Genevieve Clucky). Five years before she and another woman, Mrs. Bette Keith, had come to California from Toledo, where Jean's father was a police detective.

"Jean had recently gotten divorced from John Montgomery, a Centralia, Washington lumberjack. I paid for the divorce, I wanted to be with her that much. She was my common law wife. She had just returned from a week's visit to San Diego. When I discovered this snapshot of her and another sailor, we argued."

Dullea took the photo. It showed Jean in a jaunty little white hat with a red stripe and a silk scarf around her neck just where the noose was now.

After Jean had drunk herself into a stupor, Hughes must have knotted her cloth belt around her neck and watched her die. Afterward he had done his awful work with a straight razor.

"What do you know about the mutilation slaying of Bette Coffin two years ago?" asked Dullea.

"I don't know what you're talking about," said Hughes. He blinked rapidly and passed out. Dullea knelt and tied the prisoner's shoe so he wouldn't trip when he came to. They managed to walk the confessed killer out of the hotel, into the car, and to Kearney Street. Dullea stopped the car across from Portsmouth Square. Lights were blazing on the second floor of the old HOJ—that meant the reporters were up and prowling. A cool breeze rose. He pulled around to the rear, where three deputies waited to take Hughes to the tanks and avoid the press. At the north wing Bernard Reilly, the jail superintendent, was at the visitor's cage; when he saw them, he climbed off a high wooden bench and escorted Hughes to Judge Thomas Prendergast's court. Hughes's public defender arrived, protested that he hadn't had time to familiarize himself with the first-degree murder case, and requested a delay. "All right," said Prendergast, "I'll put the case over until September 8."

Hughes was then to endure a withering all-night third-degree interrogation about the Bay Hotel murder.

He took a seat on a rickety chair in a small room on the ground floor. Two cops entered. Hughes eyed the saps dangling by leather thongs from their wrists. One cop brought his sap down across the bridge of Ramon's nose. "Why did you do it? What about all the others? What about the Bay Hotel?" The other cop got out the rubber hose and hefted it in his palm as if to gauge its weight. Around 4:00 A.M. three guards escorted Hughes to a narrow corridor in one of the jail wings where he spent an hour pacing and biting his lips to the jibes of other prisoners in their cells.

A ferocious rivalry for exclusives drove Bay Area journalists to extremes. Reporter Willie Hale covered his crime stories armed with a revolver. The papers were as fanatical. Anytime a man went to a newspaper office to say he was guilty of murder and wanted to confess, the first thing the paper did was squirrel him away from the police. Security guards and city policemen on the newspaper payroll, then blockaded the plant until an extra packed with exclusive stories and lurid photographs was printed and loaded onto trucks for delivery. *Then* the police were notified.

Just before dawn, before any other reporter, the Iron Duke's man went to the booking sergeant on the top floor. "I've been assigned by the city editor," he said. "I want you to bring out Hughes from his cell so I can question him in the interview room." It was not a question but an order: Bill Wren wants.

"Okay," said the sergeant, "but he doesn't want to be photographed."

But Wren's man had concealed his cameraman and got a shot of Hughes, bruised, bleary-eyed, and exhausted, as he entered. "Your pictures already been taken and I can assure you it's not going to be flattering," he told Hughes. "But if you sit for a carefully lit and posed picture it might present a better image on the front page." Of course Hughes posed and gave an interview while he did.

Husted located Jean's close friend, Bette Keith, and was interviewing her when another woman, Florence Montgomery of 971 Mission Street, came to the jail and said she was Jean's sister. "We had found no local relatives of the attractive divorcee," said Husted.

Upon seeing Jean's body, she collapsed and asked to be taken to Hughes's cell so she could confront him. "When she was taken to his cell," said Husted, "she came at him with her nails. What made her outburst all the more puzzling was that she was not really the slain woman's sister."

At noon, Hughes used his pocket money to have a hamburger sent in from a nearby restaurant along with a newspaper. His face was on the front page as the long-sought Gorilla Man. Now he was completely distraught. After another grilling, he signed a complete confession admitting to slaying the Montgomery girl. He hadn't held back a fact, even seemed anxious to tell all, yet emphatically denied (just as Slipton Fell and Walker had) the murder of Bette Coffin and Mrs. Johnston in New York or the girls in San Diego, or the women in Golden Gate Park. He returned to his cell, shoulders slumped, and reread the newspaper story. He listened to the house sergeant conduct roll call, heard all the groans and sighs of the station house, the changing of shifts, and the despair of new prisoners.

An hour later, came a sharp rap on Dullea's door. He and McGinn had been discussing Pete McDonough's jailing for refusing to discuss police graft before the Grand Jury headed by Marshall Dill. "Come quickly, Captain, up to the jail," a sergeant said.

McGinn and Dullea followed and peered through the bars of Hughes's cell. His body was hanging by the neck from a noose made from his suspenders. His tongue was distended, eyes wide, and hair disarrayed. Tears on both cheeks had dried white. And that, McGinn thought, is the end of the Gorilla Man, but Dullea ordered him to sift through the records of the U.S. shipping commissioner until he found Hughes's record. They had to be sure. The next morning, McGinn got a shock. According to the shipping records and the suicide's former shipmates, Ramon Hughes had been on the high seas at the time of the Coffin and Johnston murders.

FORTY-ONE

For a century in the U.S. a large, uncouth man had been called a big ape.

—WICKED WORDS

IN Cleveland, Friday, June 5, 1936, dawned mild with warm zephyrs promising a beautiful summer. In the final days before vacation, Louis Cheeley and Gomez Ivey from the Outhwaite School ditched class. They hiked from East Sixty-fifth through the Kingsbury Run gully, tracing the NY Central tracks to slightly northeast of Jackass Hill, where Jimmy and Peter had found the two headless bodies last September. Warily, they eyed the seemingly empty boxcars and yawning doors to hobo shanties and gave them a wide berth. Coming even with the East Fifty-fifth Street Bridge spanning the gully, they observed a black willow tree growing between the rapid transit line and the tracks. A pair of brown tweed trousers had been balled into the Y of two limbs. Their weight made the slender branches droop enough for Gomez, thirteen, to reach them with his fishing pole, shake the pants and listen for a jingle. Nothing. "Wait, there might be folding money in the pockets." Another tug, and the head of a man (who resembled Ed Andrassy) rolled to his feet. Dark brown eyes looked up sightlessly at him. Rigor had fashioned the mouth into a beatific smile. The boys raced to Gomez's house. At 5:00 P.M. Mrs. Ivey found them huddled inside a closet and called patrolman Hendricks of the Fifth Precinct, who notified Inspectors Musil and

May. "It's like a game with him," said May. "Last time he left the body and took the head. This time he took the body and left the head."

At daybreak, Hogan, bird-dogging for the matching body, spiraled out from the willow. A mile away from Jackass Hill to the southwest, he reached two sets of railroad tracks at the intersection of Woodland Avenue and East Fifty-first. Two workers on a crane signaled him and pointed to a nude corpse belly down among sharp thistles. The head had been skillfully decapitated, but emasculation had not been performed. Someone had interrupted the Butcher this time.

A colorful butterfly was tattooed on the victim's left shoulder. On his left calf was the cartoon character Jiggs. On his left forearm were crossed flags, the initials "W. C. G.," and a heart and an anchor. On his right calf were the names "Helen" and "Paul," a cupid, and an anchor. On his right arm were a flag, a dove, and another anchor. The anchors suggested he was a sailor. Nevel mailed facsimiles of the tattoos to the Navy Department, eastern seaport cities, the Ohio Identification Bureau in Columbus, and the FBI's newly installed Tattoo Identification File. There was no match. The victim had probably arrived by rail and fallen asleep in the run, where the Butcher happened upon him. "First he cut his throat," Hogan said, "then hacked away at his neck. Then he undressed the victim. Stripping the victim is a maniac's trick."

A patrolman from the populous Lithuanian area between East Sixty-sixth Street and Wade Park Avenue sought out Nevel. "A man they call 'the Beast,' a strange sunken-eyed man, gaunt and bent like an animal," he said, "comes out at only night. He grovels at back doors for scraps." The Beast sounded suspiciously like Andrassy's visitor. He always told the same story—"I was once a fine doctor . . ." The Butcher's scalpel implied he might be a doctor, medical student, osteopath, chiropractor, orderly, nurse, hunter, or "a clergyman tutored in surgery and turned to excessive religiosity." He might even be a butcher. Nevel spread word among the Lithuanians. "Call us immediately, the next time the Beast appears at your door," he said.

Four days later, Nevel's phone rang. "The Beast has broken into a house on Wade Park Ave. He's still there!"

Nevel and Hogan surprised a dirty, unshaven man at the kitchen table.

His ragged clothes hung loosely on him; his face was ghastly white, his cheeks hollow, and eyes deeply buried.

"Where do you live?" Hogan snapped.

"In the slums," the Beast sobbed, giving an address Hogan recognized as a flat in a house of prostitution. "Take us there." Like Andrassy's room, his room contained only a bed and a broken chair. "I was once a fine doctor," the Beast began. "I had a wife and a child, a personal life and a great house. In one instant I lost it all."

"Go on," said Hogan. The toughest interrogator on the force had fallen oddly silent. Something in the measured way the Beast spoke held the ring of truth.

"One night in Chicago there was a holdup," he said. "I got caught up in it and was struck in the head by the holdup man. That violent blow robbed me of all my medical skill and my memory. Now I am as you see me. But once I was a fine doctor." The Beast rummaged in a trunk and returned with a doctor's bag filled with medical instruments (scalpels unused for years) and some ragged parchments. Reverently, he unfolded diplomas awarded him from major medical schools in Vienna, Paris, and Chicago.

"Just another bum steer," Hogan said outside. He was a hardhearted man, but Nevel saw him wipe his eyes.

Between June 9 and 12, Cleveland hosted the Republican National Convention, and two weeks later the Cleveland Exposition commemorated the opening of the Northwest Territory. When the big parade marched down Euclid Avenue, onlookers watched only their neighbors, wondering who among them might be the Butcher, who waited a month before dumping his next victim fifteen miles from the rest.

At 11:30 A.M., July 22, Marie Barkley, seventeen, reached a crisscrossing of railroad tracks at West Ninety-eighth and Industrial Rayon Corporation's big plant. To one side, the land slid dangerously into the swamp. Opposite, Clinton Road cut deeply into Big Creek Gully, where a nude, emasculated corpse—badly decomposed and ravaged by rats, floated. Its head lay ten feet away, severed at the third and fourth vertebrae. What skin remained on the man's fingertips was worn down as if filed. Decomposed hands with shriveled fingerprints can be recovered by soaking in hot water. Dr. Gerber meticulously peeled the rotting skin from the fingers and found a faint pattern on the underside. Fitting the reversed skin over his own fingertips, he rolled them and obtained recognizable prints that matched no missing person.

The Butcher had sanitized his male victims to erase any clues leading back to himself, but made no effort to hide the identities of his female victims. His cutting of the female genitalia only emphasized their femininity. His removal of the penes and testes of three male victims made them feminine. With this fifth victim Detectives Martin Zalewski and Peter Merylo began devoting their off-duty hours to undercover work. Camouflaging themselves as unshaven, long-haired vagrants (.38s concealed under their rags), they got into character by going sleepless and forgoing baths. Their disguises were so perfect, that cops kept arresting them. They poked through deserted tenement basements, crawled through rat-infested sewers, prowled the slums, and slept in flop houses. All they caught were lice.

At 11:15 A.M. on September 10, Jerry Harris, a transient, was sitting on the East Thirty-fourth Street bridge a half mile from Jackass Hill. A parcel wrapped in the previous week's paper lay on the rough railway abutment next to him. Idly, he watched trains traverse the gully, headed toward his St. Louis hometown. Below, the current was threading around a twenty-foot deep pool of stagnant water. Half a human torso broke the glassy film and was carried into the active currents of the run. Jerry sprinted to the Socony Vacuum Oil Company's tank station at East Thirty-seventh and alerted Leo Fields who called the police.

Nevel, Pearce, and Hogan arrived and fished in the hot sun until they snagged both halves of the torso. The newspaper bundle contained a blood-stained denim work shirt cut at the neck—the exact place where the killer had decapitated his victim. He was dressed and alive when beheaded with considerable force in the proper site for clean amputation. "The affront of the killer," said Nevel, "returning over and over to Kingsbury Run. But there has to be more to the body."

A Coast Guard boat grappled with ceiling hooks until they wrested two legs from the pool. The Fire Rescue Squad used a fire hose to flush debris down the run and drained out three million gallons of polluted water without finding the victim's head or arms. "I bet his head is on a shelf somewhere with the others," said Hogan.

After this murder the Butcher never returned to the great scar of Kingsbury Run, a region Hogan called the absolutely least enchanting spot on earth.

In Cleveland, the bone-numbing fear persisted. The hacked upper torso of a thirty-year-old mother rose in Lake Erie's ice-caked waters and washed up on the frosty beach at Beulah Park. Segments of the same disarticulated body drifted near the river's mouth. Exactly one year after Louis and Gomez turned up a head in a pair of pants, a skull was discovered wedged beneath the Lorain-Carnegie Bridge spanning the Cuyahoga. At Stone's Levee, Hogan and May dug out a lime-impregnated burlap bag containing the partial skeleton of an African American woman, Mrs. Rose Wallace, a resident of Scoville Avenue. Rose had last been seen alive in the company of "Bob," a dark-skinned white man, and shortly afterward in a car with three white men and her steady crush, "One-Armed Willie," who had also been with Flo Polillo the night before she died.

Merylo and Zalewski had by now questioned 1,500 suspects such as the "Chicken Freak," a sadistic truck driver who achieved sexual satisfaction only if his partner decapitated a live chicken during their lovemaking. Their patient, plodding work entailed spading up entire gardens for bones. East Side neighbors reported a skeleton in an old basement (a pile of chicken bones and spare ribs), bones clogging a sewer pipe (sheep bones), and a Sandusky dog dragged a human foot and leg from the brush (medical school specimens).

An attendant at the Soho refinery pump house saw an expensive black Lincoln pull onto the Jefferson Street Bridge. A short, heavyset man got out and heaved a heavy bundle into the river, where it was immediately swept away. Three weeks later, Joe Perry, a pump-house worker, observed the black Lincoln creep onto the bridge again. A month later, John Mokris and Frank Skrovan were crossing the High Level Bridge when a stranger appeared in the riverbed below. Carrying a weighty duffel bag, he crossed the slick rocks and disappeared into a brick storm drain. Over the gurgling water, they heard his steps echoing along the outflow pipes of the tunnel. They left an hour later, unfamiliar with Matowitz's theory of a secret murder lab below ground. Merylo and Zalewski were on the bridge that night, too, but after so much unrelenting work came to blows. Zalewski left the investigation and Merylo retired to work the case privately. More human flotsam, the left

foot, thighs, and headless torso of a tenth victim, appeared in the Cuyahoga River and washed ashore near Superior Avenue. Again, hesitation
marks suggested the Butcher was breaking in an apprentice. The bodies
became just another example of unidentified *disjecta membra* discovered in
Cleveland's sluggish rivers and icy lagoons and on the slopes of lonely Jackass Hill.

FORTY-TWO

Rules and Procedures gave the district captains the responsibility to report the status of their personnel and equipment. They were doing this, but in a perfunctory manner and without fear of consequences.

—RULES AND PROCEDURES, SFPD

IN San Francisco Patrolman E. J. Christal, another special-duty man from Central Station, refused to talk to the grand jury, which held him in contempt and suspended him immediately. The next witness, Lieutenant Mark Higgins, had barely opened his mouth when a bailiff whispered something to Judge Robinson. The judge cleared the courtroom. A janitor, under orders for a week to keep a lookout, had stumbled across batteries and paraphernalia strung in the attic directly above the jury quarters. Dullea got a chair, climbed up and unscrewed the plate. Resting just inside a wire mesh opening he saw an amplifier. He tracked a thin, copper wire for six hundred feet along two sides of the City Hall attic to the Polk and Grove side and dropped down into a little room with a broken lock. An empty chair had been drawn up to a cardboard box with a Dictaphone inside. It was placed there after Friday because before then the room's lock hadn't been broken.

On June 3, 1936, Sheriff Murphy took Lemon and Hoertkorn into custody. Their bail was fixed at $250 each, which both men immediately paid, and then departed. "The attitude of this commission," Roche said the next day, "is clearly and unequivocally established by their action last night in overruling Captain Lemon's objections to the proceedings and denying his motion to dismiss. Because of the lateness of the hour it would have been impossible to have completed the trial of Captain Lemon upon the charges preferred against him."

Gillen, who was "being swamped with various angles of the case," wanted to name a temporary assistant DA to act as a special prosecutor. "While a Grand Juror may not divulge what has taken place in the Grand Jury Room," he said, "there is no law that muzzles a DA who shall keep the public fully informed through the press as to what is taking place in this important investigation into a very important situation."

On June 6, 1936, Atherton asked for another $50,000. The DA told him that $25,000 might be sufficient.

Chief Quinn, seeing the way things were going, publicly abolished the special-duty men as a major police evil and returned all bucket men to uniform. On June 10 at 8:00 A.M., he organized a permanent vice squad from eight trusted special-duty men attached to his own office. "Hereafter," he said, "if an occasion arises when it is necessary to take men out of uniform for one reason or another, the captain may do so, but under a time limit of 24 hours. The same men shall not serve consecutively on this work on an immediate subsequent occasion, but others must be used. In the event this arrangement is not sufficient for investigative purposes, the new vice squad will take on the work."

The new unit, headed by Patrolman Jim McCarthy, would handle all cases affecting public morals and also function as a narcotics unit during the planned dope cleanup campaign. The chief then shook up the districts most affected by the probe.

For several months before, Captain Art Layne had been working in the personnel department at the HOJ. Abruptly and to his great joy, he was transferred to the Crime Prevention Detail. Behind the scenes, Dullea had been working hard to return this honest cop to his former position at Central Station. In response the chief sent Layne on a long vacation and named Lieutenant Ed Copeland acting captain at Central Station during Lemon's suspension. He transferred Captain Michael Riordan from Mission Station to Central to replace Copeland. Captain Bernard McDonald was transferred to Southern District, replacing Captain Hoertkorn, and Captain Peter McGee was transferred from Ingleside Station to Mission to fill Riordan's vacancy. Lieutenant Jack Sullivan of Mission Station was transferred to

Ingleside. The chief elevated two lieutenants to acting captains to fill in any remaining holes. Dullea decided not to appoint anyone to replace Lieutenant Mitchell as head of the Auto Detail until he saw how all the changes worked out and just how honest these men would prove to be.

The following day, June 12, Patrolman James Miles of Harbor Station, another special-duty man, refused to answer the Grand Jury. "Your questions are an invasion of my private affairs," he said. "I believe I might be incriminated or subject to ridicule."

Judge I. M. Golden assailed all the nontalking officers. "They are legally and morally to respond to questions affecting the welfare and security of the citizens employing them and touching upon their own integrity as law enforcement agents."

The cops had waged a long court fight to evade trial, but the tide was turning. Lieutenant Joe Mignola and Sergeant Peter McIntyre put in for retirement. "In cases where the stories of wealth do not agree with information at our disposal," Atherton expressed doubts about the testimony of Lieutenant Frank McConnell (the outstanding bunko detective in the nation), Sergeant Dan O'Neill, and Sergeant John Stelzner. "We have discovered definite discrepancies between the statements they made concerning their wealth and its sources and information in our possession. There is a misconception abroad that because an officer has testified and returns to his duties, his activities are no longer the concern of this investigation. Such belief is not well-founded."

Mayor Rossi studied Atherton's request for $50,000 more. The expenses so far were as follows: $25,000 for the primary investigation; $2,000 for the transcript; $3,500 for the Grand Jury itself; $1,000 on October 16, 1935; $2,000 on December 6; $2,000 on January 7; $2,000 on February 7; $2,000 on February 18; $2,000 on March 12; $2,000 on April 6; $2,000 on May 28; $2,000 for warrants; and $6,000 for other items.

During the graft investigations of the 1920s Roche had said, "I am going to clean up this department for the benefit of the good officers and honest men in it. The police officer's position is a hazardous one, but he is well paid for it. It has its rewards, but under no circumstances will we tolerate graft from the lowest or the highest officer."

Now he was digging deeper. "When an officer reaches the crossroads in his career," he said, "when a turn to the right means the performance of his duty as an officer, and a turn to the left means a turning aside from such duty to a stand on his constitutional right as an individual, he cannot take the left road with leaving behind him the mantle of his office. Understand, no one has any constitutional right to job."

Ed McKenzie, defense attorney for ten nontalking police officers, resigned from the bar for "confidential" reasons. Harsh criticism of his tactics were the true reason. On June 28, 1936, the call went out to find and arrest Captains Lemon and Hoertkorn, both out on a habeas corpus writ. Hoertkorn's son, Harold, was already the subject of a search.

FORTY-THREE

Keep cool during a holdup. Drop face down on the floor in the case of a gun duel between the bandits and the police, but speedy action is vital in turning in those alarms. Don't wait.

—CHIEF QUINN'S ADVICE TO BANK TELLERS

AFTER eluding a half dozen deputies, Lemon and Hoertkorn surrendered and were jailed at the HOJ. Hoertkorn's bushy gray hair had turned white; Lemon's great bulk had been reduced by thirty pounds. They were placed in the visitor's cage in the north wing of the jail, then escorted across the Bridge of Sighs by bailiff George McKeever. "Give Lemon the works! Throw Hoertkorn in the hole!" inmates awaiting trial howled as the sullen captains ran a gauntlet along their row of cells. As the chanting grew louder, deputies chased forty prisoners to the rear so the two captains could be questioned unimpeded by William Gamble, a trusty serving a term for forgery. Gamble had been arrested in the Southern District Station Hoertkorn had once commanded.

In the sheriff's office, they emptied their pockets. Lemon had $461 on his person; Hoertkorn only $200. That night, Superintendent Bernard Reilly, fearing something "might happen to them in this place," moved them into the south wing among the hookers. Both men were dismal. They refused breakfast the next day and at noon declined a lunch of corn beef and cabbage and black coffee.

On June 30, 1936, three deputy sheriffs took Lemon and Hoertkorn from their cells for a three-hour midnight hearing of the fourteen policemen who had defied the Grand Jury's graft investigation. They were the only ones not in full uniform because they could not leave jail to get them. Cases against four of the thirteen silent policemen, Lemon, DeGuire, Mino, and Brouders, were completed, and the next day Judge Robinson denied them bail.

On Friday, July 3, the Police Commission took the cases under submission at 4:00 P.M. and deliberated thirty-five minutes. They granted leniency to three who had shown a willingness to talk (Lieutenant Thomas Roche, Henry Ludolph, and Patrolman Harry Gurtler), but fired eleven policemen. Found guilty of unofficer-like conduct and disobedience were three police captains, two lieutenants, and six patrolmen. Lemon, the first fired, cocked his hat on his head and with a final tug at his empty holster, shrugged, and stalked out, followed by Hoertkorn, who did not wait to hear his name. Finally, all the "obstruction, pettifogging, and appeal to the frivolous" was at an end.

"We will have to reorganize the entire department," said Roche, his voice trembling. "We were obliged to dismiss officers with whom we have had friendly relations with over a quarter of a century. That was not easy. But I could not let my personal feelings interfere where the welfare of the entire department was at stake."

He had performed the hardest duty of his lifetime—the greatest mass ouster and departmental shakeup in any city's history.

On July 9, six more officers were shifted, including Quinn's personal aides Inspector Charles Gallivan and Frank McConnell, who were transferred out of his office back to Bunco Detail where their expertise was more suited. "Captain Dullea sometime ago requested that Gallivan be transferred to the Inspector's bureau in preparation of the coming World's Fair," explained the chief, who would not be affected by the coming reorganization. Roche had made certain of that.

The graft revelations had depressed morale, and throughout the probe honest officers had been ashamed to put on their uniforms. "The picture is so bleak," said one observer. "Short of disbanding the department and starting all over again, I don't know what can be done."

Patrolman Jim Coleman, missing on his two-month-long fishing trip, was now the object of a nationwide search by Treasury agents hell-bent to collect taxes on his $90,000 fortune. When Atherton turned in his final report, he admitted he had accomplished little. "It's kind of like a book on taxation that makes no mention of the Treasury Dept.," said Jake Ehrlich. "It carefully describes the process of collection from its earliest stages all the way up to the McDonough brothers. In a book about taxation you wouldn't expect the reader to accept the idea that all moneys collected got no further than the Department of the Internal Revenue, would you?"

Who was at the top? Atherton had quit just short of real information.

One Sunday, Patrolman George Burkhard, an expert marksman and under prosecution for falsifying documents related to the graft hearings, shot his wife and two grown daughters, then committed suicide. "Funny thing," said a cop, "that yahoo Atherton managed to louse up a lot of lives, to embarrass a whole gang of careless but not really guilty guys into retirement, to hound that poor devil into suiciding not only himself but his whole damn family and yet the bastard never really got the guy he had loaded his gun for."

But what could they do? They couldn't bring down the big guy, Chief Quinn.

"These officers received a deserved fate," said Atherton. "They were all given every opportunity to testify before the Grand Jury. They chose to flout the Police Commission, the courts, the Grand Jury and the people of San Francisco." He blamed the Grand Jury, mayor, and DA for not supporting him. "It'll all end up in a whitewash," predicted the Jack Armstrong–handsome G-man as he took the train south. By August 31, 1944, he would be dead.

FORTY-FOUR

Where there is stagnant water or in a River with a slow current, the body will likely go down where last seen.

—CRIME MANUAL OF THE PERIOD

A golden spider was spinning in the brilliant light of the Bay. Endlessly the mechanical spider shuttled back and forth, it's spinning wheel assemblies laying six strands of copper wire at each pass. Four sheaves carried a bight from reels at one anchorage across to mid-span of the Golden Gate Bridge, looped it over a shoe, then shot back across the channel. Each shoe contained 452 wires, which made up one strand. The spider laid four strands at a time, each anchored to a pair of steel bars extending deep into the concrete. When the glittering spider had twisted together sixty-one strands, it had spun one cable, which it compacted under enormous hydraulic pressure. At the end of one eight-hour shift, the spider had spun a thousand miles of wire. The spider applied narrow steel bands at intervals to bind the long cable together, wrapped it round with steel wire, and rested.

The Bay Bridge had its own diesel spider. It spun ten miles of thick cables to hold the flooring on the bridge then, at top speed, wove single strands into twenty miles of main and secondary cables to suspend the double-decker span. Forms on the San Francisco section had been placed, the painting of the first field coat was in progress, and concrete girders for the off- ramp over Harrison Street and Pier 26 were being poured. It was almost done. Watching the bridge was the Gorilla Man, his shadow snaking along the dock. His long arms swung as he boarded a freighter. His huge hands were restless.

Where there had been none before, there was a plague of Gorilla Men throughout the nation. Fascinated with these motiveless killers, LaTulipe continued to follow their activities. The same month Coroner Gerber released his report on the Butcher, LaTulipe studied a newspaper feature profiling the smiling strangler, Robert Irwin. A pictorial diagram titled "The Gorilla Man" compared his facial characteristics to a gorilla. "The small opening of the eyes show 'The Gorilla Man.' The upturned nostril . . . the straight slit in his face that goes for a lip, is also seen as an animalistic trait. Dark-blond wavy hair, low-set ears with thick lobes, a high bulging forehead, eyebrows slanting downward into his eyes in satanic fashion." The facial similarities between this erstwhile sculptor and Earle Nelson, the original Gorilla Man, were astonishing. The Butcher case intrigued LaTulipe, so much he decided to visit Ohio and learn firsthand about the methodology and psychology of a new kind of man that none of them understood.

AS Captain Dullea drove along Market Street, his wheels bumped on the raised tracks. The city's planner, Jasper O'Farrell, had insisted on Market's 120-foot width as the dividing line between the fifty-*vara*[20] lots on the north and hundred-*vara* lots to the south. Dullea turned left and passed the Ferry Building. It was bustling with activity that day, but for how much longer? Its glory days had been numbered from the moment engineers anchored the Bay Bridge to the bottom of the Bay. The south pier lay underwater on a shelf of rock extending from the Fort Point shoal; the north pier was on rocks at the water's edge. To construct the deepest foundation ever, the Oakland Moore dry dock built an open-topped steel caisson a half block in size and fitted fifty-five vertical steel cylinders into it. Workers towed it to a ridge of rock running from Rincon Hill to the bridge's central anchorage, Yerba Buena Island. As floating mixers poured in concrete, the box sank lower, the sides were built up, and the cylinders lengthened. Sharp-pointed

---

[20] The standard Mexican land measurement.

steel gads were dropped through the cylinders to anchor them to the rock a hundred feet below.

Finally the last of twenty-two million rivets was driven, and on November 12, 1936, a soaring plane wrote in the sky: "THE BRIDGE IS OPEN." After three and a half years of work, former president Herbert Hoover, a Bay Area resident, cut the ribbon amid cannonade salutes from fourteen naval ships. The skies thundered with 250 navy planes, as the first vehicles rumbled across the span at fifty miles per hour. The upper deck had six two-way lanes for cars; the lower deck had three lanes for trucks and buses and two tracks for electric trains. San Francisco had the longest (4.25 miles), tallest (519 feet above the water), and most costly suspension bridge in the world. The last section of the Bay Bridge slid, like the lid of a crypt, over the exact spot where Officer Malcolm had been shot. It was an actual grave for the bustling Ferry Building. As the sun went down that opening day, the bridge's sodium vapor and mercury vapor lights gave off the light of thirty-five full moons—a strange, glare-free light visible in the deepest fog.

MONDAY, March 8, 1937, started badly for Dullea because of a "damn freak accident" out on the Bay. Visibility was crystal clear as the *President Coolidge,* sailing from one of the two Dollar Piers at Hunter's Point, passed Alcatraz in the hands of the bar pilot. Then a fog descended. Captain Hunter was six hundred feet away from the *Frank H. Buck,* when he sighted her too late to avoid a collision. The enormous tanker hung up between Sutro Heights and Lands End on needle rocks 150 yards offshore—stern pointed into the air, crude oil gushing from her hold. Gawkers along the crumbling cliffs choked the highway. Dullea dealt with the jam, then went to lunch at the Ferry Building.

A cold wind came up at his back. The Bay was choppy. The Ferry Plaza sat in silence. Papers blowing about the empty concourse headlined: "The Old Ferry Terminal is Deserted: Gone, but not forgotten." In a few months, the S.P. ferryboat passenger service figures would be "dismal." In a year and a half Golden Gate Ferries would end auto ferry service, close the Hyde Street–Sausalito crossing, and put twenty-two ferries up for sale. The SP's *New Orleans, El Paso,* and the *Klamath* would go to the Richmond–San

Rafael ferry. In two years, the last Piedmont ferry boat would run. Within five years, ferry boats would cease running to Marin altogether. In a decade, the wide iron bridge and the Great Loop would be gone.

Dullea watched commuters arriving on the new red bridge trains, jamming the trolleys and bringing more congestion than ever to Market Street now that there were *two* bridges in the Bay. For four and a half years, he had watched this second bridge, from the construction of the pier and trestle to the sinking of the twin foundations into bedrock with dynamite. He missed the days when blazing rivets flew like meteors from tongs to buckets high above the Bay. Exactly a year before, every bell and whistle in San Francisco had sounded as the Golden Gate Bridge opened. The wind hummed, a shrill sound, through the two indestructible cables passing over the tops of the stepped-back steel towers. "The workers heard it high up in the wires," Willis O'Brien reported, "and from the towers came a deep, organlike note . . . changing, deepening, rising."

They painted the single-span suspension bridge International Orange—the color most visible in fog. Dullea missed that frenzied activity now, but the great span hadn't come without cost. In January, a toppling derrick killed one man and a wooden platform beneath the deck wrenched loose and carried nine workers 220 feet into the Bay. Miraculously, two souls dangling from the underside escaped. The two bridges were here to stay. Apparently so was Chief Quinn. Dullea still had no idea how to dislodge him. Rumors of new police corruption reached Dullea's ears daily, but as long as all three police commissioners backed the chief, Dullea was powerless.

On May 26, Quinn dropped by the St. Francis for lunch. It was dark for the first time since the '06 quake and fire, and the lobby was eerily silent. Exiting the door was comedian Oliver Hardy, out of breath and lugging his own bags. He'd never been this hungry. When the maids, desk clerks, and bellmen put on armbands reading AFL PICKET and walked out, the cooks hung up their aprons, too. The chief hated strikers. Because of them, the hotel would remain shuttered for the following eighty-seven days. By then a great many changes would have taken place in Quinn's life. Three days later, he got to crack a few heads when there was a riot in the Polk gulch area during the Golden Gate Bridge Fiesta. That lifted his spirits a little.

*   *   *

ON September 8, Captain Dullea spent Sunday morning puttering about his den, listening to the radio. At 9:00 A.M., Bobbie Rockwell read the *Chronicle* Sunday comics aloud over the air. But Dullea never cracked a smile. Some little fact still troubled him, some clue that was right before his eyes. He worked all day, and as the afternoon waned, the answer to the riddle had not become visible. A radio jingle was playing, "Coffees and coffees have invaded the West, but of all of the brands, you'll find Caswell's the best." Long shadows crept across the rug. He felt the evening coolness. At 5:30 P.M., a mocking laugh filled his comfortable room. For a year, that same laughter had been emanating over the Mutual Radio Network. *The Shadow* had made the jump from pulps to radio when San Francisco distributors McGregor & Sollie produced twenty-six fifteen-minute, transcribed episodes for the Don Lee Network. Though Orson Welles starred as the invisible sleuth, announcer Frank Readick intoned the Shadow's chilling laugh. Welles, although a great actor, could not.

Shadows all around Dullea moved, lumbering and hulking. The glow of the radio dial was faint in the dark. And there was that sibilant laugh filling the room that even the brilliant Orson Welles couldn't duplicate, but which the Gorilla Man apparently could with remarkable ease. Dullea heard that laughter in his dreams directed at himself and at his shamed department. In his mind, he saw Officer Malcolm's blood staining the dock and the bloody track of an ape's footprints trailing into the fog. The Gorilla Man turned and in his subconscious, Dullea knew that face. It just wouldn't come into focus.

FORTY-FIVE

First degree murders are those that are premeditated, committed by lying in wait, or by poison. Second degree murders are all the others.

—DETECTIVE MANUAL OF THE PERIOD

IN Cleveland on August 16, 1938, a straw boss detailed Jimmy Dawson, Ed Smith, and James McShack to clear a dump at Lake Shore Drive and East Ninth Street. When Dawson dislodged a disordered hill buzzing with insects the earth fell away to reveal a dismembered female torso wrapped in butcher's paper. Five feet away lay the head of the Butcher's eleventh victim, dead about six months. Three hours later, a passerby ferreted out a can containing a man's hair-covered skull. This twelfth victim had been killed three months before the woman. Dr. Gerber, in white shoes, tiptoed among the debris and ferreted out forty bones, a frozen fish container, a bloodstained sugar sack, and a colorful, homemade patchwork quilt.

When Nevel got to the dump at 4:40 P.M., he studied the quilt. "This is very unusual knitting," he said, "so unusual that someone is going to remember it." Charles Damyn, a barber, remembered giving it to a junkman sometime in February. "Find that junkman," Nevel ordered. Detectives Hogan, Theodore Carlson, and Herbert Wachsman found him that day. "Yes, I got the quilt from a barber," said Elmer Cummings, a fifty-six-year-old junkman, "but I sold it to the Scoville Rag and Paper Company."

Hot on the trail, Hogan rushed to the warehouse at 2276 Scoville

Avenue. "But we put it out back to dry," said William Blusinsky, "and someone made off with it." The trail went cold.

Officially, Eliot Ness had been in charge of the Butcher investigation since September 12, 1936, his first day in office as Cleveland's youngest director of public safety. He was a charismatic figure—blue eyed, brown haired, six feet tall, 180 pounds, with a firm, deep voice. A crack shot, Ness should be able to catch the Butcher—he had gotten Capone. With the passage of the Volstead Act, "Scarface" Al Capone had become the iron-handed ruler of a $120 million empire of booze, vice, and gambling. In September 1929, Ness, then a twenty-six-year-old prohibition agent, told U.S. District Attorney George Q. Johnson that only a tightly knit group of incorruptible gangbusters could break Capone's death grip on Chicago. Ness handpicked nine fearless agents of the DOJ Prohibition Detail, and for the next two years, "The Untouchables" raided Capone's breweries, confiscated his trucks, and jailed his men. With Capone's conviction on tax evasion charges, The Untouchables were disbanded, and Ness was assigned to the Northern District of Ohio in charge of the Treasury Department's Alcoholic Tax Unit, which had offices in Cleveland. "The city of Cleveland was a cesspool of crime," Oscar Fraley wrote, "the Cleveland police department was riddled by by graft and corruption."

When that city elected a reform ticket, Ness, appointed to delve into police corruption, forced two hundred resignations and sent twelve officers to prison. Now catching the Butcher was his most important mission.

"We've got to find this man," Ness told Nevel, "but frankly I just don't know how. He has great cunning and strength, a kind of monster who sets to work by a system of trial and error to find a suitable victim and once he finds a way that works he never deviates from that pattern."

He got out maps of the notorious Flats District and the run and laid them out.

"A murder lab, if one exists, is in these woods," said Nevel. "What if we took aerial photos of the murder sites from a great enough altitude to reveal any well-worn paths to and from the killer's private lair?" Ness got the Ohio governor to call out the National Guard. Within the week, pilots of the 112 Observation Squadron/37th Division were soaring over the Kingsbury Run on four photo reconnaissance flights. Nevel enlarged their detailed negatives and went over every inch with a magnifying glass. There were no worn paths.

"The stomach contents of some of the victims have been mostly fruit and vegetables," Ness said. "That is the main diet of the men of the Flats. These unemployed and unemployables live like gypsies in a cluster of shacks and tents near the railway sidings. I suspect the killer is preying on these traveling vagrants. By closing the Flats down we might be able to save some lives. If we can't catch the killer, then we can at least take away the victims."

At 1:00 A.M. on August 18, 1938, Ness led eleven police cars and twenty-five detectives over the run across the Thirty-seventh Street Bridge, where the Erie Railroad tracks crossed. Below, the convoy was reflected in a stagnant pool formed by the diverted waters. Farther up the ravine, small fires crackled among tin-roofed buildings—the shanty town. As Ness's bulldozers idled on the perimeter of the hobo jungle, a fire truck mounted with high-intensity spotlights was moved onto the hillside. His team of ten detectives took up posts at the six approaches to the camp as Sergeant James McDonald's strike team infiltrated the raiding zone. Ness gave a wide swinging arc of his flashlight (his prearranged signal), grabbed an ax handle, and led his men along the Eagle Street ramp. A battle erupted, illuminated by the powerful fire truck searchlights. Cops loaded the vagrants into Black Marias as Ness searched all thirty huts for the Butcher's curved knife. When he didn't find it, bulldozers flattened the shacks and firemen torched them. All the next day, a black cloud that could be seen from downtown, hung over the Flats. "Some of the men we brought in would have most certainly been the next victims of the killer," Ness said. "Those men are now safe."

With Ness's raid the Butcher murders ended. After three years of panic, "one of the most sinister figures in all the annals of crime. . . a genius in his chosen bloodstained field," had vanished.[21]

---

[21] There were a couple of false alarms: On August 24, a man without hands and legs washed ashore onto Gordon Park Beach on the East Side. Strands of rotting rope were entangled around the stumps, but sharp rocks and boat propellers had severed his extremities, not a killer. An amputated right foot found in the city dump turned out to be hospital refuse.

FORTY-SIX

As the ape approached the casement with its mutilated burden, the sailor shrank aghast to the rod, and . . . hurried at once home—dreading the consequences of the butchery.

—E. A. POE, "THE MURDERS IN THE RUE MORGUE"

ON Friday, August 26, 1938, the Cleveland police grilled a suspect—a Great Lake's sailor named Harry who had dated one of the victims, Flo Polillo. The AP reported:

> Police today released a suspect in Cleveland's torso slayings of the past three years. Three days of questioning had failed, Lt. Michael Blackwell said, to connect him with the crimes. Blackwell had described the man, a former hospital morgue attendant, whose hospital duties included the dissection of bodies for autopsies, as the only person among the hundreds questioned who "amounted to a nickel as a suspect."

By August 29, the Kingsbury Run Butcher had generated international headlines lurid enough to catch the attention of that world champion of murder, Adolph Hitler. The German press, under the domination of Propaganda Minister Josef Goebbels, the *Beobachter*s and *Tageblatts* and even Benito Mussolini's Fascist press editorialized how decadent life must be in a democracy where such a monster could stalk the streets without fear of capture.

The Cleveland murder sites were everywhere—on the East and West

Sides, in Kingsbury Run, and on Jackass Hill, in the streets, slums, rivers, woods, sewers, and swamps of the city, seemingly every place an inhuman fiend could eviscerate the populace for no reason at all.

An itinerant Central Avenue fruit vendor tipped Detective Hogan that "Frank Dolezal, a bricklayer, carries knives around."

Dolezal's apartment at 1908 Central Avenue SE lay 235 yards from where Flo Polillo's body was found. He had moved out the day after authorities commenced door-to-door searches along Scoville Avenue; Rose Wallace, the Lorain-Central Bridge victim, had lived a block from him at 2027 Scoville Avenue, and the quilt under the eleventh victim's torso had come from Scoville Rag and Paper at 2276 Scoville Avenue.

Local PI Lawrence J. "Pat" Lyons informed Cuyahoga County Sheriff Martin L. O'Donnell that Dolezal once lived with Mrs. Polillo, who regularly saw Wallace at her home; furthermore, a heavily tattooed sailor who visited Dolezal was not seen again. "They all knew each other," Lyons said. "Andrassy, Polillo, Wallace, and Dolezal all frequented a cheap saloon on the corner of East Twentieth Street and Central Avenue. In the guise of friendship, one gained their confidence and killed them one by one."

Lyons and two deputies gained access to Dolezal's Central Avenue rooms and took a sample of black stains on the bathroom baseboard. Lyons's chemist brother, G. V. Lyons, said, "It's blood, all right."

On July 5, 1939, Sheriff O'Donnell arrested Dolezal, who once worked at a slaughter house cutting up meat, had known Andrassy *and* Wallace, and had quarreled with Polillo. "Flo and I were in my room drinking Friday night," Dolezal explained. "She had two drinks. I had two drinks. She wanted to go out, but had no money. She grabbed $10 I had in my pocket and I argued with her because she had tried to take some money from me before. But I didn't kill her. You've got to believe me!"

"She hit you, didn't she? Didn't she?" Detective Harry Brown said.

"All right, yes!" Dolezal said. "She came at me with a butcher knife. And I hit her with my fist. She fell and hit her head against the bathtub. I thought she was dead so I put her in the bathtub around 2:00 A.M. Then I took a knife—the small one there and cut off her head. Then I cut off her legs. Then her arms."

Dolezal said he stashed her nude torso, coat, and shoes at the rear of

Hart Manufacturing along with bloody parcels containing her severed right arm, a right hand, and bisected thighs. In two baskets he carried her head, lower legs, and left arm three miles to Lake Erie. "At 4:00 A.M. I crossed the ice until I reached the breakwater in the lake and threw the contents into the open water beyond."

On the night of the murder, January 25–26, 1936, ice had formed between the shore and the breakwater, but a strong offshore breeze had scattered spots of open water. But if Dolezal had thrown Polillo's lower legs and left arm beyond the breakwater, how had they ended up behind a vacant building on Orange Avenue? Then, on July 17, Dr. E. E. Ecker, a pathologist at Cleveland's Case Western Reserve University, retested the matter from Dolezal's bathroom.[22] The scrapings were *not* blood at all. The charge against Dolezal was reduced to manslaughter, and at 1:44 P.M. August 22, Dolezal's watch left him alone in cellblock B-4. Four minutes later, the assistant jailer found him hanging like Ramon Hughes from a noose. A jail nurse attempted to revive him with insulin, but by 1:57 P.M. he was dead.

Ness had a better suspect. Chicago transient Emil Fronek told him he had barely escaped with his life after being "poisoned" by a Kingsbury Run doctor who fed him a home-cooked meal. Another hobo claimed he almost "got cut up in that house too." But neither could locate it again. Ness interrogated Dr. Francis Edward Sweeney, who had an office on the southwest corner of Broadway and Pershing near Jackass Hill. When Dr. Sweeney failed a lie detector test, Ness ran for mayor on the presumption he had solved the murders. Then, a postal inspector intercepted a letter to Chief Matowitz postmarked December 19, 1938, Los Angeles. "You can rest easy now," it concluded, "as I have come out to sunny California for the winter."

---

[22] Ecker had no idea what color G. V. Lyons's test presumptive had revealed: pink, blue, or green. Reduced phenolphthalein, potassium hydroxide, and zinc produce a pink. Benzidine combines with sodium perborate, glacial acetic acid, and peroxidase to produce a vivid blue. The leuco malachite test makes a bright green. Ecker soaked the material in saltwater, added serum from an animal immunized with human blood to the test tube, and waited in vain for a color and white ring to appear.

FORTY-SEVEN

Silverback gorillas have enlarged canine teeth and broad incisors for biting. A powerful neck gives a conical shape to the head.

—GORILLA

AT the end of 1938, the Gorilla Man talked his wife, Lydia, into selling her
small coffee shop in Brooklyn and moving back out to California. All through
1939, she labored to make a success of her new flower shop at Long Beach,
and this left her husband with free time. He shipped out or made trips to San
Francisco bankrolled by her profits. Wherever the Gorilla Man was, he continued making a monkey out of his pursuers. His big hands had a mind of
their own. With so much time on those hands, there were hours he couldn't
account for.

THROUGHOUT San Francisco, flags hanging at half-staff on city buildings
stirred as if by a breath of fresh air. An overnight death at St. Joseph's Hospital on Tuesday, February 6, 1940, set in motion a series of astonishing
events. "Beloved Police Commissioner Charles Traung has passed to his
reward," said Mayor Rossi. "He will be greatly missed, not only by myself,
but by the people of this city."

As Traung's body lay in state in the City Hall rotunda, Rossi sat alone
in his office. He had been in this chair for innumerable years. He had been
appointed mayor when Mayor James Rolph resigned to become governor,

had been mayor when the Bay and Golden Gate Bridges were built, and had presided over the building of Treasure Island and the International Exposition of 1939. But he now faced one of his biggest decisions—filling Traung's post on the Police Commission Board.

The man he appointed would break the bitter deadlock between Commissioners Ward Mailliard and Walter McGovern that had endured for years over the chief's post. Mailliard was Chief Quinn's man; McGovern wasn't.

Three days later, the mayor chose William Wobber, president of the Planning Commission. Though Wobber claimed no allegiance to either Mailliard or McGovern, rumor was he would team up with McGovern to oust the chief. Publicly, Quinn hailed Wobber's appointment, claiming a friendship dating back to when they were schoolboys at Lincoln Grammar School. Privately, he decided to go out hard. He entrusted his ally, Mailliard, to carry a threat to the mayor. "If I am ousted," Quinn warned, "the move will bring forth revelations of political maneuverings behind the scenes that might seriously embarrass City Hall."

The mayor ignored the threat.

On Wednesday, February 14, Quinn ordered Mailliard to meet with Wobber and McGovern that night and wage a bitter last-ditch fight on his behalf.

"It's up to you to settle the points in dispute," Mailliard told Wobber. "You're in the driver's seat. But I'm disappointed that a man not formally in office more than a few days should presume to become so familiar with the problems of the department and work out a program to solve them. Under your program, I can no longer serve. If a matter of this kind can be cooked up and wrapped in such a neat package my usefulness as a police commissioner is at an end because I have but one vote."

Mailliard battled far into the night. By 1:00 A.M., it was obvious the chief could not be saved. Then for another hour, he battled for the career of Deputy Chief Skelly. Wobber was definite that Quinn and Skelly must go and equally firm that Dullea must go in as chief and Captain Mike Riordan as deputy chief. "My position has always been clear concerning Quinn," McGovern told Mailliard. "Police morale is low. I believe that San Francisco needs a new Chief of Police and I also believe that Captain Dullea is the greatest peace officer in America."

"When I broke the news to Quinn," Mailliard said, "he took it like a soldier, although it was a great shock to him."

He left the chief that night, unsure if he was even going to attend the next day's Police Commission meeting. At 11:00 A.M. the following day, Quinn secluded himself in his office and refused all visitors except a few strangers stopping by City Hall. The only familiar faces were those in photos of the civilian appointees on his wall gazing sternly down upon him. Quinn couldn't decide whether to fight on or quit. He picked up the *Chronicle*, reread the headlines ("WOBBER-McGOVERN COMBINE WILL OUST CHIEF QUINN TODAY!"), and threw the paper down. What was he going to do?

By 1:00 P.M. he had made up his mind. There was really no choice. Staying on at his civil service rank of sergeant was a humiliating option. Quinn would return to private life rather than face demotion. He had been with the SFPD since 1906 and served as chief since 1929. Quinn leafed through his desk calendar. Technically, he was not eligible for retirement until May, more than three months away when he could retire on a pension. Then he realized that using his accrued vacation time and accumulated overtime he could quit immediately on a leave of absence. Afterward, he could petition the retirement board for retirement on a chief's salary—$216.66 a month for life, $7,200 a year. He smiled. That was $2,200 more than Dullea was making. Calling in his secretary, he dictated a one-page statement that slammed the door on a thirty-four-year police career.

Quinn dressed fastidiously in his full dress uniform, had his shoes shined to a high gloss, then snatched the page out of his secretary's typewriter. He signed it with a flourish, and strode down the marble corridor to the commissioners' chamber. It was now 2:30 P.M. The room was too small to accommodate the hundred interested spectators and a milling throng of officials gathered behind the rail. Filling the front row were the department captains in full dress. Dullea sat to one side against a window with his arms folded and feet crossed. Behind the commission table sat the three men who in a few minutes would take the star off Quinn's breast—Chairman Mailliard, McGovern, and Wobber, the newly appointed commissioner. Quinn took a seat near the commission table about three feet from Dullea. "Has any commissioner any new business to bring up?" Mailliard asked.

"I propose that the Commission remove Quinn as chief and appoint Captain Dullea to the chief's post," McGovern said. "The Commission is prepared to give Dullea a free hand in selecting his subordinate aids."

Wobber seconded McGovern's motion. McGovern and Wobber backed the motion, and the long deadlock was finally broken. Mailliard did not vote, but resigned in protest. "I can not stomach the program of McGovern and Wobber," he grumbled, "and I consider the ouster of Quinn a prearranged railroading."

As he passed the window seats, he reached out to shake Dullea's hand. Dullea unfolded his arms, beamed, and gripped Mailliard's hand. Then Quinn swung about in his chair, reached over and shook Dullea's hand, too. "I wish you success," he told him. Their eyes met. Quinn's face was gray and his tie was loose. "I wish to be given two weeks vacation and permission to take advantage of my accumulated overtime," he told the board, then left the room. Outside, Quinn read his short statement to the press.

"It is not easy to sever my connections with the San Francisco Police Department and its members, who association I have so much enjoyed," he said. "For 34 years I have been privileged to serve the City and County of San Francisco the last eleven years as Chief of Police." The paper shook in his hand. His voice quavered. "I have endeavored at all times to administer the department affairs honestly and faithfully and leave with pride in my accomplishments and with the firm conviction that the San Francisco Police Department is not and will never be second to any other department in the United States. First of all I want to take a rest." His eyes filled with tears.

Quinn disappeared into the office he had occupied for so many years and left the HOJ minutes later. He would be remembered for motorizing the SFPD, installing a Teletype system for interdepartmental communications, and replacing the motorcycles with radio-equipped autos that patrolled all districts all day every day. And he would be remembered for running a police department that countenanced some of the deepest graft and murderous extortion of any American city.

"The police department needs harmony and cooperation," Mayor Rossi said, "and I'm sure Dullea's selection will bring it about. I am sure the new chief will make good. We have no intention of humiliating the chief."

"I will not take the job unless I am given a free hand in the selection of any subordinates," Dullea reminded them as he took Quinn's seat. "While the chief may appoint a deputy chief from any rank, he usually is not really free to make this appointment without political pressures from the mayor or Police Commission. A new chief saddled with inherited subordinates cannot run the department as he thinks it should be run."

In the presence of the commission, all the department commanders, officers, and spectators, County Clerk Herman van der Zee swore Dullea in as chief.

Dullea returned to his tiny office. "I guess I'll have to get myself measured for a new uniform," he said, then looked into the mirror and laughed. "Maybe not." Though Dullea had been on special plainclothes duty for fifteen years, his old uniform still fit. He seemed taller, more athletic than ever, just the man for the job. He already knew the changes he would make.

Under Quinn, supervision had been poor and there was no communication between units and bureaus, which resulted in duplication of effort. Dullea detested the officer who solicited bribes and the beat patrolman who caged free meals, then vanished for the rest of his shift. Some officers slept in the station or in their cars and dressed in shabby uniforms. Their district stations were just as slovenly—squad rooms scattered with files, orders, and citation books. In basements, old records books were floating in water from leaky boilers. Hundreds of incident and accident reports filed daily were being approved automatically by unit lieutenants and rarely returned for clarification. Sick lists were not sent to unit commanders, and inquiries were not routinely made as to the justification for absences. Chief Dullea had a big job ahead.

He rolled up his shirtsleeves and began to clean out his two desks. A simple, unostentatious man, as secretary-treasurer of the Bay Peace Officers' Association he kept all their money—dollars and half dollars, bills to be paid—in a cardboard collar box. Baskets of flowers arrived as he lingered over old photos—Officer Malcolm, Frank Egan, Sergeant Oliver Hassing— all his heartbreaking cases, all solved but Bette Coffin's homicide. He took out a picture of Josie Hughes, held it at arm's length, and thought of an opportunity lost through indecision. "I can't look at it. Here, Jack, put this over in the bookcase," Dullea told his ten-year-old son. He took one last look around and, books and records under his arms, marched to the big front room. He shut the door behind, swept the ornate desk clean, and laid out his plans for the new, clean SFPD. It was just 3:00 P.M.

Fifteen minutes later, Dullea launched the SFPD's biggest upheaval in thirty years, one of the biggest police shakeups in any city's history. "The new shifts will affect the various districts," he said. They would extend from commissioned and noncommissioned personnel to the lowest beat cop on the thirteen-hundred-man force. Some officers would be assigned to captains in other districts. "These changes will be made for the purpose of achieving 100 percent efficiency, and increasing morale." Selection of inspectors had always been based on "political contacts" rather than prior record. Dullea would remedy that. "Merit and capacity to perform will be the yardsticks used to carry out these changes. Assignments to important posts beats and details should be based solely upon merit and fitness and where weaknesses are discovered because of lack of necessary qualifications to perform police duty or the negligence of a particular member, that condition must be remedied immediately."

All day heads continued to roll. Dullea demoted Deputy Chief Charles Skelly, moved Captain Michael Riordan up the corridor from the department secretary's office to the deputy chief's office; he ousted Lieutenant John Casey of the Traffic Bureau because "new blood" was needed. Casey had been the active head of the squad since the death of Captain Charles Goff. Captain Bernard McDonald of Harbor Station (formally of the Richmond Station, head of the Auto Detail and the man who brought in the Phantom) replaced Dullea as Captain of Inspectors. "Captain Dullea has built up a splendid investigating unit and I have no intention of disrupting it," McDonald said.

Dullea also had technological changes in mind. Within a year, new police cars, Ford V-8s, would replace the old Buick touring cars. He scheduled thirty-six two-man radio patrol cars to run in three shifts, 8:00 A.M. to 4:00 P.M. (daytime), 4:00 P.M. to midnight (swing shift), and from midnight to 8:00 A.M. (midnight shift). He reduced the number of gold stars and calculated the benefits, costs, and disadvantages of eliminating or consolidating precincts. The amount of district stations, vastly greater than actually needed for adequate patrol coverage, was a drain on city finances and police resources. With fewer districts and fewer captains in control, the entire department could function as a more centralized unit at less cost to the taxpayers and with less chance for graft. The actual land area of San Francisco is 41.8 square miles. How many men would he need per square mile? A leading authority on police administration, Bruce Smith, recommended in his 1937 report that the fourteen districts be cut in half. Dullea decided that nine districts: Potrero, Southern, Park, Central, Mission, Northern, Richmond, Ingleside, and Taraval, would serve the city better.

The next day, February 16, he read that his old nemesis, Dr. Nathan S. Housman, the man Egan had told of his plot to murder Josie Hughes, was at the end of his six-week trial in Judge J. E. White's court. The doctor was facing thirty counts of violations of the State Narcotics Act. Mrs. Alma E. Black, an elderly widow under his care for some time, had died of a drug overdose, yet his records showed no entry of any narcotic prescriptions for her. Dullea found it telling that Mrs. Black had left her $200,000 estate to Housman. Nate Coughlan represented the balding doctor. At one point, he lunged at prosecutor John McMahon shouting—"You're a liar—a liar!" As they rolled along the counsel table trailing punches, Bailiff Frank Burns and Narcotics Inspector Walter Creighton separated them. Two days later, the nine-woman, three-man jury found Housman guilty of three dope counts. The verdict brought a wry smile to Dr. Housman's lips that was so similar to Chief Quinn's tight little smile, that it was impossible to tell them apart. As for Chief Quinn, he went in to radio.

FORTY-EIGHT

The throat was chafed. Together with a series of livid spots which were evidently the impression of fingers [from huge hands]—throttled to death—whole body dreadfully bruised and discolored—cut with some sharp instrument—probably with a razor.

—SFPD FORENSICS REPORT

ON Tuesday, June 25, 1940, a northeast wind was sweeping the docks, shaking the Ferry Building and rocking the boats on the water. The huge clock tower above the Bay Hotel was just striking 9:00 A.M. as Chief Dullea leaned back in his chair at the HOJ and took a sip of coffee. He was grim, living as he was in the age of the human monster. Where there had been none before, sequential murderers were becoming a twentieth-century phenomenon. Dullea still did not understand them and wasn't sure he wanted to.

All the red and blue flags were cracking in that wind the day Dullea finally got his big break in the Gorilla Man case. Later he would remember every moment—how the panes had rattled and the streets had been blown clean of papers and rubbish. The odd weather pattern had not gone unnoticed. Around that time, experts had observed that a sudden northeast wind after a prevailing period of hot, mild, or not too cold weather, frequently coincided with outbursts of sexual crime. Just as Mrs. Andrassy had felt a confluence all about her before a laughing apelike visitor had appeared at her door asking for her son, Dullea felt a storm building.

His mouth was dry as cotton. He licked his lips and took another sip. So many years. "Where had his quarry been all these years?" If it hadn't been for a similar series of Gorilla Man dissections in Cleveland and

LaTulipe's obsession with the case, he would have forgotten the maniac by now. Had it really been five years since Anna Lemon left the ferry on such a blustery day, reached the darkened Bay Hotel and several hours later run back down three flights of stairs screaming? In spite of a decade of wind and rain, the stain left by Officer John Malcolm's blood on Pier 26 had still not completely washed away. So many years of waiting. So much frustration. The dread that somewhere the worst was happening and he could not stop it haunted him. The new chief went about his morning's work. His trusted aides, McGinn and Tatham, came and went, good friends, dogged hunters who never gave up. The clock tower struck noon, then one o'clock. The long-anticipated break in the New York and Bay Hotel murders came a half hour later.

A sharp rap and a patrolman burst in. "Chief, a hotel maid, Margaret Rice, found a woman jammed between the bed and wall," he said, "nude . . . unspeakably mutilated with a razor." Just like Bette Coffin. For a second Dullea couldn't move. His eyes held that sleepy, contemplative look they always did before decisive moments when he roused himself into action. Instinctively, Dullea knew the progeny of Earle Nelson had returned. This time, they would not blame the wrong man as they had with Slipton Fell. This time, there would be no tragedy like Ramon Hughes dangling from a noose in his cell. Dullea, LaTulipe at his heels, ran down the front steps and into a cruiser idling at the curb. They swung wide at the intersection, the wire radio aerial whipping like a lash, headed for 108 Fourth Street at Mission—the Hotel Irwin.

The two detectives, hearts pounding, ascended to the seventh floor and down a dimly lit hall into a double room overlooking the street. The curtains were drawn. Dullea smelled the fragrance of gardenias in the room. A fresh corsage had been trampled underfoot. Two white, waxy petals, doubled like a little sailing ship, were floating in a thin, red lake. Longtime partners George Engler and Al Corrasa (who had arrested Albert Walter) had just cracked the murder of Hewlett Tarr, a cashier at the Curren Theatre. They tracked the shooter in a stolen Yellow Cab to the Koffee Kup Restaurant three miles outside town. Now they were gathered around an overturned mattress. The killer had hidden his victim as if ashamed of what he had done. Inspector Frank Ahern and Lieutenant Michael Mitchell (head of the Homicide Squad and one of the toughest cops in the city) heaved the mattress off. Mitchell's eyes widened. He didn't feel so tough now.

Between the bed and the wall was the strangled body of a young woman clad only in black stockings, her legs sprawled in a vee. An autopsy had been conducted on her with a razor-sharp knife. The strangler had cut away a portion of her torso, flung it beside her body, then burned it with cigarettes and matches. This time the Gorilla Man had taken his time in order to enjoy himself. "One look at the victim and we saw the remarkable similarities to the Bay Hotel murder," Corrasa said. "We knew the Gorilla Man was back."

Her face was entirely covered by a girdle pulled tightly across her mouth, nose, and neck. Dullea carefully peeled it back to reveal black and blue marks around her eyes and deep claw marks on her cheeks exactly like Bette Coffin's. In life she had been a pretty girl. The cloth belt knotted around her throat had puckered her flesh as the killer slowly tightened it. Her dress, with a few of the belt loops torn away, hung over the back of a chair. Beneath the ligature were the outlines of a huge pair of hands. Like Clara Newman, the attractive young woman had been strangled *twice*.

Above her black stockings, on the woman's right thigh, was a blue eagle.

"What do you think of that?" asked Dullea. "Isn't that a U.S. Ensign?"

"Wait a minute," Ahern said. "I think I know her. I've often seen her with sailors near the Ferry Building. But I don't know her name." He saw her cheap purse on the dresser, but when he opened it found no identification, only a key to another hotel room.

"Get her fingerprints, Frank," said Dullea. "I have a hunch she's probably got a record."

LaTulipe rolled the victim's prints at the scene (which he rarely did), then discovered fingerprints on a nearly empty pint whisky bottle on the mantle. They had been deliberately smudged. The Gorilla Man was playing with them. He bagged the bottle anyway, then drove the print cards to the HOJ and turned them over to Inspector Daniel O'Neill, chief of the Bureau of Identification. LaTulipe had learned some things about the type of man they were hunting. Anatomists and mutilators are erotically stimulated by the victim's suffering and sexually gratified by inflicting the wound.

"The man and woman registered just before noon on Monday," Margaret Rice told Mitchell. "She had only a purse. I remembered he demanded a front room on the third floor but we had none." Most of the Hotel Irwin's guests had been out between 11:00 A.M. and 1:00 P.M. when the murder was probably committed. None had heard a sound or seen anything out of the ordinary. "You boys question hotel employees," Mitchell told Corrasa and Engler. "This case looks so similar to the Coffin case I'll bet we can almost guess what the hotel clerk will say. I wonder if he used the name 'Meyers' again?"

Manager Arthur Edwards said they had registered as "Mr. and Mrs. J. Wilkins of Los Angeles" around 11:00 A.M. the day before. "The only thing she carried was a purse and a corsage of gardenias," he said, and described the suspect as "30 to 35 years old, possibly 40, short, stocky, about 5', 9" and 175 to 180 pounds. He had medium light hair, almost blond—maybe from the sun, and a tanned, weather-beaten complexion. He was wearing a dark suit which fit snugly because of his broad shoulders and barrel chest. His coat collar was turned up around his neck and he wore his hat pulled low, like this." Edwards showed them. "His hands were in his pockets." The description of "Mr. Wilkins" tallied with that of "Mr. Meyers" provided by John Smeins in April 1935.

"Did he say anything?" asked Engler.

"It's an odd thing. It was just shortly after one o'clock when he came out of the elevator and said his wife was hungry and asked me where he could get some sandwiches. 'Women are funny,' he said to me. His voice was kind of soft and musical. He said, 'My wife decided she wanted me to bring her in a couple of sandwiches instead of going out for something to eat. I guess the Brass Rail right around the corner is a good as any place hereabouts, ain't it?' I told him 'yes' and he went sauntering out the door. He was whistling and laughing. It was a strange laugh. That's the last I saw of him."

"My God," thought Engler, "those are almost the identical words the Gorilla Man used at the Bay Hotel. He is unquestionably the killer."

"The way I figure it," Mitchell said, "we can cinch the Coffin killing and this murder on the same man by proving that the signatures on both registers are identical." Corrasa took the hotel register and a stat of the Bay Hotel ledger to Inspector McGinn. To his practiced eye both looked alike and analysis later that day confirmed the signatures were identical. McGinn theorized that the killer targeted red-haired women down on their luck. "I think he picks them up in some bar," he said, "and we should check those out first."

"That's already being done. But where has the Gorilla Man been all this time? Look at the tremendous time lag between his 1931 New York murders, the 1935 San Francisco killing and now this one. How has he held his compulsion in check?"

"He hasn't," said McGinn fiercely. "It just means that there are others we don't know about or haven't connected with him—yet."

"I've identified the victim's prints from the hotel bedroom," O'Neill told Dullea. "She's Mrs. Robert E. [Earl] McCarthy alias Irene Chandler and a few other monikers. She's thirty one." In April, the LAPD made an inquiry concerning the support of her boys, Harry, ten, and Ralph, nine. In 1921 she was arrested for prostitution in San Diego and over the following nine years jailed for the same offense eleven times, all in San Diego. "There's that San Diego connection again," thought Dullea. Mrs. Coffin's son had mentioned a sailor with a short name from San Diego and Dullea had a file on two San Diego murders committed by some sailor who tied unusual knots. San Diego seemed to be the logical starting point. Teletyped requests got them a photo of Irene just as O'Neill located a more current one from the local files.

"With her picture," said Engler, "we certainly ought to be able to find some bartender where she and the suspect had been drinking. At the very least we might be able to find the shop where they purchased the pint of whisky. It's unusual for many people to buy liquor in the early morning. They were probably drinking somewhere close to the hotel."

The *Examiner* headlined: "SEX MANIAC KILLS WOMAN IN HOTEL; Nude, Mutilated Victim Strangled With Belt; Drinking Companion Flees." By 6:00 P.M. the burning arc lights of the photo engraver had converted the victim's photo (stolen by a zealous reporter from her room) into a masking Velox of forty-five dots per square inch, which sulfuric acids etched onto a copper printing plate.

Dullea mapped out an area a mile square in the heart of San Francisco. "Within this zone," he said, rapping it with his knuckles, "I want you to check every bar and rooming house, question every hotel clerk and guest, and grill every bartender and beat cop. Then do it all over again." Less than twenty-four hours after Mrs. McCarthy's nude body was discovered, Lieutenant Mitchell had already visited eighty-two bars.

This first day brought no leads. No one had seen "Mr. and Mrs. J. Wilkins of Los Angeles." On the second day, Engler and Corrasa, carrying photos of the latest victim and old and new descriptions of the sadistic ripper, visited local hotels and located two where the couple had attempted to register and been turned away. Why? Was it the lack of luggage? Or had the man appeared forbidding in some way? On the third day, nearly two blocks away from the Hotel Irwin, Inspector Frank Ahern discovered a third lodging house where "Mr. and Mrs. J. Wilkins of Los Angeles" had been rejected.

Dullea's men labored for a solid week, taking little time out to eat or sleep. By Tuesday, July 2, they had covered the Embarcadero, the financial district, and south of Market with no success. Dullea read their typed reports over and ordered all the uniformed cops in the waterfront area to pitch in. Perhaps a beat cop would find something they had missed as they made another crisscross of the lowest bars.

Beat cop Carl Marcus's feet were killing him, so he stopped to rest at a tavern near his regular corner in the south of Market District. The regular bartender was not there. A relief barman was in his place. When Marcus showed him Irene McCarthy's photo he did a double take.

"Wait a minute," he said. "Wait a minute. Yeah, I recognize her. She was in here two days in a row. I worked last week too, glad to get the work. So that would make it Tuesday and Wednesday, the 23rd and 24th. I'm positive she was in here, but not with a man—with another woman—yeah, Wednesday morning."

"Not a man. Too bad." Marcus turned to go.

"Wait. Would this help? I'm certain I can locate her drinking companion." And she might know the identity of the man with huge hands who moved like an ape.

FORTY-NINE

Sgt. Tom McInerney taught fifty bank clerks at a time to shoot at the HOJ firing range. "You must realize most holdup men do not look like thugs," he said. "They will be well-dressed, wearing a cap or hat, and will enter with a briefcase or a shopping bag."

—CHIEF QUINN, *TRUE DETECTIVE* ARTICLE

OFFICER Marcus, excited, lost no time calling Chief Dullea. Within the hour, the barman had come through with the address. Dullea sent Ahern and Corrasa scurrying for their car with a warrant for arrest in hand. Speeding southwest on Mission Street, they passed the Hotel Irwin and halted in front of a hotel near Seventh and Mission. Rushing through the dimly lit lobby, they rode up in the elevator with a bellhop. A dark-haired woman dressed in lounging pajamas opened the door.

"My name is Ahern, I'm a policeman. This is Corrasa, my partner. We need to speak with you." The blinds were partially drawn and only a single lamp was burning. The woman sat down, crossed her legs, adjusted her satins, and lit a cigarette. Ahern showed her Irene McCarthy's morgue picture. "You were a friend of hers weren't you?" She glanced, shook her head, and put her hand over her eyes. "Yes, yes," she said. "That's her. Poor Irene. I had known her for several months. I want to be of help. This is such a terrible thing.

"I accompanied Mrs. McCarthy, Irene, into a bar shortly before 10:00 A.M., on June 25. We sat down and had a drink together. Then she left. A little while later a man came in and sat down at the same table with me. He had been drinking and asked me if I wanted to step out. I told him I'd think it over. When he insisted on buying me a drink, I didn't refuse. He bought several drinks and began to get confidential. When he said he was 'on the beach' here, or some-thing like that, I gathered he was a sailor. I asked him what ship he was on. He said he was looking for a berth."

"Do you know his name?" Ahern leaned forward.

She walked to the window. Faint bars of light through the closed blinds striped her face. Ahern saw her back tense. She had remembered. "I saw his name," she said. In a moment of drunken expansiveness the man had flashed his seaman's certificate to her. "Now what was that name? Wait."

They waited.

"Yes, I've got it. I'm sure his first name was 'Harry.'"

"Harry what?"

"All I can remember is Harry. I only saw his certificate a second."

"What's Harry got to do with Mrs. McCarthy?"

"She knew him. I was talking to him when Irene came in. They seemed to be old friends from San Diego . . . Irene came back in a little while and sat down beside us. They left the tavern together, saying they were going to do up the town. That was the last time I saw my poor friend alive. Poor Irene."

Ahern and Corrasa drove back to headquarters with the name "Harry" ringing in their ears. But what did they actually have? They had a first name. They had an occupation. "The name 'Harry' is a slim lead," Dullea told them, "but if there's one chance in a million then we'll get this bird."

DULLEA had put off lunch. The wind was howling outside the HOJ by the time LaTulipe brought coffee. Dullea put up his feet—his first moment of rest in a week. "Sometimes the most important clues are right in front of you," he said, "but invisible." There was the creak of his swivel chair as he leaned back. He recalled a case of Alameda County Deputy Sheriff Grover Mull's a few years back. "One bleak Sunday, a windy day like today," Dullea said, "Deputy Mull and Sheriff Doug Webb were cutting up Broadway as an oncoming rainstorm chased their cruiser . . ."

AT Tenth Street and Broadway, Oakland's main thoroughfare, Mull and Webb took a breakneck run at Hayward, fifteen miles to the east, then sped through

Fruitvale, Fitchburg, and Elmhurst towns. As they roared down bumpy roads the few streetlights leaped up in the growing dusk. Sweating in semitropical heat, they flew through the town of San Leandro and ate up ten miles of sparsely settled country. Scattered farms, fruit and nut stands, and a single filling station flashed by. At Hayward's eastern limit, they swung right onto a graveled roadway where at the far end lay 795 Pinedale Court—the Everett Richmond home with a beautiful young brunette out front. "We've just gotten home and been nearly crazy since father's shooting," Mrs. Richmond sobbed.

Inside the entry hall a pool of blood shimmered on the polished hardwood floor. The radio was playing loudly, a popular dance tune Mull knew. She clicked it off. "Father was wounded in the abdomen by a masked man hiding in the hallway," she said. "He got to a neighbor's house and was driven to the Hayward Sanitarium." Mull left Mrs. Richmond and Webb on the couch and traced the daylight shooter's escape route out the front entry hall. He had made a sharp right, then run down a side street, his arms filled with jewelry and silverware.

The northeastern storm had overtaken him. As it began to rain, lights came on in the close-by houses. Except for a gentle patter among the banana trees and tall palms, it was deathly silent. In the blueness, Mull found a single shoe print in the soft ground where the prowler had jumped down. Embedded in the angle formed by the junction of the heel and sole were tiny red particles and a metallic pellet. Getting a spade and a box from the tool shed, he carefully cut out the square of turf and got it out of the rain. He made a reverse cast, using a spoon as a baffle to break the fall of water and dry plaster of Paris from one end of the impression to the other. He took the hardened print back to Chief Silva.

"'The way I dope this out," Silva said, "the criminal picked this ore up some other place. And if we can locate where that and this bit of red earth originated we'll have our man. We'll search every square-inch of town until we find it. When we find it, we'll investigate every person, every house, every shoe, and every foot of land in that neighborhood."

Silva's men discovered the gully where the red earth and metal had come from and found the remains of a handout. A local housewife, Mary McWilliams, recognized the newspaper she had wrapped the lunch in because of a penciled notation she had made on its margin.

Still Mull felt they'd overlooked some essential clue in their preliminary investigation, but couldn't quite put his finger on it. The clue was elusive, tantalizing. A vague, yet important bit of evidence still lay undiscovered in the Richmond house. "Hold it!" Mull said. "There's something wrong here. Mrs. Richmond shut off the radio just as she sat down on the couch. Why should the radio have been playing at all? She said they had arrived home only a short time before. According to the father's testimony from his hospital bed, [he had since died] he was shot immediately after stepping into the house and so he didn't turn on the radio."

They rushed back to Pinedale Court. "Yes," Mrs. Richmond recalled, "the radio was playing when we got home. The queerest part is that the radio's been out of order for the last three days. We haven't been able to tune it at all."

"Yet it was playing perfectly last night," said Mull. "The only conclusion is that the gunman fixed it. But why? Why would he fix the radio?" Mull took the cover off the radio and explored the inside. Though the killer had wiped his prints away everywhere else in the home, he might not have wiped down the inside of the radio. He had not. Mull developed six different sets of fingerprints in the interior. He matched five of the prints to radio salesmen and repairmen and the sixth to Joseph M. Reid, a San Quentin ex-con. Mrs. McWilliams identified him as the tramp she fed.

When Mull caught Reid fencing the stolen items at a pawnshop, the fugitive dropped behind a trash can and began firing at him. As Mull lay full length on the sidewalk, he counted six shots from Reid's weapon. If Reid had a revolver Mull had him. If he had an automatic Reid would have one or more bullets left and Mull would be in a fix if he rushed him now. He took the chance. With drawn gun he charged and captured Reid trying to reload.

"While bumming through Hayward," Reid confessed, "I picked the Richmond home as a likely place to rob. Using a skeleton key, I entered by the small door on the side street. First thing I always do is turn on the radio, turn it on loud. This gives neighbors the impression some of the family is home and prevent calls to the police from neighbors who observed me through the windows. This time I found the radio not working. I used to be a radio repair man so I made a very simple repair inside the cabinet. I had to take off my gloves to do this, but I figured *no one* would think to look for prints inside the machine."

"BUT Mull did," said Dullea to LaTulipe. "An invisible clue. What do you think of that?" He paused. From the beginning he had felt there was an invisible clue in his case. But where? Was it a witness? Was it someone already in jail? Could it be another crooked officer or dishonest public official? God, there had been so many. Dullea's eyes strayed to a file cabinet standing in a shaft of rain light. It had to be there somewhere in that file. The thought nagged at him. He couldn't sleep or eat until he found it. The Gorilla Man was someone he already knew. He would bet everything on that. But who?

UNSPEAKABLE necrophiles like the Gorilla Man are propelled by an unfathomable compulsion, a misplaced desire that drives them beyond murder to the disarticulation of their victims. Though new to America, this type of woman killer had been horribly active in Europe throughout the last decade. Lord Spilsbury could name a dozen recent victims in Britain in eight of the twelve cases he was called in to help solve. "Within four years," he wrote, "the murders of four women of the streets, all strangled and all but one living in Soho, swelled the list of unsolved crimes." He attributed them to the same known hand. "The rarest class of murder, very fortunately—for it is the most terrifying to contemplate is that apparently committed for the sake of killing by a person who by all accepted standards is perfectly sane. Casual murders without motive by a maniac are intrinsically unsolvable." Sadistic crime remained at a fairly low level during the 1930s, but by 1946 would double in England. By 1956 such crimes would quadruple in the big U.S. cities and there would be a profusion of what Dullea called Gorilla Men.

OVER at the big gray stone customhouse sleepless detectives were combing through mountains of the U.S. shipping commissioner's records for the past six years. It was a daunting task. Every month more than four hundred ships left the San Francisco port with crews ranging from twenty to upward of four hundred each. All night, Engler, Corrasa, and Ahern plodded through shipping line registers of the more than forty steamship companies that signed crews out of San Francisco and scrutinized the names of all crews in the harbor at the time of the murders. Next, they compiled a list of all men whose given names were Harry and matched those with known addresses and compared their handwriting. Luckily, the commissioner required their signatures be kept on file.

"I've got a hunch," said Engler as he closed the last book without luck. "This guy Harry might have shipped out of some Pacific Northwest port— possibly Seattle or Portland. We might check there. He registered at both hotels as from LA, but might have used that only to throw us off the trail."

"It doesn't seem likely that a sailor who was almost broke," said Dullea, "would spend his dough to come here from up north, while he might do that from LA. First, though, forget about the bars for now and question as many waterfront types as possible. I figure that a sailor would hang around waterfront dives along the Embarcadero and being a drinker tend to shoot off his mouth."

A number of the old wharf rats and waterfront habitués prided themselves on knowing everyone on the waterfront. Engler and Corrasa went looking for one. The tragedy had started at the Ferry Building and might end there. In the night fog, the deserted Ferry Building and its Neoclassical Clock Tower were ghostlike. It was not hard to image it before the '06 quake—busy derricks at the base of Market Street (which then lay in cobbles), a long arcaded wooden shed with stalls for horse-drawn streetcars, and elegant carriages and coaches delivering guests to hotels.[23] At the south

---

[23] After the October 1989 earthquake, the Ferry Building's Big Clock would stop at the instant of the quake—5:07. In May 1992 the double-decked Embarcadero Freeway hiding the Ferry Building would be demolished as new ferries began steaming across San Francisco Bay to Marin again. Where the Bay Hotel had been, lush Justin Herman Plaza would stand, becoming a place where families could picnic. Farther down, the Bay Bridge still soared directly above where Officer Malcolm lost his life. Today the roar of cars passing above can be plainly heard, and if one looks closely traces of the great stain still remain.

end, Engler saw a light flare as a man cupped his hands to light a cigarette. He saw a flash of beard and a long, flushed face. He was short-legged, in boots, rolled cuffs, felt hat, and bulky jacket. They put the question to him. "I know half a dozen Harrys," he said, "but for the price of a drink I'll give it some thought." Engler and Corrasa were thirsty, too, so they adjoined to the Ensign Cafe across from the Bay Hotel. "As I said, I know several Harrys, but only one matches your description." He had another drink and scratched his beard. "That would be Harry Gordon." He had another, then turned in his seat. "He generally ships on deck as an able-bodied seaman and if I'm not mistaken he's Danish."

Engler doubted Gordon was Harry's real name but was elated all the same. Immediately, a dogged canvass ensued of all Pacific Coast Ports for any Harry Gordons. They asked the police of every Pacific Coast port to obtain a copy of Harry Gordon's signature from their local shipping commissioners. The next day, the LAPD airmailed a copy of a Harry W. Gordon's handwriting to the SFPD. As soon as it arrived, LaTulipe made a comparison with the Photostatted signatures on the two hotel registers and Harry Gordon's seaman's card. All three were written by the same man. The identity of the Gorilla Man was known at last. Harry was a simple name, the name of commoners, kings, cabbies, and killers.

Because Gordon was living in southern California, Mitchell would need assistance from local law enforcement. Dullea knew LA Detective Lieutenant Jerry Gannon would mesh well with his men and could make the actual arrest. On Friday, July 5, Gannon was officially assigned to work hand in glove with the SFPD detectives. The problem was that the only address they had for a sailor named Harry Gordon was a San Pedro seaman's union hiring hall. According to records he had used it many times before.

"He's listed to be called for work within three days," Gannon Teletyped the SFPD. "Harry Gordon is positively going to be at a union meeting on July 8."

And this time the police would be there.

FIFTY

Let him talk . . . let him discourse; it will ease his conscience.

—E. A. POE, "THE MURDERS IN THE RUE MORGUE"

IN Los Angeles on July 8, 1940, Lieutenant Jerry Gannon gathered together his strongest men. "Which route should we take?" he asked as they prepared for the raid on the San Pedro hiring hall. As the electric wall clock in the squad room ticked, a map was drawn up, and the final plan laid. At 6:00 P.M. the two recent shipping commission photos of Harry Gordon arrived from San Francisco. "O.K.," Gannon said, "here's what he looks like now." The men gathered around the two pictures. They weren't very clear. "All right, let's get started."

SIREN wailing, Mitchell and Engler raced south by car. Engler was at the wheel. As he weaved in and out of a line of produce trucks, rain began to fall and winds began to buffet them. An irrigation ditch rushing with cold water along the pitted road ran alongside them for some miles. On the first stretch of asphalt Engler pushed the throttle wide open. Cars around them were moving as fast. In the 1940s autos were capable of ninety mile per hour speeds, though many drivers were unlicensed and poorly trained. Mitchell was sure that Gordon was at the hall by now and they were missing the final act of the tragedy.

*   *   *

IN San Francisco, Chief Dullea stared at the black candlestick phone, willing it to ring. He intended to stay at his desk until the arrest was accomplished. But his eyes were heavy from lack of sleep, and he had to fight to keep awake in spite of his keen excitement.

IN San Pedro, the unmarked car containing Gannon and his men pulled up across from the hall's dimly lit entrance. The night was muggy and still. "Double up and watch closely," said Gannon.

Two of his men walked down the south side of the street. Two others flanked both sides of the building. Gannon consulted his watch. It could be a minute. It could be five minutes. The Gorilla Man might not come at all. From the shadows, he scrutinized each man entering. There was no sign of Harry Gordon. He studied the photo again. Harry's hunched shoulders and huge hands made him look formidable. Had he brought along enough men? It was now long past 8:00 P.M. The night was sinister, dirty. It began to rain.

AS the heat broke and the first fat drops of warm rain struck the pavement, an apelike figure appeared at the top of an incline. His shadow extended along the cracked sidewalk for a remarkable length. He stopped as if sniffing the hot wind and thrust his hands in his jacket. A trickle of sweat ran down his bronzed face. In spite of the heat he shivered. The blue neon of a cafe across the street had transfixed him. Head down, he crossed to the eatery. It was hot inside, so he had a beer, then another. He lost track of time in the glow of the blue neon. Finally, he remembered to look at his watch, rose unsteadily and, puppetlike, continued on to the hiring hall. Always cautious, he entered by the rear door in the alley.

OUTSIDE the San Pedro peninsula, traffic was heavier and slower moving. Engler crossed some rough pine boards that served as a bridge, saw lights ahead, and decided to use the siren a little longer, then shut down as they entered San Pedro. He passed lines of palms and slowed for a Pacific Electric big red car headed for the barns. He slammed the gears into place, stepped on the gas, skidded on the macadam, and shot forward. They mustn't miss the capture.

GANNON approached the hall entrance and crept up to a small window cut into the double doors and peered inside. The room was crowded. Gannon looked from face to face. A burly merchant seaman in the front row attracted Gannon's attention. He could see a little of his cheek now, a sloping forehead and, as the head turned—the low brow, dirty blond hair, and hooded eyes. Unmistakably, the man was Harry Gordon.

"He's here," Gannon hollered. He flung open the door shouting, "Harry Gordon, we have a warrant for your arrest on a charge of murder."

The Gorilla Man's head jerked up. His huge fists knotted and his eyes flew back. Gannon got to his side and wrestled him to the floor, but Gordon threw him off and began battling toward the front. If he made the street, he still might escape. He knocked two of Gannon's men coming up the stairs into the street. Harry was going to elude the police again.

ENGLER crossed the darkened Vincent Thomas Bridge over San Pedro Bay and covered the last blocks at high speed. He killed the siren and eyed the sawed off shotgun. They might need it. It had been a long trip to reach this spot—a maze of blind alleys, three strong suspects who were copycats yet killers, and two Gorilla Men who might just be one. They had relived the horror of Earle Nelson. They had interviewed wharf rats and b-girls and relatives, searched through a crisscross of south of Market bars, and quizzed a hundred saloon keepers. They had thumbed shipping line registers and canvassed every Pacific Coast port except this one. Finally, they were there. Ahead a terrific battle was in progress. It had spilled out onto the street and fists were flying.

GANNON and his men had finally surrounded Gordon under a streetlight. "Hit him, throw him," Gannon said. The circle of cops tightened. Harry was strong, but their sheer numbers overwhelmed him. As Engler and Mitchell pulled to a stop, Gannon had the Gorilla Man on the wet pavement and was putting cuffs on his big hands. Mitchell was in time to help hustle Harry into the back of a growler as Engler raced to find a phone to call San Francisco.

IN San Francisco, Dullea snatched up the receiver in mid-ring. "We've got him," Engler gasped when he caught his breath. "It's over." Though Dullea had been up all last night and tonight, he felt momentarily refreshed. Then exhaustion stole over him. He slumped back in his chair, let the receiver slip back on the cradle, and gave a long sigh of relief. His eyes closed. In a few minutes he roused himself and was calculating how long it would take him to reach San Pedro.

AT the San Pedro Police station Dullea joined Gannon, Mitchell, and Engler as they studied the manacled man under a naked bulb. As it had five years before, heavy rain pummeled the streets outside. Nothing had changed for Harry Gordon. It was as if he were still caught in the long shadow of the Ferry Building Clock Tower as it swept over the Bay Hotel like a scythe. He was breathing heavily and had been since his arrest. An hour earlier, he had been calling for officers and rattling his cell door with his huge hands. They were as weighty and muscular as Dullea knew they would be. Huge as an ape's and even more striking in contrast to his baby face. Harry's bow-shaped lips quivered like a child's. There came the dull rumble of thunder; his pale eyes widened. Dullea knew his face from somewhere. It would come to him.

All crimes have a motivation and Dullea was anxious to learn Harry's. But a real understanding lay decades in the future when such Gorilla Men would be more commonplace. In 1940 no one could say they understood the type with any certainty, only that they were individuals who directed their efforts to satisfying their own selfish desires. Cleveland's Coroner Pearce surmised that their Gorilla Man had committed murder as the result of his "delusions of persecution and schizophrene during some period of disassociation when the urge strikes him." Whatever the answer, they belonged to the borderline group of insanity, the constitutional psychopath such as Earle Nelson had been diagnosed.

As a matter of amenity, Dullea leaned back against the far wall and allowed Gannon to conduct the questioning. They had waited for him. In the circle of light Gannon spoke persuasively, asking several general questions about Harry's youth and getting several honest responses. Harry admitted he often flew into rages on shipboard, but insisted his life on shore had been exemplary.

"I'm pretty sure I don't go around killing women," he laughed.

"Could you have done it and not remembered?" asked Gannon.

Harry paused and rubbed the cuffs against his cheek as if scratching an itch. "I admit there are times when I can't remember where I was. I sort of feel like I may be forgetting at times. I get nervous. I get dizzy. I'm dizzy now. I'm nervous now. I'm forgetting now. When that happens I usually take a drink of water."

"Not alcohol?"

"Well," he said and licked his lips, "sometimes when I go into a bar, I can't remember doing that until somebody tells me that they've seen me there."

"How long have you had trouble remembering?"

"I can't say, but in San Francisco I would get nervous a lot." He grew rigid. "I'm remembering now." He lowered his head, then began to speak in a conspiratorial tone.

Now Gannon learned that Harry Gordon was not the suspect's real name.

The Gorilla Man's name was Wilhelm Johannsen.

"Wilhelm Johannsen?" thought Dullea, standing just outside the circle of light. "Why did that name seem familiar?"

"My father had brought me to New York City from Denmark in 1903," said Harry.

"New York City?" thought Dullea. That rang a bell, too, some connection with the Bay Hotel murderer. A New York murder case was the only one in the 1930s *exactly* like Bette Coffin's. Dullea remembered the facts.

Florence W. Johnston, a New York City housewife, had been murdered on October 21, 1933, in a Washington Heights apartment building. She had been strangled, stripped, and horribly mutilated with razor blades and a knife. The murder had ended in crude autopsy fashion—precisely like Bette Coffin's in the Bay Hotel. At the time Dullea concluded that the same fiend had absolutely committed both crimes. He recalled the unsuccessful search for her husband's body. The poor bastard! And Harry Gordon had been in New York at the same time.

"In New York I got married," Harry said. "I came home drunk one night and we argued and she bawled me out. Then she threw a flower pot at me. It hit me in the forehead and I bled like a pig. I saw a kind of blue haze." Harry spoke at length about an "irresistible impulse," a colored tide that swept over him and compelled him to do things. "I grabbed her by the throat and held her awhile, then she got limp. There wasn't any pulse any more, so I put her on the bed and autopsied her with a boning knife and a razor.

"When I came to my senses she was killed and all cut up, so I took a powder, went to Baltimore and changed my name. Ever since then I get blue hazes or flashes when I've been drinking and I get to thinking about the time I worked in the morgue. In Baltimore, I met my present wife, Lydia. Two years ago [at the same time the Butcher vanished from Cleveland forever], I persuaded her to sell her coffee shop in Brooklyn and come to California. Lydia currently operates a flower shop at Long Beach. She worked hard to build up the trade at her flower shop." The crushed roses and gardenias at the crime scenes now made sense to Dullea. In the closed room he could almost smell the flowers. "But I was out of work and last month I borrowed $250 on the car Lydia had bought and came back to San Francisco again to do my work." Matter of factly, he told of stalking San Francisco streets late at night, picking up unsuspecting Bette Coffin and taking her to the Bay Hotel.

"Why did you strangle Mrs. Coffin?" Gannon asked. Records showed that Gordon's ship had arrived in San Francisco in April 1935, and sailed right out again. "And why did you kill that McCarthy woman in San Francisco?" It was sultry in the room. All the men were sweating while Harry Gordon's skin was cold and dry. He blinked before he answered. He ground his hands together (there was a jangle from the cuffs) and puckered his lips before he began to explain. His bow-shaped mouth glistened. "Geez, I don't know," he said.

In Europe one of the Ripper ilk once exulted of the "unspeakable delight" he had in strangling women, experiencing erections and real sexual pleasure. "It satisfied me to seize the woman by the neck and suck their blood." Did this explain the scant amount of blood in Bette Coffin's hotel room; had he drunk it? "As soon as I had grabbed her by the neck, I felt sexual sensations. It did not matter the attractiveness of the woman. Choking them satisfied me. If I did not have sexual satisfaction I continued choking until I did. I choked them until they died."

LaTulipe had laid it out for Dullea: A sexual pervert derives erotic gratification from murder. A sadistic, antisocial being, he is cynical, coldly indifferent toward the horrible and derives sexual pleasure from sadistic mutilation. Sexual desire left unsatisfied can completely alter its nature. Sadistic rape is sadism, only secondarily rape. Unbridled sadism becomes in itself an object of sexual gratification; as erotic anxiety is replenished it constantly requires new fulfillment. "My God," thought Dullea, "the Gorilla Man has desires that sex can never satisfy."

"I used the money my wife, Lydia, gave me to have my teeth repaired to pay for the trip to San Francisco," continued Harry. "I was sitting at the bar when Mrs. McCarthy came in. I had known her before down south in San Diego. We had several drinks. I bought a pint of whisky and we went to the hotel. All of a sudden a kind of blue flash came over me and I just had to kill her, that's all."

"Did she scream?"

"I guess . . . a little."

"Did you choke her until she was dead?"

"I guess so, yes, sir."

"Now that it's all over, how do you feel?"

"Oh, I feel sorry for myself," Harry said. "You can see I'm in a real fix." Harry studied Gannon's face and paused. He thought hard for a normal response, sorted through his mind and decided on remorse, an emotion he had never felt. "I guess I feel sorry for those I killed," he ventured. "I just have not allowed myself to think about it too much. I couldn't think when

I was upset like that." He buried his face in his big hands. "I remember now. I remember! God, I don't give a damn if I go to the gas chamber! Not much doubt that I'm a menace. Ever since I was a child, I've been attracted to the cruel and destructive. I've killed women and I'd probably do it again unless they get me out of the way. I expect the worst, and the sooner it comes, the better."

Engler wanted to know more about the initial slaying in New York. "Why did you really kill the first woman, your wife?" he asked. "What was the real reason? There must have been some reason besides just a fight."

Harry Gordon studied his muscular hands. In the glare of the light his cupid lips shone wetly. Was that fear in his eyes at last? He shook his head. Tears welled up. "The whole thing started," Harry said, "when I worked in the basement morgue in a big New York City hospital, Mount Sinai. I'd sweep the floors and clean up around the place and also sew up the bodies. As a hospital morgue attendant my hospital duties included the dissection of bodies for autopsies. I got so I couldn't get the sight of corpses out of my mind. When that happened, I'd get drunk. Every time I got drunk I felt an urge to kill some dame and take them apart. That's how it all started." He looked up at the officers with watery-blue eyes and tried to open his slit of a mouth. It was hard for him to speak.

"You see, officers, I just couldn't get autopsies out of my mind."

Dullea stood looking at the Gorilla Man under the naked bulb. He had got it—finally. It came to him now like a ghostly touch on his shoulder, the invisible clue that had been there all along, but hidden away in his subconscious like a fingerprint inside a radio. He had known the name of the Gorilla Man from the very beginning. Harry Gordon and Wilhelm Johannsen were only two of the Gorilla Man's names. At long last he had found Mrs. Johnston's missing husband.

Acknowledgments

This six-year project was made effortless through the moral support and encouragement of Dr. Derek Penn, Dr. Elizabeth Nubla-Penn, J. D. Lester, Diane Nelson, Annie Yuen, Aaron Smith, David Smith, Margot Graysmith, Wilialak "Sow" Prakhe Smith, Rayluk Addison Smith, Harmony Manao Smith, Zoe Briao Smith, Larry and Lillian Abrusci, Steve Mortenson, Mike "Murph" Murphy, Harvey Hodgerney, Melanie Graysmith, Gary Fong, Victor Santos, Andry Muljadi, Kevin Fagan, Rick Romagosa, Brad Garrett, Maria Mendoza, the gang at Kayo Books, Kevin J. Mullen and those at the Penguin Group who made this book a tangible reality: Judy Murello, Crissie Johnson, and Julia Fleischaker.

Most especially I want to thank the professional guides who helped me track the loping stride of the Laughing Gorilla along the path of this thrilling adventure: Jaime Wolf for sage legal guidance, Candace B. Levy for amazing copyediting, Joel Gotler, the most extraordinary agent in America in both film and book, and my brilliant editors Michelle Vega, whom I could listen to all day, and Natalee Rosenstein, who has the vision and imagination of a true artist.

Author's Note

Whenever I choose a story, or more precisely when a story chooses me, I immerse myself in the time period and visit all the sites in the narrative. Sometimes I move to where the crime took place. In the six years it took to write the history of *The Laughing Gorilla*, I moved to within nine blocks of Jessie Hughes' San Francisco home, close to the former Urbano Drive home of murderous public defender Frank Egan. As I write this, I can see the El Rey Theatre from my window. In April 1932, a young couple left that movie palace to find the crumpled body of Egan's benefactor. This grim find eventually led to Captain Dullea recognizing the deep corruption within the SFPD, prosecuting the crooked cops, and beginning his battle to become the new chief of police. I still haunt the Ferry Building, which has been restored to its former greatness, and stop at the bulkhead of Piers 26 and 28 nearby where Dullea's friend, Officer Malcolm, was gunned down. I lunch at the park that replaced the Bay Hotel and have visited Dr. Housman's former office on an upper story of the Flood Building.

I worked at the *San Francisco Chronicle* for fifteen years where old-timers told me stories of the Depression era and the crooked cops and officials who once ran the city. In composing this never-before-told tale, I consulted blueprints of the Ferry Building and the *Chronicle*, studied streetcar and ferry schedules, daily weather conditions, stock market activity of 1935, city protocol, and a 1935 handbook for the St. Francis Hotel staff. I pored over period photos, books, vintage fashion books and listened to radio drama and commercials of the thirties. I consulted autopsy and police reports, court records, and the 1937 Atherton Report on Graft within the SFPD. For years I attended the Embassy Theatre on Market where Mrs. Hughes went and played Ten-O-Win games with the audience on the same wheel the Embassy used in 1928. The story of the Laughing Gorilla, never before told, is constructed in threes: the three betrayals Captain Dullea endured, the three murder suspects, and the three seemingly impossible tasks he faced: to clean up the corrupt police force, to depose Chief Quinn, and to capture the Gorilla Man.

Selected References

BOOKS:

Badal, James Jessen. *In the Wake of the Butcher. Cleveland's Torso Murders*. Kent, OH: Kent State University Press, 2001. An excellent case study.

Bassett, Burton (featuring Sheriff James J. McGrath). "The Case of the Laughing Killer." *American Detective Fact Cases* (1936), 6, No. 7.

Bayer, Oliver Weld. *Cleveland Murders*. New York: Duell, Sloan & Pearce, 1947.

Browne, Douglas G., and E. V. Tullett. *The Scalpel of Scotland Yard*. New York: Dutton, 1952.

Burchill, Detective Sergeant John. *Winnipeg Police Service, History and Museum*. Winnipeg Police Historic Files.

Crimes and Punishment. Vol. 20. Westport, CT: Stuttman, 1994.

De River, J. Paul. *The Sexual Criminal*. Burbank, CA: Bloat, 2000.

Diefendorf, Fred. "Snaring California's Sex-crazed 'Jack The Ripper.'" *Headline Detective* 3, no. 6 (1940). May 13, 1939. An important source.

Dullea, Captain Charles, and Harold J. Fitzgerald. "San Francisco's Dictograph Death Plot." *Startling Detective* 9, no. 53 (1932).

Flamm, Jerry. *Good Life in Hard Times*. San Francisco: Chronicle Books, 1997.

Forgy, M. Lee. "Passion Slaying of the Nude Red Head." *Detective World*, Mar. 25, 1950, p. 30.

Fox, Richard H., and Carl L. Cunningham. *Crime Scene Search and Physical Evidence Handbook*. Washington, DC: U.S. Department of Justice, 1973.

Fraley, Oscar. *4 Against the Mob*. New York: Popular Library, 1961.

Garvey, John. *San Francisco Police Department*. San Francisco: Arcadia, 2004.

Gilliam, Harold. *San Francisco Bay*. New York: Doubleday, 1957.

Grey, Wilton. "Cleveland's Headless Six." *American Detective Fact Cases* 6, no. 1 (1936).

Gribben, Mark. *Earle Leonard Nelson.* Court TV's Crime Library: Criminal Minds and Methods, 2004.

Harper, Hugh D. Letter to Holland Rush. July 17, 1935.

Holland, Rush L. Letter to Hugh Harper. July 15, 1935.

Hoover, J. Edgar. Letter to John Shuttleworth. Aug. 20, 1935. Reprinted *American Detective Fact Cases*, 4, no.6 (1936).

Jackson, Joseph Henry. *San Francisco Crimes: The Laughing Killer of the Woodside Glens.* New York: Duell, Sloan & Pearce, 1947. An important source.

Kemble, John Haskell. *San Francisco Bay, A Pictorial Maritime History.* Cambridge, MD: Cornell Maritime Press, 1957.

Lewis, Oscar. *San Francisco: Mission to Metropolis.* Berkeley, CA: Howell-North Books, 1966.

Lehman, David. *The Perfect Murder, A Study in Detection.* New York: Free Press, 1989.

Long, Sheriff Ray, and Frank H. Ward. "Hunting Down Ohio's Gorilla Man." *The Master Detective* 12, no. 4 (1935).

Masters, R. E. L., and Eduard Lea. *Perverse Crimes in History.* New York: Julian Press, 1963.

Martin, John Bartlow. *Butcher's Dozen.* New York, 1949. An outstanding book.

McElvaine, Robert S. *The Great Depression.* New York: Times Books, 1994.

McMahon, Inspector William, and Jack De Witt. "The Mystery of the Missing Beauty." *American Detective* 4, no. 6 (1936).

Morland, Nigel. *An Outline of Sexual Criminology.* New York: Hart, 1967.

Malloy, Lieutenant James (as told to Bennett L. Williams). "How We Solved San Francisco's Most Sensational Crime." *Famous Detective Cases* 3, no. 4 (1936).

Mull, Sheriff Brover C. (as told to Bob McLean). "California's Music Murder." *American Detective Fact Cases* 6, no. 1 (1936).

Mullen, Kevin J. *The Toughest Gang in Town.* Novato: Noir, 2005.

Nash, Robert. *Murder, America. Homicide in the U.S. from the Revolution to the Present.* London: Harrap, 1980.

———. *Bloodletters and Badmen.* New York: Warner Paperback Library, 1975.

Ness, Eliot, and Oscar Fraley. *The Untouchables*. New York: Julian Messner, 1957.

Newsom, Ted. "Confessions of a Hollywood Gorilla." *Filmfax* 16 (Aug. 1989): 30. The source for Corrigan's gorilla suit story.

Olmsted, Nancy. *The Ferry Building*. Berkley, CA: Heyday Books, 1998.

Pezet, A. W. *Greatest Crimes of the Century*. New York: Rainbow Books, 1954.

Proctor, Jacqueline. *San Francisco's West of Twin Peaks*. San Francisco: Ardcadia, 2006.

Redmond, Ian. *Gorilla*. New York: Knopf, 1995.

Rules and Procedures: Police Department. City and County of San Francisco. 1930, 1940, 1965, 1971.

San Francisco Committee on Crime. *A Report on the San Francisco Police Department*, Parts I–II. Berkley, CA: Western Star Press, 1971.

Schechter, Harold. *Bestial*. New York: Pocket Books, 1998.

Sifakis, Carl. *America's Most Vicious Criminals*. New York: Checkmark Books, 2002.

Smith, Bruce Jr. "Report of a Survey of the San Francisco California Police Department." 1957.

Starr, Kevin. *Endangered Dreams: The Great Depression in California*. New York: Oxford University Press, 1996. Source for the McCarty/Quinn conversation.

Tatham, Inspector Richmond (as told to Dean S. Jennings). "The Man in the White Mask." *True Detective Mysteries*, Feb. 1936, pp. 14–19, 66–78.

"The 1937 Atherton Report on Graft within the San Francisco Police Department." Compiled by the Mayor's Commission headed by Edwin Atherton, The San Francisco Grand Jury, Assistant District Attorney Leslie Gillan.

Time-Life editors. *Our American Century: Hard Times: The 30s*. New York: Time-Life, 1968–1998.

True Crime: Compulsion to Kill. Time-Life Books.

Wilson, Colin, and Seaman, Donald. *The Serial Killers, A Study in the Psychology of Violence*. New York: Carol Publishing Group.

Wilson, Colin, *Written in Blood*. Books I–III. New York: Warner Books, 1989.

NEWSPAPER ARTICLES

"Another big shakeup due next week," *San Francisco Chronicle*, February 17, 1940, p. 1.

"Bandits make off with Market Street Railway strong box," *San Francisco Examiner*, January 28, 1933, p. 4.

"Board fires 11 police, puts off action on trio as Roche set shakeup," *San Francisco Chronicle*, July 4, 1936. p. 1.

"Cameras to catch rare sky drama, Scientists set to 'trap' eclipse today," *San Francisco Examiner*, April 28, 1930, p. 1.

"Captain Bunner's $110,000 wealth," *San Francisco Chronicle*, May 27, 1936, p.1.

"Car believed used to crush body of Mrs. Hughes found," *San Francisco Examiner*, May 13, 1932, p. 1.

"Cases against 12 police completed, row livens trial," *San Francisco Chronicle*, July 2, 1936, p. 8.

"Chilly mountaintop Mecca, Dullea attends Easter celebration on Mount Davidson," *San Francisco Examiner*, April 21, 1935, p. 20.

"City may sue graft cops for back wages, loss of pension looms," *San Francisco Chronicle*, June 6, 1936, p. 1.

"City to have flying squad," *San Francisco Chronicle*, July 10, 1929, p. 6.

"City will postpone replacing ex-cops," *San Francisco Chronicle*, July 8, 1936, p. 6.

"'Conscience? I haven't any,' Selz says," "Flattery wrung death stories from Selz, says detective," *San Francisco Chronicle*, April 13, 1936, p. 8.

"Cops map court fight to evade trial, Board upholds right as Jury," *San Francisco Chronicle*, June 3, 1936, p. 1.

"[Cops] On their way to sheriff's office," "Roche explains Commission delay," *San Francisco Chronicle,* June 4, 1936, p. 4.

"Death suspect linked to hotel killing," *San Francisco Chronicle*, March 11, 1936, p. 1.

"Defender turned defendant," *San Francisco Examiner*, June 9, 1932, p. 9.

"Defiant witnesses refuse to talk in police graft quiz; Silent Shannon thrown out," *San Francisco Chronicle*, May 7, 1936, p. 1.

"Doran admits Egan called him," *San Francisco Examiner*, June 4, 1932, p. 1.

"Doran who drove Egan gives up," *San Francisco Examiner*, June 14, 1932, p. 1.

"Dr. Shumate, son face Graft Jury summons, McDonoughs, bail bond brokers, also expected to be called," *San Francisco Chronicle*, May 26, 1936, p.1.

"Dullea chief," *San Francisco Examiner*, February 15, 1940, p. 1.

"Dullea, the new chief happy as a kid when he changes offices, Former chief may enter radio work," *San Francisco Chronicle*, February 19, 1940, p.8.

"Egan and 2 others will make murder charge plea today," *San Francisco Examiner*, June 14, 1932, extra, p. 1.

"Egan case brings order for arrest of 2 ex-convicts," *San Francisco Examiner*, May 12, 1932, p. 1.

"Egan case ruling, Mayor's suspension of official set precedent, parallel seen as police refuse to testify," *San Francisco Chronicle*, May 20, 1936, p. 5.

"Egan ruled in contempt," *San Francisco Examiner*, June 10, 1932, p. 6.

"Egan's money woes," "Egan search extended," *San Francisco Examiner*, May 5, 1932, p. 1.

"$800,000 officer shows accounts in new jury quiz,"*San Francisco Chronicle*, June 4, 1936, p. 1.

"Farrell, cop indicted in burglary, jailed for slugging Capt. Skelly," *San Francisco Chronicle*, May 15, 1936, p. 1.

"$56,822 riches bared by Inspector Gallivan," *San Francisco Chronicle*, June 6, 1936, p. 4.

"Fingerprints may link Selz to Richmond murder," *San Francisco News-Call*, March 12, 1936, p. 8.

"4 ex-G-men chosen to aid probe police, $50,000 appropriation for costs up today," *San Francisco Chronicle*, June 29, 1936, p. 1.

"Fourteen silent police will know fate today," *San Francisco Chronicle*, July 3, 1936, p. 1.

"Frank Egan found in hospital here, guarded by police," *San Francisco Examiner*, May 7, 1932, p. 1.

"Frank Egan 'taken for ride,' mystery man informs wife," *San Francisco Examiner*, May 4, 1932, p. 1.

"'Get police slayer,' orders chief," *San Francisco Examiner*, April 30, 1930, p. 1.

"Girl identifies 'Harry,'" *San Francisco Examiner*, solving of hotel murder bares killing of first wife in N. Y. July 9, 1940, p. 4.

"Graft quiz results in shakeup," *San Francisco Chronicle*, June 10, 1936, p. 6.

"Hassing indicted in burglary," *San Francisco Chronicle*, November 20, 1935, p.1.

"Housman, guilty on 3 dope counts," *San Francisco Examiner*, February 18, 1940, p. 1.

"Housman jury locked up," *San Francisco Chronicle*, February 17, 1940, p. 6.

"Housman trial lawyers square off for fist fight," *San Francisco Chronicle*, February 16, 1940, p. 8.

"How can police board keep any of the men found guilty and face the people?" *San Francisco Examiner*, July 6, 1936, editorial page.

"Jury indicts four S. F. policemen," *San Francisco Chronicle*, May 14, 1936, p. 1.

"Killer brags of travel," *San Francisco Chronicle*, March 2, 1936, p.6.

"Laugh slayer says he saw world by being kicked around," *San Francisco News-Call*, March 12, 1936, p. 8.

"Laws that aid criminal," Captain Dullea interview, *San Francisco Examiner*, May 17, 1932, p. 8.

"Lewis Lapham, Along the Waterfront," *San Francisco Examiner*, November 18, 1934, p. 6.

"Lieut. Fogarty tells of $44,000 fortune; Hoertkorns still silent," *San Francisco Chronicle*, May 25, 1936, p. 1.

"Mayor backs up Roche in trial of cops," *San Francisco Chronicle*, May 30, 1936, p. 1.

"Monk clue fizzle, suspect denies he's Shannon's pal," *San Francisco Chronicle*, May 4, 1936, Financial section, p. 1.

"More funds demanded to probe police graft," *San Francisco Chronicle*, May 6, 1936, p. 1.

"Mrs. Hughes alive when hit by auto," *San Francisco Examiner*, May 11, 1932, p. 1.

"Mum police will face legal blast of 3 fronts today," *San Francisco Chronicle*, May 18, 1936, p. 8.

"Murder verdict in Hughes death; hold Egan and Doran, Jury asks," *San Francisco Examiner*, June 3, 1932, p. 1.

"Officer Madden bares $834,000 in bank deposits," *San Francisco Chronicle*, June 2, 1936, p. 1.

"Officer's case goes to Grand Jury tonight," *San Francisco Examiner*, November 19, 1934, p. 1.

"Police board member Traung dies," *San Francisco Chronicle*, February 6, 1940, p. 1.

"Police killer man-hunt," *San Francisco Chronicle*, April 30, 1930, p. l.

"Policeman slain in payroll holdup," *San Francisco Examiner*, April 30, 1930, p. 1.

"Police Shakeup," *San Francisco Chronicle*, February 15, 1940, p. 1.

"Police Shakeup, Dullea sworn in as chief, orders drastic changes," *San Francisco Chronicle*, February 16, 1940, p. 1.

"Police tales as to wealth questioned," *San Francisco Chronicle*, June 16, 1936, p.1.

"Police wife ill, misses Jury quiz," *San Francisco Chronicle*, May 1, 1936, p. 1.

"Quinn's order affects five lieutenants, The Chief exiles the opposition to him in the SFPD," *San Francisco Chronicle*, September 10, 1930, p. 1.

"Quinn suspends 4 more police," *San Francisco Call-Bulletin*, May 16, 1936, p. 1.

"Roche, assailed in trial of cops, offers to resign," *San Francisco Chronicle*, May 29, 1936, p. 1.

"Rossi choice expected to end deadlock," *San Francisco Chronicle*, February 9, 1940, p. 1.

"Scores see thugs murder officer, flee with payroll," *San Francisco Chronicle*, April 30, 1930, p. l.

"Seaman admits slaying 2 women,": "I don't know why I did it, 'Blue haze came over me,'" *San Francisco Examiner*, July 9, 1940, p. 4.

"Sergeant seized, freed at crime scene, jury told," *San Francisco Chronicle*, November 20, 1935, p. 1.

"Selz bares plot to poison 2," *San Francisco News-Call*, March 12, 1936, p. 8.

"Selz girl pal called tough proposition," *San Francisco News-Call*, March 12, 1936, p. 8.

"Selz given life; Poker slayer pleads guilty in surprise move," *San Francisco Chronicle*, April 13, 1936, p. 1.

"Selz linked to 4th murder," *San Francisco Examiner*, March 12, 1936, p. 8.

"S.F. cop hid $25,000 in woodpile, he says," *San Francisco Chronicle*, May 1, 1936, p. 8.

"S. F. priest swept to sea off beach," *San Francisco Call-Bulletin*, May 16, 1936, p. 1.

"S.F. sergeant is arrested as safe cracker," *San Francisco Chronicle*, November 11, 1934, p. 1.

"7 officers file report on extra cash," *San Francisco Chronicle*, July 6, 1936, p. 6.

"Sex murderer scoffs at prospect of death," "Tells how he slew 3," (photo caption)" Claiming he is ready to go to the gas chamber, Harry Gordon, seaman, yesterday told to all who would listen how he murdered three women," *San Francisco Examiner*, June 10, 1940, p. 4.

"Shannon likely to face three charges today," *San Francisco Chronicle*, May 5, 1936, p. 8.

"Shannon fired: Brouders faces sentence in jail," San Francisco Chronicle, May 19, 1936, p. 8.

"Shannon dickers with U.S. to pay up income taxes," *San Francisco Chronicle*, May 22, 1936, p. 1.

"Shaw dead? Well, no—" The great playwright comments on San Francisco, *San Francisco Chronicle*, March 3, 1936, p. 4.

"Six more officers shifted; Shakeup hits Quinn aids," *San Francisco Chronicle*, June 11, 1936, p. 1.

"Special duty men returned to beats in police shakeup," *San Francisco Chronicle*, June 10, 1936, p. 1.

"Steel on Bay Bridge 84 percent completed, span work progresses," *San Francisco Chronicle*, June 8, 1936, p. 1.

"Supervisors, trying Egan, refuse to quash charges; new murder motive cited," *San Francisco Examiner*, June 11, 1932, p. 1.

"Take police chief out of politics," *San Francisco Chronicle*, May 11, 1936, p. 1.

"Tell alls, 'dumb' police will vie as inquiry resumes," *San Francisco Chronicle*, May 23, 1936, p. 1.

"Testimony in graft trial locked up to prevent tampering," *San Francisco Chronicle*, June 22, 1936, p. 1.

"This is how I killed Mrs. Rice," *San Francisco News-Call*, March 12, 1936, p. 8.

"'This is how I killed the Bulgarian,' says slayer Selz, re-enacts murder. *San Francisco News-Call*, March 12, p. 1.

"Three more cops seal lips," *San Francisco Chronicle*, May 16, 1936, p. 1.

"3 police captains shifted by Dullea; Mailliard quits," *San Francisco Examiner*, February 16, 1940, p. 1.

"Three S. F. police jailed for burglary: Tables turned, officers jailed," *San Francisco Chronicle*, May 8, 1936, pp. 1, 8.

"Tries 4 cops; Lemon, Hoertkorn go from jail for hearing, pair face Jury today," *San Francisco Chronicle*, July 1, 1936, p. 1.

"Two captains defy quiz, Copeland bares $35,000, *San Francisco Chronicle*, May 12, 1936, p. 1.

"Two ex-felons in Egan case hunted," *San Francisco Examiner*, May 6, 1932, p. 8.

"Two officers defy Jury's graft probe," *San Francisco Chronicle*, May 5, 1936, p. 1.

"2 new policies in Egan's name," *San Francisco Examiner*, May 12, 1932, p. 1.

"Two $100,000 officers revealed in graft inquiry, Forgarty admits forgetting $16,000 item," *San Francisco Chronicle*, May 28, 1936, p. 1.

"Veteran officer murdered at Pier 28," *San Francisco Chronicle*, April 29, 1930, p. 2.

"Wobber-McGovern combine will outst Chief Quinn today!" *San Francisco Chronicle*, February 15, 1940, p. 1.

"Woman curses jury, slayer lauds counsel," [Farrington conviction] San Francisco Chronicle, September 10, 1930, p. 1.

"Woman says Egan used her as tool in looting estate," *San Francisco Examiner*, June 13, 1932, p. 1.

"W. P. Wobber named to police board," *San Francisco Chronicle*, February 10, 1940, p. 1.

WEBSITES AND OTHER SOURCES

Conversation between Dullea and Chief Quinn based on William J. Quinn's remarks in an open letter to *True Detective Mysteries Magazine*, 1931.

Earle Leonard Nelson Biography. http://www.trutv.com/library/crime/serial_killers/history/earle_nelson/7.html

The Frank Egan Case, 1932. Mullen, Kevin. City website.

The Virtual Archives of San Francisco. The Modern San Francisco Police Department 1920–1940. http://www.sfmuseum.org/sfpd/sfpd5.htm

Index

Page numbers in *italic* indicate figures; those followed by "n" indicate notes.